ADD TONER

ZINES

ISSUE #00002

FLY.

LAST GASP

ADD TONER
©2011 AARON COMETBUS

PUBLISHED AND DISTRIBUTED BY
LAST GASP OF SAN FRANCISCO
777 FLORIDA ST.
SAN FRANCISCO, CA. 94110
WWW. LAST GASP. COM

ISBN 978-0-86719-753-2

PRINTED IN CHINA

FIRST EDITION, 2011

*H*ELLO AND WELCOME. COMPILED HERE ARE THE HIGHLIGHTS FROM ISSUES 44 THROUGH 48 OF COMETBUS, PICKING UP WHERE "DESPITE EVERYTHING" LEFT OFF. THAT VOLUME CHRONICLED THE MAGAZINE'S EARLY YEARS, FROM ITS BIRTH IN 1981 THROUGH ITS ADOLESCENCE AND ACNE-RIDDEN PUBERTY. IN "ADD TONER", COMETBUS RELUCTANTLY COMES OF AGE.

THE MAGAZINE PASSED THROUGH VARIOUS PHASES AND STAGES ALONG THE WAY. FIRST IT WAS ALL ABOUT BANDS, THEN COFFEE, THEN TRAVELING, THEN ROMANCE AND PUNK. THERE WERE INTERVIEW ISSUES, ARTICLE ISSUES, COMICS ISSUES — EVEN A COUPLE AUDIO ISSUES ON VINYL AND CASSETTE. THOSE WERE ALL JUST DIFFERENT WAYS OF TELLING PEOPLE'S STORIES, AND MY OWN STORIES, TOO, AS I SLOWLY EMERGED FROM BEHIND THE SCENES. IN THE ISSUES COLLECTED HERE, WHICH ORIGINALLY CAME OUT BETWEEN 1998 AND 2002, THE DIFFERENT, DISPARATE ELEMENTS SEEM TO MERGE INTO A FLUID WHOLE, AND THE OVERALL SCOPE EXPANDS TO INCLUDE PEOPLE AND SUBJECTS THAT HAD ALWAYS BEEN PART OF THE PICTURE BUT WERE ON THE PERIPHERY.

IT WAS A PARTICULARLY FERTILE PERIOD BECAUSE I WAS ABLE, FOR THE FIRST TIME, TO RENT AN OFFICE SPACE AND FULLY DEVOTE MYSELF TO MAGAZINE WORK. THE FIRST OFFICE WAS JUST A TINY, UNHEATED LAUNDRY ROOM BEHIND MY NEIGHBORS' HOUSE, BUT WHAT A DIFFERENCE IT MADE! I REMEMBER EXCITEDLY RUNNING ACROSS THE STREET WITH THE FIRST DRAFT OF "TWO STORIES," THE OPENING PIECE IN THIS COLLECTION. IT WAS RAINING, AND THE PUDDLES IN THE GUTTERS WERE WARM ON MY BARE FEET. I HAD BEEN WORKING IN A TRANCE-LIKE STATE ALL NIGHT, AND NOW THE SUN WAS UP.

LUCKILY, SO WERE A FEW OF MY HOUSEMATES, ON THE PORCH STILL NURSING THEIR FORTIES FROM THE NIGHT BEFORE, AND I JOINED THEM TO CELEBRATE. AFTER YEARS OF FINDING IT DIFFICULT TO FOLLOW EVEN A SINGLE LINE OF THOUGHT TO ITS LOGICAL CONCLUSION, I'D SUCCEEDED IN FOLLOWING SEVERAL AT ONCE, SEEING HOW THEY INTERTWINED, AND CAPTURING THEM ALL ON THE PAGE. IDEAS WERE AS ELUSIVE AS FLIES, BUT IN AN OFFICE OF YOUR OWN YOU COULD SHUT THE DOOR SO THEY COULDN'T ESCAPE. FOR SENTIMENTAL REASONS AS WELL AS PRACTICAL ONES, I DECIDED TO KICK OFF "ADD TONER" WITH THAT STORY RATHER THAN REPRINT THE ISSUES CHRONOLOGICALLY.

OTHER OFFICES FOLLOWED. ODDLY ENOUGH, I FOUND QUIET, CHEAP PLACES TO WORK IN NEW YORK EASIER THAN I HAD ANYWHERE ELSE. WITHOUT THOSE, COMETBUS 47 PROBABLY NEVER WOULD HAVE BEEN WRITTEN. I'VE INCLUDED SOME PHOTOS OF THAT PROCESS, PLUS A BUNCH OF OTHER COOL "BONUS" STUFF: A "LANKY" GLOSSARY, A TON OF NEW ARTWORK FOR COMETBUS 46, NEW INTRODUCTIONS, AND A PILE OF PREVIOUSLY UNCOLLECTED SHORT STORIES.

WHEREAS "DESPITE EVERYTHING" CONTAINED JUST A SMALL SAMPLING OF THE ISSUES IT ANTHOLOGIZED, "ADD TONER" REPRINTS THREE ISSUES IN THEIR ENTIRETY, PLUS A LARGE CHUNK OF ANOTHER THREE. ANOTHER DIFFERENCE IS THE CONTRIBUTORS. "DESPITE" FEATURED WRITING, ART, AND PHOTOGRAPHY BY ALMOST A HUNDRED DIFFERENT PEOPLE. FOR BETTER OR WORSE, THIS ONE IS ALMOST ENTIRELY MY OWN WORK.

ENJOY.

3/11

P.S.: REREADING THESE ISSUES, I WAS REMINDED OF WHAT JOHN FANTE WROTE ABOUT THE DIFFICULTIES OF SEEING YOUR OWN WORK THROUGH FRESH EYES — A DOUBLE ENTENDRE SINCE BY THEN HE WAS BLIND. MOSTLY I WAS SURPRISED: WHAT EMBARRASSED ME WASN'T THE CONTENT BUT THE FACT THAT SO MANY OF THE PHRASES, ANALOGIES, AND IDEAS WERE THE SAME AS IN MY MOST RECENT WORK — SOMETIMES WORD FOR WORD. ALAS, THE EPIPHANIES AND FLASHES OF INSPIRATION THAT SEEMED NEW TO ME HAD APPARENTLY VISITED BEFORE. FORGIVE ANY REPITITION, PLEASE.

COMETBUS

#45 $2

1. Two Stories

MIKE AND I WERE LOOTING THE LEFTOVERS AT U.C. BERKELEY ONE YEAR AND FOUND A STATUE. DRUNKENLY, WE CARRIED IT DOWN BANCROFT. A LIFE-SIZE BUST, AFTER TWO BLOCKS IT WAS MORE HEAVY THAN AMUSING. MIKE WALKED INTO CAFE MILANO, MADE HIS WAY THROUGH THE CROWD, THEN SET IT DOWN RIGHT ON TOP OF A STRANGER'S TABLE.

TEN YEARS LATER, HE WENT ON A BLIND DATE. WHEN SHE BROUGHT HIM HOME, MIKE WAS MET WITH KNOWING EYES, STARING AT HIM STONILY FROM BETWEEN FERNS IN HER GARDEN. WHO WOULD HAVE KNOWN? ALL THOSE YEARS MIKE AND HIS DATE HAD BEEN TELLING HALF OF THE SAME STORY.

SAL AND I WERE WALKING ALONG IN THE UNDERGROWTH ALONGSIDE INTERSTATE 580 BY LAKE MERRITT. SHE TRIPPED OVER SOMETHING AND REACHED DOWN TO PICK IT UP. ANYWHERE ELSE IT WOULD HAVE BEEN A ROCK OR A HUBCAP, BUT TRUE TO FORM, THIS WAS OAKLAND. SHE PULLED HER HAND UP FROM THE IVY AND I DUCKED. MUCH TO HER SURPRISE AND MINE, SHE WAS HOLDING AN UZI. A REAL UZI. NOTHING TO DO BUT TRY TO WIPE OFF HER PRINTS AND BURY IT A LITTLE DEEPER.

AND THE BOTTLE OF GIN I DUMPSTERED? I CAN'T STAND THE STUFF, SO I GAVE IT TO JESS. EXCEPT, IT WAS NOT GIN AFTER ALL. JESS PROVED MY POINT, WHICH IS, EVERYTHING THAT'S FOUND WAS ONCE LOST, HIDDEN, OR THROWN OUT. MAYBE BETTER NOT TO KNOW WHY. BETTER NOT TO KNOW WHERE IT CAME FROM OR EXACTLY WHAT IT IS. BETTER SOME-TIMES NOT TO ASK FOR THE REST OF THE STORY, BETTER SOMETIMES NOT TO TELL. BUT HE ASKED, AND I WAS ONLY TRYING TO BE HELPFUL.

"WHAT'S THE WORST THING IT COULD BE?"

HE SAID. I PRODUCED A LIST FROM THE POISON CONTROL CENTER, AND WAS ONLY HALFWAY DOWN WHEN JESS TURNED GREEN AND WENT INTO THE BUSHES TO PUKE.

ON A WHIM, AND SORT OF AN ACCIDENT, I FOUND MYSELF IN VANCOUVER. I COULDN'T BELIEVE MY LUCK: THE LEGENDARY CANADIAN SUBHUMANS WERE DOING A REUNION SHOW THAT VERY NIGHT. IT WAS ALREADY SOLD OUT WHEN I GOT THERE, BUT THAT WAS ALRIGHT, EVEN SORT OF A RELIEF. I THOUGHT OF ALL THE GREAT BANDS I'D GONE TO SEE BUT FOR ONE REASON OR ANOTHER NEVER LAID EYES ON. UNDERAGE, BROKE, SOLD OUT, OR KICKED OUT, THOSE WERE THE BEST SHOWS OF ALL. SITTING OUT FRONT WHERE THE SOUND OF THE MUSIC BLENDED WITH THE STREET SCENE AND THE ROAR OF PASSING CARS. AS IT WAS IN THE BEGINNING, IS NOW, AND EVER SHALL BE, WORLD WITHOUT END. AMEN. I SETTLED ONTO THE PAVEMENT WITH THE OTHER PUNKS, MAKING NEW FRIENDS, TRADING STORIES AND SCHEMES FOR SNEAKING IN.

"NO STAMP? TRY WALKING IN BACKWARDS".
"DRESS UP AS THE BACK DOOR".
"SAY SOMEONE ORDERED PIZZA".
"AND ALL SIX OF US ARE HERE TO DELIVER IT? I DON'T THINK SO".
"WE'LL SAY WE'RE THE OPENING BAND".
"FUCK IT, WE'LL BE THE OPENING BAND!"
"HEY LOSERS, THE FUCKING OPENING BAND ALREADY PLAYED!"

SHE WAS RIGHT. YOU COULD HEAR THE SUBHUMANS STARTING INSIDE.

OF ALL THE TRICKS, I'D FORGOTTEN THE OLDEST IN THE BOOK. I WALKED UP THE STAIRS PAST THE SUSPICIOUS GLARE OF A HERD OF NECKLESS BOUNCERS. "GUEST LIST", I SAID, AND AS THEY LOOKED UP THE NAME I GAVE I CRANED MY HEAD AROUND LIKE A LLAMA, LOOKING OVER THEIR SHOULDERS FOR A BETTER ONE.

"NO SPIRO AGNEW ON THE LIST", THEY YELLED. "GET OUT!!"

THE HEAD BOUNCER SEIZED ME AND PICKED MY FEET OFF THE GROUND, READY TO BOWL ME HEAD-FIRST DOWN THE STAIRS AND OUT THE DOOR. I QUICKLY PUT IN A POSTSCRIPT.

"PERHAPS THEY PUT ME DOWN UNDER MY NICKNAME, 'POPO'".

THAT DID THE TRICK. INSTEAD OF THROWING ME OUT THE DOOR, THEY CROSSED POPO OFF THE LIST AND THREW ME RIGHT INTO THE PIT.

I COULDN'T BELIEVE IT, THE SUBHUMANS WERE SO FUCKING GOOD, REALLY SCREAMING AND PUMPING AND POUNDING IT OUT, NOT JUST GOING THROUGH THE MOTIONS. AND THERE WAS GERRY HANNAH, PROUDLY PLAYING HIS FIRST SHOW SINCE BEING ARRESTED AS PART OF THE VANCOUVER FIVE MORE THAN TEN YEARS BEFORE.

I CHEERED, I DANCED, I SANG ALONG. BUT IN ALL THE SWEAT AND PASSIONATE NOISE, THERE WAS A THORN IN MY SIDE. A NAGGING GUILTY FEELING I COULDN'T GET OFF MY MIND.

"WHO IS POPO?", IT ASKED. "WHERE IS POPO? DID HE SHOW UP AFTER ALL, JUST A LITTLE LATE?"

MY MOM WAS ON A DATE. TIME: THE EARLY FIFTIES. PLACE: DETROIT. THE ICY RAIN IS FALLING DOWN AND FORMING MUDDY PUDDLES. HUGE AMERICAN CARS ROLL DOWN THE ROAD AND PEOPLE RUN CROUCHED UNDER UMBRELLAS OR WRAPPED UP IN RAINCOATS. ON THE CORNER IS A RESTAURANT, FANCY BUT NOT GAUDY. THROUGH THE WINDOW YOU CAN SEE MY MOM AND SOME DUDE, FINISHING THEIR MEAL. NO FOOL, MY MOM ALLOWS HIM TO PAY THE BILL. THEY STAND UP, RETRIEVE THEIR COATS FROM THE DOORMAN, AND WALK HAPPILY TOGETHER DOWN THE STREET.

HOWEVER, IT IS NOT MEANT TO BE. A CAR RACES BY AND HITS A HUGE PUDDLE. MOM STAYS DRY BUT THE GUY IS SPLASHED HEAD TO TOE. HE TAKES OFF HIS OVERCOAT, NOW A SOAKED, RUINED, MUDDY MESS. WHAT A THING TO HAPPEN ON A DATE WITH MY MOM! BUT, EXAMINING THE DAMAGE, HE SUDDENLY LIGHTENS UP.

"WHY, THIS ISN'T MY COAT AT ALL", HE LAUGHS. "THE DOORMAN MUST HAVE GIVEN ME THE WRONG ONE!"

THEY RETURN TO THE RESTAURANT AND HAND THE DRIPPING MUDDY BUNDLE BACK TO THE HORRIFIED DOORMAN. "THERE SEEMS TO HAVE BEEN A MISTAKE", THEY SAY. "YOU GAVE US THE WRONG COAT".

INDEED, THE DOORMAN CHECKS THE TAGS AND APOLOGIZES, HANDING OVER A COAT OF A SIMILAR CUT.

HAPPY, WARM, AND DRY, THEY STROLL DOWN THE STREET AGAIN WITH A SMILE AND A GEM OF WISDOM TO PASS DOWN TO FUTURE GENERATIONS. "THAT'S THE DIFFERENCE BETWEEN A SHLEMIEL AND A SHLEMAZEL", MOM TELLS ME MANY YEARS LATER. "ANY SHLEMIEL CAN GET THEIR COAT SPLASHED IN MUD BY A PASSING CAR. BUT TO DO IT WITHOUT EVEN PUTTING IT ON OR GOING OUTSIDE, THAT TAKES A SHLEMAZEL".

POOR SHLEMAZEL. HIM AND ALL THE OTHER POPOS OF THIS WORLD, IN THEIR MUDDY OVERCOATS,

STUCK IN THE OTHER HALF OF MY FAMILY'S STORIES. PROBABLY SEVEN FEET TALL, WAITING OUTSIDE THE SHOW, IN THE RAIN, WITH AN AXE TO GRIND, LITERALLY.

ONCE I SPENT A MONTH IN STOCKHOLM, SWEDEN. UNTIL THEN, SACRAMENTO WAS THE FURTHEST I'D EVER BEEN AWAY FROM HOME AND FRIENDS. IT WAS EXCITING, BUT SO LONELY AS TO BE ALMOST UNBEARABLE. I JUST WALKED, DAY AND NIGHT, MOSTLY IN THE STREETS OF THE OLD TOWN, GAMLA STAN, WATCHING THE STREET MUSICIANS PLAY. NO CONVERSATIONS WITH ANYONE, NO HUMAN CONTACT AT ALL, JUST THE SONGS AND THE SOUND OF FOREIGN WORDS AND PEOPLE PASSING BY.

I WAS WHISTLING THE OTHER DAY WHILE I FLIPPED THE EGGS AND POURED THE MORNING COFFEE.

"WHAT'S THAT?", MY ROOMMATE JOHN ASKED, SO I TOLD HIM: A SONG A BAND OF STREET MUSICIANS PLAYED ONE DAY IN GAMLA STAN IN THE SUMMER OF '85. STILL STUCK IN MY HEAD, GODDAMMIT.

"YEAH, THAT'S FUNNY", HE SAID, MATTER-OF-FACT. "I THOUGHT I'D HEARD IT BEFORE."

MY ROOMMATES KEPT PULLING RABBITS LIKE THAT OUT OF THEIR HAT. "OH, I DIDN'T MENTION I USED TO BE A TEACHER AT A GIRLS' SCHOOL IN NEW HAMPSHIRE?", SAYS THE BEARDED SAILOR GUY. "YOU DIDN'T KNOW I HAD A TWO FOOT MOHAWK AND A FANZINE?", SAYS THE HIPPIE.

NOW IT WAS JOHN'S TURN. "STOCKHOLM? SUMMER OF '85? GAMLA STAN? YEAH, I WAS THERE AT THE SAME TIME, DOING RESEARCH ON THE SWEDISH LABOR PARTY."

MY MOUTH DROPPED AND INSTINCTIVELY BEGAN MUTTERING, "WEIRD, WEIRD, WEIRD, WEIRD" THOUGH, AS SLUGGO LIKES TO REMIND ME, IT'S ACTUALLY NOT THAT WEIRD. OUR PATHS DON'T CROSS AND INTERSECT BY CHANCE, BUT BY THE CHOICES THAT WE'VE MADE.

I WENT DOWNSTAIRS AND WENT DIGGING THROUGH OLD ISSUES UNTIL I FOUND IT, A PHOTO OF THAT WONDERFUL BAND PLAYING ON THE STREET. TWO GIRLS AND TWO GUYS, DECKED OUT AND DANCING ALL AROUND, SINGING AND STRUMMING ACOUSTIC INSTRUMENTS AND RADIATING A RARE WARMTH. A LOVE FOR PERFORMING, FOR EACH OTHER, AND FOR LIFE ITSELF SO STRONG IT SWEPT ME OUT OF MY SHELL. IN SHY STOCKHOLM, NOTHING ELSE HAD COME CLOSE TO DOING THAT.

JOHN WENT UPSTAIRS AND CAME BACK WITH A PILE OF CASSETTES. CAPTURED ON TAPE WERE THOSE FAMILIAR OLD SOUNDS: FOOTSTEPS AND FOREIGN WORDS, STREETCARS AND FALLING RAIN.

LONELY AND OUT OF PLACE LIKE ME, JOHN HAD CARRIED A TAPE RECORDER AND CAPTURED THE SOUNDS OF STOCKHOLM AS HE WALKED THROUGH IT EVERY DAY. OBSERVING PEOPLE BUT NEVER INTER-ACTING WITH THEM, AT LEAST NOT SUCCESSFULLY.

THEN HE FOUND IT, ON A TAPE OF STREET MUSICIANS. SURE ENOUGH, THE SONG I NEVER THOUGHT I'D HEAR AGAIN, BETTER EVEN THAN I REMEMBERED.

"BUT THEY WEREN'T LIKE THE OTHER STREET MUSICIANS," I PROTESTED. "I WAS IN GAMLA STAN EVERY DAY AND I SWEAR THEY WERE ONLY OUT ONCE. ONLY FOR AN HOUR, ONLY PLAYING TO FIFTEEN OR TWENTY PEOPLE AT MOST."

JOHN SAID, "I KNOW. I WAS ONE OF THOSE FIFTEEN OR TWENTY PEOPLE."

I IMAGINED I COULD HEAR THE SOUND OF MY OWN HANDS IN THE APPLAUSE BETWEEN SONGS. JOHN THOUGHT HE SAW THE CORNER OF HIS COAT IN THE CORNER OF MY PHOTO. BUT WHO KNOWS? WE WERE PROBABLY STANDING SHOULDER TO SHOULDER.

ONE DAY TOWARDS THE END OF MY STAY IN SWEDEN, A GUY CHASED ME DOWN AND, OUT OF BREATH AND IN BROKEN ENGLISH, EXPLAINED THAT HE HAD BEEN TRYING TO CATCH UP TO ME FOR THREE WEEKS, EVER SINCE THE DAY I HANDED HIM A FANZINE OUTSIDE CENTRAL STATION THEN GRUNTED AND RAN AWAY.

HIS NAME WAS DEE DEE. WE SAT EATING TOGETHER AT A LARGE LUNCH COUNTER OVERLOOK-ING THE STATION, KEEPING AN EYE OUT FOR MONGO, A SKINHEAD WHO WAS LOOKING TO BEAT DEE DEE'S BRAINS IN.

A NICE BOY, THAT DEE DEE. OUT OF A MILLION PEOPLE I'D PASSED HOPING FOR A WORD, A GESTURE, OR A CHASE, HE WAS ONE IN A MILLION. FOOLISH NOT TO REALIZE THAT EVERYONE ELSE WAS WAITING TOO, FOR SOMEONE ELSE TO MAKE THE MOVE. TO CONNECT DIFFERENT LIVES AND LOOSE ENDS, AND COMPARE STORIES.

DEE DEE HAD TRACKED ME DOWN, ASKING EVERYONE IF THEY HAD SEEN THE SHY AMERICAN FANZINE EDITOR. FINALLY ONE COUPLE SAID THEY HAD. EVIDENTLY I PASSED BY THE LICORICE SHOP WHERE THEY WORKED — NOT ONCE BUT OVER AND OVER, EVERY DAY, IN MY ENDLESS TRUDGE THROUGH OLD TOWN.

MY EARS RANG, I WAS SO HAPPY. TO BE SEEN BY STRANGERS, NOTICED BY PEOPLE WITHOUT EVEN KNOWING IT, LOOKED FOR AND REMEMBERED.

SUDDENLY I FELT MUCH LESS ALONE. IT'S GOOD TO REMEMBER THAT NOW. HOW JUST PASSING BY, WE TOUCH LIVES THAT WE DON'T EVEN KNOW, AND BECOME PART OF STORIES TOLD BY PEOPLE WE DON'T EVEN KNOW EXIST. THE WAY MONGO IS PART OF MY STOCKHOLM STORY AND HE DOESN'T EVEN KNOW I EXIST. HOPEFULLY.

2. Story of The Curse

I CAME HOME. IT WAS VERY, VERY DARK.
"POWER CUT OFF?", I CALLED OUT.
"YES" SAID A VOICE FROM THE DARKNESS. SETH KELLY.
"ANY FOOD?"
"NO". MY OTHER HOUSEMATE, J.P.
I STUMBLED AROUND THROUGH THE WRECKAGE FOR A MINUTE BEFORE I FOUND THEM. THEY STOOD IMMOBILE IN THE EERIE, FLICKERING GLOW OF A SINGLE CANDLE. THEY WERE STARING AND POINTING AT MY MONKEY.
"BOYS! NO NEED TO MAKE RASH DECISIONS! WHAT'S GOING ON HERE?"
"WE THOUGHT ABOUT THE WAY THINGS WERE GOING", J.P. SAID.
"WRONG. THE WAY THINGS WERE GOING WRONG", SETH SAID.
"IT SEEMED LIKE THERE MUST BE A CURSE".
"SO WE DECIDED TO LOOK FOR IT".
"AND LOOK WHAT WE FOUND".
THEY POINTED AT THE HORRIBLE, GRIMACING, PURPLE PAPER MACHE MONKEY. SHADOWS FELL ACROSS THE FACE OF THE ALREADY DARK AND EVIL THING, MAKING ITS GRIN AND WIDE EYES ALL THE MORE DEFIANT AND CHALLENGING. THE MONKEY POINTED BACK WITH AN OUTSTRETCHED MIDDLE FINGER, FLIPPING THEM OFF.
"SURELY YOU ARE NOT SUGGESTING THAT MY MONKEY HAS ANYTHING TO DO WITH THE UNEXPECTED TURN OUR LIVES HAVE TAKEN. WHY, IT'S JUST A SWEET PRESENT FROM MY SWEET GIRLFRIEND, MAYE."
AT THE SOUND OF THAT NAME, MY HOUSEMATES COWERED AND HISSED. DUCKED AND COVERED. PREPARED FOR LIGHTNING TO STRIKE TWICE. THEY SAID, "EITHER THE MONKEY GOES OR WE DO".

A FRIENDLY, CUDDLY LITTLE MONKEY. PEOPLE FREAK OUT OVER THE WEIRDEST THINGS. LIKE MAYE, WHEN SHE TOLD ME ABOUT SLEEPING WITH ANOTHER BOY WHILE I WAS AWAY FOR THE WEEKEND, I WAS UPSET. SHE COULDN'T UNDERSTAND WHY. I GUESS THERE'S NO TELLING WHAT WILL SET SOMEONE OFF. WHEN I MENTIONED I HAD KISSED ANOTHER GIRL, SHE GOT UP AND RAN AWAY, STRAIGHT OVER THE BACK FENCE OF THE OLD CITY HALL.

FUNNY GIRL. WHEN I RAN INTO HER TWO HOURS LATER IN ONE OF THE ALLEYS, SHE WALKED UP WITH HER HEAD HUNG LOW AND A TINY FLOWER IN HER HANDS. AN OFFERING AND AN ASKING TOO, FOR FORGIVENESS, RAPPROCHEMENT, UNDERSTANDING. FOR GIVE AND FOR TAKE. ALSO, AN OFFERING JUST FOR ITS OWN SAKE.

IT SHOULD HAVE BEEN A BAD SIGN WHEN SHE STOLE THINGS FROM HER FRIENDS TO GIVE TO ME, WHEN SHE GAVE ME THE PRESENTS FRIENDS HAD GIVEN HER, WHEN SHE TOOK THE PRESENTS I GAVE HER AND GAVE THOSE AWAY TOO, TO OTHER GIRLS WHO, MAYE SAID, LOVED ME MORE THAN SHE EVER COULD. BUT A BAD SIGN WAS LIKE A GREEN LIGHT FOR ME. A GOOD SIGN AND I WOULD HAVE BEEN THE ONE TO RUN.

FINALLY, THOUGH, IT ALL BROKE. SINCE I COULDN'T RUN I JUST SAT AT HOME SCREAMING, HITTING THE WALLS, AND TEARING OUT MY HAIR.

IN A NEARBY TOWN, MAYE BOARDED A BART TRAIN. IN HER ARMS, A LARGE PURPLE MONKEY. THOUGH THE TRAIN WAS CROWDED WITH THE MORNING COMMUTE, MAYE SAT SIDE BY SIDE WITH THE MONKEY, BOTH STARING STRAIGHT AHEAD AND FLIPPING OFF ANYONE WHO COMMENTED OR TRIED TO TAKE THE PRIMATE'S PLACE.

THOUGH I HAD SAID I NEVER WANTED TO SEE HER AGAIN, THERE SHE WAS KICKING DOWN MY DOOR. WHO ELSE WOULD SHOW UP WITH AN ANGRY PURPLE MONKEY IN AN ATTEMPT TO WIN BACK MY HEART? IT HAD BEEN AT MY APARTMENT EVER SINCE, AND SO HAD SHE, MUCH OF THE TIME.

OH, MAYE. SHE ALWAYS CHALLENGED ME, WOULDN'T EVER LET IT BE EASY. WOULDN'T LET ME GO OUT WITH HER, THEN WOULDN'T LET ME BREAK UP. SHE WOULDN'T STAND FOR MY BULLSHIT, AND THAT MADE ME LOVE HER ALL THE MORE. BUT LOVE ONLY MADE IT HARDER TO LIVE. THE LANDLORD CAME AND BOOTED US OUT INTO THE STREET. SETH LOST HIS JOB, J.P. LOST HIS GIRLFRIEND, AND I WAS SUCH A MESS I COULDN'T THINK OR SLEEP OR EAT.

IT WAS LIKE TRYING TO GET RID OF SCABIES, WHEN THERE'S NOTHING LEFT TO DO BUT SET FIRE TO ALL YOUR CLOTHES AND DRIVE OUT OF TOWN NAKED.

A COWARDLY MOVE, I KNOW. I'D ALWAYS CONSIDERED MYSELF SOMEONE WHO COULD MEET PROBLEMS FACE TO FACE. I WANTED TO BE DIFFER- ENT FROM EVERY OTHER MAN IN MAYE'S LIFE. THEY HAD ALL LEFT, STARTING WITH HER FATHER. BUT I WASN'T SO DIFFERENT.

WHEN I RETURNED, NEARLY A YEAR HAD PASSED. IN MY DAD'S BASEMENT UNPACKING, I FOUND TRACES OF RATS. THEY HAD GOTTEN INTO MY BOXES AND EATEN HALF OF MY FAVORITE T-SHIRT AND A COPY OF SNIFFIN' GLUE. I FOLLOWED A TRAIL OF PAPER AND SHIT AND CAME TO A FAMILIAR FACE: THE MONKEY— ONLY THERE WAS A HOLE WHERE ITS MOUTH HAD BEEN, AND ITS INNARDS WERE PUKED OUT IN A HORRIBLE STINKING, ROTTING MESS, AS IF THE HEART AND SOUL OF THE BEAST HAD MOVED ON AND ONLY THE EMPTY SHELL REMAINED. IT WAS THE SAME AS MY LOVE FOR MAYE, SO I KEPT THE DAMN THING. HOLLOW NOW AND DESECRATED, IT WAS ALL I HAD LEFT. I BOXED IT UP SO THAT NOTHING MORE COULD GET IN OR OUT.

I TOOK PRIDE IN THE FACT THAT MY FLEETING, AWKWARD RELATIONSHIPS ALWAYS TURNED INTO LASTING FRIENDSHIPS, MORE SATISFYING AND SWEET THAN THE ROMANCES HAD BEEN. BUT MAYE AND I WOULD NEVER BE FRIENDS. GREAT AS LOVERS, GREAT AS ENEMIES, BUT LOUSY AS FRIENDS. WE TRIED, BUT IT WAS NO USE. MAYBE I HAD FINALLY FOUND TRUE LOVE. NOT THAT TRUE LOVE IS A BITTER, ROTTEN DEAD MONKEY IN A BOX. BUT THEN AGAIN, MAYBE.

DURING OUR BRIEF ATTEMPT AT FRIENDSHIP, MAYE SAID WE SHOULD TAKE THE MONKEY DOWN TO THE PIER AND THROW IT OFF TOGETHER. BUT I SAID NO. I WASN'T READY TO LET IT GO JUST YET.

LAST YEAR I SPENT MONTHS CLEARING OUT MY DAD'S BASEMENT. LITERALLY, MONTHS. HE'S EVEN MORE OF A PACKRAT THAN ME, AND MUCH LESS ORGANIZED. UNCOVERING GHOSTS NEARLY FIFTY YEARS OLD MADE ME AWARE OF ALL THE THINGS I DON'T WANT AROUND HAUNTING ME, WAITING TO BE REMEMBERED. TIME TO TAKE OUT MY OWN TRASH.

WHEN NEIGHBORHOOD CLEANUP DAY ARRIVED, THIRTY BOXES OF CRAP WERE OUT FRONT OF MY DAD'S. I SAID MY GOODBYES — TO THE MONKEY, TO MAYE, EVEN TO THE LONG AGO DOOMED APARTMENT WITH

J.P. AND SETH. I SAID GOODBYE AND WALKED AWAY,
AND AS I LEFT I COULD ALREADY HEAR THE
SCAVENGERS WITH THEIR PICKUP TRUCKS AND
SHOPPING CARTS COMING TO PICK THROUGH THE PILE.
WHO CAN RESIST A BOX CLEARLY MARKED, "CURSE"?

3. Between the Days

IN BETWEEN THE FRANTIC, FRENZIED WEEKS
OF RUNNING AROUND GETTING READY TO LEAVE AND
THE CALM, BLISSFUL MOMENT OF ACTUALLY DRIVING
AWAY, I ALWAYS WISH THERE WAS AN EXTRA DAY.
IN BETWEEN DEPARTURE AND ARRIVAL, FAREWELL
AND BETTER TO FORGET. WHO AM I KIDDING? I WISH
THERE WAS AN EXTRA YEAR.
IF I COULD ONLY MAKE THAT MOMENT LAST.
NOT THE CRESCENDO OF BURNING DOWN THE HOUSE,
NOT THE BEGINNINGS OF BUILDING A NEW ONE IN
ITS PLACE. JUST A CIGARETTE IN THE RUBBLE TO
PAUSE AND TAKE IN THE CHANGE. BECAUSE, LIKE
SEX, THE SWEETEST PART IS NOT THE CLIMAX
BUT THE CALM AFTER THE STORM. FOLLOWED BY
THE COFFEE, CIGARETTES, THAI FOOD AND ICE
CREAM AFTER THE CALM AFTER THE STORM. SEX
AND LIFE, BOTH TOO GOOD TO LAST, YET PERHAPS
TOO GOOD TO RUSH. YES. YOU COULD ARGUE THAT
THE WORLD IS NOT A WOMAN AND LIFE IS NOT
A GLORIOUS YET EMBARRASSING ONE-NIGHT STAND.
BUT REALLY, WHAT'S THE USE IN ARGUING ABOUT IT?
IT HAPPENED TO ME, SO I KNOW. ONLY ONE
LAST THING TO DO BEFORE I LEFT TOWN, BUT IT
WAS A DOOZY. A ROOT CANAL. SO I SAID GOODBYES
AHEAD OF TIME. GOODBYE TO FRIENDS AND FAMILY,
FAREWELL TO MY FISH AND SPENGER'S AND MIDNIGHT
BASKETBALL. MY BAGS WERE EVEN PACKED IN
ADVANCE.
THE APPOINTMENT WAS AN EARLY ONE. VERY
EARLY. CRIMINALLY, INHUMANELY EARLY. BUT AFTER
WEEKS OF ANTICIPATION, THE OPERATION ITSELF
WAS A BREEZE. FAST AND ANTICLIMACTIC. MY FIFTH
ROOT CANAL, AND ONE SITUATION WHERE MY
INCREASING CALLOUSNESS AND INSENSITIVITY
REALLY PAID OFF. I WALKED OUT OF THE DENTIST
AT TEN IN THE MORNING ALL PATCHED UP AND
FEELING FINE AS WINE.
THERE WAS NOTHING TO RECOVER FROM, NO

NEED AFTER ALL TO GO HOME AND SLEEP. JUST A
NUMB MOUTH AND A WHOLE UNEXPECTED DAY
LAID OUT AHEAD OF ME. SONNY, MY RIDE, DIDN'T
LEAVE UNTIL EIGHT.

I WAS STARTING ON MY SECOND ICE CREAM
CONE WHEN I SPOTTED THE GRIMPLE BOYS OUTSIDE
THE TELEGRAPH 7-11. I YELLED AT THEM. "WHAT
THE FUCK ARE YOU GUYS DOING OUT IN THE
DAYTIME?", I SAID.

BUT IT CAME OUT MORE LIKE, "WGDLBLRRGDBDM".
MY TONGUE WOULDN'T WORK RIGHT TO FORM THE
WORDS. THEY JUST LOOKED AT ME WEIRD.

"DAMN, DUDE", THEY SAID. "WHO FUCKED UP YOUR
FACE?"

I LAUGHED AND LAUGHED, AND DROOLED. A ROOT
CANAL IS A HARD THING TO EXPLAIN, ESPECIALLY WITH
FRESH STITCHES IN YOUR MOUTH.

WALKING DOWN DWIGHT, I CAME ACROSS
YOLANDA AND COREY IN HIS FRONT YARD, KISSING. IT
WAS SWEET TO SEE, A LITTLE TENDERNESS AND
TORTURE BEFORE SHE SCURRIED OFF TO SCHOOL FOR
THE DAY. LEAVING HAS THE SAME LOOK AND FEEL
WHETHER FOR AN HOUR OR A YEAR, TO YOUR POLITICAL
SCIENCE CLASS OR TO WALK AROUND THE WORLD. IT'S
JUST A MATTER OF HOW MUCH AND HOW FAR GONE.

EASIER TO LEAVE SOMETHING YOU HATE, EASIER
TO STAY AWAY FROM SOMETHING YOU LIKE, BUT IF YOU
LOVE IT NO ONE KNOWS WHAT TO DO AND YOU FEEL
CHEATED AND CONFUSED, WHICH IS I THINK WHAT
YOLANDA WAS GOING THROUGH THAT MORNING WITH
COREY AND WHAT I'D BEEN GOING THROUGH THAT
WHOLE MONTH WITH BERKELEY, GETTING READY TO
SPLIT. TORN BETWEEN UNDERSTOOD AND UNKNOWN,
CHALLENGING AND COMFORTING. TOO MUCH FOR
COREY, THOUGH, WHO JUST NEEDED A LITTLE BIT
OF COMFORTING.

EVERYONE TURNS ON THE CHARM WHEN IT'S
TIME TO SAY GOODBYE. HOW CAN YOU HELP FALLING
IN LOVE WITH THEM ALL OVER AGAIN? HOW CAN
THEY HELP BUT RUN AND HIDE KNOWING IT WILL ONLY
MAKE YOU MISS THEM MORE? THAT'S HOW IT GOES,
NOT JUST WITH BOYS AND GIRLS, BUT EVEN WITH
MY STUPID CITY. IF ONLY IT WOULD RAIN ON ME ON
MY WAY OUT OF TOWN. BUT NO, IT WAS THE MOST
BEAUTIFUL CAREFREE SUNNY DAY I HAD EVER SEEN.
THE BAY SHINED, THE HILLS CLIMBED, AND EVERY
WINGNUT AND FLOWER WAS OUT IN FULL BLOOM.
I TOOK COREY OUT OF YOLANDA'S ARMS AND
DRAGGED HIM DOWN THE STREET. A LITTLE STROLL
TO EASE HIS TROUBLED MIND.

WE WERE TALKING. ABOUT GIRLS, AS USUAL, EXCEPT A LITTLE MORE EXPLICITLY THAN USUAL. PEOPLE OUT WATERING THE PLANTS STARED AND BLUSHED, CATCHING THE TONE OF MY SLURS IF NOT THE EXACT WORDS. I IGNORED THEM AND WENT ON, IN TEXTBOOK DETAIL.

"YOU KNOW HOW IT IS WHEN HER LEG IS UP LIKE THIS, AND YOU'RE TWISTED AROUND WITH YOUR HEAD LIKE THIS, AND THEN, YOU KNOW, SHE'S LIKE, MIND IF I DO THIS?"

"UH, SURE", COREY SAID.

"DO YOU LIKE THAT?"

I MEAN, WHAT'S THE BIG DEAL? EVERYONE TALKS ABOUT SEX, BUT NO ONE EVER REALLY TALKS ABOUT SEX, YOU KNOW? IT'S ODD. BUT I GUESS I DON'T EITHER, OR HADN'T MUCH BEFORE.

COREY OPENED ONE EYE BIGGER THAN THE OTHER AND SCRUTINIZED ME. "TELL ME", HE SAID. "DID THEY GIVE YOU ANY DRUGS AT THE DENTIST?"

"DRUGS? ME? I DON'T EVEN TAKE ANESTHESIA. NOT EVEN FOR FUN.

"BUT THIS WASN'T MY REGULAR DENTIST", I ADDED. "AND COME TO THINK OF IT, HE DID GIVE ME A LITTLE SOMETHING. SNUCK IN A SHOT QUICK BEFORE I COULD STOP HIM. MAN, I WAS PISSED. BUT I FORGOT ALL ABOUT IT UNTIL NOW. WHY DO YOU ASK?"

IF I DID DRUGS ALL THE TIME I WOULD HAVE FIGURED OUT WHAT COREY ALREADY KNEW: IT WASN'T THE STITCHES MAKING ME SLUR MY WORDS. I WAS GONE WITH THE WIND. AND COREY, I NOW NOTICED, WAS STILL IN HIS PAJAMAS.

"IT'S SUCH A NICE SUNNY DAY", I SMILED. "BUT FUCK IT, LET'S GO BACK TO YOUR BASEMENT AND JAM".

"MAYBE IF I SMOKED A FEW BONGLOADS AND TOOK HALF A HIT OF ACID, I'D BE ABLE TO ACTUALLY UNDERSTAND YOU", COREY SAID, AND SO HE DID.

WE PLAYED EVERY SONG WE'D EVER WRITTEN TOGETHER OVER THE YEARS, THEN EVERY SONG WE'D EVER WRITTEN SEPARATELY, THEN BITS AND PIECES OF EVERY SONG WE'D EVER HEARD. PLAYING DRUMS WAS DANGEROUS, SEEING AS HOW I ACCIDENTALLY HIT MYSELF IN THE FACE EVEN ON REGULAR DAYS. I JUST HOPED THE STITCHES WOULDN'T POP OUT SCREAMING ALONG LIKE THAT.

THE SUN WAS STILL OUT WHEN WE FINISHED, THE BIRDS WERE STILL CHIRPING, AND A STILL CALM HUNG IN THE AIR. TIME HELD BACK AND HAD YET TO CATCH UP. I WAS THANKFUL FOR THE

BREAK FROM THE RUSH. A PAUSE BEFORE LEAVING BUT LONG AFTER SAYING GOODBYE. A CHANCE TO LOOK BOTH WAYS.

"COREY", I SAID, "IMAGINE WAKING UP IN BETWEEN THE DAYS".

"TOTALLY".

"YOU FIND THE CAST OF CHARACTERS IN YOUR LIFE HAVING A CAST PARTY. THEY'RE MINGLING HAPPILY WITHOUT YOU TO ENFORCE THE RULES AND REINFORCE THE ROLES THEY'VE BEEN ASSIGNED".

"YOLANDA TOO?": HE LOOKED WORRIED.

"NO, FOR ONCE SHE'S RIGHT NEXT TO YOU AND STILL ASLEEP. YOU CAN SEE HER WITHOUT HAVING TO LOOK AWAY. YOU CAN BE TOGETHER FOR A WHILE WITHOUT EITHER OF YOU HAVING TO LEAVE".

"I DON'T KNOW WHETHER TO STAY IN BED", HE SAID, "OR GO AND JOIN THE PARTY. OR WAKE UP YOLANDA AND BRING HER AS MY DATE".

"I KNOW. ME NEITHER. BUT MAYBE YOU DON'T HAVE TO DECIDE. MAYBE THERE'S TIME FOR EVERY-THING".

"YOU'RE KIDDING".

"NO, JUST HIGH AS A KITE".

COREY SAID, "I KNOW YOU'RE ALWAYS WRONG. BUT JUST THIS ONCE, I REALLY HOPE YOU'RE RIGHT".

4. Tale of Two Cindys

CINDY AND CINDY WENT TO A SMALL LIBERAL ARTS COLLEGE IN CONWAY, ARKANSAS. THEY WERE NICE, THEY WERE PLEASANT, THEY WERE ENTHUSIASTIC. BUT THEY WERE PLAIN. NOT MEAN ENOUGH, SHARP ENOUGH, QUIET OR LOUD ENOUGH TO REALLY BE NOTICED. TWO LONELY LOWER UPPER CLASS ALMOST PUNK GIRLS ON A LIBERAL ARTS SCHOOL CAMPUS SADLY SET TWENTY FIVE MILES FROM THE CITY, WHERE THE REAL ACTION WAS. THEY WANTED TO BE NOTICED. WHO CAN BLAME THEM? WHO AMONG US WILL CAST THE FIRST STONE? WHO REALLY WANTS TO BE ALONE? BESIDES ME.

THEY USED TO BEAT UP GIRLS LIKE CINDY AND CINDY BACK IN THE DARK DAYS OF EARLY 80'S PUNK. THE DARK, DESTRUCTIVE, BAD, EVIL, GLORIOUS, WONDERFUL I-MISS EARLY 80'S PUNK. GIRL PUNK GANGS WOULD DESTROY THOSE POOR NORMAL GIRLS WHO DARED TO SHOW UP AT A SHOW. IT WAS

VICIOUS YET LAUGHABLE, LIKE MOST THINGS AT THE
TIME. YOU COULD SEE THE PEACE SIGN BLEACHED
INTO THE BACK OF CAROL'S HAIR AS SHE POUNDED
HER FISTS INTO THE FACE OF SOME POOR BLONDE
COLLEGE CO-ED OUTSIDE OF RUTHIE'S INN.

CINDY AND CINDY WOULDN'T HAVE LASTED LONG
AT RUTHIE'S INN, BUT THEY FIT RIGHT INTO THE
LATE 90'S LITTLE ROCK SCENE. I WOULD NEVER
WISH HARM UPON EITHER CINDY, NOR UPON MYSELF,
YET THE FACT REMAINED: NEVER IN A MILLION
YEARS WOULD I BE ABLE TO HAVE FUN AT ONE
OF THOSE SHOWS.

"WHAT DOESN'T KILL YOU MAKES YOU STRONGER",
THAT'S WHAT THEY SAY. I SAY, "DEATH IS PAINLESS,
BUT EVERYTHING ELSE HURTS LIKE HELL". WOULD
I WILLINGLY RUN THE GAUNTLET AND BE HIT BY
EVERYTHING WHICH HAS HURT ME, SHAPED ME,
AND GIVEN ME STRENGTH AND CHARACTER OVER
THE YEARS? NOT ON YOUR LIFE. I WOULD SIT ON
THE COUCH INSTEAD, RELAXING AND CATCHING UP
ON OLD MAIL. I WOULD BE A SPINELESS, FORMLESS,
BORING SCHLUB. I WOULD PAY SEVEN BUCKS TO
GET INTO THE LATE 90'S LITTLE ROCK SHOW AND,
WITH MY BACKPACK ON, SING ALONG WITH AVAIL.
NO ROUGH STUFF, THOUGH. THIS IS NO PLACE FOR
THAT.

OKAY, EACH TO HIS OWN. BUT IT WAS NO
GOOD FOR CINDY AND CINDY EITHER. TOO REMOVED
FROM THE BASE INSTINCT OF LIFE, WHICH IS,
BASICALLY, DEATH. MAYBE SEX AND DEATH. THEY
SAID, SEX AND DEATH? I WANT SOME.

BUT, POOR DISCONNECTED LIBERAL ARTS SCHOOL
COLLEGE GIRLS, THEY DIDN'T EVEN KNOW HOW TO
LIVE. DISCONNECTED FROM EVEN THE MOST BASE
INSTINCTS, THEY COULDN'T APPROACH ANYTHING
NATURALLY. TRYING IS VERY IMPORTANT, FAILING IS
ALSO GOOD, AND SUCCESS CAN DO GREAT THINGS FOR
YOUR CONFIDENCE AND ABILITY TO PERSEVERE. BUT
TRYING TOO HARD ALWAYS MAKES YOU LOOK LIKE
A BAD JOKE. WHEN THE GIRLS ANNOUNCED THEY
HAD CHANGED THEIR NAMES, I HAD TO LAUGH. "SIN"
AND "INDY"

WHY DO I HATE CINDY AND CINDY, WHOSE NEW
NAMES I COULD NEVER BRING MYSELF TO SAY? THEY
ARE FRIENDS OF MINE, THAT'S ONE GOOD REASON,
BUT THERE'S SOMETHING MORE. I HATE THEM FOR
TRYING SO HARD, I HATE THEIR DISHONESTY IN TRYING
TO CHANGE AND BE ACCEPTED INSTEAD OF JUST
ACCEPTING THEMSELVES AND WAITING FOR EVERYONE
ELSE TO CATCH ON OR FUCK OFF. MOST OF ALL I HATE

THE NAGGING LONELINESS AND THE NEED FOR ACCEPTANCE. CHANGING YOURSELF IS HEALTHY AND NECESSARY. IS IT ALSO ALWAYS DISHONEST?

WHY DOES IT SEEM SO GREAT TO ME TO BE SHAPED BY THE HARDSHIPS OF LIFE BUT NOT TO SHAPE YOURSELF TO SHORE UP AGAINST THEM? MAYBE I JUST HATE THEIR VULNERABILITY, THAT IMPATIENCE AND DESPERATION THAT MADE BOTH CINDYS CHANGE NOT ONLY THEIR NAMES BUT ALSO THE WAY THEY DRESSED, THE WAY THEY LIVED, AND THE PEOPLE THAT THEY KNEW.

WHAT CAN I SAY? THE WORLD SEES SIN AND INDY, EXCITING AND BOLD IN THEIR SEPARATE WAYS. I SEE THE TWO CINDYS UNDERNEATH IT ALL, BACK WHEN THEY WERE INSEPARABLE. I'M SAD AT THE WORLD BECAUSE IT'S SO HARD TO CHANGE AND STILL STAY TOGETHER. BECAUSE WHAT BROUGHT THE TWO CINDYS OUT OF THEIR SHELL ALSO SERVED TO SET THEM FURTHER AND FURTHER APART. IN THE RUSH TO RECREATE, THE FRIENDSHIP WAS CAST ASIDE, FORGOTTEN LIKE THEIR OLD NAMES.

5. Me Too

LITTLE SLEEVELESS SHIRTS THAT SAID "PUNK RULES", SAFETY PINS AND BURNING DISCO RECORDS AT THE SCHOOL. DOWN IN THE BUSHES BEHIND THE BLACKTOP WE SOAKED THEM WITH GASOLINE AND WATCHED THEM GO UP IN FLAMES. GIGGLING HIPPIE GIRLS WERE MORE THAN READY TO TRADE IN THE SUGAR HILL GANG FOR OURS. TROY, JOHN, TIM, AND JOEY SMILING THROUGH THE THICK BLACK SMOKE. ME TOO, BUT I WAS JUST TAGGING ALONG, A YEAR YOUNGER AND NOT YET WISE TO GIRLS OR THE WAYS OF THE WORLD.

"PUNK RULES? YEAH RIGHT! MORE LIKE, PUNK SUCKS!" THE GUY AT THE HARDWARE STORE WAS ALWAYS YELLING AT US. "PUNK BITES. PUNK IS BUNK", HE SAID, RACING FROM BEHIND THE COUNTER TO FOLLOW US THROUGH THE STORE. BUT, ALAS, TOO LATE. WE ROUNDED A CORNER AND SHOVED CASES OF BUBBLE GUM IN OUR SOCKS, DOWN OUR PANTS, IN OUR POCKETS AND MOUTHS IN SECONDS FLAT, THEN CURLED OUR LIPS AND SNEERED BACK: FUCK YOU.

WE RODE BIKES TROY AND I BUILT WITH

SPARE PARTS AND A HAMMER, NOTHING ELSE. IF PEOPLE WERE GONNA LAUGH, WE MIGHT AS WELL BE FUNNY. MINE HAD NO PEDALS AND A YELLOW BANANA SEAT WITH AN A.M. RADIO GLUED UNDERNEATH. RIDING TO SEVEN-ELEVEN AND BACK FOR SLURPEES AND MORE SPRAYPAINT, FLINSTONES-STYLE ACROSS THE ASPHALT WITH NO BRAKES AND THE STATIC TURNED UP ALL THE WAY.

THE T.O. YARD HAD ALWAYS BEEN THE STAGE. SCHOOLED THERE FROM KINDERGARTEN TO THIRD GRADE, THEN ON TO FIREWORKS, GRAFFITI, MOTOR-CROSS AND WEED. NOW WE FOUND PUNK WHILE THE TEENAGERS JUST FOUND NEW WAYS TO BE MEAN. THEY BLEW UP A GIRL'S FACE ONCE, PUT A LADYFINGER IN HER CIGARETTE AND WERE STILL LAUGHING A WEEK LATER. NOT MY FRIENDS, BUT THE OTHER DEAD-ENDS. THEY BROKE INTO THE SCHOOL THROUGH A SKYLIGHT AND RACED MOTOR-CYCLES DOWN THE HALLS. STOLE ALL THE SCHOOL'S RECORDS AND THREW THEM AT EACH OTHER IN THE DARKNESS OF THE SCHOOLYARD. THE NEXT MORNING THE WHOLE BLACKTOP WAS COVERED WITH BROKEN BLACK VINYL SHARDS.

LET THE OLDER TRASH LAUGH IN THEIR TRANS-AMS, YELLING "FAGGOTS" AT US. EVEN ON BANANA SEAT BIKES WITH NO PEDALS WE LOOKED TOUGH. A CUT ABOVE THE REST BECAUSE WE WERE ONTO SOMETHING NEW. TIM POINTED HIS CIGARETTE LIKE A KNIFE, SAYING, "YEAH, BUT HAVE YOU HEARD THE DEAD BOYS, MOTHERFUCKERS?"

6. Lost Boy Raised by DJ's

GROWING UP, I LEARNED SIX THINGS FROM MY PARENTS. ONE, DON'T WATCH "HOGAN'S HEROES" BECAUSE IT MAKES THE HOLOCAUST INTO A JOKE. TWO, DON'T MAKE FUN OF PEOPLE FOR BEING INTELLECTUALS. THREE, DON'T LET ANYONE TAKE YOUR FINGERPRINTS. FOUR, DON'T PLAY WITH GUNS, EVEN SQUIRT GUNS. FIVE, DON'T RIDE IN THE OPEN BED OF A TRUCK OR YOU MIGHT FLY OUT AND DIE LIKE THAT HAPPY COUPLE AT THE KIBBUTZ BACK IN '51. SIX, BEWARE AGENT PROVOCATEURS.

THEY WERE ALL VALUABLE LESSONS, AND YET, THEY SEEMED ARBITRARY AND DISCONNECTED TO ME. THE LARGER MORAL FRAMEWORK AND MEANING OF LIFE REMAINED A MYSTERY. IT MIGHT HAVE FOREVER

HAD IT NOT BEEN FOR KALX, NINETY POINT SEVEN ON THE DIAL. THAT WAS WHERE I LEARNED DIGNITY, RESPECT, AND UNDERSTANDING. IT TOOK THE ENTIRE STATION STAFF TO HAMMER IN WHAT MY PARENTS HAD ONLY HINTED AT.

IT SEEMS STRANGE NOW, BUT KALX USED TO BE LOCATED AT THE LAWRENCE HALL OF SCIENCE, UP ON TOP OF THE BERKELEY HILLS. IN THE CORNER OF THE LAWRENCE HALL SNACKBAR, NEXT TO THE VENDING MACHINES, HUGE PLATE GLASS WINDOWS DISPLAYED BLINKING LIGHTS AND WHIRLING MOTORS. JUST ONE MORE SCIENTIFIC EXHIBIT, EXCEPT THIS ONE HAD HUMANS IN IT — A REAL LIVE RADIO STATION. LIKE ALL DISPLAYS UP AT THE HALL, IT WAS INTERACTIVE. A BOX MOUNTED TO THE FRONT HAD A BUTTON AND A SPEAKER: "PUSH TO HEAR THE DISC JOCKEYS".

I RAPPED ON THE GLASS OF THE OVERSIZED FISHTANK, POINTING AT SIGNS I'D TAPED UP FACING IN: "PLAY BLACK FLAG", "PLAY THE RAMONES". I PUSHED THE BUTTON BUT THE ONLY THING TO COME OUT WAS AIR SUPPLY AND KANSAS. I WAS PACING AROUND THE SNACKBAR IMPATIENTLY WAITING WHEN A SIDE DOOR OPENED AND THE DJ STUCK HER HEAD OUT. "IF YOU WANT TO HEAR IT SO BAD", SHE SAID, "YOU CAN PLAY IT".

ONCE I'D GOTTEN IN THE DOOR, I DIDN'T LET IT CLOSE ON ME AGAIN. SOON, I WAS THERE EVERY SPARE HOUR OF THE DAY, FILING RECORDS AND BUGGING THE POOR FOLKS JUST TRYING TO DO THEIR SHOWS. SNIVELING, SCRATCHING, AND BEGGING FOR ATTENTION, I BECAME THE KALX DOG.

MY PARENTS HAD ALWAYS BEEN SUPPORTIVE, BUT KEPT OUT OF MY PERSONAL BUSINESS. LESS OUT OF PERMISSIVENESS, I THINK, THAN THE FACT THAT THEIR OWN PARENTS HAD NEVER GIVEN THEM THE PRIVACY THAT KIDS NEED. AS A RESULT, I WAS INDEPEN-DENT AND SELF-ASSURED, BUT I WAS ALSO A SNOT-NOSED BRAT WITH NO IDEA OF HOW TO LIVE OR HOW TO TREAT OTHERS. MY NEW FAMILY WAS ALSO INCREDIBLY SUPPORTIVE, FIRST JUST BY TAKING ME SERIOUSLY AT ALL, THEN LATER BY TAKING ME INTO THEIR CONFIDENCE AND UNDER THEIR WINGS. BUT THE KALX FAMILY WAS DIFFERENT. MORE SAPPY, MORE DIVERSE, MORE VOLATILE, MORE SENSITIVE.

"WHAT WAS THAT LAST SONG YOU PLAYED?", I ASKED JUSTINE ONE DAY. "IT REALLY SUCKED".

SHE SNAPPED AT ME. "YOU DON'T NEED TO TELL ME THAT", SHE SAID. "IT'S LIKE TELLING YOUR MOM HER DRESS IS UGLY".

SHE HAD TO SIT ME DOWN AND EXPLAIN THE DIFFERENCE BETWEEN BEING HONEST AND JUST BEING

RUDE. IT WAS HARD TO UNDERSTAND, BECAUSE IN MY FAMILY CRITICIZING SOMEONE'S TASTE WASN'T CONSIDERED RUDE. OF COURSE, IN MY FAMILY WE HAD PRETTY SIMILAR STANDARDS, SO IT WAS USUALLY SOMEONE ELSE WHO RECEIVED THE CRITICISM. JUSTINE USED A BAD EXAMPLE, BECAUSE NONE OF MY MOM'S DRESSES WERE UGLY TO ME. BUT THAT WAS THE POINT: EVERYONE HAS DIFFERENT FAMILIES, DIFFERENT STANDARDS, AND DIFFERENT TASTES.

NOEL CORNERED ME ONE DAY WITH A JOAN ARMATRADING ALBUM. "IS THIS YOUR WORK?", SHE ASKED.

THE COVER WAS BARELY VISIBLE UNDERNEATH THE SCRAWLING OF A HUGE BLACK MARKER: A DRUNK LOOKING FISH, THE LOGO OF MY FAVORITE BAND. THE SAME FISH WHICH LOOKED ON FROM SCRAWLED DRAWINGS ON MY SHIRT, MY HAND, AND MY SHOES. I'D TAKEN THE LIBERTY OF BEAUTIFYING SOME OF THE KALX LIBRARY, RECORDS SO LAUGHABLY STUPID-LOOKING THAT NO ONE WOULD EVER WANT TO PLAY THEM. AS IT TURNED OUT, I'D PICKED THE MOST POPULAR RECORDS AT THE STATION.

"DON'T STOP WRITING ON THEM", SAID NOEL. "BUT HAVE RESPECT. USE A SMALLER PEN"

I LEARNED FAST, THINGS I'D NEVER LEARNED FROM MY PARENTS OR SCHOOL. JUSTINE TAUGHT ME HOW TO SLIP CUE AND BACK ANNOUNCE, HOW TO MAKE TAPE SPLICES AND LOOPS. SHE ALSO TOLD ME BRAVE AND MATTER-OF-FACT ABOUT BEING RAPED. DOUG TOLD ME ABOUT HIS TIME IN VIETNAM. HE ALSO TAUGHT ME HOW TO SEGUE SMOOTHLY BETWEEN CARTS, TURNTABLES, AND REEL-TO-REEL. IT WAS ALL PART OF THE LEARNING PROCESS, AND THE PROCESS OF BECOMING PART OF THE KALX FAMILY.

JOEY DESOTO WAS THE STATION BAD BOY, ALTERNATELY CHASTISED AND ADMIRED FOR BREAKING EVERY RULE IN THE BOOK. HE DRANK A CASE OF BEER AND PLAYED FLIPPER LIVE TAPES FOR HOURS ON END WITHOUT EVEN SAYING THE REQUIRED HOURLY STATION IDENTIFICATION. HIS CONSTANT STREAM OF OBSCENITIES WAS THE REASON THE BOX MOUNTED IN THE SNACK BAR WAS NOW TUNED, NOT TO KALX, BUT KBLX, THE LOCAL 'EASY LISTENING' CHANNEL. JOEY EPITOMIZED MUCH OF WHAT IS GREAT, AND USUALLY MISSING, FROM RADIO. BUT I DIDN'T ADMIRE HIM, EVEN IF WHAT THEY SAID ABOUT LYDIA LUNCH AND THE LAWRENCE HALL BATHROOM WAS TRUE. I ADMIRED RON WURTZ, THE SOFTSPOKEN TALK SHOW

HOST INSTEAD.

I LIKED RON'S SHOW ENOUGH TO WAKE UP AND WALK ALL THE WAY UP THE HILL EARLY SUNDAY MORNING WHEN THE BUSSES HADN'T STARTED TO RUN. RON KNEW HOW TO TALK, BUT ALSO HOW TO LISTEN. HIS QUALITIES BROUGHT OUT THE QUALITIES IN RADIO WHICH MAKE IT UNIQUE. THE INTIMACY OF BEING ALLOWED INSIDE SO MANY HOMES, THE ANONYMITY OF BEING HEARD AND NOT SEEN, THE GIVE AND TAKE AND TEASE WITH THE LISTENERS OVER THE AIR AND THE PHONE LINES. IT WASN'T JUST PERFORMING LIKE JOEY DESOTO'S ONE MAN SHOW. A DYNAMIC, OVER-BEARING PERSONALITY DRAWS YOU IN BY STRENGTH OF CHARACTER ALONE. THAT'S AN EXCITING AND IMPORT-ANT PART OF RADIO, BUT NOT WHAT MAKES IT DIFFERENT FROM ALL OTHER MEDIUMS. RON WAS A MASTER AT STIMULATING CONVERSATION AND MOODS AND IDEAS, NOT JUST CONTROLLING THEM. I THOUGHT IT WAS FUNNY TO KEEP HANGING UP ON ANNOYING CALLERS WHEN I CO-HOSTED THE SHOW, BUT RON TOLD ME TO STOP. "NO ONE WANTS TO HEAR JUST YOUR VOICE FOR HOURS", HE SAID. "NO MATTER WHAT YOU HAVE TO SAY".

BANDS STOPPED BY TOO, OBSTENSIBLY TO FILL IN THE DEAD HOURS OF TOUR, BUT REALLY TO TEACH ME OTHER IMPORTANT LESSONS IN LIFE. THE MISFITS STOLE A BUNCH OF ANIMAL SKULLS OUT OF ONE OF THE LAWRENCE HALL OF SCIENCE DISPLAY CASES, ALMOST RESULTING IN KALX GETTING KICKED OUT. REALLY TOUGH, GUYS. BLACK FLAG CAME AND STOLE ALL THE TSOL RECORDS. THEY WERE LATER RETRIEVED AT ANOTHER RADIO STATION, IN THE URINAL. WHY? BECAUSE TSOL WORE MAKEUP. HMMM. HÜSKER DÜ CAME TOO, AND THEY WERE NICE, BUT THEIR ROADIE WAS THE ONE TO ILLUSTRATE AN IMPORTANT MAXIM. IT WAS NONE OTHER THAN D. BOON. HE SAT EATING FRIED CHICKEN, DRINKING BEER AND JUST LAUGHING AND LAUGHING, SAYING SOMETIMES IT'S BETTER JUST TO BE ALONG FOR THE RIDE.

THERE WERE OTHERS — OTHER BANDS, OTHER DAYS, AND MANY MANY OTHER DJ'S. I STUCK AROUND THERE FOR YEARS, THROUGH TRAINING, OFFICIAL AND UN-OFFICIAL, AND EVEN WENT TO THE KALX SOFTBALL GAMES. BUT I NEVER GOT A HANDLE, NO COOL ON-AIR NAME LIKE "ACNE KING" OR "THE TEENAGE TROTSKY". I NEVER DID BECOME A DISC JOCKEY MYSELF. I LOVED BEING PART OF IT, BUT PERHAPS LIKE D. BOON, I WAS HAPPIEST BEHIND THE SCENES.

7. Martov

ONCE I WAS IN A BAND WITH A BUNCH OF GRUMPY OLD MEN. THAT WAS NICE — I GOT TO BE THE YOUNG IRRESPONSIBLE ONE FOR A CHANGE. THE BAND WAS CALLED "MARTOV," AFTER THE GREAT MENSHKEVIK LEADER WHO LOST THE BID FOR POWER AFTER THE BOLSHEVIKS TOOK OVER RUSSIA IN 1917. A POLITICAL BAND, BUT STRANGELY, ONLY POLITICS FROM ABOUT 80 YEARS, AND 8000 MILES AWAY.

OUR FLIERS AND RECORD COVERS FEATURED THAT STYLE OF ART KNOWN AS SOCIALIST REALISM, HARDLY DISTINGUISHABLE FROM THAT OTHER STYLE KNOWN AS FASCIST PROPAGANDA. BOTH FEATURE STURDY, DETERMINED LOOKING MEN WITH HIGH CHEEKBONES DIGGING DITCHES, SWINGING PICKAXES, AND OTHER MENIAL TASKS THOUGHT TO LIFT THE SPIRIT AND CONSCIOUSNESS OF THE MASSES. A BARTENDER, A WRITER, AND THE COUNTER GUY AT A COOKIE STORE, WORKING BUT NOT EXACTLY WORKING CLASS, GLORIFYING THE WORK WE WOULD BE THE FIRST TO AVOID. THE BASSIST WAS EMPLOYED AT THE POST OFFICE, BUT THAT DIDN'T REALLY COUNT; HE WAS A LINE BOSS, NOT A LABORER. HE SAT ON HIS STOOL TELLING EVERYONE TO WORK FASTER, THEN CAME TO REHEARS-AL AND COMPLAINED HOW STUPID HIS WORKERS WERE. I ADMIT, I'VE NEVER LIKED BASSISTS MUCH.

"THIS SONG IS ABOUT THE DECEMBRISTS," I YELLED FROM BEHIND MY DRUMS. "ZHELIABOV, MIKHAILOV, AND MOROZOV."

"YOU JUST GOTTA BE A WISE ASS, DON'T YOU?," THE SINGER SPIT. "ACTUALLY, IT'S ABOUT THE NARODNIKS. MAY THE SPIRIT OF THOSE MARTYRS GUIDE US IN OUR STRUGGLE!"

IT'S IMPORTANT TO LEARN FROM EXAMPLES, BUT THERE IS SOMETHING TO SAY FOR PUTTING THINGS INTO CONTEXT. AS TROTSKY SAID, "THE ART OF LANDSCAPE PAINTING WOULD NOT HAVE ORIGINATED IN THE SAHARA DESERT." TUESDAY NIGHT IN A SAN FRANCISCO BAR, THE THINNING CROWD SCRATCHED THEIR THINNING HAIR. ALL EXCEPT A DRUNK SLAVIC LANGUAGES MAJOR FROM S.F. STATE WHO HECKLED US ABOUT THE PRONOUNCIATIONS.

I MISSED POLITICS BEING MORE A PART OF PUNK, BUT MARTOV WAS ALMOST A PARODY OF A POLITICAL PUNK BAND. DISCORDANT, MONOTONOUS SONGS ABOUT IRRELEVANT, HOPELESS CAUSES. HEARTFELT

BUT KINDA SUCKY. I LIKED IT, THOUGH, EVEN IF NO ONE ELSE DID. HISTORY IS LIKE PORNOGRAPHY FOR ME, ESPECIALLY THE HISTORY OF RUSSIAN COMMUNIST ANARCHISTS, SO I WAS HAPPY. IN TURN, A HAPPY, LIVELY DRUMMER WITH STYLE AND A FRESH APPROACH CAN BRING ANY MUSIC TO LIFE. NOT TO BRAG, BUT IT'S TRUE.

THE SINGER TURNED AROUND OCCASIONALLY TO YELL, "SLOWER! SLOWER! SLOWER!". I'D LEARNED THE SONGS LISTENING TO THE OLD MARTOV RECORD, WITH THEIR OLD DRUMMER. IMPATIENT, I PLAYED IT AT A HIGHER SPEED, AND PERHAPS WAS STILL PLAYING THE SONGS THAT WAY. BUT TELLING A DRUMMER TO SLOW DOWN IS LIKE TELLING A GUITARIST TO TURN DOWN. LIKE TELLING A MARXIST TO RESPECT A DIFFERING OPINION.

"PEOPLE WHO GREW UP IN BERKELEY WITH AN ECONOMICS PROFESSOR AS A DADDY", THE SINGER LAUGHED INTO THE MICROPHONE, "MAY NOT UNDER-STAND THIS SONG. BUT THE PEASANTS IN PETROGRAD DIDN'T NEED A BUNCH OF BOOKS TO UNDERSTAND ECONOMICS".

"THIS NEXT SONG IS FOR STALIN", I SHOUTED. GUITARISTS MAY HAVE THE MIC, BUT THEY ALWAYS FORGET YOU CAN'T START A SONG WITHOUT DRUMS. "BUT LET'S NOT FORGET POL POT, HOXHA, MAO, AND THE REST OF THE GREATS WHO ALSO KNEW HOW TO PUT INTELLECTUALS IN THEIR PLACE".

THE BAND TURNED TO SNEER AND THE SLAVIC LANGUAGES MAJOR BEGAN TO CHOKE ON HIS OWN VOMIT, BUT I'D MADE MY POINT: NOT ONLY IS ANTI-INTELLECTUALISM BY INTELLECTUALS REPREHENSIBLE AND DISHONEST, IT'S ALSO BEEN THE DOWNFALL OF NEARLY EVERY SOCIAL MOVEMENT IN HISTORY.

PART BAND, PART STUDY GROUP, PART DEBATE TEAM. WE ARGUED AND BICKERED, BUT WHAT ELSE WOULD YOU EXPECT FROM GRUMPY OLD MEN? AT LEAST, FOR ONCE, IT WAS SOMETHING WORTH ARGUING ABOUT.

OUR SHINING MOMENT CAME AT A CIVIC CENTER RALLY FOR HOMES NOT JAILS. THE CROWD MILLED ABOUT ACROSS FROM CITY HALL WHILE DOWN THE STREET, IN A RENTED FLATBED TRUCK, WE AWAITED THE SIGNAL.

GO! JORDAN FIRED UP THE GENERATOR. LITTLE TOM STARTED THE TRUCK'S ENGINE AND TOOK OFF DOWN FOLSOM STREET. WE LAY FLAT ON THE FLATBED, OUR EQUIPMENT CONCEALED BY BANNERS HANGING OFF THE TRUCK'S WOODEN GRATING: "APPLES, FIVE FOR A DOLLAR". "WATERMELON, TEN CENTS A POUND".

AS WE PULLED IN DIRECTLY ACROSS FROM THE MAYOR'S OFFICE, I CUT THE CORDS, FLIPPING THEM OVER, REVEALING THE SCRAWLED MESSAGES ON THE UNDERSIDE: "HOUSING ON DEMAND! SHELTER, A RIGHT NOT A PRIVILEGE! STOP THE CITY!"

A FEW SPEAKERS CLIMBED ABOARD, DELIVERING QUICK AND CONCISE PLANS AND A LIST OF DEMANDS. THE CROWD RAISED THEIR CROWBARS AND CHEERED, NOT JUST ANOTHER SYMBOLIC MARCH. BEING DENIED A PERMIT FOR A P.A. HADN'T STOPPED THEM. NOW, BEING DENIED HOUSING WHILE HUNDREDS OF BUILDINGS IN THE PRESIDIO SAT VACANT WOULDN'T STOP THEM EITHER.

BUT FIRST, A FEW SONGS FROM MARTOV. JUST A FEW, TO RALLY THE TROOPS AND FILL THEM WITH REVOLUTIONARY FERVOR. AS WE PLAYED, THE POLICE CARS BEGAN TO ARRIVE AND THE BLINDS OF CITY HALL PARTED TO MAKE WAY FOR NERVOUS EYES. I COULD FEEL THE REAL POWER OF MUSIC AND THE REAL POWER OF HISTORY TOGETHER FOR THE FIRST TIME, NOT OUT OF CONTEXT AT ALL.

8. Folklore

PUNK ALWAYS HAD A STRONG SENSE OF STORY, AN ORAL TRADITION PASSED ON AND PASSED DOWN WHICH SHAPED THE WAY WE TALKED ABOUT, AND THOUGHT ABOUT, OURSELVES. STRANGELY, THE MUSIC ITSELF NEVER REALLY REFLECTED THAT. THE SONGS WERE PART OF OUR LIFE BUT NOT VICE VERSA. FOR EVERY HUNDRED SONGS ABOUT EL SALVADOR, THERE WAS ONLY ONE ABOUT OKI-DOGS.

NO GOOD TO BE SO WRAPPED UP IN YOUR OWN LIFE AND IMMEDIATE SURROUNDINGS THAT YOU IGNORE THE REST OF THE WORLD, BUT THE OTHER EXTREME IS JUST AS SKEWED A PERSPECTIVE. "YOU CAN'T EVEN SKATEBOARD IN LEBANON", SAID THE SINGER OF DEADLY REIGN, A BAND I INTERVIEWED MANY YEARS AGO. THOUGH IT'S NATURAL TO DEFINE YOURSELF IN NEGATIVE TERMS, IT LEADS TO UNANSWERED QUESTIONS. WHAT CAN YOU DO IN LEBANON? WHERE CAN YOU SKATEBOARD? I HAPPEN TO BE STUDYING LEBANON CURRENTLY AT THE COLLEGE LIBRARY, BUT NOWHERE CAN I FIND BOOKS

ON THE CULTURE AND HISTORY OF DEADLY REIGN AND THE OLD CONTRA COSTA PUNK SCENE. SEE WHAT I MEAN?

NOW SO MANY STORIES NEVER GET TOLD. WHY? BECAUSE PEOPLE ARE SCARED TO TELL THEM. IT'S ONE THING TO SHOW OFF FADED SLAYER TATTOOS AND PASS AROUND PHOTOS OF YOURSELF IN A DIFFERENT STAGE OF LIFE, WEARING AN ARMY UNIFORM OR WEDDING DRESS. BUT IF YOUR OLD STORIES AND PICTURES ARE PUNK, EVERYONE RUNS THE OTHER WAY. "OH NO", THEY SAY. "NOT ANOTHER JADED BLOWHARD TALKING ABOUT THE GOOD OLD DAYS". IT'S SAD BECAUSE FOR SOME OF US IT'S IMPOSSIBLE TO TALK ABOUT OUR PERSONAL HISTORY WITHOUT TALKING ABOUT THE PAST, AND PUNK.

ED AND SHANTELL GREW UP IN THE CITY OF TUOLOMNE, POPULATION 1,700, TEN MILES EAST OF SONORA. ED WALKED FROM HER HOUSE ON THE WRONG SIDE OF THE TRACKS, SHANTELL FROM HER HOUSE ON THE RIGHT SIDE. HALFWAY BETWEEN WERE THE STEPS WHERE THE TWO GIRLS WOULD MEET AND SIT ALL DAY, WATCHING THE TRAFFIC PASS AND WAITING TO GET PICKED UP BY THE CLASH. ED HAD READ AN INTERVIEW WHICH MENTIONED THEIR VAN, A HIGH-DOME CHEVY WITH A LIGHT BLUE STRIPE.

SOME DAYS A VAN OF THAT DESCRIPTION PASSED, AND ED AND SHANTELL JUMPED UP AND DOWN WAVING THEIR ARMS. UNLIKELY THAT THE CLASH WOULD FIND THEMSELVES IN TUOLOMNE, TEN MILES EAST OF SONORA. BUT THEN AGAIN, YOU NEVER KNOW. YOU HAVE TO HAVE HOPE IN SOMETHING.

ROGER JOINED THE JUNIOR AVIATION LEAGUE IN SIXTH GRADE. THE PLAN WAS TO STEAL A PLANE, FLY TO ENGLAND, AND FIND JOHNNY ROTTEN. JOHNNY HAD RAVED ABOUT AIRPLANES, OR YOUNG RUNAWAYS, OR BOTH, IN AN INTERVIEW ROGER HAD READ.

"YOU WEREN'T SERIOUS", I ASK.

"DEAD SERIOUS", HE SAYS. "WE LEARNED, TOO. BUT THEY KEPT THE IGNITION KEYS LOCKED UP WHERE WE COULDN'T GET TO THEM. WE KEPT TRYING, UNTIL THE FIRST PUBLIC IMAGE RECORD CAME OUT. THEN WE GAVE UP ENTIRELY".

THE LAST TIME I PASSED THROUGH DAVIS, I STOPPED BY TO VISIT ROGER. HE PULLED OUT A FILE. "GUESS WHAT THIS IS", HE SMILED. ONE LOOK AND I COULD TELL. BACK WHEN I LIVED AT HOME,

THE ONLY WAY I KNEW HOW TO CLEAN MY ROOM
WAS TO GATHER UP ALL THE CRAP, TAKE IT TO A
SHOW, AND THROW IT OUT INTO THE AUDIENCE.
PUNKS WILL CATCH ANYTHING THROWN OFF A
STAGE — EVEN PEOPLE.

ROGER TOOK FLIERS OUT OF THE FOLDER ONE
BY ONE, AND LAID THEM ON THE TABLE. MOST
WERE FLIERS I HAD MADE, AND I WAS PROUD OF
THEM. BUT THEY REMINDED ME OF BANDS, NOT
THE SPIRIT OF THOSE TIMES. THEY DIDN'T TELL ME
HOW WE HAD ALL COME TOGETHER OR THE SEPARATE
DIRECTIONS WE WENT AFTER THE SHOW. I WISHED
I HAD THE STORY OF THAT LAST BUS HOME INSTEAD
OF A RECORD BY THAT LAST BAND. I WISHED WE
HAD WRITTEN IT ALL DOWN. NOT TO ELEVATE THE
TRIVIAL TO GRANDIOSE HEIGHTS, BUT I'D RATHER
LISTEN TO ED OR ROGER'S STORIES THAN LISTEN TO
THE PISTOLS OR THE CLASH, ON MOST DAYS.

"HERE'S THE GOOD PART", ROGER SAID. HE BEGAN
TURNING OVER THE OLD FLIERS I HAD TOSSED, AND
MUCH TO MY HORROR, THERE WAS WRITING ON THE
BACK OF EACH ONE, RANGING FROM LOVE LETTERS TO
NOTES TO MY PARENTS ASKING THEM TO WAKE ME
UP FOR A DENTIST APPOINTMENT.

"WOULDN'T IT BE COOL", ROGER ASKED, "IF
EVERY FLIER HAD WRITING ON THE OTHER SIDE
LIKE THAT?"

BUT I DIDN'T ANSWER. I WAS MORTIFIED. MY
MIND REELED AT THE POSSIBILITIES OF WHAT OTHER
PRIVATE NOTES I MIGHT HAVE LET GO.

"WEREN'T YOU JUST SAYING", HE LAUGHED, "HOW
YOU WISH OUR DAY-TO-DAY LIFE HAD BEEN SAVED
AND WRITTEN DOWN?"

"OUR DAY-TO-DAY LIFE, YES. BUT MINE, NO. IT'S
EMBARRASSING. GIVE ME THOSE NOTES BACK!"

THERE WAS A FANZINE FROM LOS ANGELES
CALLED "DESTROY". THERE WAS ALSO A FANZINE
FROM FLORIDA BY THE SAME NAME. FLORIDA HAD
SENIORITY, SO THE WEST COAST VERSION YIELDED TO
PRESSURE AND ADDED INITIALS. FROM THEN ON IT
WAS KNOWN AS "DESTROY L.A.". UNFORTUNATELY,
THE POSTMASTER GENERAL HAPPENED UPON A COPY
AND DREW THE WRONG CONCLUSIONS ABOUT THE
NEW NAME.

FUNNY TO THINK OF THOSE KIDS PLOTTING TO
"DESTROY LOS ANGELES", BUT TO THE FBI IT WAS NO
JOKE. THEY SHOWED UP AT THE DOOR WITH A SEARCH

WARRANT AND A CHARGE OF SEDITION. THE AGENTS BROUGHT ALONG A FILE FILLED WITH EVERY LITTLE DETAIL OF THEIR LIVES, EVEN XEROXES OF THEIR LAST SIX MONTHS OF MAIL. WISH I HAD A COPY OF THAT FBI FILE NOW, INSTEAD OF A COPY OF THE FANZINE.

9. Three Things

I WENT TO HEAR A TALK BY JERRY BROWN, THE MAN WHO PUT THE WINGS ON "WINGNUT".

"TWO THINGS I WANT TO MAKE CLEAR", HE SAID. "NUMBER ONE, OAKLAND IS A REAL PLACE. NUMBER TWO, IF YOU WANT TO GET REAL, THIS IS THE PLACE TO BE. THIRD, AND LASTLY, WHERE THE HELL IS DUBLIN ANYWAY?"

THAT'S HOW TO PICK OUT A WINGNUT IN A CROWD: THEY ARE INCAPABLE OF HAVING TWO SEPARATE IDEAS. ANY TWO IDEAS MUST BE TURNED INTO AN EQUATION THEN ADDED, SUBTRACTED, OR DIVIDED TO MAKE A THIRD.

WE USED TO EXPLAIN THE PHENOMENON LIKE THIS. A: GOT A SMOKE, STONE? B: PULLING AN ALL-NIGHT ROT AT GUD FUD. FURTHERMORE, AND THEREFORE, X: ONE PLANT TWO FEET TALL, ONE PLANT FOUR FEET TALL, ONE PLANT SIX FEET TALL. PERFECTLY LEGAL.

IT'S A PARTICULAR COMBINATION OF CRITICAL THINKING, POP PSYCHOLOGY, MATH, AND BAD ACID. ITS NATURAL HABITAT? THE BAY AREA, OF COURSE. ITS ORIGINS? CONCEIVED ON THE STEPS OF THE UNITARIAN CHURCH ON THE CORNER OF VINE AND WALNUT IN BERKELEY, WHERE I USED TO SEE MS. SABERHAGEN, THE FREAKIEST OF ALL THE BERKELEY SCHOOL SYSTEM'S FREAKY SUBSTITUTE TEACHERS, SITTING STONED OUT OF HER GOURD READING POETRY ALOUD TO A CAT. FROM THERE IT SPREAD AS A FLU-LIKE VIRUS VIA PEET'S COFFEE. HALF UCB, HALF SLA, PLUS TWO THIRDS EST, IT DUG IN ROOTS AT THE LOGICAL CROSSROADS, TELEGRAPH AND HASTE.

FAITHFUL BELIEVERS NOW FLOCK FROM FAR AND WIDE TO VISIT THE CRADLE OF WINGNUT CULTURE. BUSSES ARRIVE IN A STEADY PROCESSION EVERY SUMMER, HASTILY DISCHARGING THEIR LOADS. LIKE

A MODERN-DAY BERLIN AIRLIFT, ONLY BACKWARDS. THE NEW ARRIVALS DESCEND UPON THE HALLOWED GROUND, CHANTING.

"WE, THE BERKELEY LIBERATION FRONT", THEY CHANT, "HAVE TWO NON-NEGOTIABLE DEMANDS.

"ONE, FREE THE LAND. TWO, SMASH THE MAN. NOT TO MENTION, CONSEQUENTLY, AND OF COURSE INCLUDING THE DISTRIBUTION OF ALL SURPLUS WEALTH, FREEDOM FOR ALL POLITICAL PRISONERS, AND LEGAL-IZATION OF ALL NATIVE PLANTS, INCLUDING HEMP! HEMP! HEMP!"

EVEN THE BAY AREA COPS HORN IN ON THE ACT. I MEAN, EVEN THE OPPRESSOR TRIES TO CO-OPT OUR CULTURE. "JUST TELL ME TWO THINGS", THEY SAY, "I'M REAL CURIOUS. DIDN'T YOU SEE THAT 'STOP CLEARCUTTING' SIGN BACK THERE? WHAT MAKES YOU THINK YOU CAN BREAK THE LAW? NOW WHAT IF YOU'D GOTTEN HIT BY CRITICAL MASS WHEN CROSSING THE STREET? YOU'D PROBABLY CALL THE COPS, SMART GUY, AND COME TO US CRYING ABOUT TRAFFIC ENFORCEMENT. DO YOU REALLY THINK THAT'S FAIR? HOW DO YOU THINK THAT MAKES US FEEL?"

"OFFICER, WITH ALL DUE RESPECT", I SAY, "EAT SHIT. SUCK MY ASS. DIE, PIG. P.S.: I PLEAD THE FIFTH".

IT JUST SO HAPPENS THAT THE FIRST GIRL I EVER KISSED IS NOW A JAILER IN THE OAKLAND JAILS, SO WHEN WORST COMES TO WORST AND I GO FEDERAL, MAYBE I'LL STILL HAVE A CHANCE TO GET LUCKY, YOU KNOW? THIS TIME I'LL BE READY. AND TALLER THAN HER. WHICH REMINDS ME, USUALLY OF ANOTHER GIRL OR DIFFERENT JAIL OR A COMPLETE-LY UNRELATED STORY.

I WALK INTO THE CAFE AND CATCH THE EYE OF THE BOMBSHELL BEHIND THE COUNTER. "THERE'S ONLY TWO THINGS I NEED IN THIS WORLD", I SAY. "AND YOU HAVE BOTH OF THEM".

SHE LOOKS UP. "COFFEE AND A BEER".

"THAT'S RIGHT", I SMILE. "AND CASEY, IT'S ALWAYS GOOD TO SEE AN OLD FRIEND AGAIN".

COMETBUS
ST. LOUIS STORIES

CB44 $2

1. Lessons

WHEN I WAS THIRTEEN, I LEARNED ABOUT GUILT.
JESSE HAD TO TEACH ME. I HAD NO NATURAL INSTINCT
FOR IT AT ALL. EVEN LEARNING WAS DIFFICULT, BUT
JESSE WAS SUCH A GUILT-RIDDEN KID AND HE WALKED
ME THROUGH IT STEP BY STEP.

WHEN I WAS TWENTY-THREE, MAYE TAUGHT ME
ABOUT ANXIETY. YOU COULD SAY SHE WALKED ME THROUGH
IT STEP BY STEP ALSO, ALTHOUGH, JUST LIKE GUILT WITH
JESSE, I WAS THE ONE WHO HAD ASKED.

ABOUT A YEAR LATER, I STARTED SIGHING.
IT WAS IN A TEXAS SQUAT THAT MY FIRST SIGH CAME.
LIKE A SHIP LEAVING HARBOR, AS I HAVE SAID BEFORE.
HEAVY WITH SADNESS AND YET THOROUGHLY SATISFYING.

SIGH. MY BEST FRIEND LEFT AND THEN MY GIRL-
FRIEND LEFT, BUT THE ANXIETY AND GUILT STAYED. WHY?
BECAUSE LIFE IS STUPID. WHAT DID I DO? NATURALLY,
I CAME TO ST. LOUIS, RENTED A BASEMENT ROOM,
PROMPTLY LOST MY MIND AND NEARLY ENDED UP IN
THE HOSPITAL.

OH, I HATED THAT HOUSE. IT WAS THE WORST EVER.
TERRIBLE. LIFELESS. LONELY. AND JOEL'S DAD THE
CREEPY TRAVELING SALESMAN WAS ALWAYS HANGING
OUT ON THE COUCH. THAT WAS THE FOURTH TIME I'D
LIVED IN ST. LOUIS, AND MY LAST TIME EVER. WHEN I
LEFT I VOWED NEVER TO RETURN.

THREE YEARS LATER I ENDED UP MOVING BACK,
RIGHT ACROSS THE STREET.

IRONIC, BUT NOT WEIRD. WEIRD WAS THAT I FORGOT
THE VOW COMPLETELY UNTIL A FEW DAYS AGO.

"WOW", I SAID. "I'M SURPRISED I DIDN'T VOW TO LEAVE
HERE YEARS AGO AND NEVER RETURN. OH, OOPS."

2. Brendan

BRENDAN SAID, "I'M SURPRISED TO SEE YOU BACK.
YOU WERE ALWAYS WHINING ABOUT HOW DIFFERENT IT
WAS HERE, HOW YOU DIDN'T FIT IN."

"I WAS NOT WHINING", I SAID. "JUST STATING A FACT."

"NO", HE SAID. "YOU WERE WHINING."

"IT'S CALLED PASSION, BRENDAN. IT MAY SOUND
STRANGE TO YOUR MIDWESTERN EARS, BUT THAT'S HOW WE
TALK WHERE I'M FROM. WE SHOW OUR EMOTIONS
INSTEAD OF BOTTLING THEM UP. A CRISIS AND GRIPE
SESSION IS A SIMPLE WAY OF SAYING HELLO, BUT NO!
HERE YOU HAVE TO KEEP IT TO YOURSELF AND ACT ALL

SOLEMN. WHAT THE HELL IS WRONG WITH YOU PEOPLE, ANYWAY? NO WONDER YOU'RE ALL ALCOHOLICS!"

BRENDAN LOOKED AT ME FUNNY. HE SAID, "ALRIGHT, ALREADY, I MISSED YOU".

I SAID, "DON'T CRY TO ME ABOUT IT. JUST BUY ME A BEER".

IN THE DUMPSTER IN THE ALLEY, FILLED WITH BIKE PARTS, WE WERE HAPPILY DRAINING OUR FORTIES AND GETTING REAQUAINTED. "JUST ONE THING", HE SAID. "WHAT BRINGS YOU BACK TO TOWN?"

"I LOST A BET".

"THAT'S WHAT YOU SAID LAST TIME"

"YUP. I'M BACK BECAUSE I LOST THE BET. I LOST IT BY COMING HERE LAST TIME".

"DAMN", SAID BRENDAN. "THAT'S CONFUSING! WHAT HAPPENED TO THE LUCKY GUY WHO WON THE BET?"

3. Fill in the Blank

THE GOOD THING ABOUT HAVING FRIENDS WHO WORK AT CAFES IS I CAN TELL THEM TO TURN THE FUCKING MUSIC DOWN. HEY CASEY, TURN THAT SHIT DOWN. I'VE GOT SOME SERIOUS THINKING TO DO. SEE THAT BOOTH IN THE CORNER? BRING ME COFFEE EVERY FIFTEEN MINUTES AND A FORTY OF KING COBRA EVERY HOUR ON THE HOUR.

"I'LL BET YOU'VE BEEN WAITING YEARS TO SAY THAT", SHE SAYS.

"I'VE BEEN WAITING YEARS FOR EVERYTHING".

"THEN ONE MORE DAY", SHE SMILED, "WON'T KILL YOU".

THAT'S THE GOOD THING ABOUT FRIENDS WHO WORK AT CAFES: THEY'RE BUSY WITH THEIR OWN WORK, TOO BUSY TO PAY MUCH ATTENTION TO YOU. JUST LIKE CHESS. A SMILE, A WINK, MAYBE A SHARED SMOKE ON BREAK. A CHANCE FOR TIME TOGETHER WITHOUT TOO MANY WORDS.

THAT'S THE GOOD THING ABOUT BEING IN A BAND. COMMUNICATING THROUGH GLANCES AND SIGNALS AND RHYTHM. IF ONLY ALL FORMS OF FRIENDSHIP HAD SUCH A FRAMEWORK. SAYING JUST A FEW THINGS, PRACTICING OVER AND OVER TO SAY THEM TOGETHER, TO SAY THEM WELL.

MUSIC KEEPS US FROM FEELING ALONE. THAT'S WHY NOWADAYS YOU HEAR IT EVERY SINGLE PLACE YOU GO. IT BLOTS OUT THOSE NAGGING THOUGHTS, IT FILLS IN THE BLANK. CHASING AWAY THAT AWKWARD SILENCE, IT KEEPS US FROM EVER REALLY GETTING USED TO BEING ALONE TOGETHER.

WHAT'S THAT CASEY? WHY DOES PLAYING MUSIC IN

THE BASEMENT BRING US TOGETHER BUT BLASTING IT
AT THE CAFE, CO-OP, LAUNDROMAT, AND COPY SHOP ONLY
SERVE TO KEEP US IN OUR SHELLS? I DON'T KNOW.
     BUT TURN THAT SHIT DOWN. THEN WE CAN SING
OUR OWN SONGS.

4. Harmony

ONLY IN THE MIDDLE WEST COULD A SOUR HARMONY
BE TRACED BACK TWO GENERATIONS. I HAD TO STOP THE
SONG HALFWAY THROUGH AND SEPARATE THE TWO
SINGERS. ONE AT A TIME NOW, I SAID.
     EMMET, IRISH FROM CHICAGO, AND ALISON, GERMAN
FROM WISCONSIN. I PAY ATTENTION TO THESE THINGS.
BECAUSE I'M FASCINATED BY THE PATHS OF IMMIGRATION,
AND BECAUSE MY AMATEUR STUDIES OF SOCIOLOGY PROVIDE
A GOOD EXCUSE TO MAKE NEW, WEIRD GENERALIZATIONS.
     WHEN IN HISTORY HAVE GERMAN PROTESTANTS
AND IRISH CATHOLICS SANG TOGETHER? WHEN INDEED
HAVE THEY SUNG THE WORDS OF A POLISH JEW? NOT ONLY
ARE WE MAKING MUSIC, WE'RE MAKING HISTORY.
THERE'S BOUND TO BE DIFFICULTIES.
     IT DOESN'T MATTER THAT I'VE NEVER BEEN TO
POLAND, THEY'VE NEVER BEEN TO GERMANY OR IRELAND.
AMERICANS, ALL THREE OF US, WITH NO PERSONAL
CONNECTION TO ANY OTHER GROUP OF PEOPLE. CROSSED
THAT OCEAN LONG AGO AND DOWN THE STAIRS INTO
THIS DINGY BASEMENT. BUT, LISTENING TO THEM SING
SEPARATELY, IT WAS OBVIOUS THEY HAD COME OFF TWO
SEPARATE BOATS. NOT A SINGLE WORD DID THEY
PRONOUNCE OR ACCENTUATE THE SAME.
     EVERYONE HAS THEIR OWN VOICE, AND SHOULD
USE IT. BUT WHEN YOU WANT A SONG TO SOUND LIKE A
SONG INSTEAD OF A WOUNDED ANIMAL OR THE WAITING
ROOM AT ELLIS ISLAND, A LITTLE FINE TUNING MAY BE
NECESSARY. IN THIS CASE, I GOT EMMET TO IMITATE
ALISON. HER PRONUNCIATION, ENUNCIATION, AND THAT
SING-SONG WISCONSIN INFLECTION.
     ALONE, EMMET SOUNDED RIDICULOUS SINGING
LIKE THAT. BUT ONCE ALISON JOINED IN, IT WAS A
BEAUTIFUL HARMONY. MORE THAN THE SUM OF THE
PARTS, AS THEY SAY.

5. Ziporah

ZIPORAH, WIFE OF MOSES, AND AARON, HIS BROTHER.
TREACHEROUS TO BE TOGETHER LIKE THIS, AND YET MY

GRANDMOTHER WOULD BE PROUD. WE WALK ALONG THE SHADED PATHS OF RIVER DES PERES WRAPPED UP IN OUR OWN WORLD. WHILE I CHASE THE DOG, ZIPORAH SINGS.

NO MATTER HOW THEY START, HOW HIGH-PITCHED AND FAST PACED THEY BECOME, JEWISH SONGS ALWAYS END IN AN EXAGGERATEDLY LOW-PITCHED SLOW AND SOLEMN GROAN, NOT UNLIKE A TUGBOAT. THAT'S THE WAY I LEARNED, AT LEAST, AND I LIKE TO APPLY IT TO EVERYTHING, NOT JUST SONGS. ZIPORAH SINGS AN UPBEAT TUNE, "THE WHOLE WORLD IS BUT A NARROW BRIDGE". UPBEAT FOR JEWS IS DIFFERENT THAN FOR OTHER PEOPLE.

PERHAPS I AM OVERPLAYING THE CULTURAL HERITAGE CARD AND IT'S ONLY BY CHANCE THAT I PUT MY SAD SONGS TO HAPPY MUSIC AND VICE VERSA, THAT MY PARTIES ARE PURPOSELY MISERABLE, AND I LIKE PEOPLE BEST AFTER A FUNERAL. IS IT CHANCE, OR THE FACT THAT I'M JEWISH? ASK GOD, WHO DOESN'T EXIST.

I WANT TO BE CAREFUL THOUGH, NOT TO FALL BACK ON ETHNICITY AS MY WHOLE CULTURAL IDENTITY, THE WAY MANY OF MY FRIENDS ARE DOING AS THEY GET OLDER. LOOKING TO ESTABLISHED COMMUNITIES BECAUSE THE ONES WE'VE WORKED TO CREATE HAVE FALLEN APART. BECAUSE PUNK DIDN'T HAVE THE SAME LASTING SPIRITUAL QUALITY AS BLOOD OR RELIGION, IT DIDN'T INSTILL THE SAME LOYALTY AS FAMILY AND TRADITION.

NOW THEY USE ETHNICITY AS A WAY TO CLOSE THE DOOR AND RETURN TO THE MORE TRADITIONAL FAMILY THEY ONCE FOUGHT SO HARD TO ESCAPE. OF COURSE, IT IS NOT FOR ME TO JUDGE. BUT, SINCE JEWS ARE NOTORIOUSLY CRITICAL AND JUDGEMENTAL, I DON'T FEEL AS BAD SAYING, IT IS WRONG.

MAYBE IT'S MY OWN EXPERIENCE THAT MAKES ME HEARTSICK FOR NEW YORK CITY AS IF IT WAS THE PROMISED LAND, THAT MAKES MY HUGE BURDENS AND LONG LIST OF WORRIES JUST DISAPPEAR WHEN ZIPORAH BRINGS ME MATZOH BALL SOUP, A GOOD BOOK, AND HALF A LOAF OF LIGHT RYE. BUT I LOOK BEHIND ME AT THE LONG LINE OF BEARDED WEIRDOS WINDING BACK FOR THOUSANDS OF YEARS, AND I HAVE TO WONDER. JUDAISM IS AN UNDENIABLE PART OF MY CHARACTER AND MY LIFE.

BUT, I ALSO CAN'T DENY THE RAMONES AND THE NEW YORK DOLLS. ZIPORAH AND I MAY SING TOGETHER, BUT SHE'S NOT A PUNK. WE'LL NEVER KISS.

6. Songwriting

I'VE HAD THE SAME SONG STUCK IN MY HEAD NOW

FOR A YEAR. DON'T ASK WHAT SONG — YOU DON'T WANT TO KNOW. PEOPLE TELLING YOU THEIR DREAMS IS BAD, AND PEOPLE TELLING YOU THE SONG STUCK IN THEIR HEAD IS WORSE. SONGS ABOUT DREAMS, DREAMS ABOUT SONGS, BOTH BAD. NATURALLY, MY SOCIALIST UTOPIA WOULD HAVE NO MUSIC AND NO SLEEP, THE TWO THINGS THAT ALWAYS MESS WITH EMOTIONS.

JEWS ARE GENERALLY KNOWN FOR HAVING A LIMITED AMOUNT OF SONGS, BUT AN UNLIMITED AMOUNT OF MELODIES FOR EACH ONE. "TWO JEWS, THREE OPINIONS", AS THEY SAY, AND AT LEAST FOUR MELODIES. IT MAKES SINGING TOGETHER DIFFICULT, BUT MAKES HOLIDAYS LIKE PASSOVER, WHEN YOU'RE REQUIRED TO DRINK AT LEAST FOUR GLASSES OF WINE AND TAKE AS LONG AS POSSIBLE TO TELL THE STORIES AND SING THE SONGS — IT MAKES THAT EASY.

BUT NOT ME. I HAVE MANY SONGS, ALL TO THE SAME TUNE. EIGHT YEARS OF HEBREW SCHOOL, ALL FOR NAUGHT. BUT IF I MIGHT TAKE A MOMENT TO PARA-PHRASE A BIT OF THE YOM KIPPUR SERVICE WHICH REALLY TOUCHED ME:

"TO RECALL THE PAST YEAR, ITS EXULTATIONS AND DISILLUSIONMENTS. TO REMEMBER THAT OUR LIFE IS BUT A PASSING SHADOW. BETWEEN MEMORY AND HOPE, BETWEEN THE KNOWN AND UNKNOWN."

TO ME, THAT IS A BEAUTIFUL SONG. BUT, A LOUSY ANTHEM. AND THAT'S THE PROBLEM I'M HAVING TRYING TO WRITE SONGS THESE DAYS.

BEFORE IT WAS SIMPLE: WHAT HAPPENED TO YOU? YOU'VE CHANGED.

NOW IT'S LIKE, WHAT HAPPENED TO YOU? IT'S FREAKY AND KIND OF HORRIBLE AND SORT OF INTEREST-ING, AND I THINK I LIKE YOU BETTER NOW.

"WHO CAN RETELL THE THINGS THAT BEFELL US? WHO CAN RETELL? IN EVERY AGE A HERO OR SAGE CAME TO OUR AID." THAT'S ANOTHER SONG I LEARNED IN HEBREW SCHOOL.

A BEAUTIFUL, ROUSING ANTHEM IF I'VE EVER HEARD ONE. UNFORTUNATELY, IT'S JUST NOT TRUE.

7. Joseph

I WAS STUNNED AND THRILLED WHEN JOSEPH INVITED ME TO A BARBECUE AT HIS HOUSE. TOTALLY DISPROPORTIONATE TO THE ACTUAL EVENT OR CIRCUM-STANCES, I FELT TRIUMPHANT. A SMALL VICTORY AFTER YEARS OF COMING BACK TO THIS STUPID TOWN WHERE NO ONE WOULD EVEN OFFER YOU A CIGARETTE, LEST THEY BE REJECTED. THEY WOULD SAY, "THOSE ARE MY CIGARETTES, YOU ARE WELCOME TO SMOKE THEM", OR "I AM GOING TO

VISIT THE HOBOS AT THE BRICK FACTORY, YOU CAN COME ALONG IF YOU WANT TO." THEY WOULD NEVER GIVE YOU A CHANCE TO SAY NO.

IN A WAY IT WAS A RELIEF. COMPARED TO CALIFORNIA, WHERE EVERYTHING IS A QUESTION. "DO YOU FEEL THAT WAY? HAVEN'T YOU EVER FELT THAT WAY? BECAUSE I FEEL THAT WAY, LET ME TELL YOU."

ALWAYS SEEKING APPROVAL, THAT'S NEEDY AND SPINELESS. YOU KNOW? BUT ALWAYS ACTING ALOOF AND UNCARING DIDN'T SEEM MUCH BETTER.

MEET SOMEONE FROM CALIFORNIA, THEY'LL BE NICE TO YOUR FACE, BUT IT'S FAKE. MEET SOMEONE FROM THE MIDWEST AND THEY'LL BE AN ASSHOLE, BUT GET TO KNOW THEM AND THEY'LL BE YOUR FRIEND FOR LIFE.

SO THEY SAY. AN AMAZING RATIONALE FOR THE FACT THAT PEOPLE IN THE MIDWEST ARE UNBEARABLE SNOBS AND PRETENTIOUS ASSHOLES.

STILL, THERE WAS SOME TRUTH IN WHAT THEY SAID. I WAS NICE, AND JOSEPH WAS AN UNBEARABLE PRICK. IT ALMOST SEEMED LIKE HE'D BE MY FRIEND FOR LIFE. BUT IN ALL THE YEARS WE'D KNOWN EACH OTHER, I HAD NEVER BEEN TO HIS HOUSE. I HAD NEVER INVITED HIM TO MY HOUSE EITHER, BUT THAT'S DIFFERENT. DIFFERENT, I GUESS, BECAUSE I'M FROM CALIFORNIA.

FUNNY TO KNOW SOMEONE THAT LONG AND NOT SEE WHERE THEY LIVE. BUT, I'D NEVER EVEN CONSIDERED IT BEFORE. WE ALREADY SHARED THE SAME KITCHEN, BATH-ROOM, AND LIVING ROOM EVERY DAY AT OUR HOME AWAY FROM HOME, THE CAFE. FRANKLY, WE HAD EVEN USED THE ROOF AS A BEDROOM ON OCCASION. BUT A LITTLE PRIVACY AND MYSTERY IS GOOD FOR PEOPLE, AND FOR FRIENDSHIPS. WE DIDN'T NEED TO SHARE THE SAME BED.

WE'D MET ON THE STREET AND GOTTEN TO KNOW EACH OTHER AT THE CAFE, THEN CONTINUED YEAR AFTER YEAR THAT SAME WAY. TWO PRIVATE PEOPLE WHO LIVED MOST OF OUR LIVES IN PUBLIC. IF YOU DO YOUR PRIVATE THINGS IN PUBLIC, WHAT DO YOU DO IN PRIVATE? BETTER NOT TO ASK.

SINGING THE PRAISES OF SELF-SUFFICIENCY AND SOLITUDE, YET WORKING TO BUILD A VIBRANT PUBLIC LIFE AND A GENUINE CIVIC-MINDED COMMUNITY FEELING. THAT WAS THE ST. LOUIS SCHIZOPHRENIA, AND JOSEPH AND I PERHAPS PARTICULARLY SUITED FOR LIVING IT. WHEREAS FRANCE HAS "LIBERTY, FRATERNITY, EQUALITY", ST. LOUIS HAS TWO FLAGS: "SURLY, SELF-SUFFICIENT, CYNICAL" ON ONE, AND "COMMUNITY, CULTURE, AND CO-DEPENDENCE" ON THE OTHER.

SALUD! BUT WHICH FLAG TO BURN AT THE BARBECUE?

8. Paths

IT WAS RAINING ONE MORNING AND I WAS OUT WALKING. PROBABLY I WAS DEPRESSED. I GOT TO FOLLOWING A TRACE OF PRINTS IN THE MUD. UNDER FENCES, THROUGH BUSHES, AND UP TO MY ANKLES IN SLUDGE. ACROSS FEDERAL PROPERTY AND A FEW SCARY BACKYARDS, I FOLLOWED.

UPHILL THROUGH BRAMBLES AND BRANCHES AND SPIDER WEBS FROM SPIDERS SO MASSIVE THAT THE WEBS MADE A SOUND WHEN THEY SNAPPED ON MY FACE, I TRIPPED AND FELL INTO A TANGLE OF THORNS. BUT THERE WAS NO POINT SCREAMING IN AGONY. NO ONE WAS AROUND TO CARE. LIKE A TREE FALLING IN THE FOREST, MY VERY EXISTENCE WAS QUESTIONABLE.

IT WAS EARLY AFTERNOON WHEN I CAME TO AN END. A TALL WALL, A LARGE HOLE. GOPHERS. I'D SPENT ALL DAY FOLLOWING A GODDAMN GOPHER. THE WORLD IS A STUPID PLACE, AND EVEN SO, I STAND OUT AS BEING PARTICULARLY DUMB.

THE ONLY OTHER WAY TO GO WAS A CLIFF WITH A TWO HUNDRED FOOT DROP-OFF. I HAD TO THINK IT OVER. A GOOD SHORTCUT, AFTER ALL. I WAS TEMPTED TO JUMP OFF JUST TO KEEP FROM GOING BACK THE WAY I CAME. THAT'S ONE THING I CAN'T STAND.

TODAY, I FOUND ANOTHER NICE PATH. ALONG THE TRACKS, ALONG THE SHORE OF THE MISSISSIPPI, THEN THROUGH A WILDERNESS PRESERVE. IT LED TO A CLEARING WHERE A BLACK BUTTERFLY FLAPPED AROUND AS BIG AS A BAT. STRANGE THAT A PATH SHOULD LEAD HERE, I THOUGHT. BUT NICE.

I THOUGHT BACK UPON THE BEST FIVE MINUTES OF MY LIFE. IT WAS IN THIRD GRADE, WHEN A DRAGONFLY LANDED ON MY FINGER. FOR A WEEK IT WAS THE TALK OF THOUSAND OAKS. NOT A DAMSELFLY, THEY SAID, BUT AN HONEST-TO-GOD METALLIC GREEN DRAGONFLY, THE HARLEY-DAVIDSON OF INSECTS.

THEN IT WAS FORGOTTEN, PUSHED BY THE WAYSIDE BY A GIRL WHO PULLED DOWN HER PANTS UNDER THE FALSE PROMISE OF A NEW BEST FRIEND. SAD. BUT I NEVER FORGOT.

JUST A FEW MONTHS AGO, IT HAPPENED AGAIN. I WAS IN BERKELEY, SITTING ON MY ROOFTOP OVERLOOKING THE BAY. I WAS TIRED, ANGRY, BITTER, HUNGOVER, DISGUSTED, HORRIFIED, I HAD A HEADACHE, I WAS IN A BAD MOOD, HOPELESS, DESPONDENT, UGLY, UNHEALTHY, AND I THINK SOMEONE HAD USED THE LAST OF THE CREAM NECESSARY FOR MY MORNING COFFEE. THEN A TIGER SWALLOWTAIL CAME DRIFTING BY, RIDING THE WIND.

I LIFTED MY HAND. GENTLY, LIKE THIS. WITH ONE FINGER OUT, LIKE IN THIRD GRADE. AND THE TIGER SWALLOWTAIL SWEPT DOWN AND LANDED AS IF ON CUE.

ITS LEGS TICKLED MY FINGER, WHICH MADE ME GIGGLE AND FEEL GIDDY. UNSHAVEN AND UNWASHED, WITH A HUGE BUTTERFLY ON MY FINGER, I FELT LIKE A HIPPIE. AND YET, NO ONE WAS AROUND TO CARE, SO I SMILED. ALL THE POINTLESSNESS, THE INANITY, THE STUPIDITY AND BEAUTY OF IT ALL. I LOOKED AT THE BUTTERFLY AND THE BUTTERFLY LOOKED AT ME. ALL MY TIME CHASING BUTTERFLIES, I HAD NEVER SEEN ONE SO CLOSE. MAJESTIC BLACK AND YELLOW, GRACEFUL YET FORCEFUL.

IN A FLASH, ANOTHER SWALLOWTAIL SWOOPED DOWN AND THEY TOOK OFF TOGETHER IN A RUNNING, ROLLING RIOT THROUGH THE SKY. STUMBLING, TUMBLING, CLAWING AND KISSING AND BARELY MISSING MY NEIGHBOR'S ANTENNAS. I LOOKED ON, RUBBED MY EYES, SHOOK OFF MY OWN BULL-SHIT, SHAVED, AND WENT BACK TO REALLY LIVING.

I MOVED TO ST. LOUIS AND STUCK OUT MY FINGER AGAIN, THIS TIME FOR THE BIG BLACK BAT OF A BUTTERFLY. BUT WHO WAS I KIDDING? TWICE IN A LIFETIME WAS LUCKY, LIKE LIGHTNING. GOOD OR BAD, IT'S STILL LUCK.

9. Binge Purge

I GOT MY $15 BIKE AT UNIQUE THRIFT ON HALF-OFF DAY. YES, A MERE $7.50. IMAGINE, INSTEAD OF PAYING NEXT MONTH'S RENT, ME AND EMMET COULD GET THIRTY OF SUCH BIKES. TALL, RUSTY, AND PROUD, JUST ONE MAKES ME FEEL LIKE A MILLION BUCKS. INSTEAD OF WHAT I HAD BEEN FEELING LIKE, WHICH WAS ABOUT FOUR.

"WE COULD RIDE THEM ACROSS THE COUNTRY," I SAID, "FIFTEEN BIKES EACH." BUT JOSEPH'S IDEA WAS BETTER: GET THIRTY FRIENDS AND RIDE THEM ACROSS TOWN.

JOSEPH'S IDEA OF A PARTY WAS DIFFERENT THAN MINE, AND THANKFULLY SO, BECAUSE WHO COULD SURVIVE ANOTHER ONE OF MY BIRTHDAY PLANS? WE WERE TO MEET UP AT 9:00 P.M. AND GO TO EVERY BAR ON THE SOUTHSIDE ON BIKES. A GOOD PLAN, EXCEPT MY NEW SLEEPING SCHEDULE WAS ALREADY SCREWED UP. I WOKE UP AT 11:00.

ROLLING THROUGH TRAFFIC AND UP AND DOWN THE ALLEYWAYS, THE CLOUDS CLEARED OUT OF MY HEAD. FOR THE FIRST TIME IN WEEKS, MY RACING BRAIN LOST THE RACE. I MOVED FASTER THAN MY THOUGHTS. WHAT A RELIEF. SPLIT-SECOND INTUITIVE DECISIONS INSTEAD OF THE MULLED-OVER LONGTERM KIND.

AFTER AN HOUR OF TRYING TO FIND THE MOBILE PARTY, IT FOUND ME. THERE WERE PAINTERS AND BLUE-

GRASS BANDS, WRITERS AND TEACHERS AND SMALL BUSINESS OWNERS, ALL LOOKING SHARP AND SLY ON TWO WHEELS, AND ALL MAKING IT HARD TO STEER FOR THIS PARTICULAR GUY, BECAUSE MOST OF THEM WERE SOME MIGHTY MIGHTY FINE WOMEN. IS THIS, I ASKED, WHAT GROWING UP IS ALL ABOUT?

TWENTY FIVE OF US IN ALL, AND JOSEPH WITH THE WHISTLE AROUND HIS NECK CALLING TIME AFTER FIFTEEN MINUTES IN EACH PLACE. NOTHING PLEASES ME MORE THAN BEING IN THE COMPANY OF A CONTROL FREAK. IT MEANS I CAN TAKE THE DAY OFF.

FIRST I WAS SHOWING JOSEPH HOW TO RIDE DOUBLE AND SWITCH POSITIONS WITHOUT STOPPING. NEXT THING I KNEW JOSEPH WAS GONE AND I HAD ONE GIRL ON THE SEAT AND ONE ON THE HANDLEBARS, RIDING DOWN THE MIDDLE OF THE STREET.

IT'S ALL FUN AND GAMES UNTIL SOMEONE GETS HURT, AND, DAMN, I WAS ONLY STARTING TO WAKE UP. WHEN THAT GIRL LET GO OF MY HAND, GOT OFF THE BARS, AND JUST WALKED AWAY, I HEARD SOMETHING BREAK.

10. Birthday

"WHAT'S GOING ON?", CASEY ASKED, SIDLING UP NEXT TO ME AT THE COUNTER AND POURING A BIG CUP OF COFFEE.

"OH, SAME AS USUAL", I SAID. "WORK ALL NIGHT, THEN PUT ON MY HULK SUIT IN THE MORNING AND RUN AROUND THE LAKE IN THE BRIGHT WARM SUN. GET ALL WARM AND HAPPY ABOUT HUMANITY, THEN GO TO THE CAFE AND FLIRT WITH THE PRETTY GIRLS."

I WINKED. SHE LEERED BACK AT ME, A LITTLE TOO CRUDE AND LOUD TO FIT THE ROLE AS CAFE GIRL. NOT ALOOF, COY, OR COORDINATED WHATSOEVER, WHICH IS WHY IT'S FUN TO SEE CASEY IN THOSE SURROUNDINGS.

"YOU KNOW ME, CASEY. DRINK FREE COFFEE, SIT GLOWERING AND FIDGETING AT THE BACK TABLE TRYING TO DRUM UP SOME HATE. WRITE A COUPLE SONGS ABOUT HOW I CAN'T STAND MY FRIENDS. THEN GO HOME AND SEE IF ANY OF THEM HAVE CALLED OR WRITTEN."

"SO WHY SO BLUE?"

"BECAUSE, I CAN'T WRITE ANY SONGS TODAY. I CAN'T CONCENTRATE OR EVEN SIT STILL. I QUIT EVERYTHING I LOVED, EVERYTHING BESIDES COFFEE. NOW I'M JUST A WRECK."

"WHY'D YOU DO THAT FOR?", SHE ASKED.

"FOR MY BIRTHDAY."

"OH, THAT MAKES A LOT OF SENSE."

"I'M GLAD SOMEONE UNDERSTANDS", I SAID, "BECAUSE I COULD SURE USE SOME UNDERSTANDING. I CAN'T

THINK STRAIGHT AT ALL. BETWEEN THE QUITTING AND THE FUCKING LOUD MUSIC IN HERE, MY NERVES ARE SHOT."

"DARLING," SHE SAID, "I'M NOT EVEN PLAYING MUSIC RIGHT NOW."

"CASEY," I SAID. "YOU KNOW WHAT I MEAN."

11. St. Louis Classified

AM I TOO EASTBAY FOR YOU? TOO WEST COAST AT LEAST? NEUROTIC, I WEAR MY HEART ON MY SLEEVE. SECRETS ARE THE LAST THING I WOULD WANT TO KEEP. I DO ALL MY THINKING OUT LOUD. NOT LIKE YOU, TALKING IN A LOW RUMBLING GROWL AND NOT VERY OFTEN AT ALL. NOT ENOUGH. I THINK I LOVE YOU, OR AT LEAST A HUGE CRUSH LONG LEGS BIG EYES BIG EVERYTHING AND YOU WON'T EVEN GIVE ME THE TIME OF DAY, EXCEPT ONCE YOU SAID, "MAYBE," AND SMILED. THAT'S ALL, ONE WORD, BUT A BEAUTIFUL ONE.

CASEY SAID, "THAT JENNA GIRL WAS LOOKING AT ME EVIL CUZ I WAS WITH YOU."

"I DON'T LIKE THE WAY SHE WALKS," CASEY SAID. SOMETHING ABOUT IT BUGS ME."

I SAID "OH YEAH, ME TOO. IT DRIVES ME CRAAAZY."

HORSE FACED BITCH: I MET YOU AT THE BIRTHDAY BASH. YOU WERE CONDESCENDING AND RUDE. YOU MAY AS WELL HAVE JUST SPIT IN MY FACE. MAYBE NEXT TIME? WHAT'S THE POINT? YOU PROBABLY CAN'T EVEN READ. GET OUT OF MY LIFE, BUT DON'T LEAVE TOWN BEFORE THIS MAKES IT INTO THE RIVERFRONT TIMES MISSED CONNECTIONS. YOU'RE NOT AS COOL AS YOU THINK YOU ARE AND EVERYONE WILL LAUGH AT YOU SOMEDAY WHEN YOU FALL FOR ME.

12. Jenna

"I DON'T KNOW WHAT HAPPENED TO MY LIFE," JENNA SAID.

SHE LOOKED AT ME ALL FRANTIC WITH WILD EYES AND HAIR LIKE A TIDAL WAVE, DIRTY HANDS DRAGGING THROUGH IT. SHE PACED AROUND, DUMPING OUT HER DRAWERS.

"NOTHING HAPPENED TO YOUR LIFE," I SAID. "WHAT IS IT? CAN'T FIND A SPOON? AM I RIGHT?"

I WAS RIGHT. EVERYONE'S LIFE IS A MESS, BUT AS LONG AS THEY HAVE SOMETHING TO HOLD ON TO, THEY DON'T NOTICE MUCH. A PEN TO WRITE WITH, A SPOON TO STIR THE COFFEE. A BOOK, A GUITAR PICK, A BEER, A BOY. WHATEVER. IT REMINDED ME OF AN OLD JEWISH PRAYER:

HAD THE LORD GIVEN US SUGAR, THAT WOULD SUFFICE.
HAD HE GIVEN US CREAM BUT NO SUGAR, THAT WOULD
SUFFICE. HAD HE GIVEN US COFFEE BUT NO CREAM AND
SUGAR, WE COULD LEARN TO LIVE WITH IT. BUT IF THE
LORD OUR GOD, KING OF THE UNIVERSE, FATHER OF
ABRAHAM, ISAAC, AND JACOB WERE TO TAKE AWAY
OUR COFFEE, WE WOULD SMASH HIS PRETTY FACE AND GO
BACK TO WORSHIPPING IDOLS AND THE GOLDEN CALF.

"NO CREAM OR SUGAR?", SHE SAID. "BOY, YOU'RE REALLY
DROPPING YOUR STANDARDS FAST."

"STANDARDS CAN BE DROPPED", I SAID. "BUT DROP YOUR
MATCHES, YOUR GLASSES, YOUR HAT, AND YOU'RE LOST,
MAN, LIKE THE ISRAELITES. IT'S THOSE LITTLE THINGS
THAT COUNT. ONE DAY YOU'RE IN LIKE FLYNN AND THE NEXT
IS LIKE FORTY YEARS IN THE DESERT."

"ONE DAY YOU'RE STUCK WITH A BOY WHO WON'T
SHUT UP", SHE SAID. "AND THE NEXT YOU'VE TRADED HIM
FOR A SWEET YOUNG THING WHO DON'T DO NOTHING
BUT STIR YOUR COFFEE AND SMILE. THINK ABOUT THAT!"

13. Working for the Man

I WOKE UP, GROPED FOR THE LIGHT SWITCH, THEN
STUMBLED THROUGH THE DUST TOWARDS MY COFFEE-
MAKER. THE DOG WAS WAITING THERE FOR ME, STARING
WITH BIG SAD EYES. EYES LIKE LIMPID POOLS, LIKE THEY
TELL YOU ABOUT IN THE ROMANCE NOVELS BUT YOU NEVER
FIND ON A GIRL. HUNGRY EYES.

I CAME TO ST. LOUIS TO GET SOME TIME TO MYSELF.
INSTEAD, WHAT DID I RUN OUT AND GET? A DOG. REALLY
SMART. IT BEGS, IT BARKS, AND I CAN'T MAKE IT FEEL
GUILTY FOR BEING DEMANDING LIKE I CAN WITH MY
GIRLFRIEND. IT IGNORES MY EXPLANATIONS AND
EXCUSES.

"YOU GOTTA BE CRAZY", I SAY, "IF YOU THINK I'M
GOING OUT TO GET YOU FOOD BEFORE I'VE MADE COFFEE
FOR MYSELF."

CAN'T ARGUE WITH A DOBERMAN, THOUGH. AND SO,
SLEEPLESS AND SORE I AM SOON SEEN DRAGGING MY ASS
OVER TO THE TEXACO. THAT'S ONE OF THE PROBLEMS
WITH LIVING DOWNTOWN, NOWHERE ELSE TO GET
GROCERIES FOR MILES, AND ALL THEY'VE GOT IS GENERIC
DOG FOOD. THE MUTT SNIFFS AND FROWNS. EVEN THE
DOGS ARE YUPPIES THESE DAYS.

TIME TO MYSELF WITHOUT HAVING TO ANSWER TO
ANYONE ELSE'S NEEDS, DEMANDS, OR EXPECTATIONS.
THAT'S WHAT I SAID. WHAT DID I GET? FIRST A BAND,
THEN A GIRLFRIEND, THEN A DOG, AND THEN A FUCKING
JOB. I DIDN'T EVEN KNOW I WAS OUT LOOKING, BUT I

MUST HAVE BEEN LOOKING FOR SOMETHING BECAUSE I FOUND ALL FOUR.

INNOCENTLY ENOUGH, I WENT TO A PARTY AND MET JENNA. THEN, AS MY SONG SAYS, "I TOOK A WALK TO CLEAR MY HEAD, BUT DOWN AT RIVER ROAD I RAN INTO YOU INSTEAD. OH SHIT!"

WHEN SHE LEFT TOWN FOR A COUPLE WEEKS TO VISIT HER FOLKS BACK EAST, SHE LEFT HER STINKING CANINE WITH ME.

NO PROBLEM, REALLY. WE WALKED AROUND TOGETHER GROWLING AND WHINING. THERE WAS AN EXTRA MOUTH TO FEED, BUT I STILL HAD LOTS OF TIME ON MY HANDS. THAT WAS BEFORE I STARTED WORKING FOR THE MAN.

LATE ONE NIGHT WE SAW A FLIER FOR A 24-HOUR RECORD SALE. TWENTY JEFFERSON AVENUE, THE FLIERS SAID, BUT AT EIGHTEEN JEFFERSON A GUY WAVED THROUGH THE WINDOW, TELLING US TO COME IN.

"IS THIS THE RECORD SALE?", I ASKED.

"NO", HE SAID. "BUT I HAVE A PROPOSITION FOR YOU!"

WELL, HELL, I HADN'T WORKED FOR ANYONE BUT MYSELF IN YEARS, AND AS GREAT AS THAT MAY SOUND, LET ME TELL YOU, NO MATTER WHO YOU WORK FOR, YOU HATE THE BOSS.

NOW HERE WAS A GUY OFFERING FIFTEEN BUCKS TO GO DUMPSTERING WITH HIM. SAYS THERE'S A BUNCH OF OFFICE EQUIPMENT IN THE GARBAGE A BLOCK AWAY, SO I SAID OKAY. TEN FOR ME AND FIVE FOR THE MONGREL. LET'S GO. LET'S GET DOWN TO BUSINESS.

MY BOSS SMILED AND TOOK SOME CLOTHES OFF THE RACK AND CHANGED. "NO SENSE GETTING MY OWN CLOTHES DIRTY", HE SAID. MY KIND OF GUY.

HIS WHOLE STORE WAS FULL OF SIMILARLY SALVAGED TRASH. OLD CLOTHES, APPLIANCES, OFFICE SUPPLIES, EVEN A LITTLE FOOD. A TEMPORARY STOREFRONT SET-UP RENTED FOR JUST ONE MONTH. DECEMBER.

"OPEN TWENTY FOUR HOURS A DAY?", I ASKED. "DON'T YOU NEED TO SLEEP SOMETIME?"

"YES, SIR", HE SAID. "I SURE DO."

SIMPLE AS THAT. ME AND JENNA'S BASTARD HOUND WITH THE SAD EYES SET UP OFFICE IN THE JUNKSHOP WHILE THE MAN WENT AND SPENT THE NIGHT IN HIS TRUCK.

IT'S BEEN THAT WAY ALMOST EVERY NIGHT SINCE, AND ONE OF THE DAYS, WORKING FOR A LITTLE CASH BUT MOSTLY TRADE. WINTER CLOTHES, A DESK, A LAMP, AN EXTRA COFFEEMAKER JUST TO BE SURE. RENT AT THE WAREHOUSE IS CHEAP ENOUGH TO SCRAPE BY WITHOUT A STEADY JOB, BUT A LITTLE EXTRA COFFEE AND DOG FOOD MONEY DOESN'T HURT, AND HONESTLY, I WAS GETTING A LITTLE LONELY AND SICK OF MYSELF INSIDE THAT CAVE, CUT OFF FROM THE REST OF THE WORLD.

EXCEPT FOR THE FEW ODD CUSTOMERS, NIGHTS ARE

JUST AS QUIET HERE AT THE SHOP, BUT IT'S DIFFERENT. THE HUM OF THE LIGHTS, THE OCCASSIONAL BICKERING AND BARGAINING. THE FLICKER OF WET STREETLAMPS SHINING THROUGH THE WINDOW AND THE SLOW BUT STEADY PASSING OF CARS DOWN THE AVENUE IN THE RAIN. IT'S COMFORTING. ROMANTIC.

TONIGHT THE STREETS ARE TRULY DESERTED, WIDE OPEN AND QUIETER THAN EVER BEFORE. THE LAST OF THE LAST MINUTE RUSHING IS ALL OVER. TIME TO TAKE THE DOG OUT FOR A LITTLE ROMP AND RACE THROUGH THE SNOW.

MIGHT AS WELL CLOSE UP THE SHOP FOR THE NIGHT, BUT I PUT THE "BACK IN FIFTEEN MINUTES" SIGN UP INSTEAD. YOU NEVER KNOW WHO MIGHT BE OUT LOOKING FOR A BROKEN DUSTBUSTER OR AN UGLY LAMP AT 4:00 A.M. ON CHRISTMAS EVE.

14. Last Words

LIFE IS LIKE ONE OF ED'S STORIES. TWO TANGENTS FOR EVERY TANGENT, AND AS THE HOURS PASS I'M BURNING WITH IMPATIENCE. WHAT IS THIS ABOUT? HOW DID IT START AND WHAT COULD IT POSSIBLY MEAN? HOW CAN I HURRY UP AND GET TO THE END WITHOUT BEING RUDE?

ED'S STORIES ARE NEVER FUNNY, BUT HE ALWAYS HAS A GOOD LAUGH AT THE END. IS LIFE LIKE THAT, A JOKE THAT'S NOT FUNNY? A STORY THAT DOESN'T MAKE SENSE? MAYBE HE HAS THE RIGHT ATTITUDE, LAUGHING ANYWAY. MAYBE LIFE ISN'T THE JOKE AT ALL, BUT JUST THE PUNCH-LINE WHICH MAKES THE JOKE STUPID. WHEN I DIE, WILL ED LAUGH? WILL I?

I THINK LIFE MAY BE A BOOK WITH THE LAST PAGES MISSING, OR A SONG CUT OFF AT THE END OF THE TAPE. STRUCK DEAD IN THE MIDDLE OF ONE OF ED'S STORIES, WOULD IT COME AS A RELIEF, OR WOULD THE FEELING OF WITHDRAWAL BE TORTUROUS? I HATE TO LEAVE ANYTHING UNFINISHED. BUT, ALAS, THAT IS PROBABLY THE VERY ESSENCE OF LIFE. FEELING INCOMPLETE. LIKE ED'S STORIES, ENDING BUT NEVER COMING TO A CONCLUSION.

I WILL HAVE TO INTERRUPT ED ON MY DEATHBED TO GET IN MY FAMOUS LAST WORDS. "I DON'T WANT THEM TO UNDRESS ME, I WANT YOU TO UNDRESS ME" IS WHAT I PLAN TO SAY, NO MATTER WHO IS AROUND. THOSE WERE TROTSKY'S LAST WORDS, SPOKEN TO N. SEDOVA, AND AMONG THE SWEETEST SENTIMENTS I'VE EVER HEARD. BUT INTERRUPTING ED IS NO EASY TASK. SO, MY LAST WORDS WILL PROBABLY BE, "GIVE ME A CHANCE TO SAY SOMETHING JUST THIS ONCE", OR, SIMPLY, "EXCUSE ME."

COMETBUS

THE DEAD END

#46
$2.00

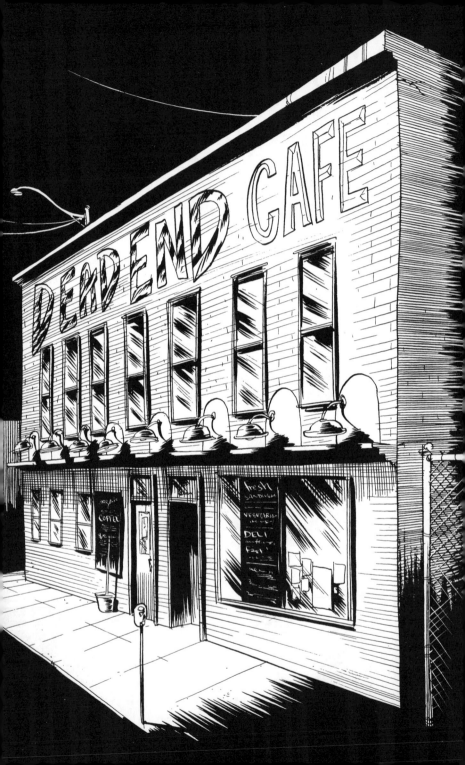

the TRUTH
ABOUT
COMETBUS 46!

IN THE WINTER OF 1999, A NAGGING LITTLE IDEA
ENTERED MY HEAD AND GREW INTO AN OBSESSION.
I'D TOLD PEOPLE'S STORIES IN DIFFERENT WAYS OVER
THE YEARS, AND TRIED TO DOCUMENT THE MORES AND
MOODS OF WHOLE SCENES — YET SOMETHING WAS
STILL MISSING. THE MAGAZINE DIDN'T REFLECT THE
VARIETY AND INTENSITY OF THE LIVES GOING ON
AROUND ME.
I COULDN'T CAPTURE THE VOICES OF THE PEOPLE
WHO WERE MOST INTERESTING, AND THEY WOULDN'T
WRITE DOWN THEIR OWN STORIES FOR ME TO PRINT,
NO MATTER HOW I PESTERED AND BEGGED. NATURAL
STORYTELLERS, THEY FROZE UP WHEN CONFRONTED
WITH THE BLANK PAGE. WHEN THEY TRIED, THE
WORDS DIDN'T MAKE SENSE OR CONTAIN THE
DELICIOUS, GOSSIPY RING OF TRUTH. IT WASN'T
LIKE TALKING TO THEM FACE-TO-FACE.
AND SO, I DECIDED TO RETURN TO DOING INTER-
VIEWS. COMETBUS HAD BEEN ENTIRELY INTERVIEWS
IN THE EARLY YEARS, MOSTLY OF SMALL BAY AREA
PUNK BANDS. WHAT I WANTED NOW WAS A DIFFERENT
KIND OF GROUP, ONE LARGER AND MORE DIVERSE,
YET WITH THE SAME KIND OF SHARED PURPOSE AS
A BAND, AND THE SAME INTERNAL CONFLICTS ALWAYS
THREATENING TO BREAK IT UP. I'D ALWAYS BEEN
FASCINATED WITH GROUP IDENTITY — HOW INDIVIDUALS
FROM DIFFERENT BACKGROUNDS AND WITH DIFFERENT
TEMPERAMENTS JOIN TOGETHER TO FORM SOMETHING
LARGER THAN THE SUM OF THEIR PARTS.
I WANTED TO FIND SOME KIND OF COLLECTIVE,
COMMUNAL ENTERPRISE AND RECORD THE STORIES OF
EVERYONE INVOLVED AS WELL AS THE WAYS THEIR
LIVES INTERSECTED AND OVERLAPPED. MULLING OVER
THE IDEA IN MY HEAD AND TALKING IT OVER WITH MY
PEERS, THE EXAMPLE THAT KEPT COMING UP WAS THE
HARD TIMES CAFE IN MINNEAPOLIS. IT WAS BURSTING

WITH LIFE, AT THE CROSSROADS OF MANY DIFFERENT CULTURES, AND FULL OF PEOPLE WITH DYNAMIC, IF NOT OVERBEARING, PERSONALITIES—AND MANY OF THEM WERE MY OLD FRIENDS.

THE HARD TIMES, HOWEVER, WAS JUST AN EXAMPLE OF WHAT I WAS LOOKING FOR. IT WASN'T THEIR STORY IN PARTICULAR I WAS ITCHING TO TELL. BESIDES, IT WAS WINTER AND I WAS SETTLED IN SNUG AND WARM. WHO IN THEIR RIGHT MIND WOULD CHOOSE THAT TIME FOR A VISIT TO THE MIDWEST?

AS IT TURNED OUT, THE HARD TIMES WAS A BAD EXAMPLE TO PICK. MUCH AS I WRACKED MY BRAINS, NOTHING COULD TAKE ITS PLACE. FINALLY I BUNDLED UP MY QUESTIONS AND HEADED EAST. I RENTED A BASEMENT ROOM AND BEGAN THE LONG, STRANGE, AND COLD PROCESS OF CONDUCTING INTERVIEWS. IT WAS A HOMECOMING OF SORTS FOR ME—A LONG OVERDUE RETURN, FOR WHICH I'LL NEED TO ROLL BACK TIME TO EXPLAIN.

MINNEAPOLIS WAS THE FIRST CITY I EVER MOVED TO ON MY OWN. I WAS 22 AND WORKING A CRAPPY JOB TO PAY OFF THE PRINTING DEBT ON A PREVIOUS ISSUE OF COMETBUS. EVERY WAKING HOUR NOT WORK-ING WAS SPENT WALKING THE STREETS TRYING TO MAKE FRIENDS, WITH VERY LITTLE LUCK.

AFTER A FEW MONTHS, FLIERS BEGAN APPEARING ON TELEPHONE POLES ANNOUNCING THE OPENING OF A NEW ALL-NIGHT CAFE. I COULD SENSE A LIGHT AT THE END OF THE TUNNEL. "GET A GRIP ON REALITY," THEY READ. COOL. I NEEDED ONE BAD.

ONE COLLECTIVE MEMBER I INTERVIEWED DESCRIB-ED REGULAR CUSTOMERS WHO SEEMED TO HAVE NOWHERE ELSE TO GO, WHO CAME TO THE CAFE EVEN ON HOLIDAYS. SHE MAY AS WELL HAVE JUST USED MY NAME. I WAS ONE OF THOSE REGULARS, PERMAN-ENTLY HAUNTING THE PLACE. IT WAS A SAFE HAVEN AND A LITTLE SLICE OF HEAVEN FOR ME, EXACTLY WHAT I NEEDED TO CONNECT WITH OTHER PEOPLE AND MAKE MINNEAPOLIS START TO FEEL LIKE HOME.

THE CAFE WENT THROUGH SEVERAL DIFFERENT INCARNATIONS. AT FIRST IT WAS MORE OF A LOAN THAN A ROOM OF ONE'S OWN. THOUGH THE PHRASE MAKES ME SHIVER, IT TRULY WAS A TEMPORARY AUTONOMOUS ZONE. A GROUP OF WORKERS AT A HIPPIE-STYLE EATERY CALLED THE URBAN PEASANT CONVINCED THEIR BOSS TO LET THEM RENT OUT THE PLACE DURING THE HOURS THE RESTAURANT WAS

CLOSED. THE INMATES RAN THE ASYLUM AT NIGHT AND CALLED IT "CAFE GLOBAL".

IT WAS A SUCCESS, AND SOON THE YOUNG UPSTARTS WERE ABLE TO BUY OUT THE OLD OWNER AND TAKE OVER FULL-TIME. BUT BEFORE THE PAINT ON THE NEW SIGN HAD A CHANCE TO DRY, THERE WAS A PALACE COUP AND ANOTHER NAME CHANGE. THE GLOBAL BECAME THE HARD TIMES, A WORKER-OWNED COLLECTIVE.

BETWEEN THE OPENING OF THE GLOBAL AND THE WINTER I RETURNED TO CONDUCT INTERVIEWS, NEARLY A DECADE HAD PASSED. I DIDN'T KNOW THE NEWER COLLECTIVE MEMBERS WHO MADE UP THE BULK OF THE HARD TIMES' STAFF. APPROACHING THEM WITH A TAPE RECORDER AND A LIST OF INVAS-IVE QUESTIONS WASN'T GOING TO BE EASY—NOT IF THE GOAL WAS TO WIN THEIR TRUST AND GET THEM TO REVEAL THEMSELVES. MINNESOTANS ARE LEGENDARY FOR THEIR SHYNESS AND RESERVE, AND THE HARD TIMES STAFF WAS A PARTICULARLY SECRETIVE AND GUARDED BUNCH. PART OF DEVELOPING A GROUP IDENTITY IS DISTANCING YOURSELF FROM, AND BEING DISTRUSTFUL OF, EVERYONE ELSE. THEY HAD REALLY EXCELLED AT THAT.

EVEN THE COLLECTIVE MEMBERS I CONSIDERED OLD FRIENDS WERE NOT THE TYPE TO TALK AT LENGTH OR CASUALLY SHARE THEIR FEELINGS. THEY DIDN'T WEAR THEIR HEARTS ON THEIR SLEEVES LIKE ME. I'D ALWAYS BEEN AN OUTSIDER AMONGST THEM, BUT ONE WHO FELT WELCOMED AND ACCEPTED INTO THEIR GROUP. YET WOULD OUR OLD FAMILIARITY AND TRUST BE FORCE ENOUGH TO GET THEM TO OPEN UP?

AS IT TURNED OUT, MY FEARS WERE TOTALLY UN-FOUNDED. THE MOMENT I HIT PLAY AND RECORD, THE COLLECTIVE MEMBERS LINED UP TO DIVULGE THEIR SECRETS, EVEN THE NEWER MEMBERS I'D NEVER MET. THEY BLOSSOMED LIKE FLOWERS, THEY BABBLED LIKE CALIFORNIANS. THEY STEERED DIRECTLY TOWARD THE TOPICS I WAS SCARED TO EVEN BRING UP. THE FACT THAT I WAS AN OUTSIDER NO DOUBT HELPED, FOR IT'S EASIER TO REVEAL YOURSELF TO SOMEONE SEEING YOU WITH FRESH EYES. STILL, THEY TOOK A RISK BY COMMITTING THEIR WORDS TO TAPE, AND I WAS—AND AM—GRATEFUL TO THEM FOR GIVING MY PROJECT A CHANCE.

TO GUARANTEE PRIVACY, I CHANGED EVERYONE'S NAMES. UNFORTUNATELY, I WENT FURTHER THAN THAT—TOO FAR, IN FACT. I CHANGED THE NAME OF THE HARD TIMES AND EVERY OTHER BUSINESS AND

LANDMARK WE TALKED ABOUT. I CHANGED THE NAME OF THE NEIGHBORHOOD AND ENTIRELY LEFT OUT THE NAME OF THE CITY IN WHICH THE CAFE IS LOCATED, CAUSING MANY READERS TO ASSUME IT WAS BERKELEY THAT WAS BEING DISCUSSED. I WANTED THE STORY TO BE UNIVERSAL, AND EVEN MAKE PEOPLE WONDER IF IT WAS A WORK OF FICTION.

IN HINDSIGHT, THAT WAS A MISTAKE—AND THAT WAS JUST THE START. MY LAYOUT DIDN'T HAVE ENOUGH CONTRAST TO CONVEY THE RHYTHMIC BACK-AND-FORTH OF CONVERSATION. WITHOUT VISUAL CUES, IT WAS HARD TO DIFFERENTIATE BETWEEN THE DIFFERENT COLLECTIVE MEMBERS. NATE'S COVER ART, WHILE STUNNING, FAILED TO REFLECT THE ETHNIC DIVERSITY OF THE CAFE'S CLIENTELE—AND THE COUP DE GRACE WAS DELIVERED BY THE PRINTER, WHO DID A SHITTY JOB ON SOMETHING ALREADY SERIOUSLY FLAWED.

WHEN I RETURNED TO THE INTERVIEW FORMAT FOR ISSUE 48, I TOOK A DIFFERENT APPROACH, AND LEARNED FROM MY PREVIOUS MISTAKES. EVER SINCE, I'VE LONGED TO GIVE "THE DEAD END" THE SAME TREATMENT. WITH THIS REPRINT, I FINALLY HAD THE CHANCE. I ENTIRELY REDID THE LAYOUT, AND NATE PROVIDED BEAUTIFUL NEW PORTRAITS TO COMPLETE IT, TAKEN FROM HIS IMAGINATION.

THERE WAS ONE UPSIDE OF MY INITIAL MISTAKE. IN EARLY 2000, THE HARD TIMES WAS RAIDED AND BUSTED FOR DRUGS. TWO RIVAL CAMPAIGNS BEGAN IN THE COMMUNITY AND IN THE PRESS, ONE TO SAVE THE PLACE AND THE OTHER TO PERMANENTLY SHUT IT DOWN. THE LAST THING THE HARD TIMES NEEDED WAS THE RELEASE OF AN 80-PAGE WRITTEN CONFESSION OF ALL ITS SORDID MISDEEDS, BUT THE COMETBUS CONTAINING THEIR INTERVIEWS HAD ALREADY BEEN SHIPPED OUT. IT TURNED OUT TO HAVE BEEN A STROKE OF LUCK THAT THE NAMES WERE CHANGED.

IN THE END, AND AGAINST ALL ODDS, THE HARD TIMES AND ITS SUPPORTERS WON THE FIGHT. THE STRUGGLE HELPED UNIFY AND GALVANIZE THE STAFF, AND THE VICTORY PROVIDED A RENEWED SOURCE OF ENERGY AND PRIDE. DESPITE THE SKEPTICISM THEY EXPRESSED ABOUT GROWING OLDER TOGETHER, MANY OF THE COLLECTIVE MEMBERS I INTERVIEWED ARE STILL THERE, AND THE PLACE CONTINUES TO THRIVE.

CB46: THE CRITICS RAVE!

Zine Review;
"Cometbus"
–RWW

Back when I lived in Kansas and published "Backroads Bicycling", I saw a review of this other 'zine called "Cometbus" in the old "Factsheet Five" review publication and sent for a copy.

It was a great read. I mean, Aaron, the author, was a punk in the literal sense of the word, the 'zine was hand-printed and photo-copied, but I really enjoyed reading about Aaron's travels, seeing his world through the eyes of a very talented author. I would've subscribed, but Aaron doesn't accept subscriptions, so, although I MEANT to keep getting it, things happened and I never did.

Until, that is, the last ARG we got. I saw "Cometbus" was still being published, so sent Aaron three bucks, cash, for a copy. We didn't hear from them for over a month, and I honestly thought that somebody aside from Aaron needed my money more than he did, so was ready to write it off; that is one of the risks of sending cash through the mail.

Well, not long ago, I got a copy of "Cometbus #46". It consisted entirely of interviews of the patrons and workers of a co-operative café in Berkely called "The Dead End". Barb and I were tortured with stories of drug use, wanton sexual activity, one case of a worker smashing an aquarium because he didn't want to clean it any longer, another incident of the same employee/owner smashing an espresso machine for the same reason, and it got worse. I have never read about a more worthless group of people in my life!

It is total downer with no optimism, or sense of purpose, whatsoever, no direction, humor, or hope. **DO NOT WASTE YOUR MONEY ON THIS TRASH!!!**

In short, "Cometbus" might have been a great 'zine at one time, but from what we saw in #46, it has really become a waste of ink and paper, and that is a crying shame.

Foreword

About the Series

These case studies in cultural anthropology are designed to bring to students in the social sciences insights into the richness and complexity of human life as it is lived in different ways and in different places. They are written by men and women who have lived in the societies they write about, and who are professionally trained as observers and interpreters of human behavior. The authors are also teachers, and in writing their books they have kept the students who will read them foremost in their minds. It is our belief that when an understanding of ways of life very different from one's own is gained, abstractions and generalizations about social structure, cultural values, subsistence techniques, and the other universal categories of human social behavior become meaningful.

1. Joseph

X: HOW DID YOU GO FROM HANGING OUT HERE TO HAVING A STAKE IN RUNNING THE PLACE?

J: IT WAS ALL PART OF A MASTER PLAN THAT ME AND NATHAN AND REX HAD. IT WENT LIKE THIS: WE SPENT MONTH AFTER MONTH AFTER MONTH OF JUST HANGING AROUND HERE AND DRINKING BEER ON THE SLY OUT OF WATER CUPS AND AT NIGHT MOPPING FLOORS AND HELPING THROW OUT DRUNKS. JUST BASICALLY MAKING A NUISANCE OUT OF OURSELVES.

NATHAN WAS THE FIRST ONE TO GET A JOB HERE, AND THEN I FOLLOWED SUIT. BASICALLY HOW I GOT THE JOB WAS, WELL, FOR A WHILE THEY HAD A DOORMAN CHARGING PEOPLE A ONE DOLLAR COVER TO GET IN.

X: BECAUSE OF PROBLEMS WITH THE COPS?

J: WELL, YEAH, DRUG DEALERS AND SHIT LIKE THAT.

X: WOULDN'T THE DRUG DEALERS PAY A DOLLAR TO GET IN?

J: YEAH, THEY WOULD. WELL, WE ENDED THAT PROGRAM AFTER A WHILE. BUT ANYWAY, WHAT HAPPENED WAS, I STAYED DOING THAT FOR A LITTLE WHILE, AND THEN THERE WAS A POSITION OPEN FOR A BARTENDER. I SAID, SINCE I'M ALREADY ON THE PAYROLL AND HALFWAY IN THE DOOR, WHY DON'T YOU JUST HIRE ME AS A BARTENDER? I'D ALREADY APPLIED A FEW TIMES AND AFTER A WHILE IT JUST BECAME KIND OF LIKE A JOKE. BUT THIS TIME, IT SEEMED TO WORK, AND I GOT IN. AND I'VE BEEN HERE EVER SINCE.

X: BY BARTENDER, YOU MEAN A COFFEE BARTENDER.

J: YEAH, LIKE A BARISTA. SERVING COFFEE AND ATTITUDE.

X: MORE COFFEE OR MORE ATTITUDE?

J: IT DEPENDS ON THE CUSTOMER. MOST OF THE BARTENDERS HERE HAVE A PRETTY SHITTY ATTITUDE, BUT OUR COFFEE IS SO GODDAMN FUCKING GOOD AND THICK AND ADDICTIVE THAT PEOPLE JUST DON'T CARE WHAT THEY GOTTA GO THROUGH TO GET A CUP OF OUR COFFEE. THEY'D GO THROUGH A TOTAL TONGUE LASHING. A TOTAL BREAKDOWN OF THEIR WHOLE PERSONALITY, THEIR WHOLE PERSONA, JUST TO GET A CUP OF OUR COFFEE. REDUCED TO JUST A CRYING HEAP OF SELF-CONSCIOUSNESS.

X: DO PEOPLE GET MAD IF YOU'RE IN A GOOD MOOD?

J: I DON'T GET AS GOOD OF TIPS. THIS IS MY MOM, SHE'S STONED.

JOSEPH'S MOM: YEAH, I'M STONED, I'M NOT DRUNK.

X: EVEN THOUGH IT WAS A MASTER PLAN, DID YOU WAKE UP ONE DAY AND REALIZE YOU HAD TO DEAL WITH MORE THAN YOU HAD INTENDED TO?

J: ACTUALLY, I WOKE UP ONE DAY AND I REALIZED THAT I WAS STUCK IN A LOW-PAYING, CRAPPY, STRESS-INDUCING JOB THAT WAS TAKING YEARS OFF OF MY LIFE AND SUCKING MY SOUL AND TURNING ME INTO A BITTER, RESENTFUL PERSON. NOW I SPEND MOST OF MY TIME IN A DELUSIONAL HOMICIDAL STATE. SO, NO, THE MASTER PLAN NEVER WORKED OUT.

ME AND NATHAN AND REX ARE STILL WORKING HERE, AND THAT WAS OUR MASTER PLAN IN THE FIRST PLACE, TO GET THE THREE OF US WORKING HERE AND KIND OF TAKE IT OVER. BUT THEN WE REALIZED THAT IT WAS SUCH A MESS AND JUST SO DISORGANIZED AND SO CHAOTIC AND SO CRAZY, IT WAS BEYOND OUR CONTROL. BEYOND ANYTHING WE COULD EVEN COMPREHEND OR EVEN TRY TO PUT A FINGER ON. WE JUST GOT IN TOO DEEP. IT WAS HORRIBLE.

2. Nathan

X: HOW DID IT START FOR YOU?

N: I GUESS I STARTED JUST HANGING OUT HERE BECAUSE IT WAS THE ONLY PLACE YOU COULD SIT DOWN AND NOT FEEL HARRASSED. NOT FEEL LIKE YOU WERE SOME KIND OF A NUISANCE AND YOU SHOULD LEAVE. SO ME AND JOSEPH AND REX JUST SAT IN BACK AND DRANK BEER. PRETTY SOON THEY COULDN'T GET RID OF US. THEN WE STARTED INFILTRATING.

X: DID MARCO REALLY LAUGH AT YOU GUYS WHEN YOU FIRST TRIED TO GET JOBS?

N: HE SAID, "YOU'RE NEVER GOING TO WORK HERE."

X: WERE YOU PART OF THE ORIGINAL GROUP THAT KICKED MARCO OUT AND FORMED THE COLLECTIVE?

N: NO.

X: WERE YOU AROUND HERE AT THE TIME?

N: I DON'T REALLY REMEMBER. I THINK I MIGHT HAVE BEEN IN JAIL THEN, ACTUALLY.

X: HOW HAS THE PLACE CHANGED SINCE THEN?

N: I THINK IN A LOT OF WAYS IT'S STAYED THE SAME. I DON'T KNOW, I THINK IT SEEMED MORE LIKE FAMILY WHEN IT FIRST STARTED. NOW IT'S A LOT OF DIFFERENT PEOPLE. A LOT OF NEW PEOPLE WORK HERE TOO. BUT I THINK OUTSIDE THINGS LIKE THE CITY MADE MORE OF THE CHANGES. BECAUSE YOU'RE KIND OF PUSHED, YOU HAVE TO MAKE COMPROMISES.

X: WHAT KIND OF COMPROMISES?

N: LIKE THE CITY DOESN'T WANT PEOPLE TO LOITER OUT FRONT. BUT THEY HAD THE BUS STOP RIGHT OUTSIDE

OF THE DINING ROOM WINDOW. SO, THE CITY MOVED IT TO THE CORNER ACROSS THE STREET. THEY HAD TO CHANGE THE LANES OF TRAFFIC, CHANGE THE SIGNS, SO THE BUS COULD GO THAT WAY.

X: JUST TO KEEP PEOPLE FROM HANGING OUT IN FRONT HERE?

N: YEAH. I TOLD THE COUNCIL LADY, "I'M SURE YOU'RE GOING TO PUT A HEATED BUS SHELTER OVER THERE, SINCE PEOPLE USE OUR DOORWAY AS A HEATED BUS SHELTER. NICE PEOPLE, WITH RESPECTABLE JOBS DOWNTOWN".

X: YOU GO TO THE COUNCIL MEETINGS?

N: NO, THE BUSINESS ASSOCIATION MEETINGS. AND THE NEIGHBORHOOD GROUP, THE COMMUNITY COALITION.

X: ARE YOU TREATED AS AN EQUAL WITH THE OTHER BUSINESSES?

N: AT LEAST TO YOUR FACE. I'M SURE A LOT OF PEOPLE WHO DIDN'T LIKE THE PLACE STILL DON'T LIKE THE PLACE, BUT THE CITY AND THE NEIGHBORS HAVE KIND OF BACKED OFF. I THINK A LOT OF THAT IS THEY CAME TO REALIZE THAT WE'RE NOT GOING AWAY, AND THEY ARE NOT GOING TO PUT US OUT OF BUSINESS, SO THEY HAVE TO DEAL WITH IT IN SOME WAY.

    I USED TO TAKE MY BABY TO THE MEETINGS, WHEN SHE WAS LITTLE. THEY HAD TO ATTACH A YOUNG CUTE BABY FACE ON THE NAME DEAD END, I THINK THAT INADVERTENTLY HELPED. IT KIND OF FUCKED UP THEIR PERCEPTION OF THE PLACE. THE OLD LADIES WERE LIKE, "HOW'S OUR BABY TODAY?"

X: DO YOU SEE A RESPONSIBILITY TO THE CITY AND THE COMMUNITY? LIKE THE COMMUNITY HAS A RESPONSIBILITY TO YOU AND YOU HAVE A RESPONSIBILITY TO IT AS WELL?

N: THAT WAS THE WEIRD THING. I THOUGHT WE WERE MORE IN TUNE WITH THE COMMUNITY THAN THE PEOPLE THAT WERE REPRESENTING THE COMMUNITY, THAT WERE ATTACKING US. INCLUDING THE COUNCIL LADY, THE PEOPLE FROM THE COMMUNITY DEVELOPMENT CORPORATION, THE BUSINESSPEOPLE, A LOT OF RESIDENTS WHO WERE OLDER. IT SEEMED LIKE THIS PLACE CARED MORE ABOUT THE COMMUNITY THAN MOST OF THE BUSINESSES.

    YOU'D SEE THE BUSINESSES AT THE MEETING, AND THEY WOULD BE THERE FOR A TOTALLY TRANSPARENT,

SELFISH REASON. THEY WANTED TO BE FUNDED BY
THE COMMUNITY DEVELOPMENT ASSOCIATION FOR
THIS OR A GRANT FOR THAT OR A LICENSE FOR
WHATEVER. OUR MAIN REASON TO GO TO THE
MEETINGS WAS TO DEFEND OURSELVES. BUT OTHER
THAN SELF-DEFENSE, OUR ONLY CONCERN WAS THE
GOOD OF THE COMMUNITY AND THE NEIGHBORHOOD,
WHEREAS OTHER PEOPLE WERE IN IT COMPLETELY
FOR THEMSELVES. AND IT DIDN'T SEEM LIKE THEY
REALIZED THAT.

YOU'D SEE THE PEOPLE THAT WORKED HERE OUT
SWEEPING THE SIDEWALK RELIGIOUSLY EVERY DAY,
OR MOPPING THE FLOOR EVERY NIGHT. IT DOESN'T
NEED TO BE MOPPED EVERY NIGHT PROBABLY, BUT THEY
TOOK A PRIDE IN DOING THAT. BUT STILL PEOPLE WANTED
TO BLAME VANDALISM, BLAME DRUGS, BLAME WHATEVER
ON THIS PLACE. WHEN IT SEEMED LIKE THIS PLACE
WAS MORE IN TUNE WITH THE COMMUNITY.

THAT WAS ONE OF THE MAIN REASONS I LIKED
THE CAFE, BECAUSE IN THE DINING ROOM YOU COULD SEE
ALL DIFFERENT KINDS OF NATIONALITIES REPRESENTED,
ALL DIFFERENT KINDS OF LIFESTYLES REPRESENTED. OLD
PEOPLE, YOUNG PEOPLE, KIDS, BABIES. PROFESSIONAL
PEOPLE, BUMS. YOU'D SEE A WINO AND A COLLEGE
PROFESSOR SITTING THERE TALKING ABOUT THE
HISTORY OF THE CITY OR SOMETHING. THAT WAS THE
MAIN THING I THOUGHT WAS COOL ABOUT THIS PLACE,
AND WHY I LIKED IT. BECAUSE YOU DIDN'T FEEL OUT OF
PLACE, NO MATTER WHO YOU WERE.

3. Rex

X: IS KRVR STILL ACROSS THE STREET?

R: YUP. THEY UPPED THEIR VOLTAGE SO NOW THEY CAN BE HEARD FURTHER OUT EVEN. THEIR PROGRAMMING HAS EXPANDED, THERE'S A HMONG HOUR WHICH IS REALLY COOL. HMONG NEWS PROGRAMS, HMONG MUSIC PROGRAMS. IT'S STILL COMMUNITY BASED. THEY'VE BEEN GOING FOR TWENTY YEARS NOW.

X: DO YOU SEE DJ'S BEFORE THEY GO IN ON THEIR SHIFTS, OR CALLING OVER HERE IN THE MIDDLE OF THE NIGHT BEGGING FOR COFFEE?

R: YEAH. WE'VE EVEN CATERED COFFEE AND DRINKS OVER TO THEM. WE'LL CALL THEM UP, "DO YOU GUYS NEED ANYTHING? COULD YOU PLAY THIS?"

X: ARE THERE ANY OTHER GROUPS OF REGULARS WHO DON'T HANG OUT HERE, BUT COME BY LIKE CLOCK-WORK TO GET THEIR COFFEE?

R: THE DENNY'S EMPLOYEES. IT USED TO BE, WHEN THEY GOT OFF THEIR SHIFT, THEY'D COME HERE. THEY WERE SOME OF THE BEST TIPPERS. THE WHOLE ENTIRE SHIFT WOULD GET OFF AT TWO IN THE MORNING AND THEY WOULD COME HERE.

X: DO YOU GO OUT OF THE WAY TO MAKE PEOPLE FEEL COMFORTABLE HERE?

R: WE DON'T GO OUT OF OUR WAY. IT'S LIKE, YOU SHOW US RESPECT, WE'LL SHOW YOU RESPECT. YOU TREAT OUR PLACE, OUR BUILDING, OUR PROPERTY, AND THE OTHER CUSTOMERS WITH RESPECT, YOU'LL GET IT. YOU DON'T, YOU GET THROWN OUT. YOU GET 86'D, TOUGH LUCK. WHERE ARE YOU GONNA GO AT TWO IN THE MORNING? DENNY'S?

X: WHERE DOES THE CAFE DRAW ITS LINE? AT THE DOOR? OUT ON THE SIDEWALK OUT FRONT? IF SOMEONE'S 86'D, YOU'RE NOT GOING TO LET THEM BE RIGHT OUTSIDE THE DOOR. BUT AT THE SAME TIME, HOW FAR OUTSIDE THE CAFE'S DOORS ARE YOU TAKING RESPONSIBILITY FOR PEOPLE'S WELL BEING?

R: THAT'S AN AMBIGUOUS QUESTION, BECAUSE THAT CHANGES CONSTANTLY. LIKE, NATHAN. A COP CAME IN ONE DAY AND BITCHED AT NATHAN ABOUT THE PARKING LOT. NATHAN WAS LIKE, "THAT'S NOT OUR RESPONSIBILITY. THAT'S NOT OUR PARKING LOT. IT'S OWNED BY THE CITY AND IT'S LEASED OUT TO THIS COMPANY. THEREFORE, IT'S YOUR RESPONSIBILITY, NOT OURS. DON'T BLAME US FOR DRUG DEALING IN THE PARKING LOT".

X: BUT, FRANKLY, DON'T YOU CONSIDER IT YOURS?

R: YEAH, IN A WAY WE DO CONSIDER IT OUR PARKING LOT. SEE, THAT'S WHY IT'S AN AMBIGUOUS QUESTION. WE DO KIND OF SPREAD A LITTLE FURTHER.

X: HOW FAR?

R: PRETTY MUCH FROM THE STREET NEXT TO THE VULTURE BAR, UP TO AND BEYOND THE CHINESE RESTAURANT.

4. Brent

X: DO YOU FIND YOURSELF HAVING DREAMS ABOUT THE CAFE?

B: I'D HAVE TO SAY NO, AND I COULD QUALIFY THAT BY SAYING I'M HERE SO MUCH, AND HAVE BEEN ON THIS BLOCK SO MUCH EVEN BEFORE I WAS A WORKER-OWNER HERE, OR STARTED WORKING HERE IN EARNEST, SO I HAVE SOME SEPARATION DISCIPLINE. I DON'T CARRY THIS OVER INTO MY SUBCONSCIOUS, FORTUNATELY.

X: WHEN A CUSTOMER WALKS UP, DO YOU FIND YOURSELF JUDGING THEM? OR GUESSING ABOUT THEIR LIFE?

B: I JUDGE PEOPLE MORE INTUITIVELY AND EMPATHICALLY THAN VISUALLY OR FROM WHAT THEY MAY BE SAYING. THERE ARE PEOPLE I WILL TALK TO AND PEOPLE THAT I JUST END UP NEVER TALKING TO, ALTHOUGH I WILL PUT A NICE K-MART SERVICE FACE ON IT. NOT TO BE OVERLY, WHAT DO THEY CALL THAT? OBSEQUIOUS? NO. IT'S NOT CHEESY, IT'S NOT A PUT-ON, BUT...

X: FROM BEING AROUND PEOPLE A LOT, ARE YOU MORE QUICKLY ANNOYED OR QUICKLY IN TUNE WITH THEM?

B: SOMETIMES I'LL WAKE UP AND THIS IS THE FIRST PLACE I'LL HIT. MORE OFTEN THAN NOT, THERE'S SOMETHING TO BE UPSET ABOUT. I RECOGNIZE THIS, AND I GO BACK TO WHAT I LIKE TO CALL "CRAFTY AMORPHISMS". I DON'T KNOW IF YOU'RE INTO ROBERT FRIPP AT ALL, BUT ONE OF THE THINGS THAT CAME OUT OF FRIPP WAS, IT'S NICE TO BE IRRITATED. BECAUSE THAT LETS YOU KNOW YOU'RE ALIVE. AND YOU DON'T GET A SENSE, I'VE NEVER HAD A SENSE OF COMPLACENCY ABOUT THIS PLACE CUZ IT'S JUST TOO FUCKING ENTROPIC.

X: ARE YOUR SENSES SO OVERLOADED HERE THAT

B: GETTING AWAY FROM THIS PLACE IS LIKE TASTING FINE WINE. NO, SERIOUSLY. BECAUSE I'VE BEEN IN THIS NEIGHBORHOOD SINCE 1980. I'VE BEEN IN THIS CAFE BEFORE IT WAS THE GOOD INTENTIONS, WHATEVER IT WAS BEFORE THAT. AND THEN THE DEAD END, HELPING PEOPLE START IT AND FINALLY ENDING UP WORKING HERE. IT'S GOT ITS OWN, UH, OH GOD, THAT'S THE PROBLEM WITH STREAM OF CONSCIOUSNESS. IT SOMETIMES FADES. WHAT WAS THE QUESTION?

X: FINE WINE. GETTING AWAY.

B: YEAH, BECAUSE I'M HERE EVERY DAY, AND I ALSO HAVE ANOTHER JOB. SO I WORK TWO JOBS, AND I HAVE A BAND, AND WHATEVER ELSE HAPPENS. AND BECAUSE I'VE ONLY BEEN REALLY WORKING AND HAVING INCOME FOR THE PAST FOUR OR FIVE YEARS, AS OPPOSED TO BEING AN ITINERANT ARTIST DRUMMER, WHAT THEY CALL "SCHNORRER" IN YIDDISH, WHICH IS SOMEONE WHO TAKES ADVANTAGE OF YOUR HOSPITALITY.

X: MY MOM USED TO SAY, WHAT KIND OF CIGARETTE DOES A SCHNORRER SMOKE? SOMEBODY ELSE'S.

B: OH YEAH. HERE ESPECIALLY. WHICH IS WHY I DON'T EVER BEGRUDGE ANYONE A ROLLIE.
    BUT I GUESS, TO TIE THAT IN WITH THE FORMER QUESTION, IT'S REALLY WEIRD NOT TO HAVE A DIVISION BETWEEN WORK AND LIFE. BECAUSE THIS PLACE IS SO INGRAINED. I'VE BEEN ACTUALLY TRYING TO GET AWAY FROM HERE. I THINK FOUR YEARS HERE I'VE BEEN THROUGH THREE GIRLFRIENDS, ONE WHO TURNED INTO A MARRIAGE, WHO TURNED INTO A DIVORCE, AND THAT WAS THROUGH THIS CAFE. IN THE CAFE.

X: YOU MET THEM ALL HERE?

B: WELL, I MET MY EX-WIFE AT A MAY DAY PARADE A LONG, LONG TIME AGO. THAT DIDN'T DO ANYTHING, BUT ALL THINGS COME AROUND. SHE STARTED WORKING HERE WHEN SHE WAS MY GIRLFRIEND AND I TRIED TO BE A PROGRESSIVE MALE ABOUT IT. IT TURNED OUT IT WASN'T WORKING FOR ME AND IT WAS WORKING FOR HER. THAT KIND OF STARTED THE WHOLE WEIRDNESS. IT'S PRETTY MUCH ALL RESOLVED, BUT AT THE SAME TIME IT'S LIKE, HOW MUCH MORE SHIT DO I HAVE TO GO THROUGH IN THIS ONE PLACE?
    THAT, AND I ALSO, IN THE CAFE, DON'T FEEL THE SENSE OF UNITY THERE WAS ONCE. FOR VARIOUS REASONS.

X: WHY WAS THERE MORE BEFORE AND WHAT CAN BUILD MORE NOW?

B: WHEN THE DEAD END FIRST STARTED OUT IT WAS ABOUT FIFTEEN PEOPLE WHO WERE WORKING FOR SOMEONE WHO GOT TOO FAR IN OVER HIS HEAD.

X: YOU'RE TALKING ABOUT MARCO.

B: YEAH, YEAH. WHO I STILL CONSIDER A FRIEND. I REMEMBER WHEN MARCO CAME OVER TO WHERE EVERYONE USED TO HANG OUT DOWNTOWN AND STARTED CHATTING UP EVERYBODY, AND GOT THROWN OUT OF THE REGAL BEAN.

THE GUY'S LIKE, "YOU CAN'T BE TALKING ABOUT STARTING NO CAFE IN HERE, GET OUT OF HERE!"

MARCO'S LIKE, "I'M GONNA PUT YOU OUT OF BUSINESS, MAN!"

IT TURNS OUT HE WAS WRONG, BUT ALL THE PEOPLE WHO USED TO HANG OUT OVER THERE DID END UP COMING HERE.

5. Dean

X: IS IT TRUE THAT THE DEAD END BUILDING USED TO BE THE CITY MORGUE?

D: I THINK IT WAS ACTUALLY THE BUILDING NEXT DOOR. I DON'T REALLY KNOW, BUT THAT WAS A GREAT LITTLE MYTH TO USE.

X: WITH THE STATE'S ONLY CONVICTED GRAVE ROBBER SERVING COFFEE?

D: YES. SPARROW. BUT HE DIDN'T WORK AT THE CAFE UNTIL AFTER I'D ALREADY LEFT.

X: LET'S GO BACK TO THE START OF YOUR INVOLVEMENT AT THE CAFE. DID YOU KNOW MARCO BEFOREHAND?

D: YEAH, WE WENT TO HIGH SCHOOL TOGETHER. WE WERE BOTH JUST TOTAL FREAKS AND NEITHER ONE OF US REALLY FIT IN, AND THEREFORE WE KIND OF REPELLED EACH OTHER. YOU KNOW WHAT I MEAN? BUT THERE WAS A COUPLE TIMES WHEN WE CLICKED.

THEN, THIS IS EMBARRASSING, BUT I WAS KIND OF DRIFTING AROUND LOST AFTER HIGH SCHOOL AND I WENT TO THIS RAINBOW GATHERING. AND I GOT MY MIND TOTALLY BLOWN OPEN. I CAME BACK TO MY JOB SERVING TROPICAL VANILLA CAPPUCCINOS IN THE MALL THE NEXT DAY, AND I JUST COULDN'T DO IT. RUNNING NAKED THROUGH THE WOODS TRIPPING MY BRAINS OUT ON SUNDAY AND THEN MONDAY MORNING, SIX A.M., I'M WEARING CHINOS AND WINGTIPS AND SERVING TROPICAL VANILLA COFFEE.

SO I QUIT. I HAD ALL THESE CRAZY PEOPLE STAYING AT MY HOUSE, AND I WAS TRYING TO FIND A JOB, AND I DIDN'T KNOW WHAT TO DO. I DROVE PAST THE VILLAGE IDIOT AND I SAW A BUNCH OF PEOPLE

HAVING THIS CRAZY DRUM JAM IN THERE. I WAS NEVER REALLY A HIPPIE BUT I LIKED THE IDEA OF, YOU KNOW, I WAS TRYING TO INTEGRATE THE PUNK ROCK PHILOSOPHY INTO THE FREE LOVE THING. A HYBRID. I HATED THE GRATEFUL DEAD THOUGH, I COULDN'T EVER GET PAST THAT.

X: LET'S GET THAT OUT IN THE CLEAR RIGHT NOW.

D: I JUST PULLED OVER THERE, AND I WENT IN, AND SAID, "I WANT A JOB HERE".

I GOT THIS PHONE CALL ASKING ME TO COME IN FOR AN INTERVIEW. THE GUY'S LIKE, "SO YOU KNOW MARCO HANSON, RIGHT? HE SAID YOU WERE A GREAT GUY AND I SHOULD GIVE YOU A JOB".

I'M LIKE, "YEAH! I LOVE MARCO!!" I MEAN, I HADN'T TALKED TO THE GUY IN TWO YEARS, AND I DIDN'T REALIZE WHAT A FAVOR HE WAS DOING ME.

AND SO, I GOT THE JOB. I STARTED WAITING TABLES AT THE IDIOT, AND MARCO WAS A COOK. AND SOMEHOW, I ENDED UP MOVING IN WITH HIM. AND, UM, WE WERE WALKING DOWN THE RAILROAD TRACKS AND HE SAYS, "HEY, LISTEN, MY GRANDMOTHER'S GONNA LOAN ME FIFTEEN THOUSAND DOLLARS AT NINE PERCENT TO DO SOMETHING CONSTRUCTIVE WITH MY LIFE. WILL YOU HELP ME?"

I WENT, "SURE".

I'D BEEN WORKING IN COFFEESHOPS, BUT THAT WHOLE DEAL WAS PRETTY NEW BACK THEN. THERE WASN'T A WHOLE LOT OF PEOPLE WHO KNEW WHAT TO DO OR HOW TO RUN IT OR WERE ANY GOOD AT MAKING ESPRESSO. REMEMBER THAT? I WAS OBSESSED WITH COFFEE AT THE TIME. I THOUGHT IT WAS MY JOB, MY DUTY, TO MAKE THE BEST COFFEE FOR EVERYBODY.

MARCO BOUGHT THE BUSINESS. HE CHANGED THE NAME, AND WE SPLIT IT UP. THE GOOD INTENTIONS CAFE. OF COURSE MARCO HAD T-SHIRTS PRINTED TWO MONTHS BEFORE WE WERE EVEN OPENED. SUCH A BOY THING, YOU KNOW? MAKE THE T-SHIRTS BEFORE IT EVEN FUCKING OPENS.

WE OPENED TOTALLY BY THE SEAT OF OUR PANTS. WE DIDN'T EVEN HAVE A CASH REGISTER. WE WERE BOTH JUST SO EXCITED ABOUT WORKING THERE AND ABOUT HAVING SOMETHING TO DO. YOU KNOW, WE WERE NINETEEN.

X: I THINK HE WAS TWENTY.

D: YEAH, HE WAS TWENTY. AND I WAS NINETEEN. SO WE BOTH INSISTED ON WORKING TWELVE HOUR

SHIFTS, MIDNIGHT TO NOON AND NOON TO MIDNIGHT.
WE HIRED ON A COUPLE PEOPLE, AND WE JUST DID IT.
THERE WAS NO RULES, IT WAS WHATEVER WE
WANTED TO DO. WE DIDN'T EVEN HAVE A FUCKING
PERMIT TO BE OPEN TWENTY FOUR HOURS. I THINK
EVENTUALLY WE GOT A CONDITIONAL USE PERMIT,
BUT FOR THE FIRST COUPLE YEARS I KNOW WE
WEREN'T SUPPOSED TO BE OPEN BUT WE JUST DID
IT ANYWAY.

TERRY TRAUMA STARTED WORKING THERE, THE
GUY THAT WAS LIVING IN MY ATTIC, THEN HE WAS
SLEEPING IN THE CLOSET, THEN HE WAS WORKING
FOR US. YOU'D LEAVE AND COME BACK AND FIND OUT
THAT HALF OF THE PEOPLE HAD BEEN THREATENED
WITH MURDER. AND THE ESPRESSO MACHINE WAS
BUSTED. IT WAS NUTS.

THAT WAS MY LIFE, AND I DIDN'T DO ANYTHING
BUT WORK THERE AND THINK ABOUT IT AND TRY TO
MAKE IT WORK FOR A SOLID YEAR. IT WAS A
CRAZY, CRAZY TIME.

6. Joseph

X: HOW MUCH DO YOU DEFINE YOURSELF IN TERMS OF THIS PLACE? HOW MUCH OF THE DEAD END DO YOU BRING HOME WITH YOU?

J: I TRY TO KEEP THIS PLACE AS FAR AWAY FROM MY HOME LIFE AS POSSIBLE. I WOULD NEVER HAVE SEX WITH A CO-WORKER.

X: HAVE YOU BROKEN THAT RULE?

J: OCCASIONALLY. I'M NOT QUITE SURE IF IT REALLY HAPPENED OR IF IT WAS JUST SOME SORT OF DREAM. I DO KNOW I WAS PRETTY DRUNK AT THE TIME. WE MIGHT HAVE JUST RUBBED UP AGAINST EACH OTHER. I DUNNO, IT WAS WEIRD. I DIDN'T LIKE IT.

X: DO YOU STILL SEE MARCO OR DEAN OR ANY OF THE ORIGINAL PEOPLE HERE?

J: I'VE SEEN MARCO AT BURNING MAN FESTIVAL, OUT IN BLACK ROCK DESERT, OUT IN NEVADA. SEEN HIM OUT THERE, HE WAS A COOK AT ONE OF THE MANY KITCHENS. AND DEAN, I'VE SEEN HIM OCCASIONALLY. AND DAVEY COMES IN ALL THE TIME. HE'S A BITTER OLD MAN. HE INSTALLS CABLE NOW.

X: SO THE OLD GUARD IS STILL ON RELATIVELY GOOD TERMS?

J: YEAH. THEY STILL COME IN AND HANG OUT, AND THEY STILL CONSIDER THE PLACE THEIRS. BUT LIKE I SAID, THIS PLACE JUST SUCKS YOUR SOUL AND TURNS YOU INTO A BITTER EVIL OLD PERSON.

X: DO YOU GET POSSESSIVE ABOUT IT?

J: NO. IF YOU SPEND ANY AMOUNT OF TIME AT THE CAFE AND HAVE DONE ANYTHING FOR THE CAFE, IT'S YOURS. SOMEONE MIGHT BE HERE ALL NIGHT ONE NIGHT AND JUST HELP MOPPING FLOORS. SOME-ONE MIGHT BE HERE WHEN A FIGHT BREAKS OUT

AND HELPS BREAK UP THE FIGHT. OR HELPS TO RUN CRACKHEADS OFF. A LOT OF THE CUSTOMERS FEEL THAT IT'S THEIR PLACE TOO, AND NOT ONLY BECAUSE THEY BUY COFFEE AND FOOD HERE AND HANG OUT HERE ALL THE TIME, BUT BECAUSE THEY CHIP IN IN THOSE WEIRD PLACES THAT YOU DON'T REALLY THINK ABOUT WHEN YOU THINK ABOUT RUNNING A COFFEESHOP.

X: WHAT'S INSTILLED THAT SENSE OF COMMUNITY RESPONSIBILITY?

J: IT'S KIND OF A WEIRD EXAMPLE, BUT SAY YOU'RE IN A NEIGHBORHOOD, RIGHT? AND THERE'S A PARK IN THE NEIGHBORHOOD. AND YOU AND YOUR BUDDIES HANG OUT AT THE PARK. AND YOUR BUDDIES' FRIENDS AND THEIR KIDS AND EVERYBODY KIND OF HANGS OUT AT THE PARK, AND IT'S A COMMON GROUND FOR PEOPLE TO JUST BE AND DO THEIR THING, AND EVERY-BODY ENJOYS IT.

BUT THEN THEY SEE SOMETHING THREATENING THAT SPACE OF THEIRS, THAT COMMON GROUND. THEY SEE SOMETHING FUCKING IT UP. PEOPLE LITTERING, OR PEOPLE SELLING DRUGS THERE. PEOPLE OVER-DOSING, OR PEOPLE LIKE RUNNING AROUND NAKED HALF-DRUNK IN THE MIDDLE OF THE AFTERNOON. IN A WAY THEY KIND OF BAND TOGETHER AND SAY, "THIS IS OUR PLACE. AND WE'RE GONNA TAKE CARE OF IT."

EVEN THOUGH IT BELONGS TO THE CITY, AND THE CITY SHOULD BE THE ONES TAKING CARE OF IT. WELL, THEY'RE NOT. THEY'RE NOT THERE. THEY'RE NEGLECT-ING IT, SO THESE PEOPLE JUST SORT OF TAKE IT OVER.

X: HOW DOES THAT SENSE OF GROUP MORALITY DEVELOP?

J: OVER TIME.

X: YOU MENTIONED SOMEONE RUNNING AROUND NAKED AND HALF DRUNK IN THE MIDDLE OF THE DAY. THAT WOULD PROBABLY BE FINE HERE.

J: LIKE I SAID, IT WAS A BAD EXAMPLE.

X: BUT WHAT I'M SAYING IS, IN ANY COMMUNITY PEOPLE ARE GOING TO HAVE A GROUP IDEA OF WHAT'S RIGHT AND WRONG. BUT IN THIS COMMUNITY, THERE ARE TWO SETS OF RULES, THE OFFICIAL RULES OF THE BUSINESS AND THE OTHER RULES WHICH ARE UNSAID BUT UNDERSTOOD.

J: I DON'T KNOW IF I WANT THOSE RECORDED. THEY'RE UNSPOKEN, SO I THINK THEY SHOULD REMAIN UNSPOKEN.

7. Ed

X: PLEASE INTRODUCE YOURSELF.

E: MY NAME IS ED. SOME PEOPLE REFER TO ME AS "DOWNTOWN STANDING AROUND AGAIN ED", BUT I'VE BEEN TRYING TO GET RID OF THAT NICKNAME FOR YEARS NOW.

X: AREN'T YOU DOWN IN THIS PART OF TOWN A LOT MORE NOWADAYS?

E: YES.

X: WHEN DID YOU START COMING IN HERE?

E: ABOUT NINE YEARS AGO. I DIDN'T ACTUALLY START SOMEWHAT WORKING UNTIL FOUR YEARS AGO.

X: WAS THAT A BIG CHANGE?

E: NOT REALLY, BECAUSE I WOULD HELP OUT A LITTLE BIT. THERE WOULD BE TIMES MANDY WOULD BE LIKE, "HEY ED, I'LL GIVE YOU A CUP OF COFFEE IF YOU GO AND BUS THE DINING ROOM FOR ME". OR BEING HERE ALL NIGHT AND BORED AND HELPING DAVEY SWEEP AND MOP. SO I HAD ALREADY HELPED OUT.

X: WHAT DO YOU DO HERE NOW?

E: I BUS DISHES, SCRUB DISHES. I'M THE EMERGENCY COOK, SUCH AS IF I GET HERE AND THERE IS NO COOK, OR IF A COOK HAS TO LEAVE EARLY BECAUSE THEY'RE SICK.

X: DOES EACH MEMBER OF THE COLLECTIVE HAVE SEPARATE DUTIES?

E: THE ONLY REAL CHORES ARE PROBABLY THE ORDERING. LIKE ONE PERSON WOULD BE IN CHARGE OF ORDERING ALL THE SODA. SOMEBODY ELSE MIGHT HAVE TO DEAL WITH THE CIGARETTE DISTRIBUTOR. SOMEBODY ELSE MIGHT BE IN CHARGE OF THE COFFEE DISTRIBUTOR.

E: BECCA. ONE OF THE PEOPLE THAT WORKS HERE. SHE DOES ALL THE BOOKS.

X: WHAT ABOUT FIXING THINGS WHEN THEY BREAK?

E: WE DO HAVE A PERSON NAMED BRENDAN THAT HANGS OUT QUITE A BIT, AND HE DOES A LOT OF THE MAINTENANCE. BUT, PRETTY MUCH, WHOEVER.
LIKE UP HERE, IN THE OFFICE. WHO PRETTY MUCH CLEANS UP HERE? ME. BECAUSE NOBODY ELSE DOES. SO, AROUND HERE PEOPLE MAY BE IN CHARGE OF ONE PARTICULAR THING, BUT THAT IS NOT REALLY BECAUSE THEY HAVE BEEN APPOINTED BUT, MORE OR LESS, BECAUSE NOBODY ELSE WILL DO IT.

X: DOES EVERYTHING PRETTY MUCH GET TAKEN CARE OF THAT WAY?

E: SOMETIMES. THE PLACE IS A COLLECTIVE, WORKER-OWNED, AND EVERYBODY HAS THEIR OWN OPINIONS AND THEIR OWN WAY OF LOOKING AT THINGS. SO, SOMETIMES THINGS DO COLLIDE. THE PLACE DOES BECOME DYSFUNCTIONAL BECAUSE OF THAT.

X: IS THERE A PROCESS WHERE PEOPLE ARE TAKEN TO TASK AND HELD ACCOUNTABLE?

E: YEAH, THERE IS. THE MEETINGS. SOMETIMES THEY DO TURN INTO BITCH SESSIONS. THAT'S WHERE PEOPLE BRING UP PROBLEMS SUCH AS, "YOU DON'T MOP THE FLOORS WHEN YOU DO OVERNIGHT".

X: ARE THERE ANY RULES?

E: LIKE HOW SO?

X: LIKE MOST PLACES MIGHT HAVE POSTED RULES, YOU KNOW?

E: PAINTED ON THE DOOR, WE ACTUALLY HAD SOME, BUT THAT WAS TAKEN DOWN, I DON'T REMEMBER WHY. YEAH, THERE ARE I SUPPOSE YOUR TYPICAL, BASIC BUSINESS RULES. YOU KNOW, LIKE, NO PANHANDLING. NO SMOKING CRACK IN THE BATHROOM.

X: ARE THOSE RULES ALL BROKEN?

E: SOMETIMES. AT LEAST THE SECOND ONE I SAID USED TO BE A PROBLEM, BUT NOW MAY NOT BE AS MUCH OF A PROBLEM AS IT ONCE WAS.

8. Nathan

X: DOES EVERYONE IN THE COLLECTIVE GET PAID THE SAME?

N: THE BAKERS GET A DOLLAR MORE BECAUSE THEY DON'T GET A CUT OF THE TIPS. THE BOOKKEEPER GETS A LITTLE MORE BECAUSE THEY DON'T GET ANY TIPS. BUT OTHER THAN THAT, EVERYONE GETS PAID THE SAME. WELL, AFTER SIX MONTHS. FIRST YOU'RE ON PROBATION FOR SIX MONTHS, THEN YOU GET VOTED INTO THE COLLECTIVE, THEN YOU GET A QUARTER RAISE OR SOMETHING. IT'S SUCH A SMALL DIFFER-ENCE. WE GAVE OURSELVES RAISES, THEN TOOK THEM AWAY RIGHT AFTER THAT WHEN WE REALIZED WE COULDN'T AFFORD THEM. WHICH PROBABLY DIDN'T HELP ANYONE'S ATTITUDE.

X: WHERE DOES THE FOOD COME FROM?

N: WE'VE PICKED COLLECTIVES OR COOPERATIVES AS DISTRIBUTORS WHERE IT WAS POSSIBLE, AND THEN SMALL LOCAL BUSINESSES WHERE IT WASN'T. UNTIL RECENTLY, WHEN WE STARTED GETTING STUFF LIKE HERSHEY'S CHOCOLATE SYRUP FROM A PLACE THAT GOT BOUGHT OUT AND BECAME ONE OF THE LARGEST FOOD DISTRIBUTORS IN THE COUNTRY. WHICH I STILL HAVE A PROBLEM WITH, SORT OF.

   IT'S THE SAME AS PEOPLE ARGUING, WHY DO WE SELL MARLBORO CIGARETTES? IT WAS A TRADE OFF. PEOPLE WANT MARLBORO CIGARETTES AND PEOPLE ARE EXTREMELY BRAND LOYAL WITH CIGARETTES. SO, DO WE GIVE THESE PEOPLE WHAT THEY WANT, OR DO WE HAVE THIS HIGH MORAL STANCE, LIKE, "FUCK YOU, YOU CAN'T HAVE MARLBORO LIGHTS. YOU CAN ONLY HAVE AMERICAN SPIRITS."

WHICH IS WHAT I THINK WE SHOULD DO, TO A POINT.
BUT IT'S HARD. WE'VE ALWAYS REFUSED TO SELL
COKE AND PEPSI. BUT THEN WE SELL MARLBORO
CIGARETTES, WHICH SEEMS PRETTY QUESTIONABLE.

X: WHAT'S YOUR FAVORITE TIME OF DAY HERE? THE
PERFECT TIME?

N: IT DEPENDS. I LIKE IT WHEN IT'S BUSY. NOW WE'VE
STARTED HAVING A DJ HERE ON SATURDAY AND
HAVING MOVIE NIGHT ON SUNDAY. LAST SUNDAY,
YESTERDAY I GUESS, IT WAS SPIT'S BIRTHDAY,
SO JOSEPH, WHO'S DOING THE MOVIES, DIDN'T DO
THE MOVIES.

X: AND RIPPED SPIT'S HOUSE TO SHREDS INSTEAD.

N: YEAH, WHICH WAS IMPORTANT. BUT I LIKE THE
IDEA OF THE MOVIES, AND I CAME HERE AND
KIND OF MISSED THAT. BECAUSE THE LIGHTS ARE
DIMMED, SO THAT MAKES PEOPLE A LITTLE FREER
TO TRY TO GET AWAY WITH WHAT THEY TRY TO
GET AWAY WITH ANYWAYS. PEOPLE ARE IN THE
DARK, MORE OR LESS, SO THEY CAN FEEL REAL
SNEAKY. EVEN THOUGH MOST PEOPLE WHO ARE
DOING STUFF ARE SO BLATANTLY OBVIOUS.

X: DO YOU EVER WORK ALL NIGHT, FINALLY GO HOME,
THEN HAVE DREAMS ABOUT THE CAFE?

N: I DON'T REMEMBER MY DREAMS, BUT REX WOULD
BE THE ONE TO ASK. HE GOT IN THIS THING OF
MAKING SOUP, EVEN THOUGH HE'S NOT A COOK.
HE'D MAKE "REX'S ZESTY POTATO SOUP". HE'D
MAKE A BIG POT OF IT. HE'D MAKE IT HERE, AND
HE DIDN'T HAVE A PLACE TO LIVE, SO HE WAS
SLEEPING IN THE OFFICE.
ONE DAY HE WASN'T EVEN WORKING, HE MADE
SOUP FOR NO REASON. I MEAN, WE NEEDED SOUP,
BUT IT WASN'T HIS JOB. HE WASN'T GETTING PAID,
HE WAS JUST MAKING SOUP OUT OF THE GOODNESS
OF HIS HEART.
SO HE GOES UPSTAIRS AND GOES TO SLEEP. HE
COMES STUMBLING IN AT FIVE IN THE MORNING
LOOKING LIKE A ZOMBIE, AND HE'S LIKE, "I HAD A
DREAM THAT THE SOUP HEATER WAS EMPTY, SO I
CAME DOWN AND IT WAS".
SO HE FILLED IT UP WITH SOUP AND THEN
STAGGERED BACK UPSTAIRS. I THINK THAT MIGHT
HAVE BEEN A RECCURING DREAM FOR REX.

9. Rex

X: REX, DO YOU ACTUALLY RESPECT THE CUSTOMERS, OR MERELY TOLERATE THEM? OR JUST IGNORE THEM?

R: DEPENDS ON WHO THEY ARE AND WHAT'S GOING ON. I'VE WATCHED SOME INTERESTING THINGS HAPPEN IN THE CAFE. WORKERS STANDING UP FOR PEOPLE THEY BARELY KNOW. LIKE A GUY SCREAMING AT A WOMAN AND HE GRABS HER, AND ALL OF A SUDDEN PEOPLE JUMP ON HIM AND ARE LIKE, "YOU DON'T DO THAT IN HERE. YOU DON'T DO THAT EVER."

X: WHAT ABOUT CONFLICTS THAT ORIGINATE SOMEWHERE ELSE? IF THAT SAME SITUATION HAD HAPPENED LAST WEEK AT THE VULTURE BAR? THEN, TONIGHT, THE WOMAN AND MAN ARE BOTH HERE AT THE CAFE, AND HIS MERE PRESENCE MAKES HER FEEL UNCOM-FORTABLE AND UNSAFE?

R: I'VE DEALT WITH THAT BEFORE. ACTUALLY, THAT'S HAPPENED TWICE IN THE LAST MONTH WITH WOMEN I'VE KNOWN. AND I'VE BEEN ASKED A COUPLE OF TIMES, "THIS GUY'S CREEPING ME OUT, CAN YOU COME AND SIT AT MY TABLE AND JUST TALK WITH ME?" AND I SAY, "SURE."
    DEAF JOHN HAS DONE THAT TOO. HE WRITES NOTES OCCASIONALLY. IT'LL BE LIKE, "THIS MAN BAD." YOU DON'T KNOW WHY, OR WHAT'S GOING THROUGH JOHN'S HEAD, SO YOU GOTTA WRITE HIM A NOTE, "WHY?" THEN HE'LL WRITE YOU ANOTHER NOTE WHICH IS EVEN MORE CONFUSING.

X: SO WHAT DO YOU DO?

R: GO OUT AND TALK TO THE PERSON AND BE LIKE, "JOHN'S HERE. JOHN'S ONE OF OUR EVERYDAY PEOPLE.

HE'S PART OF THE CAFE. WHY DOES HE NOT LIKE YOU?"
A LOT OF IT COMES DOWN TO BEING ABLE TO GO UP
AND TALK TO PEOPLE AND BE LIKE, "OKAY, WHAT'S
YOUR SIDE OF THIS?"

NATHAN IS REALLY GOOD AT THAT. I'VE WATCHED
NATHAN BREAK UP FIGHTS WHERE PEOPLE ARE
READY TO KILL EACH OTHER, AND HALF THE TIME
HE'S INSULTING BOTH PEOPLE. IT'S FUNNY TO WATCH
HIM BECAUSE HE USES WORDS THAT HAVE A DUAL
MEANING. I'VE WATCHED HIM DO IT WHILE I WORKED
WITH HIM, JUST SAT THERE AND BEEN AMAZED
THAT NOT ONLY HAS HE MANAGED TO BREAK UP
THE FIGHT, GET AT LEAST ONE OF THE PERSONS OUT
OF THE CAFE, BUT INSULT BOTH OF THE PEOPLE AT
THE SAME TIME.

X: HAVE YOU LEARNED WAYS TO DIFFUSE SITUATIONS?

R: NO, USUALLY I JUST WANT TO PUNCH PEOPLE. BUT
I'VE LEARNED. INSTEAD OF BEING PHYSICAL ABOUT
THINGS I'VE GONE MENTAL A LOT MORE. I DAYDREAM.
I HAD TO WRITE A NOTE, "DO NOT PUNCH THE MILK
COOLER ANY LONGER". BECAUSE, THAT'S WHY MY
KNUCKLES LOOK LIKE THIS. I'LL TURN AROUND AND
PUNCH THE MILK COOLER.

X: INSTEAD OF THE PERSON.

R: YEAH. NOT A GOOD IDEA. I KEEP BREAKING MY
KNUCKLES.

10. Dean

X: WHEN DID MARCO LEAVE?

D: OKAY, WE FIRED MARCO. BECAUSE WOMEN WERE
AFRAID TO COME IN. BECAUSE HE WAS SCAMMING
ON CHICKS.

THAT WAS A TURNING POINT IN THE PLACE. AND
BECAUSE OF THE FACT THAT THERE WAS NO CASH
REGISTER, THERE WAS JUST A DRAWER, YOU KNOW
WHAT I'M ALLUDING TO. MONEY WAS HARD TO KEEP
TRACK OF. AND I TOOK THAT PERSONALLY.

SO WE FIRED HIM AND I BECAME MANAGER.
I WAS LIKE, ALRIGHT, WE HAVE THIS REALLY COOL
THING. IT WOULD BE REALLY GREAT IF WE COULD
DO A COLLECTIVE. BUT NOBODY HAD ANY MONEY TO
DO IT.

I'M LIKE, I DON'T WANT TO BOSS MY FRIENDS
AROUND. IF WE HAVE THIS PART OF IT, WHY CAN'T
WE FINISH IT OFF AND DO IT FOR REAL WHERE
EVERYONE IS EQUAL AND WE DON'T HAVE THE
TRADITIONAL HIERARCHY OF "I AM THE BOSS"?

BECAUSE, INSTANTLY, I BECAME THE SYMBOL
OF WHAT YOU'RE NOT SUPPOSED TO DO, OR WHAT
YOU ARE SUPPOSED TO DO. EVEN THOUGH WE WERE
ALL FRIENDS. AND THE SAME AGE. AND DID EVERY-
THING THE SAME.

X: AND THEN?

D: I GOT A TRIP TO EGYPT. I WAS LIKE, FUCK THIS.
I'M OUTTA HERE.

X: I REMEMBER THAT. WHAT WAS GOING ON? YOU
WERE AT THE END OF YOUR ROPE AND YOU LOOKED
IN THE WANT ADS AND...

D: IT SAID, "FREE TRIP TO EGYPT. DISABLED WRITER

NEEDS AMIGO TO PUSH HIS WHEELCHAIR". I KNOCKED
MARCO OUT OF THE WAY AND I FUCKING WENT AND
GOT ON THE PHONE. "YEAH, I'M ATHLETIC! YEAH, I'M
SIX FEET TALL!"

AT THAT POINT I THOUGHT THE CAFE WAS
TOTALLY GOING TO GO UNDER WHILE I WAS GONE.
I DIDN'T KNOW WHO THE FUCK WAS GOING TO
STEP IN, STEP UP TO THE PLATE ON THAT ONE. I
HAD THIS VISION OF COMING BACK AND TRYING TO
CALL AND IT JUST BEING THIS RINGING PHONE JUST
RINGING AND RINGING. I DON'T KNOW HOW MUCH
OF THAT WAS SELF-IMPORTANCE AND HOW MUCH
WAS REAL CARE, BUT IT MADE IT. IT ALL WORKED
OUT. IT BECAME A COLLECTIVE FINALLY. THE DREAM
BECAME REALIZED ABOUT WHAT IT WAS ACTUALLY
SUPPOSED TO BE THROUGH ALL THIS PAINFUL CHANGE
AND PEOPLE GETTING SCREWED OVER LEFT AND RIGHT.
I WAS REALLY HAPPY. BUT BY THAT TIME I WAS
ALREADY CONSIDERED A PARIAH. BECAUSE EVERYONE
THERE KNEW I WAS USING THE NEEDLE.

X: BECAUSE WHAT?

D: BECAUSE I WAS SHOOTING UP.

11. Spit

X: HOW'S EVERYTHING LOOKING IN THE DINING ROOM TONIGHT?

S: FINE, FINE.

X: WOULD YOU LIKE TO INTRODUCE YOURSELF?

S: MY NAME'S CEDRIC, BUT MY GOOD FRIENDS AROUND HERE CALL ME SPIT. IT'S AN OLD NICKNAME THAT'S KIND OF STUCK WITH ME.

X: WHY DO YOU LOVE THIS JOB?

S: I THINK IT'S THE PEOPLE. I'M REALLY AN ANTI-SOCIAL PERSON BUT FOR SOME REASON I LIKE THIS TYPE OF SOCIAL ATMOSPHERE. THERE'S NO PRESSURE TO CONFORM HERE. THAT'S WHAT'S NICE ABOUT IT, YOU CAN JUST BE WHOEVER YOU WANT TO BE AND BE AROUND ALL THESE OTHER PEOPLE WHO ARE DOING WHATEVER THEY WANT TO DO.

X: HOW DID YOU FIND IT?

S: A FRIEND OF MINE HAS BEEN WORKING HERE SINCE LAST SEPTEMBER. I WAS HANGING OUT WITH HIM THIS SPRING, AND I SPENT A LOT OF TIME HERE, AND THEY NEEDED COOKS BADLY. MY FRIEND SAID, "WELL, YOU CAN COOK. YOU SHOULD GET A JOB HERE". I SAID, "NO NO NO NO NO NO NO NO. I KNOW I CAN COOK, BUT I CAN'T WORK AS A COOK".

X: DID IT TAKE A WHILE TO PROVE YOURSELF?

S: YEAH, IT TOOK A WHILE. PEOPLE DIDN'T THINK I WAS GOING TO MAKE IT. AT FIRST I DIDN'T EITHER.

X: IS IT HARD COMING INTO SOMETHING WITH A LONG HISTORY AND BEING THE NEW PERSON?

S: YEAH. THERE'S A PAST HERE AND YOU HAVE TO LIVE UP TO THAT.

X: DOES EACH PERSON HAVE A DIFFERENT VERSION OF THE PAST WHEN THEY TELL YOU ABOUT IT?

S: YOU KNOW, IT'S BEEN REALLY GOOD, FROM WHAT I GATHER. I DON'T THINK I'M GOING TO BE ABLE TO MAKE THAT BIG OF A CHANGE HERE. I DON'T REALLY WANT TO.

X: BUT IF YOU DID, WHERE WOULD YOU START?

S: NEXT SUMMER I REALLY WANT TO GET A DEAD END BUS GOING, WITH A MOBILE ESPRESSO BAR. BE ABLE TO TRAVEL AROUND THE COUNTRY AND SHIT. THAT'S PROBABLY THE ONLY WAY TO GET OUT OF HERE, TO TAKE A VACATION. BECAUSE YOU CAN'T EVER GET ANYONE TO COVER YOUR SHIFTS. I WENT ON A LITTLE VACATION A COUPLE WEEKS AGO TO GO BACK UP NORTH, AND THERE WAS NO ONE HERE COOKING.

ED: I COOKED A COUPLE OF THOSE SHIFTS. BUT A COUPLE OF THOSE SHIFTS I COULD NOT DO. BECAUSE I'M MORE OR LESS THE EMERGENCY COOK, YOU KNOW. I WAS GETTING FED UP, LIKE EVERY DAY BEING AN EMERGENCY.

X: YOU'RE NOT USED TO EVERY DAY BEING AN EMERGENCY?

S: EVERY DAY IS AN EMERGENCY. ESPECIALLY THE OTHER NIGHT WHEN WE HAD THAT FIRE. THAT WAS FUN.

X: BACK HERE IN THE KITCHEN?

S: NO, IT WAS IN THE WALL. BETWEEN THE BATH-ROOM AND THE OUTSIDE WALL. THE PLACE WAS FILLING UP WITH SMOKE. IT WAS FUNNY, YOU KNOW, WE'RE FIGHTING THE FIRE BACK THERE AND PEOPLE ARE STILL ORDERING THEIR LATTES AND QUESADILLAS AND SHIT. SOMEBODY ASKED, "CAN I USE THE BATHROOM?"
  NATHAN SAID, "NO, THERE'S A FIRE IN THERE". THEY SAID, "WELL, WHEN'S IT GONNA BE DONE?"

12. Jody

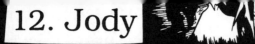

X: DOES THIS PLACE FOSTER GOOD VALUES?

J: SURE, IN LITTLE WAYS. ONE EXAMPLE IS, I USED TO SMOKE, BACK WHEN THE CAFE FIRST OPENED. AND I SMOKED MARLBOROS. ONE DAY DEAN SAID, "MAN, HOW CAN YOU TAKE YOURSELF SERIOUSLY SMOKING THAT SHIT, SUPPORTING THAT?"

I'D HEARD IT BEFORE, AND IT WAS TRUE. BUT, YOU KNOW, PEOPLE LIKE TO BE A LITTLE CONTRADICTORY. A LITTLE HYPOCRITICAL. OR AT LEAST, THEY GET DEFENSIVE ABOUT IT, AND NEED A HELPING HAND.

DEAN THREW A POUCH OF TOBACCO AT ME AND SAID, "LEARN TO ROLL".

AND SO, I DID. WHICH IS JUST A LITTLE THING, BUT IT FELT GOOD NOT TO BE GIVING MY MONEY TO PHILIP MORRIS ANYMORE.

ANOTHER EXAMPLE IS, A GUY CAME IN WEARING A T-SHIRT OF A NAKED WOMAN. A BOSS HOG T-SHIRT. AND HE WAS CONFRONTED BY A GROUP OF WOMEN WHO WERE OFFENDED BY IT. NOT OFFENDED, JUST, IT MADE THEM FEEL UNCOMFORTABLE. THEY FOUND THE SHIRT DEMEANING, AND THE GUY COULDN'T UNDERSTAND WHY. HE REFUSED TO TAKE IT OFF.

THAT ARGUMENT CARRIED OVER INTO A HUGE ARGUMENT WITHIN THE COLLECTIVE, AND THAT WENT ON FOR MONTHS. BECAUSE SOME PEOPLE THOUGHT THAT THE WOMEN HAD HANDLED THINGS IN A REACTIONARY WAY. AND OTHER PEOPLE THOUGHT THE WOMEN DESERVED MORE SUPPORT AND THEIR FEELINGS DESERVED MORE RESPECT IN THE FIRST PLACE.

: HOW HAD THEY HANDLED IT?

: WELL, THEY CHASED THE GUY DOWN THE STREET AND BEAT HIM DOWN. RIPPED THE T-SHIRT OFF. BLOOD AND EVERYTHING, IT WAS A MESS.

13. Gary

X: IT SEEMS LIKE A LOT OF PEOPLE ONLY WANT TO TAKE ON A BIG PROJECT IF THEY'RE SURE IT WILL FAIL. YOU KNOW WHAT I MEAN? THEY DON'T WANT SOMETHING GOOD TO LAST.

G: WE'VE EXPERIENCED PEOPLE HERE WHO FEEL THIS IS A GOOD IDEA WITH A SHORT LIFE EXPECTANCY, BUT I DON'T FEEL THAT WAY. I THINK IT'S REALLY IMPORTANT TO LOOK AT IT IN A LONG-TERM WAY. I THINK OUR CHANCES ARE AS GOOD TO MAKE SEVENTY YEARS AS THEY ARE TO MAKE TEN. AND WE'VE ONLY GOT THREE LEFT TO MAKE TEN.

X: WHAT ARE THE LONGTERM GOALS?

G: PEOPLE COME INTO A COLLECTIVE WITH SO MANY DIFFERENT NOTIONS OF WHAT A COLLECTIVE IS. WE HAVE A UNIQUE SITUATION HERE, AND IT'S NOT EASILY DEFINABLE BY REGULAR BUSINESS STANDARDS. THAT'S PART OF THE LONGTERM PROCESS, DEFINING WHAT WE ARE FROM WITHIN, RATHER THAN BEING DEFINED FROM WITHOUT.

PERSONALLY, I BELIEVE THIS KIND OF BUSINESS IS A UNIQUE KIND OF TRAINING. IT GIVES PEOPLE THE OPPORTUNITY TO GO ON AND DO OTHER THINGS. IT HELPS PEOPLE BECOME ASSERTIVE FOR THEIR OWN LIFESTYLES. BECAUSE WE STRUGGLE WITH COMMUNICATION, TO UNDERSTAND ANYTHING, TO GET TO KNOW ANYTHING, YOU HAVE TO PURSUE IT. AND BECAUSE YOU'RE AT LEAST NOMINALLY AN OWNER, GENERALLY IT GROWS ON YOU.

THERE ARE ONLY A FEW PEOPLE WHO'VE BEEN HERE WHO HAVE FELT THE NEED TO BE TOLD WHAT TO DO. AND THEY USUALLY HAVEN'T LASTED TOO LONG. THE MAJORITY OF PEOPLE I THINK ARE THOSE WHO HAVE TO DISCOVER THE PROCESS OF COLLECTIVE WORK AND HAVE TO DISCOVER WHERE IT COMES FROM IN THEM.

X: DOES HAVING BEEN HERE A LONGER TIME AND BEING OLDER THAN OTHER PEOPLE HERE GIVE YOU A DIFFERENT INSIGHT OR A DIFFERENT TAKE ON THINGS?

G: IT DEFINITELY GIVES ME A DIFFERENT ACCUMULATION OF EXPERIENCES HERE, WHICH I SUPPOSE LEAD TO INSIGHT. BUT AS FAR AS AFFECTION FOR THE PLACE AND AGGRAVATION WITH SOME THINGS THAT HAPPEN HERE, I THINK I'M RIGHT IN THE MIDDLE, AVERAGE WITH EVERYBODY.

WHY I'VE STAYED HERE SO LONG, WHY I'VE BEEN ASSOCIATED WITH THE PLACE SO LONG, I REALLY CAN'T DEFINE. MAYBE BECAUSE WHEN I FIRST WORKED HERE THE BOSS PICKED A FIGHT WITH ME. I DON'T LIKE TO LEAVE A SITUATION WHERE THERE'S ACRIMONY THAT WAY, AND SO, I INSISTED ON STAYING HERE AND MAKING FRIENDS.

I FIND THAT HAPPENS ALL THE TIME. THERE ARE NUMEROUS OCCASSIONS TO BACKTRACK AND MAKE FRIENDS OUT OF ANTAGONISTS OR ENEMIES, OR WHATEVER PEOPLE DEFINE THEIR CONFLICTS WITH OTHER PEOPLE AS.

I DON'T HAVE A PROBLEM WORKING WITH PEOPLE I'M IN CONFLICT WITH. TO ME IT'S PART OF THE PROCESS OF COLLECTIVISM, MAKING CONSENSUS. I DON'T AGREE WITH A LOT OF DECISIONS THAT ARE MADE HERE, BUT THEY'RE NOT IMPORTANT ENOUGH FOR ME TO OBSTRUCT THOSE DECISIONS.

14. Beth

X: HOW HAS THE CAFE CHANGED OVER TIME?

B: IT USED TO BE INFESTED WITH HIPPIES EVERYWHERE.
THERE'S A LOT OF DIFFERENT KINDS OF PEOPLE WHO
WORK HERE NOW. WE'RE KIND OF OPENING UP AND
LETTING NEW PEOPLE COME IN WHO HAVEN'T HUNG
OUT HERE FOR YEARS UPON YEARS. I REALLY LIKE
THAT. I'M STILL GETTING A FEEL FOR ALL THE NEW
PEOPLE.

X: WHERE DOES THE SHARED SENSE OF VALUES COME
FROM?

B: I DON'T KNOW BECAUSE I WASN'T AROUND. I'VE
ONLY BEEN HERE FOR FOUR YEARS, FIVE YEARS
MAYBE. I THINK IT'S ALWAYS KIND OF BEEN THIS
WAY. WHEN I FIRST CAME TO TOWN I WAS TOLD TO
GO TO THE DEAD END CAFE BECAUSE THAT WAS THE
COOL PLACE TO HANG OUT. SO I CAME HERE. IT
WAS THE FIRST PLACE I CAME WHEN I GOT OFF
THE GREYHOUND. AND I WAS LIKE, "WOW, EVERYONE'S
JUST MELLOW AND LAID BACK AND INTO THEIR OWN
THING AND NOT TOO CONCERNED WITH THE OUTSIDE
WORLD". I THINK THAT'S THE WAY IT'S ALWAYS
BEEN HERE.

X: HOW MUCH DOES BEING A COLLECTIVE HAVE TO DO
WITH THE OVERALL ENVIRONMENT?

B: WELL, IT CREATES MORE CHAOS. THERE'S SO MANY
DIFFERENT CONFLICTING VIEWS THAT IT'S HARD TO
GET A DECISION ON A LOT OF IMPORTANT MATTERS.
WE DON'T REALLY VOTE AS OFTEN AS WE SHOULD,
AND WHEN WE DO VOTE THAT DOESN'T NECESSARILY
MEAN THAT'S WHAT'S GOING TO HAPPEN. WE'LL VOTE
ONE WAY ONE WEEK AND THEN IT'LL COME UP

AGAIN AT THE NEXT MEETING. EVERYONE WILL
HAVE CHANGED THEIR IDEAS OR HAD SECOND
THOUGHTS.

X: DOES EVERYONE HAVE AN EQUAL SAY?

B: YEAH. YOU WORK HERE FOR SIX MONTHS, AND AFTER
SIX MONTHS YOU HAVE THE RIGHT TO VOTE. ALTHOUGH
SOME PEOPLE'S VOICES ARE LOUDER THAN OTHERS
AND SOMETIMES THEIR VIEWS GET HEARD MORE
THAN OTHERS. SOMETIMES PEOPLE DON'T HAVE A BIG
SAY JUST BECAUSE THEY DON'T LET THEMSELVES BE
HEARD.

X: DOES THE DECISION MAKING PROCESS WORK?

B: SOMETIMES IT DOES AND SOMETIMES IT DOESN'T.
IT DEPENDS ON HOW IMPORTANT PEOPLE FEEL THE
ISSUE TO BE.

X: WHAT ARE SOME OF THE IMPORTANT ONES?

B: A LOT OF THE ISSUES HAVE BEEN WITH CRACKHEADS
THAT COME IN HERE. THAT'S BEEN A BIG DEAL
FOR ME BECAUSE I DON'T WANT THIS PLACE TO BE
A DRUG ENVIRONMENT. AND IT IS. IT JUST NATURALLY
IS, IT ALWAYS HAS BEEN.
    I DON'T MIND IF PEOPLE DO DRUGS. I LIKE TO
HAVE FUN AND DO STUFF TOO. BUT I DON'T WANT
PEOPLE TO KNOW THAT THIS IS THE PLACE TO GET
DRUGS, TO DO DRUGS, TO BE ON THEM. IT'S BAD, THE
POLICE WANT TO COME IN HERE WHEN IT GETS
CRAZY LIKE THAT, AND WE DON'T WANT THE POLICE
HERE, EVER.

15. Ed

X: WHAT'S THE COOLEST THING YOU'VE EVER FOUND HERE?

E: I'VE FOUND INTERESTING THINGS. I'M GOING TO TRY TO MAKE THIS AS QUICK AS POSSIBLE. WELL, ONE THING IS, I HAVE MY OWN TIP JAR. AND IN MY OWN TIP JAR I HAVE FOUND, OF COURSE MONEY, BUT ALSO CANDY, AND CIGARETTES. I FOUND A WATCH IN MY TIP JAR ONCE. ONE TIME IN THE KITCHEN HERE, I WALK OUT AND FROM THE DISTANCE I NOTICE THAT MY TIP JAR IS HIGH UP, AS IF IT'S ON SOMETHING. AND I GET OUT THERE AND NOTICE THAT IT'S SITTING ON TOP OF A SIX-PACK OF BEER.

X: DAMN!

E: WHAT ELSE? I'VE FOUND COKE IN MY TIP JAR, JOINTS. ANOTHER EXAMPLE IS THAT, ONE TIME IN THE DINING ROOM, I SEE SOMETHING OUT OF THE CORNER OF MY EYE. IT WAS A LITTLE PACKAGE WITH CRACK IN IT. I HATE THAT STUFF, BUT I STILL HAD TO JUST PICK IT UP AND GET RID OF IT. WHO KNOWS WHO WOULD HAVE FOUND IT IF I HADN'T DONE THAT?
WE ALSO HAVE A FREE BOX HERE AND I'VE FOUND SOME PRETTY...

X: DID YOU FIND THE CRACK IN THE FREE BOX?

E: NO, BUT ONE TIME ACTUALLY I FOUND A JACKET IN THE FREE BOX, AND I'M CHECKING THE POCKETS, AND I PULL OUT A SACK OF POT. AND OF COURSE, TURNED AROUND AND GAVE IT AWAY. BUT A WEEK LATER I FIND A JACKET IN THE FREE BOX AND CHECK THE POCKETS AND PULL OUT A TWENTY DOLLAR BILL.

X: HOW DO YOU FEEL ABOUT DRUGS IN THE CAFE?

E: DEPENDS. I MEAN, ARE YOU TALKING ABOUT CO-WORKERS OR CUSTOMERS? WITH CO-WORKERS, THERE'S BEEN SOME PROBLEMS. A COUPLE PEOPLE WHICH SOMETIMES GET OUT OF CONTROL. IF THEY'RE DRINKING ON THE JOB, SOME PEOPLE DO GET A LITTLE OUT OF HAND SOMETIMES.

CUSTOMERS? OF COURSE WE GET DRUNKEN IDIOTS. OR PEOPLE MAY DISRESPECT THE PLACE AND USE IT AS A BUSINESS.

X: YOU MEAN, USE THE PLACE FOR THEIR OWN BUSINESS?

E: LET ME TELL YOU A LITTLE STORY. NOT TOO LONG AGO, THESE TWO GUYS COME IN HERE AND THEY SIT AS FAR AS POSSIBLE AWAY FROM THE FRONT DOOR. THEY SIT DOWN AND TWO MINUTES LATER THE POLICE WALK IN AND DRAG THEM OUT.

I WALKED OVER TO WHERE THEY WERE SITTING. A FELLOW EMPLOYEE WAS ALREADY THERE, PICKING UP EVERYTHING THAT THEY HAD DITCHED. OF COURSE, SO THEY WOULDN'T GET IN TROUBLE FOR HAVING WHAT THEY HAD ON THEM. EITHER TAKE A TOTAL LOSS OR GET ARRESTED FOR IT. AND OF COURSE, THE EMPLOYEE'S MENTALITY WAS LIKE, "YOUR STUPIDITY IS MY GAIN".

16. Joseph

X: WHAT ABOUT THE NEIGHBORHOOD?

J: I'VE BEEN IN ALMOST EVERY MAJOR CITY IN THE UNITED STATES, AND I THINK THIS NEIGHBORHOOD HERE IS ONE OF THE BEST. IT'S SO DIVERSE, AND PEOPLE ARE REALLY TIGHT. THEY CALL THIS NEIGHBORHOOD "THE LITTLE VILLAGE IN THE CITY", WHICH IT REALLY IS IN A WAY. BECAUSE WE TAKE CARE OF OUR OWN.

THERE'S A LOT OF BUSINESSES AROUND HERE THAT ARE SELF-RELIANT, NOT ONLY AS FAR AS CUSTOMER RELATIONS GO, BUT AS FAR AS POLICING THEMSELVES GOES. I MEAN, THE POLICE ARE HERE BECAUSE THEY'RE GETTING PAID, NOT BECAUSE WE NEED THEM. WE DON'T NEED THE POLICE, WE CAN TAKE CARE OF OURSELVES.

X: DOES THE CAFE REFLECT THE NEIGHBORHOOD?

J: THE CAFE IS A MAJOR PART OF THE NEIGHBORHOOD. A LOT OF STUFF GOES ON HERE. WE GOT, ON ANY GIVEN NIGHT, ETHIOPIAN EX-GENERALS FROM THE WAR PLAYING CHESS WITH BURNT OUT ALCOHOLIC PROFESSORS FROM THE UNIVERSITY. AND THEN SEVENTEEN-YEAR-OLD RUNAWAY KIDS WAITING IN LINE TO PLAY CHESS WITH THEM. ALL OF THESE PEOPLE HANG OUT IN THE NEIGHBORHOOD. IT'S LIKE A WHOLE NEIGHBORHOOD FULL OF CHARACTERS. IT'S LIKE IF YOU HAD A WHOLE BUNCH OF ACTORS WHO WERE OUT OF WORK BUT THEY WERE STILL PLAYING SOME KIND OF A PART, AND YOU HAD A PARTICULAR PLACE WHERE THEY LIVED IN THE CITY, THIS WOULD BE IT. THIS IS WHERE THEY'D BE HANGING OUT. THEY'D BE HANGING OUT AT THE CAFE. AND WE TALK TO EACH OTHER LIKE...

JOSEPH'S MOM: DOES THIS LOOK LIKE A QUARTER?

J: WELL, I GUESS. IT LOOKS A LITTLE HEAVY.

JOSEPH'S MOM: YOU GUYS WANT TO SMOKE SOME?

J: NAH, I DON'T DO DRUGS, MOM.
BUT LIKE I SAID, SAY I'M WORKING THE AFTERNOON SHIFT. SAY MY BUDDY IS WORKING UP AT CHANDLER'S BAR. AND HE THROWS SOME DRUNK GUY OUT. HE'LL CALL ME UP AND SAY, "HEY, I JUST THREW SOME DRUNK GUY OUT OF THE BAR AND HE MIGHT BE HEADED YOUR WAY".
I'LL BE LIKE, "HEY, THANKS FOR THE TIP".
AND THEN LIKE, MY MOM, YOU KNOW. SHE WALKS AROUND AT NIGHT, SHE FEELS TOTALLY SAFE. SHE FEELS LIKE NO ONE'S GONNA FUCK WITH HER. BECAUSE THEY KNOW WHO SHE IS. LIKE YOU WERE SAYING BEFORE, IT'S THIS WEIRD UNWRITTEN, UNSPOKEN THING. IT'S THIS WEIRD NEIGHBORHOOD POLICY, CERTAIN PEOPLE YOU CAN FUCK WITH AND CERTAIN PEOPLE YOU CAN'T. IT'S A LOT ABOUT FAMILY, TOO. A LOT OF PEOPLE AROUND HERE, WE CONSIDER EACH OTHER LIKE FAMILY. WE TAKE CARE OF EACH OTHER AND DO THINGS FOR EACH OTHER, AND WE DON'T REALLY HAVE ANYONE ELSE. ALL WE HAVE IS EACH OTHER.

X: WITH THE NEIGHBORHOOD, THE CAFE, OR BOTH?

J: WITH BOTH. PEOPLE FROM THE NEIGHBORHOOD, PEOPLE FROM THE CAFE, PEOPLE THAT HAVE BEEN AROUND HERE FOREVER THAT DON'T REALLY HAVE NOWHERE ELSE TO TURN TO, SO THEY TURN TO EACH OTHER. WE'VE CREATED THIS FAMILY, AND NO ONE CAN FUCK WITH THAT FAMILY.

17. Gary

X: A LOT OF PEOPLE HAVE SAID IT'S LIKE FAMILY HERE. BUT A COLLECTIVE IS DIFFERENT BECAUSE IT'S BY CHOICE.

G: YEAH, IT'S DEFINITELY AN INTENTIONAL COMMUNITY. AND THE INTENTIONS WE DEVELOP HERE FOR COLLECTIVISM APPLY TO OTHER THINGS. PEOPLE HAVE MOVED ON, AND IF THEY'RE NOT ENGAGED IN THOSE OTHER THINGS THE WAY THEY WERE ENGAGED HERE, THEY MISS IT HERE.

THAT'S AT THE CORE OF IT, THE POTENTIAL TO BE FULLY ENGAGED. THAT'S SOMETHING YOU CAN GET IN AN INHERITED SITUATION, BUT IN A DELIBERATE SITUATION, IT'S NOT A GUARANTEE. YOU HAVE TO WORK AT THE COMMUNICATION.

X: IT SEEMS EASY TO LOSE SIGHT OF THE HIGHER PURPOSE.

G: THERE'S A TRANSFORMATION IN EVERYBODY. THE PLACE CHANGES YOU, SOMETIMES IN SUBTLE WAYS. TO ME, THAT'S A PURPOSE. BECAUSE IT'S NOT JUST A JOB WHICH CAN BE EASILY SEPARATED IN PEOPLE'S MINDS FROM A LIFE-SHAPING EXPERIENCE.

X: YOU BROUGHT UP DEFINING YOURSELF FROM WITHIN RATHER THAN FROM WITHOUT. BUT, BEING PART OF A COMMUNITY, THERE'S GOING TO BE AN INTERPLAY BETWEEN THOSE TWO THINGS. HOW MUCH DO YOU ADAPT TO OTHER PEOPLE'S NEEDS?

G: THAT'S SOMETHING WE END UP WORKING ON INTERNALLY, AND NOT ALWAYS IN PLEASANT WAYS.

NUMBER ONE, THIS COMMUNITY HAS A THOUSAND RESIDENTS WITH SOME SORT OF CHRONIC AND DEBILITATING MENTAL ILLNESS. IT'S ONE OF THE NEIGHBORHOODS WHERE RONALD REAGAN WAREHOUS-

ED PEOPLE WHEN HE DECIMATED SOCIAL SPENDING. THEY ARE A REGULAR PART OF OUR CLIENTEL, AND WE HAVE MADE ADJUSTMENTS TO ACCOMODATE THEM. PSYCHOLOGICAL ADJUSTMENTS AND BUSINESS PRACTICE ADJUSTMENTS. THERE ARE SOME PEOPLE WE TRUST TO BUILD UP A CREDIT DEBT WITH US THAT THEY'LL PAY OFF AT THE FIRST OF THE MONTH. IT'S NOT A GOOD CYCLE FOR THEIR BUDGETS, BUT THEY COME THROUGH, AND WE ACCOMMODATE THAT SO THEY'RE LIKELY TO HANG OUT HERE MORE. AND JUST THEIR HANGING OUT MAKES THE PLACE SOMETIMES LIKE A DAYROOM AT A PSYCH WARD.

THE IMMIGRANT CLIENTEL CREATES NOT ONLY LANGUAGE PROBLEMS, BUT CULTURAL PROBLEMS EXIST TOO. SOME ARE REAL BASIC, LIKE IN SOME CULTURES YOU DON'T FORM A LINE. LESS THAN A YEAR AGO I WAS WORKING WHEN TWO DIFFERENT AFRICAN CULTURES CLASHED OVER THAT ISSUE. THERE WAS ONE GUY WHO HAD BEEN WAITING IN LINE, WITH HIS HANDS AROUND ANOTHER GUY'S THROAT, AND THEY WERE CUSSING EACH OTHER OUT IN DIFFERENT VERSIONS OF BROKEN ENGLISH.

AND THESE GUYS, THEY BRING THEIR CLAN CONFLICTS WITH THEM. ETHIOPIA WAS AT WAR FOR THIRTY-ODD YEARS WITH SECTIONS OF THE NORTH AND EAST OF THAT COUNTRY. AND SOMALIA, EVERYONE IS FAMILIAR WITH THEIR CIVIL WAR. SOUTHEASTERN EUROPE HAS GOT THE SAME ISSUES WITH CLAN PROBLEMS, AND WHEN THOSE GROUPS LEAVE THOSE AREAS, THEY DON'T LEAVE THEIR CLAN AFFINITIES BEHIND. SO WE HAVE TO ADJUST TO THAT, AND REFEREE SITUATIONS.

THERE'S INDIVIDUALS WHO WOULD RATHER NOT UNDERSTAND, WHO WOULD RATHER JUST KICK EVERY-BODY OUT. BUT, YOU KNOW, THAT'S NOT OUR POLICY.

SO YOU HAVE PEOPLE WHO ARE INCAPACITATED BY INDIVIDUAL INTERNAL CONDITIONS. YOU HAVE DIFFERENT PEOPLE WHO HAVE CULTURAL CONFLICTS. AND YOU HAVE DIFFERENT PEOPLE THAT HAVE CONFLICTS FROM DIFFERENT NOTIONS OF HOW TO BEHAVE. WE HAVE ALL OF THAT, WHICH AFFECTS THE WAY WE AS INDIVIDUALS WORK. SO WHEN WE GIVE EACH OTHER FEEDBACK INTERNALLY, THERE IS A LOT OF DISCUSSION ABOUT THESE KINDS OF THINGS, AND HOW YOU RESPOND TO THOSE SITUATIONS. AND THAT'S PART OF THE PROCESS OF CHANGING. PART OF INDIVIDUAL GROWTH.

18. Brent

X: HOW DID YOU FIRST COME HERE?

B: I CAME FROM THE SUBURBS, BUT I BAILED OUT OF
THE SUBURBS EARLY ON. I DIDN'T REALLY HAVE
COMMUNITY SUPPORT OR ANY SENSE THAT THERE
WERE ANY MORE FREAKS UNTIL I STARTED HANGING
OUT HERE. BETWEEN HERE AND DOWNTOWN AND
CAMPUS PROTEST ACTIVITIES I WAS INVOLVED WITH
IN THE EIGHTIES. IT GAVE ME A SENSE THAT, OKAY,
THERE IS AN ALTERNATIVE TO REALITY AS YOU
THOUGHT IT WAS GOING TO BE.

X: HOW DID YOU BECOME INVOLVED?

B: I WAS GOING THROUGH THIS BREAKUP OR, NOT
BREAKUP BUT GETTING-DUMPED-THING, AND
BECAUSE OF THE WAY MY SELF-ESTEEM WAS,
I WAS JUST TOTALLED. I'D STARE AT THE POST,
HANG AROUND AND HAVE COFFEE. AFTER TWO
YEARS OF THAT, DAVEY'S LIKE, "LOOK, YOU'VE GOT TO
GET OFF YOUR ASS AND DO SOMETHING. HERE'S A
BROOM. SWEEP THE FLOORS."
    SO I BASICALLY BECAME DAVEY'S TRAIN-IN TO
BE THE OVERNIGHT. HE WAS TRAINING ME IN ON
THE SLY. WHILE I WOULD BE CLEANING THE FLOORS,
WHICH I DID FOR A YEAR STRAIGHT, HE WOULD GO
FIX STUFF IN THE CAFE. PEOPLE WOULD BE LIKE,
"HE'S NOT DOING THE FLOORS, HE'S NOT DOING HIS
JOB". I'M LIKE, "WHO DO YOU THINK DOES THE
FUCKING MAINTENANCE HERE?"

X: HOW HAS IT CHANGED?

B: THERE WAS A GROUP OF FIFTEEN PEOPLE WHO HAD
A UNIFIED SENSE OF PURPOSE. THEY WANTED TO
CREATE A CAFE OF THEIR OWN OUT OF THE ASHES
OF WHAT MARCO HAD HAPPEN. AND ALL OF US
FRIENDS WERE READY TO DIVE IN AND HELP OUT IN
ONE WAY OR ANOTHER.

X: YOU'RE COUNTING YOURSELF AS ONE OF THE FIFTEEN
PEOPLE?

B: NO. OH, NO. I'D BE LIKE THE THIRD RING OUT. THERE'S THE FIRST CORE GROUP, AND THEN THEIR PERSONAL ASSOCIATES, AND THEN, AT THE TIME, I WAS ON THE FRINGE BECAUSE NOBODY COULD FIGURE ME OUT. I DIDN'T HAVE A WORK ETHIC UNLESS IT INVOLVED GOING TO PLAY DRUMS SOMEWHERE. NOW IT'S WEIRD BECAUSE I'VE BEEN OFFERED JOBS AS A BAKER BECAUSE OF MY REPUTATION HERE THAT COULD MAKE ME DOUBLE AND GET RID OF A LOT OF MY STRESS. BUT I HAVEN'T TAKEN THEM BECAUSE I'M USED TO BEING MY OWN BOSS.

THE UNITY THING IS, SINCE I'M NOW AN OLDER FART...

X: A VETERAN.

B: A VETERAN OF THE WAR HERE, FIGHTING AGAINST ENTROPY AND OTHER THINGS, I PERSONALLY DON'T HAVE THE SAME SENSE OF SELFLESSNESS THAT I USED TO HAVE WITH THIS PLACE, BECAUSE I FINALLY FIGURED OUT THAT MY TIME IS WORTH MONEY IN SOME SITUATIONS. AND I ALSO GOT HIP TO EQUITABLE EXCHANGE. IDEALLY, YOU'RE DOING THINGS FOR THE COOPERATIVE, AND THE COOPERATIVE RETURNS THE FAVOR.

I DON'T WANT TO DISRESPECT A LOT OF PEOPLE. MOST OF THE PEOPLE WHO WORK HERE NOW ARE VERY GOOD AT WHAT THEY DO, BUT SOME JUST THOUGHT THEY WERE GOING TO WORK AT THE COOL COFFEESHOP. IT'S HARD TO GET THESE PEOPLE TO MOVE ON. BECAUSE WHAT ARE WE GOING TO DO FOR A BARTENDER IF WE GET RID OF THAT PERSON WHO'S NOT DOING SO WELL? HOPEFULLY THEY'LL CHANGE.

X: YOU'RE SAYING, HOW DO WE FIRE PEOPLE IN THE COLLECTIVE? OR HOW DO WE MOTIVATE THEM?

B: ABOUT A YEAR AGO I STARTED NOTICING THERE WAS THIS TENDENCY TO PARTY AND WORK A LITTLE, WHEREAS FOUR YEARS AGO WE WORKED VERY HARD SO WE COULD HAVE A PLACE TO PARTY, AND CELEBRATE LIFE, AND THE STRUGGLE. AND WHATEVER GOES ON WITH LIFE AND THE STRUGGLE IN LIFE.

NOW, THE CAFE IS STILL A UNIQUE WEIRD MELTING POT, BUT A LOT OF THE QUALITY CONTROL IS GONE. THAT'S JUST ME AND WHAT I'M PROJECTING ALSO. THINGS CHANGE, THEY CAN'T REMAIN THE SAME, BUT I WOULD HAVE LIKED TO HAVE THOUGHT THERE WAS SOME KIND OF CONSISTENCY AVAILABLE

19. Chad

X: WERE YOU PART OF THE BIKE CLUB?

C: YEAH, ME, JOSEPH, AND NICKEL. FOUNDING MEMBERS OF THE DEAD END BIKE CLUB. ME AND JOSEPH, WE USED TO GO UP AND DOWN ALLEYS AND JOUST WITH THE BIKES AND FUCK EACH OTHER UP. WE WERE PRETTY MUCH ATTACHED TO OUR BIKES.

X: HOW MUCH DID THE CLUB HAVE TO DO WITH THE CAFE?

C: I DON'T KNOW, NICKEL NAMED IT THAT. I DIDN'T THINK IT WAS A CLUB AT ALL, BUT WE JUST DID IT. IT JUST HAPPENED. AND SUDDENLY WE WERE FIFTY, SIXTY STRONG AND WE'RE RIDING DOWN THE FUCKING STREET STOPPING TRAFFIC AND SHIT. I MEAN, WE WERE CAUSING CAR ACCIDENTS.

X: EVEN IF THE NAME WAS SORT OF ARBITRARY, IT SEEMS LIKE IT DOES RELATE TO THE CAFE.

C: THAT'S JUST BECAUSE THAT'S WHERE OUR CLUB, THAT'S WHERE WE ALL HUNG OUT TOGETHER. I MEAN, I'VE KNOWN JOSEPH SINCE WE WERE EAST END GUTTERPUNKS. THAT ESTABLISHED BECAUSE WE WERE ALL ON THE EAST END AND WE WERE LIVING IN THE GUTTER AND WE WERE PUNKS.

X: DON'T YOU THINK THAT'S ABOUT MORE THAN JUST A LOCATION?

C: I DON'T KNOW, DO YOU?

X: WHEN THE BIKE CLUB WENT ON TOUR, IT WAS STILL THE DEAD END. YOU BROUGHT A PIECE OF THE PLACE WITH YOU, A PARTICULAR STYLE.

C: WELL, YEAH. ANYTHING THAT COMES FROM ITS

ORIGIN DOES. LIKE, MY GRANDFATHER WAS IRISH, AND YOU COULD FUCKING TELL HE WAS, BECAUSE HE CAME FROM THERE.

X: SO WHEN DOES IT STOP BEING A CAFE AND START BEING A CULTURAL IDENTITY? OR A CULTURE?

C: THAT'S KIND OF A HARD QUESTION, DUDE. TO ME IT'S JUST SOMETHING THAT MANIFESTS ITSELF BECAUSE YOU'RE WITH YOUR CREW OF PEOPLE, AND YOU'RE TIGHT, AND YOU'RE FAMILY. IT WAS A SIGNIFICATION OF THE FACT. PLUS, JOSEPH IS AN OWNER OF THE DEAD END, AND SOME OF THE OTHER MEMBERS WERE OWNERS OF THE DEAD END.

I DON'T KNOW IF YOU'RE TRYING TO SAY THE NAME HAS ANYTHING TO DO WITH IT. I DON'T EVEN KNOW HOW THEY CAME UP WITH THE NAME. I PERSONALLY THOUGHT IT WAS STUPID AT FIRST, BUT NOW IT'S JUST NATURAL.

BUT I MEAN, YOU CAN'T LOOK AT ME AND GO, "THAT GUY'S FROM THE EAST END, HE MUST HANG OUT AT THE DEAD END". BUT IF SOMEONE SPOTS ME RIDING DOWN A HUGE HILL WITH MY BRAKE PADS BURNING OFF, OR JOUSTING AND COVERED IN BLOOD, OR WHATNOT, THEY'D SAY, "HEY! YOU'RE ONE OF THOSE DEAD END BIKE CLUB DUDES!"

I'M DEFINITELY ASSOCIATED TO A LOT OF PEOPLE BECAUSE OF THAT. WHICH IS LIKE, EVERYBODY LOOKS FOR SOME KIND OF TRIBALISM, SOME PLACE TO BASE THEMSELVES OUT OF. EVERYBODY.

20. Jody

X: WHAT MAKES THIS PLACE UNIQUE?

J: I REALLY DON'T KNOW. WE DEFINITELY HAVE OUR OWN CULTURE, OUR OWN LITTLE SOCIETY. BUT IT'S TOO MYOPIC, TOO MUCH TUNNEL VISION TO TELL THE BIGGER PICTURE FROM WHERE I'M STANDING.

X: FROM INSIDE THE TUNNEL.

J: WELL, I THINK OF IT AS MORE OF A DRAIN. OR, WHAT DO THEY CALL IT? A SINKHOLE. BECAUSE THAT BETTER EXPLAINS HOW EVERYONE I'D MET IN OTHER PLACES ENDED UP HERE. A DOWNWARD SPIRAL.

X: DOES THE FOCUS ON COFFEE INSTEAD OF ALCOHOL MAKE A DIFFERENCE?

J: IT MAKES A BIG DIFFERENCE TO ME. FOR ONE THING, NOBODY IS GOING TO MAKE FUN OF YOU FOR READING A BOOK IN HERE. AND NOBODY IS GOING TO ASSUME I WANT TO BE TALKED TO. AND IN A NEIGH-BORHOOD FULL OF BARS, IT'S IMPORTANT TO HAVE SOMEWHERE NON-DRINKERS AND RECOVERED ALCOHOLICS CAN GO TO. WHICH ISN'T JUST A.A., OR CHURCH, OR WHATEVER.

X: BUT YOU'RE NOT A RECOVERED ALCOHOLIC?

J: ME? NO. NEITHER. I DRINK. BUT I HATE DRUNKS. AND I TEND TO LIKE RECOVERED ALCOHOLICS. THEY HAVE THIS CERTAIN QUALITY, LIKE HARDENED AND WORN OUT YET KIND OF FRESH AND ENTHUSIASTIC IN A REALLY YOUTHFUL WAY. YOU KNOW? EXCITED TO BE LOOKING AT THINGS CLEARLY FOR THE FIRST TIME. GOOD CHESS PLAYERS.

X: THEM AND PEOPLE WHO WERE IN PRISON FOR A LONG TIME.

J: RIGHT, AND THAT'S IMPORTANT TOO. BECAUSE WHAT YOU SEE HERE, WHO YOU SEE HERE, IS NOT THE WHOLE PICTURE. BECAUSE PEOPLE GET CAUGHT UP IN THINGS, WHETHER IT'S DRINKING OR DRUGS OR FAMILY OR TRAGEDY OR WHATEVER. OR JUST, THEY GET CAUGHT UP IN THEMSELVES FOR A WHILE. IT CAN BE A GREAT THING EVEN, BUT THEY MAKE DECISIONS THAT ALTER THE COURSE OF THEIR LIFE IN MAJOR WAYS.

THAT'S LIFE. EVERYONE MAKES THOSE DECISIONS. AND LIKE ANY RISK, SOMETIMES YOU LOSE. AND SOMETIMES YOU WIN BUT YOU LOSE TRACK OF WHERE YOU'RE GOING AND WHERE YOU STARTED FROM. IT'S IMPORTANT TO HAVE SOMEWHERE PEOPLE CAN LAND, SOMETHING STABLE PEOPLE CAN COME BACK TO AND PLUG INTO. AND THE FACT IS, THEY DO COME BACK. OR AT LEAST CHECK IN FROM TIME TO TIME. AND THAT'S IMPORTANT.

X: IF THE CITY IS THE COMMUNITY'S HOUSE, WOULD THIS BE THE LIVING ROOM, KITCHEN, BEDROOM, OR BATHROOM?

J: I'D HAVE TO SAY BATHROOM.

X: YOU THINK IT'S AS PRIVATE AS A BATHROOM?

J: LET ME PUT IT THIS WAY. I REMEMBER ONE TIME, MY FRIEND THALIA CAME TO THE CAFE. WAIT, AM I ALLOWED TO SAY THIS? WELL, ONE NIGHT THALIA BROUGHT DEAN HOME WITH HER. AND WHEN THEY WERE DONE, ALL CUDDLED UP AND ABOUT TO TURN OFF THE LIGHT, HE'S LIKE, "SEE YA!"

SHE'S LIKE, "WHAT?? IT'S FOUR IN THE MORNING! GET BACK IN BED. WHERE THE HELL ARE YOU GOING?"

HE'S ALL, "HEY, THAT WAS FUN, BUT THERE'S NO POINT STICKING AROUND ALL NIGHT".

THALIA WAS DUMBFOUNDED, MORE SHOCKED THAN OFFENDED. DEAN GOT DRESSED AND CALLED A CAB. AND WHERE DO YOU THINK HE WENT? RIGHT BACK TO THE DEAD END.

21. Lincoln

X: HAVE YOU EVER PICKED UP ANYBODY AT THE DEAD END?

L: YEAH. I'VE PICKED UP ALL KINDS OF PEOPLE. LET ME THINK BACK.

OKAY, I WAS DRIVING FOR ABC CAB AT THE TIME, AND QUITE OFTEN WE WOULD GET CALLS FOR THE CAB STAND FOR THE DEAD END AND THE VULTURE BAR. IF I WAS ON THIS SIDE OF TOWN I'D GO PICK UP THE CALL, HOPING IT WOULD BE MORE FROM THE DEAD END THAN FROM THE VULTURE.

ONE TIME IT WAS A DRUNKEN GUY THAT WANDERED OVER FROM THE VULTURE INTO THE DEAD END, AND THEY HAD CALLED HIM A CAB. HE WAS SINGING OUT LOUD IN THE DEAD END. SOMETHING THAT GOT ON EVERYBODY'S NERVES.

THAT'S THE THING ABOUT CAB DRIVING: WHEN THEY DON'T WANT TO CALL THE COPS, THEY CALL A CAB DRIVER CUZ THEY JUST WANT YOU TO GET RID OF THE PERSON. WHEN I FIRST WOULD DRIVE CAB, I WOULD TAKE THOSE KIND OF CALLS. I DIDN'T KNOW YOU COULD REFUSE THOSE KIND OF CALLS, AND I WAS HALFWAY INTO JUST SEEING WHERE IT WOULD GO.

SO I PICKED UP THE GUY, AND I REMEMBER, HE LIVED NOT TOO FAR, OFF OF EAST WASHINGTON. THAT'S THE OTHER THING WEIRD ABOUT CAB DRIVING, YOU CAN REMEMBER WHERE YOU DROP PEOPLE OFF AND WHERE YOU PICK THEM UP. IF I GET SOMEONE IN MY CAB TWO TIMES, I KNOW WHERE THEY'RE GOING.

X: DO YOU EVER SEE THEM ON THE STREET LATER AND KNOW EXACTLY WHERE THEY LIVE, BUT THEY DON'T RECOGNIZE YOU?

L: SOMETIMES. I RODE THE BUS WITH THIS GUY FOR THREE MONTHS, AND HE'S LIKE, "WHERE DO I KNOW YOU FROM?"

X: YOU REMEMBER EMBARRASSING THINGS WHICH THEY DON'T REMEMBER?

L: THAT'S THE OTHER THING ABOUT DRIVING CAB. AT NIGHTTIME, WHEN I DRIVE, NINETY PERCENT OF THE PEOPLE YOU PICK UP ARE TOTALLY DRUNK. I'VE GOT TO VEER AWAY FROM THE DRUNK GUY THOUGH, BECAUSE ACTUALLY HE WAS KIND OF BORING AND I JUST TOOK HIM HOME.
  I PICKED UP THIS ONE OLDER PUNK GUY THAT WAS LIKE THE GRANDFATHER GAY GUY, AND THEN THERE'S THE YOUNGER GAY PUNKS TAKING HIM BACK, AND THEY'RE ALL KIND OF HALF IN THE BAG.

X: HALF WHAT?

L: DRUNK. HALF IN THE BAG. YOU'VE NEVER HEARD THAT?
  OKAY, THEY WENT OUT TO... NO, THAT CALL'S BORING. THEY JUST WENT BACK TO THAT GUY'S PLACE, AND THEY WERE ALL TRYING TO PICK ME UP. THAT WAS KIND OF AN UNCOMFORTABLE RIDE BECAUSE THEY WERE CATCALLING THE WHOLE WAY. CATCALLING ME.
  SO ANYHOW, THIS OTHER GUY, THIS ONE I REMEMBER FROM THE DEAD END. HE LOOKS LIKE A BLONDE SURFER GUY. I STILL HAVE HIS I.D. BACK AT MY HOUSE.

X: WHAT DO YOU MEAN?

L: WELL, HE GOT IN THE CAB, AND THIS IS LIKE FOUR IN THE MORNING. IT'S WINTERTIME, SO THE SUN IS JUST STARTING TO COME UP. AND HE GOES, "JUST GET ON THE HIGHWAY".
  THIS GUY SEEMS REALLY STRANGE TO ME. I'M GOING, "WHAT THE HELL IS UP WITH THIS GUY?"
  I SAID, "WELL, WHAT ARE YOU DOING UP HERE IF YOU LIVE THIRTY MILES SOUTH?", AND HE SAID, "WELL, I JUST SOLD A CAR".
  OF COURSE I DIDN'T BELIEVE HIM. I WAS TRYING TO GUESS IF HE HAD MONEY FOR A THIRTY MILE CAB RIDE IF I WAS GOING TO TAKE HIM THAT FAR. AND HE SAID, "ALL I GOT IS A CHECK. WE'LL WAIT TILL THE BANK OPENS. I'LL PAY YOU THEN AND I'LL BUY YOU BREAKFAST. I'VE GOT TWENTY BUCKS ON ME AT LEAST".
  I'M THINKING, "WELL THIS IS COOL BECAUSE

I GET OFF AT NINE IN THE MORNING ANYWAY. THAT'LL BE FINE".

X: HOW COULD IT BE FINE? THAT'S FIVE HOURS.

L: YOU'LL HEAR IT WHEN I GET TO THE END OF THE STORY.

SO ANYWAY, WE GO OUT THERE AND THE GUY'S TOTALLY ACTING LIKE A BIG CRACKHEAD. HE'S ACTING ALL NERVOUS AND ASKING ME ALL KINDS OF QUESTIONS LIKE, "DO CAB DRIVERS CARRY GUNS?"

AT THIS POINT I'M BEING REALLY VAGUE AND I'M REALIZING RIGHT NOW WE'RE OUT IN THE MIDDLE OF NOWHERE AND IT'S STILL KIND OF DARK. AND HE'S TRYING TO GET ME TO PULL OVER ON THE ROAD CUZ HE WANTS TO TAKE A PISS. AND I'M REALIZING, "THIS IS NOT A GOOD SITUATION".

SO THEN HE SAYS, "THERE'S A CONVENIENCE STORE COMING UP". NO, I WAS THE ONE WHO SAID, "LET'S GO THERE CUZ I WANT A LIGHTED PLACE. YOU CAN TAKE A PISS THERE".

HE GOES, "HEY MAN, CAN YOU LOAN ME FIVE BUCKS TO GET A CUP OF COFFEE?"

I SAID, "I THOUGHT YOU HAD A TWENTY", AND HE'S LIKE, "WELL, I GUESS I REALIZED I DON'T".

I SAID, "WELL, I'LL GIVE YOU FIVE BUCKS IF YOU GIVE ME YOUR I.D."

HE GOES IN THERE. AND THEN I JUST TOOK OFF. LEFT HIM OUT IN THE MIDDLE OF NOWHERE. IT WAS REALLY EARLY MORNING AND COLD OUTSIDE AND I KIND OF FELT LIKE CRAP, BUT I KIND OF FELT LIKE THE GUY WAS GOING TO ROB ME ANYWAY, SO FUCK IT.

X: HOW ABOUT AWKWARD COUPLES?

L: THE MOST AWKWARD COUPLES I WOULD PICK UP WOULD BE PEOPLE THAT HAVE JUST MET AT A CLUB AND THEY'RE GOING TO GO HAVE SEX. THEY'RE TRYING TO HAVE SEX IN THE CAB.

X: ANY FROM THE DEAD END?

L: AWKWARD COUPLES FROM THE DEAD END? MMM, NO. ACTUALLY, THE DEAD END ONLY GETS FIVE OR SIX CALLS A YEAR THAT I WOULD GO TO. THEY'RE USUALLY PUNKS, NOT GOING FAR. THEY DON'T HAVE MONEY FOR A CAB RIDE IN THE FIRST PLACE. THERE WERE SOME RAD PUNK GIRLS I WOULD PICK UP THAT I THOUGHT WERE KIND OF HOT. AND ACTUALLY, THERE WAS ONE GIRL THAT I PICKED UP FROM THE 'STRIP BAR EARLIER ON IN THE WEEK. A PUNK ROCK STRIPPER GIRL, HANGING OUT AT THE DEAD END.

THERE WASN'T ANYTHING REALLY STRANGE ABOUT THE PEOPLE I WOULD PICK UP FROM THE DEAD END. THEY WERE MOSTLY WELL-BEHAVED. NOT TOO MUCH DRAMA.

I DUNNO, WANT TO HEAR A CRAZY CAB DRIVER STORY?

X: SURE.

L: I'LL TELL YOU ABOUT THE MOST MEMORABLE ONE.

IT WAS THE THIRD WEEK ON THE JOB. I WAS DOWNTOWN AND I PICKED UP THIS GUY WHO LOOKED LIKE THE WRESTLER MACHO MAN RANDY SAVAGE, EXCEPT HE HAD BLONDE HAIR AND NOT BROWN. AND HE GETS IN MY CAR. AND HE GIVES ME A HUNDRED DOLLARS. AND HE SAYS, "I WANT TO DRIVE AROUND FOR A LITTLE".

SO I SAID, "THAT'S FINE".

HE SAID, "YOU DON'T NEED TO TURN ON YOUR METER". HE'S LIKE, "I WANT TO GO PICK UP A PROSTITUTE AND GO BUY SOME CRACK".

ON ONE HAND I WAS LIKE, THIS IS REALLY STRANGE. THIS IS TOTALLY A MOVIE OR SOMETHING. THIS IS THE TOTAL STEREOTYPICAL BAD CAB RIDE. BUT IT WAS MY THIRD WEEK ON THE JOB AND I WASN'T SURE WHERE THIS WAS GOING. SO I WAS JUST LIKE, "OKAY".

SO WE'RE DRIVING AROUND ONE OF THE SEEDIER PARTS OF SOUTH STREET, AND HE PICKS UP THIS PROSTITUTE AND BUYS SOME CRACK. HE'S LIKE, "TAKE US TO A QUIET PART OF TOWN".

I KIND OF PUT MY FOOT DOWN. I WAS LIKE, "THAT'S FINE IF YOU WANT TO GET A BLOWJOB AND YOU WANT TO SMOKE CRACK, BUT I'M NOT GONNA BE HERE WHEN YOU DO IT".

SO, ANYHOW. WE PULL OFF TO ONE OF THESE SIDESTREETS, AND I'M FEIGNING LIKE THERE'S SOMETHING THE MATTER WITH MY CAR. LOOKING AT MY ENGINE WHILE THIS IS GOING ON. THE GUY'S HOPPED UP, AND HE'S TRYING TO GET ME TO GET A BLOWJOB, AND I'M LIKE, "NO, THAT'S FINE. I DON'T REALLY WANT ONE. THAT'S NOT REALLY MY THING".

SO, WE DROP OFF THE GIRL, AND HE GIVES ME ANOTHER FIFTY BUCKS. HE'S LIKE, "I GOTTA GO HOME". AND ON THE WAY HOME HE'S TELLING ME ABOUT HIS GIRLFRIEND WHO'S A REFORMED PROSTITUTE, AND HE'S GOING THROUGH THIS MENTAL BREAKDOWN, LIKE, "WHY DO I DO THIS?" TOTALLY COMING APART AT THE SEAMS.

SO NOW I GOT A HUNDRED AND FIFTY, AND I'VE ONLY SPENT ABOUT FORTY-FIVE MINUTES WITH THIS GUY. WE'RE IN THE BACK OF HIS APARTMENT AND...

X: YOU WENT INTO HIS APARTMENT??

L: NO NO NO, I'M LIKE IN THE ALLEY BEHIND IT. HE GIVES ME THIS FIFTY TO HOLD ONTO. HE GOES, "I'M GONNA GO INSIDE. I'M GONNA GO START A FIGHT WITH MY GIRLFRIEND". HE'S WORKING IT ALL OUT IN HIS HEAD, AND HE TELLS ME, "YOU JUST WAIT RIGHT HERE, I'M GONNA BE RIGHT BACK OUT".

THE MINUTE HE WENT IN THE HOUSE, I DROVE OFF. I'M LIKE, "THIS IS TOO CRAZY. I CAN'T BELIEVE THIS IS HAPPENING. THIS IS MY THIRD WEEK ON THE JOB".

AND THEN I WAS TALKING TO OTHER CAB DRIVERS, AND THEY'RE LIKE, "MAN, I'VE NEVER HAD A CALL LIKE THAT".

22. Joseph & Chad

X: WHAT ABOUT THE SCAVENGER HUNTS?

J: I HAVEN'T DONE A SCAVENGER HUNT IN A LONG TIME. THE LAST ONE I DID, THERE WAS JUST A LITTLE TOO MUCH CONTROVERSY. THE FIRST SCAVENGER HUNT THAT I DID, WE ALMOST GOT BUSTED FOR RACKETEERING. WE WERE CHARGING PEOPLE A DOLLAR TO GET IN, THEN WE WERE SUPPOSED TO TAKE ALL THE MONEY AND GIVE IT BACK TO THE WINNER. A NON-PROFIT KIND OF THING. BUT WE ENDED UP TAKING THE MONEY AND GOING AND BUYING BEER AND GETTING DRUNK. THEN WHEN THE TIME CAME AND THE WINNER WAS CHOSEN, WE TOLD HIM WE WOULD MAIL HIM THE MONEY.

X: THERE WASN'T ANY BEER LEFT?

J: OH NO, WE DRANK THE BEER. WE NEVER PLANNED ON GIVING ANYBODY ANY MONEY. THEN ABOUT SIX MONTHS WENT BY AND THEY WERE LIKE, "WHERE'S OUR MONEY?" I JUST YELLED AT THEM. I SAID, "WASN'T IT ENOUGH THAT I HAD A SCAVENGER HUNT FOR YOU ASSHOLES?"
   SO THOSE PEOPLE DIDN'T JOIN THE SCAVENGER HUNT THE NEXT YEAR. THE NEXT YEAR I DID IT FOR FREE, BUT I STILL HAD NO PRIZE.

X: WHAT DID YOU DO WHEN EVERYBODY BROUGHT ALL THE STUFF IN?

J: MADE THEM BRING IT HOME WITH THEM. A LOT OF IT GOT LEFT AT THE CAFE.

X: LIKE WHAT STUFF?

J: I DON'T KNOW. LIKE TAXI CAB DOORS AND BOWLING BALLS AND SHOPPING CARTS AND...

C: OLD LADY WIGS.

J: STUFFED ANIMALS.

C: USED CONDOMS.

J: YEAH. STOP SIGNS.

C: YOU SHOULD HAVE SEEN THE LIST. IT'S HILARIOUS. YOU KNOW GORDY, THE OLD BUM? HE WAS ON THE LIST.

J: THERE WAS ACTUALLY A FEW PEOPLE ON THE LIST. CHESTER WAS ON THE LIST. YOUR MOM WAS ON THE LIST.

X: HOW MANY PEOPLE BROUGHT IN YOUR MOM?

J: QUITE A FEW. NOT MY MOM,"YOUR MOM". THAT WAS KIND OF A HAZE, THOUGH. I DON'T REALLY REMEMBER THE SECOND SCAVENGER HUNT TOO MUCH.
THE THIRD SCAVENGER HUNT WAS TOTALLY SET UP. ONE GROUP OF PEOPLE WERE ALREADY GOING TO WIN BECAUSE THEY AGREED THAT THEY DIDN'T WANT A PRIZE, THEY JUST WANTED TO DO IT FOR THE FUN OF IT. SO I SAID, OKAY, YOU CAN WIN.
I PRETENDED THERE WAS THIS BIG HUGE PRIZE BUT THERE REALLY WASN'T. SO ALL THESE PEOPLE JOINED IN. ABOUT TEN TEAMS AND TEN PEOPLE ON EACH TEAM. BUT THEN ALL THESE PEOPLE FOUND OUT IT WAS SET UP AND THEY GOT REALLY PISSED, BECAUSE I HAD THEM GETTING WHOLE LILAC BUSHES AND TOILETS AND REALLY HEAVY STUFF.

X: WHAT ABOUT THE BEER HUNT?

J: THAT'S ROCKY'S DEAL. I'M NOT REALLY IN THE BEER HUNT.

X: IT'S NOT AT THE CAFE TOO?

J: IT'S NOT AT THE CAFE, IT'S JUST AROUND THE CAFE, IN THE NEIGHBORHOOD. LAST YEAR WHEN ROCKY DID IT, WE JUST FOLLOWED HIM AROUND AND WATCHED HIM HIDE THE BEERS, AND THEN COLLECTED THEM ALL AND GOT DRUNK AND WENT AND LAUGHED AT HIM. AND THEN HE WOULDN'T GIVE US THE PRIZE, AND THE PRIZE WAS THIS BIG, NEW MOUNTAIN BIKE AND FIFTY BUCKS.

X: HE DIDN'T KNOW YOU WERE FOLLOWING HIM?

J: HE THOUGHT WE WERE FLYING KITES. HE DID IT DOWN BY THE RIVER AND WE WATCHED HIM DO IT BUT WE WERE PRETENDING TO FLY KITES.

X: WHAT ABOUT THE OTHER SPECIAL EVENTS YOU CLOSE THE CAFE FOR?

J: WE HARDLY EVER CLOSE THE CAFE. WE USED TO CLOSE FOR SOLSTICES, BUT NOW THE ONLY TIME WE REALLY CLOSE IS FOR THE CAFE'S BIRTHDAY PARTY, AND MY BIRTHDAY PARTY SINCE THEY'RE SO CLOSE TOGETHER. IT'S USUALLY A GOOD TIME. WE SERVE LIQUOR AND HAVE BANDS PLAY.

X: I WANTED TO ASK ABOUT THE CROSS-GENERATIONAL NATURE OF THE PLACE. I SEE YOUR MOTHER AND YOUR DAUGHTER BOTH HANGING OUT HERE.

J: WELL, MY MOM WAS DOWN HERE BEFORE I WAS. THEN I STARTED HANGING OUT DOWN HERE. AND THEN MY DAUGHTER. WHAT'S THERE TO SAY? IT'S KIND OF IRRITATING SOMETIMES.

C: SOMETIMES YOU JUST WANT TO GET AWAY FROM EVERYONE.

J: THERE'S REALLY NO WAY TO DO THAT ON THE EAST END. EVEN TO THINK THAT FOR A SECOND IS JUST RIDICULOUS.

X: DO YOU THINK THE NEIGHBORHOOD HAS CHANGED A LITTLE BIT WITH EVERYONE HAVING KIDS?

J: NAH. I THINK WE'VE ALL GOTTEN A LITTLE OLDER AND WISER, BUT I DON'T THINK IT'S CHANGED VERY MUCH. IT'S PROBABLY A LITTLE MORE KID-ORIENTED. PEOPLE DON'T CARRY GUNS AS OFTEN, COMMIT VIOLENT CRIMES AS OFTEN AS THEY WOULD.

X: HAS THE CAFE MATURED WITH AGE?

J: I WAS THINKING ABOUT THAT EARLIER TODAY, THAT'S WEIRD YOU SHOULD MENTION IT. I WAS THINKING ABOUT WHEN I WAS EIGHTEEN. LIKE, WHO ARE THOSE PEOPLE NOW? WHO'S HANGING OUT DOWNTOWN AND DRINKING UNDER THE BRIDGES? WHO'S DOING ALL THE THINGS I USED TO DO? I WANT TO MEET THESE PEOPLE. I WANT TO GO OUT AND FIND THESE EIGHTEEN-YEAR-OLD PUNK ROCK KIDS THAT ARE OUT THERE DOING WHAT I USED TO DO, AND SEE HOW THEY'RE DOING IT. SEEING IF ANYBODY IS STILL OUT THERE DOING IT. BECAUSE IT SEEMS A LOT OF TIMES LIKE THERE ISN'T. AND IT SEEMS LIKE THERE SHOULD BE.

X IF THEY'RE THE SAME AS YOU WERE THEN, MAYBE

THEY WOULD BE DOING SOMETHING COMPLETELY DIFFERENT NOW.

J: I DON'T THINK THEY'D BE DOING IT EXACTLY THE SAME. THEY MIGHT NOT BE DRINKING, OR THEY MIGHT NOT BE UNDER A BRIDGE. BUT, YOU KNOW, I WANT TO SEE IF ANYONE'S STILL OUT THERE DOING WHAT I USED TO DO WHEN I WAS A KID, OR IF THAT SPACE THAT I LEFT IS JUST EMPTY AND VOID. IF IT'S JUST A WHOLE DIFFERENT THING NOW.

C: IT ALSO DEPENDS ON HOW MUCH THE COPS CAUGHT ON TO WHAT WE WERE DOING. HAVING HUGE FIRES AND SHIT. WE USED TO GO DOWN THERE IN PACKS OF TWENTY PEOPLE, NEVER HAD ANY PROBLEMS. HAD FIRES. IT WAS FUCKING BEAUTIFUL. JOSEPH GOT ARRESTED NOT LONG AGO, JUST FOR GOING DOWN UNDER THE BRIDGE AND HAVING A BEER.

J: YEAH, I ACTUALLY WENT DOWN THERE TO JUST CHECK IT OUT AND REMINISCE. I WAS DOING LAUNDRY AND I WENT DOWN THERE. AND THE FUCKING COPS SHOWED UP AND ARRESTED ME. FOR TRESPASSING.

23. Chad

X: DO YOU WANT TO TAKE OVER FOR A FEW MINUTES AND TELL ME ABOUT BEING A BUSINESS OWNER ON THE EAST END?

C: SURE, WHY NOT? EVERYBODY, THIS IS CHAD, JOSEPH'S BROTHER, AND I JUST BOUGHT A BUSINESS CALLED THE FOOTLONG. THE EAST END IS A PLACE I GREW UP IN. MINE AND JOSEPH'S PARENTS HUNG AROUND HERE SELLING DRUGS, DOING DRUGS. OUR PARENTS AND OUR PARENTS' FRIENDS AND ALL THE OLD-TIMERS THAT USED TO BE DOWN HERE.

WHEN WE STARTED GETTING INTO BARS, THE BARS WERE FULL OF OLD-TIMERS. WELL, THEY'VE BEEN DYING OFF LIKE FUCKING RATS IN A PLAGUE BECAUSE THEY'VE BEEN DRINKING THEMSELVES TO DEATH FOR THIRTY YEARS. SO NOW THE BARS ARE FILLING UP WITH THE YOUNGER GENERATION. ME AND JOSEPH HAVE INTEGRATED A LOT OF OUR FRIENDS HERE FROM THE DOWNTOWN AREA TO SHOW THEM THAT THERE'S A REAL CITY IN THIS GOD FORSAKEN TOWN OF POLICE ENFORCEMENT AND MAJOR FUCKING CORPORATE ENTITIES.

THE EAST END, IT'S INTRA-CULTURAL. IT'S PEOPLE FROM ALL OVER. EAST AFRICANS. CUBANS. IRISH, NORWEGIAN, POLISH. NATIVE AMERICAN. PEOPLE THAT HAVE SOME IDEA OF THEIR BACK-GROUND IN HISTORY. SO IT'S BECOMING A REALLY POPULAR PLACE FOR A LOT OF ALTERNATIVE THINGS TO HAPPEN.

THEY GOT THE PANIC PUPPET THEATER HERE NOW. THERE'S THE OAK STREET CULTURAL CENTER. THE 911 ALWAYS HAS GOOD SHOWS. THE BURNING BUSH, THEY DO A LOT OF REGGAE. I OWN MY OWN BUSINESS. AND THERE'S THE DEAD END, OF COURSE, WHICH IS PRETTY FAMOUS.

BUT IT'S ONLY A TWO SQUARE BLOCK RADIUS, THIS LITTLE HUNK OF FUCKING STREET THAT KIND OF FEELS LIKE YOU'RE IN NEW YORK. LIKE A REAL CITY, WITH SOME CHARACTER. ANYTHING OUTSIDE OF THAT, I DON'T EVEN REMEMBER. I DON'T EVEN KNOW ABOUT BECAUSE I NEVER FUCKING LEAVE THE NEIGHBORHOOD. I SLEEP IN THE BASEMENT OF MY RESTAURANT. IT'S A HOT DOG STAND. IT'S THE VIENNA BEEF PLACE, ORIGINALLY STARTED IN CHICAGO AS A KOSHER HOT DOG CUZ IT'S ALL BEEF.

THEN, WHO ELSE HAS STARTED A BUSINESS DOWN HERE?

X: THERE'S BLACK CAT BOOKS.

C: YEAH, THERE'S BLACK CAT BOOKS, WHICH IS THE TOTALLY FUCKING ANARCHIST BOOKSTORE. THAT GUY EATS AT MY RESTAURANT ALL THE TIME. HE ORDERS TWO CHEESEBURGERS, AN ORDER OF FRIES. TO GO. EVERY FUCKING DAY. I KNOW ALL THESE PEOPLE'S DIETS.

X: DO THE PEOPLE FROM THE DEAD END SNEAK OVER TO YOUR PLACE TO EAT MEAT?

C: SHIT, MORE THAN HALF THE PEOPLE WHO WORK AT THE DEAD END. THEY'LL COME OVER FOR LUNCH. I GOT PEOPLE FROM THE BARK AND GRASS. A LOT OF THEM DON'T EAT MEAT BUT THEY'LL STILL EAT FISH, WHICH I THINK IS KIND OF FUNNY.

X: IS IT A NEW PERSPECTIVE ON THE NEIGHBORHOOD, OWNING A BUSINESS?

C: YEAH. IT'S A LOT MORE ANNOYING FIRST OF ALL. WHEN YOU WALK INTO THE BAR, EVERYONE'S LIKE, "HOW'S BUSINESS?", LIKE THAT'S ALL YOU ARE. I JUST GOT THE PLACE EIGHT MONTHS AGO, SO THAT'S GOING TO CHANGE. EVENTUALLY I'M JUST GONNA BE CHAD, I'M GONNA BE THE GUY I ALWAYS HAVE BEEN. I SHOULDN'T GET SO ANNOYED BECAUSE THEY'RE JUST HAPPY FOR ME, WHICH IS A COOL THING. A LOT OF THE OLD-TIMERS ARE EXCITED TO SEE SOMEONE LIKE THEM THAT'S NOT AFRAID TO SIT IN A ROOM WHERE PEOPLE ARE SMOKING WEED OR WHATEVER, AND JUST HANG OUT.

X: DO YOU SEE YOURSELF CARRYING ON A TRADITION?

C: OH, FUCK YEAH. WE'RE KEEPING IT ALIVE. THAT PARTICULAR BUSINESS HAS BEEN THERE FOR TWENTY YEARS, AND I DIDN'T WANT TO CHANGE

IT. I'D BEEN GOING THERE SINCE I WAS A KID. I DON'T REALLY LIKE THE NAME, BUT I DIDN'T EVEN WANT TO CHANGE THE NAME.

X: HOW DO YOU KNOW HOW MUCH TO CHANGE AND HOW MUCH TO STAY THE SAME IN ORDER TO KEEP THE BUSINESS GOING AND KEEP THE CULTURE GOING?

C: WELL, THE CULTURE'S ALWAYS GOING TO CHANGE. YOU WANT CHANGE. CHANGE IS HEALTHY. BUT YOU ALSO WANT A PLACE TO STAY STABLE. IT'S NOT JUST BECAUSE I CAN'T HANDLE CHANGE. SOME THINGS SHOULD CHANGE. BUT SOME THINGS SHOULD STAY THE SAME. AND I OFFER SOMETHING, SO DOES THE DEAD END, THAT YOU CAN'T GET ANYWHERE ELSE. THERE'S NO PLACE ELSE IN THIS TOWN FOR SURE.

I JUST THINK IT'S A PERFECT PLACE. IF ANYONE'S TRAVELING, THEY CAN COME TO THE EAST END BECAUSE ALL THE FREEWAY SYSTEMS ARE AROUND HERE. IT'S FAR ENOUGH AWAY FROM DOWNTOWN. THERE'S A COLLEGE CAMPUS OVER THERE. THERE'S A LOT OF SCHOOLKIDS. THERE'S A LIBRARY, ANY INFORMATION YOU NEED TO FIND. THE SQUATTING IS HORRIBLE. I SQUATTED IN THE LAST HOUSE WHICH WAS BEHIND EL GLOBULO, WHICH IS NOW THE RED CARPET. THEY'VE RIPPED DOWN ALL THE SQUATS, WHICH KIND OF BITES, I THINK. I THINK THEY SHOULD LEAVE A COUPLE ABANDONED HOUSES UP AND LET PEOPLE SQUAT THEM.

X: HOW DOES A HOT DOG STAND CONTRIBUTE TO THE NEIGHBORHOOD?

C: EVERY SINGLE ONE OF MY CUSTOMERS THAT COMES IN WHEN I OPEN AT ELEVEN IS IN A REALLY HORRIBLE, GRUMPY MOOD. AFTER THEY'RE DONE EATING, THEY'RE THANKING ME UP AND DOWN THE WALL. THEY'RE TOTALLY HAPPY, AND THAT'S THE REWARDING PART ABOUT GIVING SOMEBODY SOME-THING. IT'S LIKE MAKING MAGIC, MAN.

I MEAN, MY FOOD IS NOT THE HEALTHIEST FOOD. IT'S A SNACK PLACE. I WOULDN'T RECOMMEND EATING THERE FIVE DAYS A WEEK OR YOU'RE GONNA END UP WITH COLON CANCER OR SOME SHIT. BUT IT'S A GOOD PLACE TO GO AND HAVE A GOOD FUCKING SNACK, YOU KNOW? AND I ALSO SUPPLY THE VEGGIE-DOGS WITH ALL THE TRIMMINGS ON THEM. I GOT VEGGIE-BURGERS AND SHIT LIKE THAT....

24. Debbie

X: WHAT ORIGINALLY BROUGHT YOU TO THE CAFE?

D: I GUESS WHEN I WAS AROUND SEVENTEEN, I CAME TO THE CAFE BECAUSE I MOVED TO THOUSAND OAKS. AND I WOULD COME HERE BECAUSE ME AND MY MOM DIDN'T GET ALONG, AND IT WAS KIND OF A SMALL SPACE.

X: WHAT'S 'THOUSAND OAKS'?

D: THE HIGHRISE BUILDING ACROSS THE STREET ON OAK STREET.

X: THE PROJECTS?

D: YEAH, THE PROJECTS. THERE'S MAYBE A POPULAT-ION OF FIFTEEN THOUSAND PEOPLE THERE. IT'S NOT REALLY THAT DANGEROUS, BUT IT IS SORT OF A WEIRD PLACE. IT'S KIND OF ISOLATED. CONCRETE. STRANGE.

X: WHAT DO YOU MEAN, ISOLATED?

D: EVERY PERSON IS KIND OF ISOLATED FROM EACH OTHER. NO ONE REALLY INTERMINGLES WITHIN THE BUILDING. BASICALLY, THAT'S WHAT THE DEAD END IS FOR, IN A WAY. FOR THE PEOPLE WHO LIVE IN THE BUILDING TO COME TOGETHER AND HANG OUT. OBVIOUSLY NOT ALL FIFTEEN THOUSAND PEOPLE THAT LIVE THERE DO, BUT A LOT OF PEOPLE WHO FEEL THE NEED TO GET OUT OF THE CONFINES OF THOSE APARTMENT BUILDINGS.

X: AND OTHER KINDS OF CONFINES...

D: I WAS TALKING TO MY FRIEND NOEL, AND SHE KIND OF ENDED UP HERE FOR THE SAME REASONS I DID. BECAUSE SHE COMES FROM THIS SOMEWHAT

DYSFUNCTIONAL FAMILY, AND HER FATHER DRINKS, AND THIS IS A GOOD PLACE FOR HER TO COME AND HANG OUT, AWAY FROM HOME.

ANOTHER KID, J.J., HE WAS THROWN OUT OF HIS HOUSE. SOMETIMES PEOPLE GET DOWN ON HIM FOR NOT TRYING ENOUGH, BUT HE IS ONLY FIFTEEN, AND IT'S GOOD THAT HE HAS SOMEPLACE TO GO. AND IT'S IMPORTANT TO ME TO LOOK OUT FOR HIM AS MUCH AS I CAN. NOT DO EVERYTHING FOR HIM, BUT AT LEAST MAKE IT SO HE CAN HAVE SOME PLACE TO BE AND NOT BE ENDANGERED.

IT'S KIND OF FUNNY TO THINK WHERE THOSE PEOPLE WOULD GO IF THEY DIDN'T HAVE A DEAD END. LIKE THIS IS WHERE PEOPLE END UP IN THEIR LIVES IF THEY REALLY HAVE NOWHERE ELSE TO GO. I'VE SEEN PEOPLE ON HOLIDAYS HERE AND YOU WONDER WHY THEY'RE HERE AND NOT AT HOME, YOU KNOW?

X: IS IT STRANGE TO BE IN EVERYONE'S LIVING ROOM, AND BE IN CHARGE OF IT?

D: YEAH, CERTAINLY. YOU HAVE TO PICK AND CHOOSE WHO YOU'D LIKE TO ASSOCIATE WITH ON A PERSONAL LEVEL, AND IT GETS HARD TO MAKE THOSE KINDS OF DECISIONS. YOU HAVE TO BE FAIRLY SOCIAL AND OUTGOING BUT STILL HAVE A SORT OF STANDOFFISH PERSONALITY. A PERSONA OF BEING A STRONG PERSON. AND SOMETIMES PEOPLE THINK YOU'RE AN ASSHOLE. I HEAR THAT A LOT.

X: WHERE IS THE LINE BETWEEN YOUR PRIVATE AND PUBLIC LIFE?

D: I WAS THINKING ABOUT THAT YESTERDAY. I HANG OUT AT WORK A LOT, YOU KNOW? I'M ALWAYS HERE. THIS IS THE PLACE I HANG OUT, AND I HUNG OUT HERE BEFORE I WORKED HERE. BUT I DIDN'T KNOW MANY OF THE EMPLOYEES. I KNEW THEIR FACES, I KNEW THEIR NAMES, BUT I DIDN'T REALLY KNOW THEM AS FRIENDS OR HAVE ANY CLOSE TIES WITH THEM. SO IT WAS WEIRD TO CROSS THAT LINE MYSELF. YOU HAVE TO MAKE RESPONSIBLE DECISIONS ABOUT THAT, OTHERWISE PEOPLE GET A LITTLE WARY OF YOU.

X: RIGHT. WHAT DO YOU MEAN?

D: I REALLY SHOULDN'T BE SAYING THIS.

X: I'LL CHANGE THE NAMES.

D: WELL, PEOPLE WERE WARY ABOUT A GROUP OF PEOPLE ONE OF THE EMPLOYEES WANTED TO HANG OUT WITH, BECAUSE THEY'RE AVOWED TO BE THE

NEIGHBORHOOD CRACK DEALERS. AND THEY HAVE BEEN CONSIDERED A NUISANCE. AND IN A WAY, SHE LET THEM INTO HER PRIVATE LIFE.

YOU ALWAYS HAVE THAT FEELING OF BEING PUBLIC PROPERTY. LIKE YOU'RE NOT JUST MAKING A DECISION FOR YOURSELF, YOU'RE MAKING A DECISION FOR YOUR BUSINESS, WHO YOU CHOOSE TO ASSOCIATE WITH. YOU DON'T FEEL LIKE YOUR PRIVATE LIFE IS VERY PRIVATE. EVERYONE IN THE COLLECTIVE KNOWS WHO YOU'RE WITH AND WHO YOU'RE HANGING OUT WITH, AND HAS A SAY IN IT TO SOME EXTENT. IF YOU'RE MAKING A BAD DECISION.

X: HOW HAS BEING PART OF THE PLACE CHANGED YOUR FUTURE PLANS?

D: I THINK WORKING AT THE CAFE HAS MADE ME FEEL A LOT MORE OF A SENSE OF FREEDOM I DIDN'T HAVE BEFORE. AND A SENSE OF SECURITY THAT WASN'T THERE BEFORE. AND IT GIVES ME THE IDEA THAT I CAN BRANCH OUT MORE AND DO WHAT I WANTED TO DO. BECAUSE BEFORE I WAS WORKING FOR CORPORATIONS I DIDN'T AGREE WITH AND IT WAS TAKING A LOT OF MY ENERGY AWAY FROM THINGS I WANTED TO DO, LIKE GO TO COLLEGE.

X: ARE YOU GOING TO COLLEGE?

D: WELL, I WANT TO, DEFINITELY. IT SEEMS LIKE I HAD TO FIGURE OUT THE JOB THING FIRST. BECAUSE THAT WAS A REAL ISSUE FOR ME, BEING KIND OF DEPRESSED THAT I WAS WORKING AWAY MY LIFE AND IT WASN'T GETTING ME ANYWHERE.

X: IS IT AN EMOTIONAL, MENTAL SENSE OF FREEDOM, OR A LITERAL THING?

D: I THINK IT'S EMOTIONAL, MENTAL, AND ALSO THAT YOU'RE NOT OWNED BY THE CORPORATION OR THE BUSINESS. YOU'RE PUTTING IN ALL THIS ENERGY BECAUSE IT IS YOUR BUSINESS.

X: SO YOU ARE OWNED BY IT.

D: WE OWN IT, SO THEREFORE WE KIND OF ARE OWNED BY IT, BECAUSE IT'S OUR LIVELIHOOD.

X: OTHER JOBS YOU CAN QUIT.

D: WELL, I CERTAINLY COULDN'T LEAVE, THAT'S THE THING. WHERE WOULD I GO? I COULD QUIT, BUT NOT LEAVE.

25. Dean

X: WHERE DID YOU GO AFTER THE CAFE?

D: WELL, I WAS GOING TO KEEP TRAVELING UP THROUGH EUROPE AFTER EGYPT, BUT I WAS SO LOVESICK WITH THIS GIRL, TSHOMBE, THAT I CAME BACK. I WANTED TO GO SOMEPLACE WARM THAT WAS VAGUELY OUT OF THE COUNTRY. SO, WE MOVED TO NEW ORLEANS.

I DID A LOT OF THINGS THERE, REALLY GREAT CREATIVE THINGS, LIKE I DID A FREE PRESS, AND I STARTED DOING SPOKEN WORD PERFORMANCES.

AND THEN I STARTED DOING HEROIN. AND COCAINE.

AND THEN I MOVED BACK HERE TRYING TO GET AWAY FROM THERE. IT JUST BECAME THIS RUNNING AWAY THING. WITHIN A YEAR OF SHOOTING DOPE I ENDED UP H.I.V. POSITIVE AND IN TREATMENT.

SO I GET OUT OF TREATMENT, BUT I'M GOING TO BARS STILL, I'M DRINKING LIKE CRAZY, I HAVE NO IDEA HOW TO NOT USE AND BE HAPPY.

THE FRAIL EELS WERE GOING TO PLAY. WE WERE FRIENDS WITH THE DRUMMER, EVA, SO WE GO DOWN THERE. TSHOMBE AND ALL HER ANARCHIST AFFINITY GROUP FRIENDS ARE ALL STANDING AROUND IN THE DRESSING ROOM AND EVA PULLS OUT THIS CARMEX CONTAINER WITH A BUNCH OF CRYSTAL IN IT.

THIS IS THE DRUG THAT DROVE ME TO TREATMENT FINALLY, SO I FREAK OUT. EVERYONE'S LOOKING AT ME. I'M SLAMMING DOWN DRINKS, AND THEN I JUST LEAVE. I GO TO THE BIG CLUB NEXT DOOR. AND I JUST, I DO A LINE.

I'M ALL HIGH ON CRYSTAL. AND THIS FINNISH GIRL STARTS CHATTING ME UP. THE SINGER OF THE BAND PLAYING THAT NIGHT, WHO I'VE NEVER HEARD OF. SHE ASKS ME TO COME BACK TO HER HOTEL. WE HAD THIS THREE-DAY FLING. AND NOW

I'VE RELAPSED, SO EVERYONE'S PISSED OFF.

I DIDN'T REALLY HAVE ANYTHING GOING ON. THE WHOLE HOUSE IS FALLING DOWN AROUND ME AND SHE SENDS ME THIS TICKET TO LOS ANGELES. I'M LIKE, FUCK IT. SHUT THE DOOR, THE HOUSE COMPLETELY CRUMBLES, AND I RUN TO THE FUCKING AIRPORT. I'M OUT OF THERE. I'M LIKE, "I CAN'T BELIEVE THIS IS HAPPENING".

SO SHE FLEW ME OUT THERE, AND I GOT THE FAKE ROCKSTAR LITTLE THING GOING ON. SHE INTRODUCED ME TO ALL THESE PEOPLE. I JUST KEPT MOVING, I WAS A TOTAL PARASITE. I HAD NO HOPE. I WAS GOING OUT THERE TO DIE, BASICALLY.

X: GOOD PLACE FOR IT.

D: YEAH, REAL EASY TO. I HAD THIS GRANDIOSE VISION OF PERISHING IN LOS ANGELES. I ENDED UP TRICKING, YOU KNOW, AND DOING ALL KINDS OF DRUGS. I RAN INTO MY OLD ROOMMATE FROM NEW ORLEANS AND HE WAS WORKING FOR TIMOTHY LEARY. COME HOME AND THERE'S THIS VOICE MAIL MESSAGE, "HEY GUYS, THIS IS TIM, JUST WONDERING WHAT'S GOING ON". THE SIXTEEN YEAR OLD IN ME IS LIKE, "OH MY GOD, TIMOTHY LEARY". AND THE OTHER PART OF ME IS LIKE, "ALRIGHT, IT'S L.A., EVERYONE'S FUCKING FAMOUS".

I DON'T KNOW, WE WERE GOING TO GET MARRIED, THIS SINGER GIRL AND I. SHE WENT BACK TO FINLAND, THEN TO CHICAGO TO DO SOME RECORDING. I DROVE ALL THE WAY THERE. THE DOOR OPENS. YOU KNOW HOW IT IS WHEN YOU DRIVE ALL NIGHT, IT'S FIVE A.M. AND THE DOOR OPENS AND YOU KNOW IT'S JUST OVER. LIKE THERE'S NOTHING YOU CAN DO?

X: TOTALLY.

D: SO I TRIED TO HANG OUT. I DIDN'T REALIZE BY THIS TIME I'D GOTTEN A HEROIN HABIT. I'D MET THIS OTHER GIRL WHO I'D BEEN DOING HEROIN WITH, AND I DIDN'T REALIZE. I'D ALWAYS BEEN REAL CAREFUL AND NOT DONE IT EVERY DAY. AND I'D BEEN DOING IT EVERY DAY FOR A MONTH AND DIDN'T EVEN REALIZE IT.

SO THERE I AM WITH THIS GIRL I DON'T LOVE, KICKING. I'M COLD AND SWEATY AND SHE'S LIKE, WHAT'S GOING ON?

I'M TRYING TO ACT LIKE I'M STILL INTO THIS THING BECAUSE I REALLY WANTED TO STAY FRIENDS WITH HER BECAUSE SHE'S SO GREAT. BUT I DIDN'T WANT TO SLEEP WITH HER ANYMORE. IT WAS THE WEIRDEST THANKSGIVING I'VE EVER HAD.

I END UP THINKING I'M SUPPOSED TO TAKE CARE OF THIS JUNKIE GIRL. I STILL FELT LIKE I WAS GOING TO DIE REALLY SOON, YOU KNOW? I THOUGHT MAYBE THIS IS WHAT I'M SUPPOSED TO DO, TAKE CARE OF THIS PERSON. I ENDED UP TRYING TO GET OUT OF THAT RELATIONSHIP, I ROBBED THE FUCKING PLACE. AND THAT'S WHEN I ENDED UP IN SAN FRANCISCO.

IT WAS A PROCESS OF JUST TRYING TO GET CLEAN. I WORKED AS A YOUTH WORKER, AN HIV-STD YOUTH WORKER FOR A WHILE. AND THEN I WENT OUT AND STARTED USING AGAIN. AND THEN I GOT CLEAN, SO I WAS A NANNY FOR A YEAR AND A HALF.

I WOULD GO TO THE EAST END AND I WOULD SEE PEOPLE I KNEW, AND I WOULD BE REALLY HAPPY TO BE CLEAN. BUT MY CLOSEST FRIENDS THERE DIDN'T REALLY GET THE WHOLE THING. THEY DIDN'T REALLY KNOW THE DEAL. LIKE, "YOU CAN STILL DRINK, RIGHT? YOU CAN STILL SMOKE POT, RIGHT?" AND IT'S SO HARD, BECAUSE THESE ARE THE PEOPLE WHO DEFINED MY EXISTENCE. WE ALL HELPED EACH OTHER GROW UP. HAVING TO SAY GOODBYE TO THAT WAS REALLY, I HAD A REALLY HARD TIME DOING THAT. AND I THINK MAYBE THAT'S WHY I ALWAYS CREATED SUCH DRAMA. SO IT WAS MUCH EASIER TO LEAVE.

X: I USED TO THINK YOU WERE VERY LUCKY. YOU ARE LUCKY, BUT IT'S MADE ME RE-THINK WHAT THAT MEANS.

D: I AM LUCKY THAT I'M NOT IN PRISON AND I'M LUCKY I'M NOT DEAD. I AM.

26. Ed

X: WHAT IS THE DIFFERENCE BETWEEN THIS PLACE AND THE GENTLE FAWN, WHEN THAT WAS AROUND?

E: THE FAWN WAS NICE BECAUSE IT WAS QUIET, IT WAS LOW-KEY. I KNOW PEOPLE WHO WOULD GO OVER THERE BECAUSE IT WAS NO SMOKING. BUT OF COURSE A LOT OF PEOPLE CHOSE TO COME OVER HERE THAT COULD SMOKE HERE. THIS PLACE MAY BE A LITTLE MORE ACTIVE, A LITTLE MORE PLUGGED IN COMPARED TO THE FAWN, AND IT SEEMED LIKE THEY WOULD CATER, NOT JUST TO MORE OF A MELLOW CROWD, BUT ALSO MORE OF A MORNING AND LUNCH CROWD.

X: DID THE FAWN CLOSING AFFECT THINGS HERE?

E: OH, IT AFFECTED US BECAUSE WE GOT THEIR CUSTOMERS.

X: DID ANY OF THE COLLECTIVE MEMBERS FROM THERE COME OVER HERE?

E: YES, BUT THE PEOPLE WHO WORKED HERE WHO HAD ONCE WORKED AT THE FAWN STARTED WORKING HERE BEFORE THE FAWN CLOSED DOWN.

X: THEY HAD BEEN AROUND A LONG TIME, HADN'T THEY?

E: LIKE TWENTY PLUS YEARS.

X: DO YOU KNOW WHY THE DEAD END WAS SUCCESSFUL WHILE THEY WERE FAILING?

E: IF I REMEMBER RIGHT, THE FAWN CLOSED BECAUSE OF FINANCIAL REASONS. THE PERSON WHO HAD BEEN DOING THE BOOKS EITHER TURNED THE BOOKS OVER TO SOMEBODY ELSE, OR QUIT, AND IT JUST WENT DOWN THE TUBES. SOMEBODY MADE

SOME BAD DECISIONS, SUCH AS TAKING OUT A LOAN BECAUSE OF GOING INTO A SLOW PERIOD AND BOUNCING CHECKS. TAKING OUT A LOAN SO THEY WOULD STOP BOUNCING CHECKS AND THEN A LOAN TO PAY BACK THE LOAN. AND EVENTUALLY GOING DOWN THE TUBES.

X: HAVE YOU BEEN ABLE TO LEARN FROM THEIR MISTAKES, OR THE MISTAKES OF OTHER COLLECTIVES?

E: WHEN THE DEAD END BECAME A COLLECTIVE, A COUPLE OF THE MEMBERS WOULD ACTUALLY GO AND HANG OUT AT THE FAWN'S MEETINGS TO KIND OF LEARN HOW A COLLECTIVE WORKS.

X: OR DOESN'T WORK.

E: YES. AND IF I REMEMBER RIGHT, THE FAWN WAS VERY SUPPORTIVE.

X: WHAT ABOUT YOUR RELATIONSHIP WITH THREE RIVERS CO-OP AND THE OAK STREET CULTURAL CENTER?

E: WE'RE PRETTY MUCH CATERING. THE OAK STREET CULTURAL CENTER, WE SUPPLY THEM WITH COOKIES, AND, UM, BROWNIES. MAYBE EVEN MUFFINS, I'M NOT SURE. AND THE CO-OP, IT'S A LITTLE MORE THAN THAT. WE ALSO SUPPLY THEM WITH WHOLE SALADS, OR PASTA SALADS, MAYBE EVEN SOUP.

X: HOW ARE THINGS WITH THE LANDLORD?

E: HE'S SUPPORTIVE. WE'RE ON GOOD TERMS WITH HIM, FOR THE MOST PART.

X: DO YOU SEE A DISTANT FUTURE WITH THESE PEOPLE? DO YOU PLAN ON GETTING OLD TOGETHER?

E: IF ANYBODY DOES, I DON'T BELIEVE WE REALLY DISCUSS IT.

X: WHAT ABOUT THE NAME? IS IT A SELF-FULFILLING PROPHESY?

E: I DON'T KNOW, PROBABLY. I ALWAYS REFER TO THIS PLACE AS "THE BITTER END".

27. Nathan

X: WHAT HAPPENS WHEN A NEWER, YOUNGER, LOUDER PLACE MOVES INTO THE NEIGHBORHOOD AND YOU BECOME "THE ESTABLISHMENT"? WHEN THE DEAD END BECOMES THE STATUS QUO?

N: I SEE WHAT YOU'RE SAYING. JUST BECAUSE, BEING PART OF A GROUP, YOU HAVE TO MAKE COMPROMISES WITHIN THE GROUP. BUT THEN TO MAKE COMPROMISES WITH THE CITY AND MAKE COMPROMISES WITH THE NEIGHBORHOOD ACCELERATES THAT. BUT AS YOU GET OLDER, IT PROBABLY NATURALLY COMES.

THAT'S THE WEIRD THING, BECAUSE IT WOULD BE BETTER OFF IF IT WEREN'T AN OFFICIAL BUSINESS AND YOU DIDN'T HAVE TO ABIDE BY SO MANY RULES. IF IT WAS JUST SET UP AT A SQUAT, THOUGH YOU'D HAVE TO BE MORE CAREFUL ABOUT SOME THINGS, YOU'D BE MORE FREE IN A LOT OF WAYS.

I DON'T KNOW, IT IS A COMPROMISE. BECAUSE, I GO TO THE BUSINESS MEETINGS, AND THE POLICE ARE THERE. HOW WOULD IT LOOK IF I GOT CAUGHT SPRAYPAINTING SOMEWHERE? YOU KNOW, I NEVER SPRAYPAINT ON THE EAST END, WHY SHIT IN YOUR OWN BACKYARD? BUT SAY I GOT ARRESTED FOR SPRAYPAINTING DOWNTOWN. WHAT CAN I SAY WHEN THEY BITCH ABOUT GRAFFITI AND TRY TO BLAME GRAFFITI ON THE DEAD END?

28. Beth

X: HOW MUCH WOULD THE CAFE CHANGE JUST TO SURVIVE?

B: LIKE WHAT KIND OF CHANGE?

X: IF THERE WAS A DROP IN BUSINESS, WOULD YOU CHANGE IN ORDER TO ATTRACT NEW CUSTOMERS?

B: I'D LIKE TO SEE THAT HAPPEN. BECAUSE IT'S IMPORTANT FOR US TO KEEP THIS PLACE OPEN. BUT THERE'S A LOT OF HARDHEADS HERE AND I DON'T KNOW IF IT WOULD BE POSSIBLE TO CHANGE. PEOPLE ARE PRETTY STUBBORN AND THEY ARE STUCK IN THE WAY THIS PLACE IS RUNNING RIGHT NOW.

WE'VE TRIED ALL SORTS OF STUFF, LIKE KEEPING THINGS A LITTLE CLEANER, OR HAVING DIFFERENT KINDS OF ARTWORK UP. THE MUSIC, THERE'S ALWAYS BEEN FIGHTS ABOUT THAT. BUT THERE ARE SO MANY HARDHEADS THAT I REALLY DON'T THINK WE ARE ABLE TO CHANGE, AS MUCH AS I WOULD LIKE TO AND OTHER PEOPLE WOULD LIKE TO. EVERYBODY'S GOT DIFFERENT IDEAS OF WHAT THEY WANT TO CHANGE.

LIKE LAST SUMMER, WE WERE HAVING REALLY BAD BUSINESS. INSTEAD OF CHANGING THE ATMOS-PHERE, WE STARTED WHOLESALING FOODS. WE'VE EXPANDED THE KITCHEN SO WE'RE NOT GETTING MUCH MORE BUSINESS AT THE COUNTER, BUT WE'RE SELLING MORE OF OUR FOOD OUTSIDE OF HERE. SO WE'RE GETTING MORE BUSINESS, BUT IT'S A DIFFERENT KIND OF BUSINESS.

X: HOW HAS BEING INVOLVED WITH THE CAFE CHANGED YOU?

B: I DON'T FEEL SO TIED DOWN. I'M NOT SO STRESSED OUT, LIKE, "I HAVE TO GO TO WORK EVERY DAY AND I HAVE TO MAKE MONEY SO I CAN LIVE". IF I DON'T HAVE A PLACE TO LIVE I CAN COME AND STAY HERE, YOU KNOW? IT REALLY IS A COMFORT BLANKET FOR ME.

29. Spit

X: DO YOU SEE A LONGTERM FUTURE HERE?

S: PERSONALLY, I PLAN ON STAYING. I'M REALLY A RAMBLING MAN. BORN UNDER A WANDERING STAR. I'VE JUMPED AROUND FROM JOB TO JOB, STATE TO STATE ALL AROUND...

X: DIDN'T YOU TELL ME YOU WERE A LUMBERJACK FOR TEN YEARS?

S: YEAH.

X: THAT DOESN'T SOUND VERY RAMBLING.

S: WELL, NOT WORKING FOR THE SAME GUY. I NEVER HELD THE SAME JOB FOR MORE THAN FOUR OR FIVE MONTHS. BUT I ALWAYS STAYED IN THE WOODS. IT WAS WHAT MY DAD DID AND HE TAUGHT ME HOW TO DO IT. AND I MISS THE WOODS, I MISS THE OUTDOORS. ANIMALS AND TREES. NOW WHENEVER I GO BACK IT'S LIKE A GIANT REPRIEVE. LIKE GETTING OUT OF JAIL.

X: WHAT ABOUT THE FOCUS HERE ON VEGETARIAN AND HEALTHY FOOD?

S: I APPRECIATE THAT A LOT. HEALTHY EATING. AND HAVING A CHANCE TO COOK HERE WHERE IT'S ALL VEGETARIAN, IT'S NICE.

X: SO IT SEEMS STRANGE THAT WHENEVER THE PLACE IS CLOSED, ALL OF YOU HAVE DEER OR GOATS ROASTING IN THE KITCHEN. ARE YOU ONLY VEGETARIANS DURING BUSINESS HOURS?

S: WELL, WE TRY TO KEEP OUR CUSTOMERS HEALTHY. I LOVE MEAT, MYSELF. I WAS RAISED ON IT. WE HAD MEAT THREE MEALS A DAY.

X: IT SEEMS LIKE MOST OF THE PEOPLE WORKING HERE AREN'T VEGETARIANS.

S: YEAH, IT'S KIND OF ODD. WE HAVE A FEW WORKERS

WHO ARE VEGETARIAN, AND VEGAN TOO. I THINK THERE'S TWO VEGANS STILL.

X: HOW MANY COLLECTIVE MEMBERS ARE THERE?

S: I'M NOT EVEN SURE. WE'RE UP TO SIXTEEN OR SEVENTEEN NOW. SOMETHING IN THAT RANGE.

X: WANT TO TALK ABOUT SOME OF THE DIFFERENT SPECIES YOU'VE ROASTED UP IN THE KITCHEN?

S: UH, VENISON, GOAT, SOMEONE HAD A DUCK IN HERE ONCE. I'M ALWAYS BRINGING IN BACON. OF COURSE, I DON'T LIKE SWINE THAT MUCH...

ED: I COOKED UP A DRAGON ONCE.

S: YOU LIE. WHERE'D YOU GET A DRAGON, THE SHORE-LINE ZOO?

X: EVERYONE HAS TALKED ABOUT HOW THIS IS SOMEWHERE WHERE DIFFERENT CULTURES AND DIFFERENT UP-BRINGINGS CAN COME TOGETHER, BUT I THINK ONCE IT'S COME TOGETHER, IT'S MAKING SOMETHING ELSE. IT'S NOT JUST OIL AND WATER.

S: IT'S ALMOST A NEW CULTURE BORN BY THE MIXING OF THE CULTURES. WE'VE GOT OUR OWN LITTLE EAST END CULTURE GOING HERE. IT SEEMS INTERNATIONAL, BUT IT'S ALSO HOMEY. THERE'S A HOMETOWN FEELING. I CAN WALK AROUND THE BLOCKS AND SAY HELLO TO ALL THESE DIFFERENT PEOPLE I KNOW PERSONALLY.

X: HOW FAR DOES IT GO? THREE BLOCKS?

S: MAYBE SIX. THEN I GO DOWN TO MY NEIGHBORHOOD, I LIVE IN THE AVENUES. I DON'T HARDLY KNOW ANYONE DOWN THERE, JUST A FEW OF MY CLOSE NEIGHBORS.

X: DOES BEING AROUND PEOPLE SO MUCH HERE MAKE YOU BETTER AT DEALING WITH PEOPLE? OR MAKE YOU WANT TO BE AROUND PEOPLE LESS?

S: NO, MY COMMUNICATION SKILLS HAVE REALLY GROWN. I USED TO BE VERY ANTI-SOCIAL. WELL, I STILL AM, I JUST DON'T SEE HOW I FIT IN HERE. MAYBE CUZ WE'RE ALL A BUNCH OF MISFITS. EVERYBODY ELSE IS ANTI-SOCIAL TOO. WE ALL GET TOGETHER AND HATE EVERYONE IN UNISON.

30. Nathan

X: WHAT CAN'T BE CHANGED, CAN'T BE COMPROMISED?

N: I THOUGHT WE SHOULD STILL BE OPEN TWENTY FOUR HOURS, AND THAT'S ALREADY BEEN CHANGED. THAT'S THE PROBLEM WITH THE GROUP. IF IT'S A DEMOCRATIC GROUP YOU REACH THE LOWEST COMMON DENOMINATOR GENERALLY. DEMOCRACY CAN ONLY REACH AVERAGE, OR SO IT SEEMS. RIGHT NOW IT'S AT A STANDSTILL. MEETINGS DON'T REALLY HAPPEN VERY WELL, AND IF THEY DO THEY DON'T REALLY ACCOMPLISH ANYTHING THAT MATTERS BECAUSE PEOPLE ARE TOO SCATTERED IN WHICH DIRECTION THEY'RE GOING FOR. SO YOU'RE PULLING AND PUSHING EACH OTHER. IT'S AT A STANDSTILL RIGHT NOW. IT HAS BEEN FOR A WHILE.

X: DO THINGS HAVE TO BE MOVING IN A DIRECTION TO BE RELEVANT? YOU DON'T WANT TO BE STRUGGLING ALL THE TIME.

N: IT SEEMS TO ME THAT IT WOULD BE BETTER TO BE FIGHTING MORE, BECAUSE THEN YOU WOULD HAVE A FOCUS. IF YOU HAVE A COMMON ENEMY, THAT PROMOTES UNITY, ANYWAY, AMONG PEOPLE THAT HATE EACH OTHER.

X: UNITY IS NOT NECESSARILY THE GREATEST THING.

N: NO. IT WOULD MAKE THINGS EASIER THOUGH. YOU CAN'T DO ANYTHING BECAUSE PEOPLE ARE NEVER GONNA AGREE. IF YOU HAVE TWO PEOPLE IN A GROUP YOU'RE GONNA DISAGREE. IF YOU HAVE THIRTEEN PEOPLE YOU'RE GONNA DISAGREE A LOT MORE.

X: I'D CHALLENGE THAT. IF YOU HAVE TWO PEOPLE YOU'LL DISAGREE, AND THIRTEEN YOU'LL BE ABLE TO FIND MORE OF A COMMON GROUND, OR YOU'LL BE ABLE TO COMPROMISE MORE.

N: OR YOU'LL GET FRUSTRATED AND SKIP THAT.

X: NOT THAT THERE'S ANYTHING WRONG WITH LOOKING AT THE NEGATIVE ASPECT OF THINGS, BUT I'M SEEING SOMETHING A LITTLE DIFFERENT.

N: NO, IT'S NOT ALL NEGATIVE. BUT WHEN YOU'RE IN THE THICK OF IT, BECAUSE YOU LOOK AT THE POTENTIAL, AND THEN LOOK AT WHAT YOU HAVE, AND TRYING TO SOLVE PROBLEMS, HOWEVER BIG OR SMALL, IF YOU FOCUS ON THE PROBLEM IT'S GOING TO COME ACROSS AS NEGATIVE ANYWAY. BUT REALLY I THINK I'M MORE POSITIVE, BUT IT COMES ACROSS AS NEGATIVE BECAUSE YOU SEE WHAT IT COULD BE. AND THE GAP IN BETWEEN WHAT IT COULD BE AND WHAT I WANT IT TO BE.

X: SORRY, BUT I SEE THE PROBLEM SOLVING AS A POSITIVE THING TOO.

N: IT IS A POSITIVE THING.

X: BUT WHAT DO YOU WANT THE PLACE TO BE?

N: WELL, FOR ONE, IT SHOULD BE AN EXAMPLE. WHEN WE USED TO ADVERTISE, EVERYTHING SAID, "WORKER OWNED", "WORKER MANAGED", "COLLECTIVE", WHATEVER, WHICH COULD SHOW PEOPLE THERE'S A BETTER WAY, OR A DIFFERENT WAY, ANYWAY. SO PEOPLE COULD LOOK AT THAT AS AN EXAMPLE, AND THAT IN AND OF ITSELF WOULD BE HELPING PEOPLE.

X: HOW LONG WILL YOU KEEP STRUGGLING?

N: I LOOK AT IT LIKE, IS THAT HEAVEN OR IS THAT HELL? BECAUSE, DO I WANT TO BE WORKING HERE WHEN I'M FORTY THREE?

X: DO YOU?

N: YEAH, PROBABLY. SEE, WHEN I STARTED WORKING HERE, WHEN I APPLIED HERE, IT WAS LIKE THE END OF THE LINE. LIKE WHERE ELSE WOULD I WANT TO WORK IN THIS CITY? AND I'D LOOK AT THIS CITY LIKE ANY OTHER CITY IN THE WHOLE COUNTRY. THIS WAS THE ONLY PLACE I COULD THINK OF THAT I EVEN HAD THE SLIGHTEST DESIRE TO WORK AT. BUT, BECAUSE I SAT BACK THERE AND DRANK BEER ALL NIGHT, AND WE TRIED TO MAKE IT A TRADE OFF, TO HELP CLEAN AND HELP OUT A LITTLE BIT TO MAKE UP FOR THE NUISANCE THAT WE WERE. KIND OF A TRADE OFF. I THINK THAT WE GOT THE BETTER SIDE OF THE DEAL, BUT WHATEVER.

BECAUSE OF THE DRINKING, THERE WAS A LOT OF HESITATION TO EVEN GIVE ME A CHANCE. BUT I QUIT DRINKING RIGHT AFTER THAT. I REALIZED I HADN'T EVEN DRUNK A BEER IN LIKE A WEEK. IT KIND OF FREAKED ME OUT. BUT THEN I DIDN'T REALLY HAVE THAT MUCH DESIRE TO DRINK.

31. Rex

X: WHAT'S YOUR ROLE AT THE CAFE?

R: I FILL IN FOR PEOPLE NOW. I GAVE UP MY COLLECTIVE MEMBERSHIP. VOLUNTARILY. BECAUSE I REALLY, REALLY GOT SICK OF THE PLACE. I GOT SICK OF THE CUSTOMERS. AT THAT POINT, STANDING BEHIND THE COUNTER, I PLANNED OUT HOW I COULD KILL EVERYONE IN THE CAFE.

X: HOW WAS THAT?

R: WELL, IT WAS KIND OF FUNNY. I HAD THREE DIFFERENT WAYS, AND THEY WERE ALL REALLY COOL. AFTER I QUIT, AFTER I GAVE UP MY COLLECTIVE MEMBERSHIP AND QUIT, THEY ASKED ME BACK TO ONE OF THE COLLECTIVE MEETINGS TO FIND OUT WHY.

    I WAS LIKE, "WELL, IF YOU UNDERSTOOD THAT WHEN I WORK, ALL I WANT TO DO IS PUT A BAR ON THE BAR".

    PEOPLE LOOKED AT ME AND WENT, "WHAT?"

    I'M LIKE, "DO YOU KNOW WHAT A B-A-R IS? IT'S A BROWNING AUTOMATIC RIFLE. IT'S A THIRTY CALIBRE BELT-FED MACHINE GUN ON A BI-POD, AND I COULD SLAP IT ON THE COUNTER AND START IN ONE CORNER OF THE CAFE. START IN THE NO SMOKING SECTION AND JUST GO BRU-B-B-B-B-B-B-B-B".

    BUT THEN I THOUGHT, "TOO MUCH OF A MESS. I'M GONNA HAVE TO CLEAN IT UP".

    ONE OF MY OTHER IDEAS WAS HAVING A BOX OF HAND GRENADES. AND A BOTTLE OF SUPERGLUE. AND WHEN IDIOTS ASK ME FOR TO GO CUPS OF COFFEE, INSTEAD OF TO GO CUPS I COULD JUST PULL THE PIN, HOLD THE HANDLE OF THE HAND GRENADE, PUT SUPERGLUE ON ONE EDGE, SLAP IT INTO THEIR HAND, AND TAKE THE PIN WITH ME. AND DROP BEHIND THE COUNTER. THE COUNTER IS ACTUALLY THICK ENOUGH

TO DEAL WITH A GRENADE EXPLOSION. OH YES IT IS. IT WOULD DEAL WITH IT.

X: THAT'S TWO.

R: THE THIRD IS, BOUNCING BETTIES AND TOE POPPERS.

X: WHICH ARE?

R: MINES. LITTLE TINY MINES. I WANTED TO PUT THEM UNDER THE FLOOR TILES IN THE DINING ROOM.
EVERYONE AT THE MEETING WAS LIKE, "OKAY, WELL MAYBE YOU DO NEED SOME TIME OFF."

X: BUT YOU CAME BACK.

R: YEAH, I CAME BACK. I'VE COME BACK TWICE. I'VE QUIT TWICE AND COME BACK TWICE.

X: WHY?

R: BECAUSE I DON'T WANT TO SEE THE PLACE DIE.

32. Nathan

X: BEING BEHIND THE COUNTER, DO YOU WITNESS THINGS LIKE CASES OF MISTAKEN IDENTITY, OR AWKWARD DATES, OR PARENT AND CHILD REUNIONS?

N: ONE THAT COMES TO MIND IS THIS LADY WHO I THINK WAS STRUNG OUT ON CRACK. YOU SAW HER DETERIORATING RAPIDLY. BUT SHE HAD A GOOD HEART, SHE WAS A NICE LADY, YOU FELT LIKE TRYING TO HELP HER AND BE PATIENT WITH HER. AND SHE WAS GETTING WORSE AND WORSE, TO THE POINT OF BEING SUPER DEPRESSING. THEN ONE DAY HER DAUGHTER SHOWED UP. SHE LOOKED LIKE SHE WAS TWENTY YEARS OLD, AND CLEAN. PREPPY, A LITTLE. SHE LOOKED LIKE SHE CAME FROM THE UNIVERSITY OR SOMETHING, AND SHE CAME SEARCHING FOR HER MOM TO SAVE HER.

X: WHAT ABOUT PEOPLE EMBARRASSING THEMSELVES? FALLING ON THEIR FACE, SAYING THE WRONG THING, DOING THE WRONG THING?

N: OH, THERE'S ONE GUY WHO LOOKED, NOT LIKE A TROLL, BUT SIMILAR TO A TROLL.

X: NOT UNLIKE A TROLL.

N: YEAH, HE LOOKED LIKE HE LIVED IN THE WOODS, I DON'T EVEN THINK HE HAD A TENT OR ANYTHING. THEN HE'D CRASH WITH HIS FRIENDS WHEN HE CAME TO THE CITY. BUT HE CAME IN HERE, AND HE'D BE SO DRUNK OR HIGH OR WHATEVER. HE CAME IN HERE AND PASSED OUT IN THE FREE BOX.

WE WERE ALL LIKE, "IT'S MORE TROUBLE THAN IT'S WORTH TO DEAL WITH. HE'S A NICE GUY, LET'S JUST IGNORE HIM". WE PUT SOME SHIRTS ON TOP SO HE WASN'T SO NOTICEABLE.

AND THEN HE GETS UP, HE SUDDENLY JERKS UP.

AND HE JUST STARTS PEEING IN THE CORNER IN THE FREE BOX. I'M ABSOLUTELY POSITIVE THAT HE THOUGHT HE WAS IN THE WOODS. HE PROBABLY EVEN SAW TREES, YOU KNOW? HE DIDN'T REALIZE FOR A FEW MINUTES THAT HE WAS IN A WELL-LIT PLACE WITH PEOPLE EATING FOOD.

BUT HE ACTUALLY MOPPED IT ALL UP, EVEN THOUGH HE DIDN'T SEEM TOO CLEAR ON WHAT HE DID. I IMAGINE THAT WAS EMBARRASSING.

ONE TIME DOWNTOWN STANDING AROUND AGAIN ED CAME UP TO ME AND HE GOES, "UH, UM, UM, UM, I THINK UH, UM, SOMEONE'S UH, JACKING OFF IN THE DINING ROOM."

I LOOKED AT THE GUY. HE LOOKED LIKE THE KIND OF PERSON WHO WOULD BE JACKING OFF IN THE DINING ROOM. HE LOOKED SWEATY AND KIND OF LITTLE AND OUT OF BREATH. HE HAD ON A JACKET WITH NO SHIRT AND HE JUST LOOKED REALLY OUT OF PLACE NO MATTER WHERE HE WOULD BE.

I WENT AND LOOKED AT HIM, AND YOU COULDN'T TELL. SO I LOOKED UNDER THE TABLE, AND SURE ENOUGH, HE WAS.

SO I SAID, "PUT THAT THING AWAY! WHAT DO YOU THINK YOU'RE DOING?"

HE SORT OF CHUCKLED AND PANTED AND PUT IT AWAY AND LEFT WITHOUT TOO MUCH ARGUMENT. THEN I APOLOGIZED TO THE GIRLS SITTING AT THE TABLES NEXT TO HIM, AND THEY SAID, "FOR WHAT?" THEY WERE TOTALLY OBLIVIOUS.

THEN HE COMES BACK THE NEXT NIGHT. I SAW HIM COMING ACROSS THE STREET, SO I HEADED HIM OFF AT THE DOOR. HE'S LIKE, "ARE YOU OPEN?"

I SAID, "NOT FOR YOU. IF PEE WEE HERMAN CAN'T DO IT, NEITHER CAN YOU."

AND HE JUST LAUGHED AND WENT ON HIS MERRY WAY. BUT THAT WAS EMBARRASSING. FOR ME.

X: WHAT ABOUT CHANGE SCAMS? PEOPLE COME IN AND TRY TO PULL THOSE?

N: THEY USED TO TRY. "COULD I GET CHANGE FOR THIS?" AND THEY GIVE YOU A TWENTY. YOU GIVE THEM ONES AND THEY'D ASK FOR QUARTERS AND THEN BE LIKE, "I THOUGHT I GAVE YOU A ONE." THEN "GIVE ME BACK THAT" THEN "GIVE ME THIS". THEN TRY TO WALK OUT WITH ALL THE MONEY.

OR THERE'S PEOPLE WHO CUT OFF THE ENDS OF TWENTIES AND TAPE THEM ON ONES. AND WE'VE HAD A FEW ACTUAL COUNTERFEIT BILLS. AT LEAST THAT'S WHAT THE BANK SAID. BUT MAYBE THE BANK IS JUST

RIPPING US OFF.

I DON'T KNOW IF IT WAS THE PRESIDENT OF THE BANK OR THE OWNER, BUT ONE OF THEM GOT EXTREMELY OFFENDED. HE CAME IN HERE ONE DAY AND STARTED SCREAMING, I THINK AT GARY, BECAUSE SOMEONE OUTSIDE ASKED HIM IF HE HAD A QUARTER. YOU KNOW, THE PRESIDENT OF THE BANK GETS OFFENDED THAT SOMEONE ON A PUBLIC STREET ASKS HIM FOR A QUARTER IN A NEIGHBORHOOD WHICH IS NOTORIOUS FOR THAT. AND SOMEHOW, IT'S OUR FAULT FOR SURE.

X: ANYTHING HERE THAT'S REALLY OBVIOUS BUT IT TOOK YOU TWO OR THREE YEARS TO NOTICE?

N: I DON'T KNOW IF IT'S BEEN OBVIOUS. MOSTLY IT'S INVOLVED BREAKING THINGS. LIKE I WAS DEMON- STRATING TO SOMEONE WHY THE RECYCLING BIN SHOULDN'T BE NEAR THE HOT WATER PIPE. I SHOWED HER, IT KNOCKS OVER THE WATER FILTER WHICH BANGS ON THE PIPE. THE THIRD TIME I BANGED ON THE PIPE, IT BROKE. I HAD TO CRAWL THROUGH THE CRAWLSPACE THAT GOES ALL THE WAY UNDERNEATH THE CAFE. I LEARNED A LOT ABOUT THE STRUCTURE OF THE BUILDING JUST DOING THAT.

AND YOU KNOW HOW YOU SAY THINGS AT THE HEAT OF THE MOMENT? OR SAY THINGS YOU MEAN AT THE TIME BUT ONLY TEN MINUTES LATER YOU WOULDN'T MEAN? BUT THEN PEOPLE TELL YOU YOU'RE A HYPOCRITE, OR YOU DON'T FOLLOW THROUGH ON WHAT YOU SAY?

ANYWAY, I SAID SOMETHING ABOUT HOW I WAS GOING TO SMASH THE ESPRESSO MACHINE. SO I FELT COERCED INTO DOING IT, BECAUSE I SAID IT. YOU KNOW. AND I REGRETTED IT AS I PUSHED IT. I THINK A LOT OF THE PEOPLE WHO ARE NEW HERE DON'T REALIZE IT'S A FIVE THOUSAND DOLLAR MACHINE, AND WHAT I WAS ATTEMPTING WAS BASICALLY ATTEMPTED MURDER TO THE CAFE. BECAUSE I KNOW FOR A FACT THAT THE CAFE COULDN'T AFFORD TO BUY ANOTHER.

SO I PUSHED IT. BUT I REGRETTED IT AS IT FELL, AND, YOU KNOW, WATER STARTED SHOOTING OUT OF IT.

IT DIDN'T ACTUALLY BREAK, BUT I FELT BAD. SO I CALLED THE COFFEE PEOPLE AND TOLD THEM THAT I HAD JUST THROWN THE MACHINE ON THE FLOOR. THE GUY CAME OUT. BUT I LEARNED ALL KINDS OF THINGS ABOUT THE INSIDE OF THE MACHINE THROUGH THAT. AND THE REPAIR GUY, THE NEXT TIME HE NEEDED TO FIX SOMETHING, HE ASKED WHEN I WAS WORKING, BECAUSE HE WANTED TO COME WHILE I WAS WORKING. FOR SOME REASON, HE LIKED ME.

I'VE BROKEN A LOT OF THINGS HERE. WE USED TO HAVE A BIG AQUARIUM. I PUT MY FOOT THROUGH IT BECAUSE I WAS TIRED OF CLEANING IT MYSELF AND IT DIDN'T SEEM LIKE ANYONE ELSE WAS GONNA CLEAN IT. IT JUST LOOKED DISGUSTING, AND IT WAS RIGHT NEXT TO WHERE YOU GET YOUR FOOD.

X: THERE WEREN'T FISH IN IT?

N: THERE WAS A COUPLE.

X: YOU PUT YOUR FOOT THROUGH IT WITH THE FISH STILL IN THERE??

N: I TRIED TO SAVE THE FISH. BUT THAT WAS A FUTILE EFFORT. AND I FELT BAD ABOUT THAT.
BUT SEE, THE THING WAS, I'D SOLVED THE PROBLEM OF THE AQUARIUM NOT BEING CLEAN. YOU KNOW? I'D SOLVED THE PROBLEM. AND THE ESPRESSO MACHINE, I LEARNED FROM THAT. AND THE PIPE BEING BROKEN? NOW THE PIPE IS NEW, AND IT'S BETTER THAN IT WAS.

X: SO WHAT IS THE LESSON TO BE LEARNED? SMASH EVERYTHING?

N: WELL, YOU LEARN FROM YOUR MISTAKES. I THINK.

33. Joseph

X: WHAT IS EACH PERSON'S RESPONSIBILITY TO THE FAMILY, OR THE NEIGHBORHOOD, OR THE COMMUNITY?

J: JUST TO TAKE CARE OF EACH OTHER. TO LOOK OUT FOR AND TAKE CARE OF EACH OTHER. LIKE IF MY BROTHER COMES UP TO ME AND SAYS, "HEY BRO, GOT A COUPLE BUCKS SO I CAN GO TO THE BAR?", I'LL GIVE HIM A TEN DOLLAR BILL AND I DON'T THINK TWICE. I'LL SAY, "HEY BRO, YOU GOT A COUPLE BUCKS SO I CAN GET SOMETHING TO EAT?" AND HE SAYS, "OH, COME DOWN TO MY RESTAURANT" AND HE FEEDS ME TIL I PUKE.

WE JUST TAKE CARE OF EACH OTHER. AND WE DO THINGS, LIKE I SAID, THAT I DON'T REALLY WANT TO PUT ON TAPE, BUT WE DO THINGS TO TAKE CARE OF EACH OTHER AND TO MAKE SURE THAT EVERYBODY ALWAYS HAS A HOME, FOOD, WHATEVER THEY NEED. CIGARETTES. OR JUST A FEELING OF SAFETY, A FEELING OF WELL-BEING. IT'S LIKE THE INNER-CITY WALTONS ON DRUGS.

X: BUT PEOPLE NEED MORE THAN JUST FOOD AND A ROOF OVER THEIR HEADS. THEY NEED TO BE INTELLECTUALLY STIMULATED, THEY NEED A CREATIVE OUTLET, THEY NEED TO BE EXPOSED TO NEW IDEAS.

J: THERE'S SOME THINGS LIKE THAT AROUND HERE. THERE'S THE EAST END SCHOOL OF ART...

X: I THINK THIS PLACE IS LIKE THAT.

J: YOU THINK THIS PLACE IS LIKE THAT?? YEAH, I SUPPOSE, IN A WAY IT IS. PEOPLE DO MEET OTHER PEOPLE HERE AND EXCHANGE CREATIVE IDEAS OR COMBINE CREATIVE IDEAS. I'VE SEEN PEOPLE MEET HERE AND A YEAR DOWN THE ROAD THEIR PARTNERSHIP HAS FLOURISHED

INTO SOMETHING INCREDIBLY COOL, WHETHER IT BE A PERSONAL RELATIONSHIP, A BUSINESS RELATIONSHIP, OR AN ARTISTIC RELATIONSHIP. PEOPLE DO MEET EACH OTHER HERE, PEOPLE COME IN HERE AND THEY PAINT OR THEY DRAW OR THEY WRITE OR THEY TAKE PHOTOGRAPHS. PEOPLE EVEN FILM MOVIES HERE. THERE'S BEEN THREE OR FOUR MOVIES THAT HAVE BEEN FILMED HERE. WEIRD PEOPLE COME IN WITH CAMERAS ALL THE TIME FILMING SHIT. I DON'T BUG THEM.

X: THAT'S AN UNWRITTEN RULE SOME PLACES, NO PHOTOGRAPHS.

J: I THINK IT'S KIND OF FUNNY SOMETIMES, THESE PEOPLE COME IN WITH CAMERAS AND START SNAPPING PICTURES AND PEOPLE GET UP AND KICK THEIR ASSES. I JUST KIND OF SIT BACK AND WATCH IT.

X: ABOUT PEOPLE MEETING HERE, DO YOU SEE...

J: I'VE SEEN PEOPLE TRY TO FUCK IN HERE. RIGHT ON THE TABLES IN THE DINING ROOM. CUSTOMERS. AT FOUR IN THE MORNING, THEY'RE LIKE RIPPING EACH OTHER'S CLOTHES OFF, READY TO GO AT IT. I TOLD THEM, "GO IN THE BATHROOM, MAN. WHAT, DO YOU WANT US TO WATCH?"

X: IS IT WEIRD TO SEE PEOPLE SHOW UP NEW AND MEET PEOPLE AND START ROMANCES AND START FAMILIES?

J: I THINK IT'S BEAUTIFUL WATCHING THAT.

X: THEN THEY PASS THROUGH THE PLACE AND YOU'RE STILL HERE?

J: IT'S PRETTY WEIRD SOMETIMES. I MEAN, I'VE HAD, EVERY RELATIONSHIP I'VE HAD FOR THE PAST EIGHT YEARS HAS BEEN WITH SOMEONE THAT I'VE MET HERE.

X: YOU SAID YOU KEPT THE CAFE AWAY FROM YOUR HOME.

J: AND I ALSO SAID THAT I BROKE THAT RULE. I JUST DON'T LIKE TO THINK ABOUT WORK WHEN I'M AT HOME. ABOUT THE FACT THAT I WORK HERE OR I'M AN OWNER OF THIS PLACE. I AM PROUD OF IT IN SOME ASPECTS. BUT IN OTHER WAYS, LIKE, I WAS AT A FUCKING PARTY, AND I WAS TALKING TO THIS GUY, AND IT WAS SOME KIND OF FUCKING HIGH-COLLAR, NOSE IN THE AIR, HIGH-FALUTIN', SIX-SHOOTING KIND OF PARTY. SOME DOWNTOWN PARTY, YOU KNOW? I WAS HANGING OUT, DRINKING SOME FREE BOOZE, AND MIXING UP WITH EVERYBODY, AND SOME GUY IS LIKE, "OH, WHAT DO YOU DO FOR A LIVING?", ALL KIND OF SNOTTY.

I SAID, "WELL, I OWN A RESTAURANT", RIGHT BACK AT HIM.

HE SAID, "OH REALLY?" HE SEEMED ALL COOL WITH IT. "WHAT RESTAURANT?"

"THE DEAD END"

HE WAS LIKE, "OH, THE DEAD END", JUST LIKE THAT. "OH, THE DEAD END".

HE WALKED AWAY ALL DISGUSTED. I JUST STARTED LAUGHING. LIKE, GODDAMN, ARE WE REALLY THAT BAD?

The ▮▮▮ End

Some background on CB46½...

MY BEST FRIEND CINDY LEFT THE BAY AREA AND HEADED TO ITHACA TO FIND LAND FOR HER SISTER TO START A FARM. UNFORTUNATELY, SHE GOT DISTRACTED ON THE WAY THERE—PROBABLY BY A TALL GUY IN TENNESSEE—AND ENDED UP IN ASHEVILLE INSTEAD. I'D PROMISED TO JOIN HER IN SIX MONTHS, AND DECIDED TO STICK TO THAT PLAN EVEN IF RELOCATING TO RURAL NORTH CAROLINA WAS MY IDEA OF HELL.

IT WAS AS IF WE WERE HITTING OUR OWN PERSONAL 1970: TWO LATTER-DAY HIPPIES ESCAPING THE CITY AND OUR HOME SCENE JUST AS BOTH BEGAN TO TURN SOUR. TO PREPARE MYSELF I WENT TO THE LIBRARY AND READ "TOTAL LOSS FARM," THE FOLLOW-UP TO RAYMOND MUNGO'S SIXTIES MEMOIR "FAMOUS LONG AGO." THE STORY STARTS WITH THE MAOISTS TAKING CONTROL OF THE LIBERATION NEWS SERVICE AND FORCING ITS FOUNDERS OUT. MUNGO AND HIS BEST FRIEND RETREAT TO A FARM WHERE THEY READ THOREAU, MAKE BONFIRES, AND DRINK CHEAP RED WINE. BUT THEIR RETREAT IS NOT A HAPPY ONE. WITHOUT A COMMON ENEMY OR THE DISTRACTIONS OF THE CITY, THEY HAVE TO FACE THEIR OWN DEMONS. BY THE END OF THE BOOK, MUNGO'S FRIEND HAS COMMITTED SUICIDE.

IT WAS A CAUTIONARY TALE, AND HAUNTINGLY FAMILIAR: REPLACE THE LIBERATION NEWS SERVICE WITH EASTBAY PUNK, AND THE MAOISTS WITH APOLITICAL OPPORTUNISTS AND SPEED FREAKS, AND YOU'D HAVE ME AND CINDY SETTING OUT TO BUY THE FARM. TO SAY I ARRIVED IN ASHEVILLE WITH A BAD ATTITUDE WOULD BE PUTTING IT LIGHTLY, ESPECIALLY WHEN I FOUND THAT THERE WASN'T EVEN A FARM, JUST A TRAILER WITH NO YARD, FIVE MILES OUTSIDE OF TOWN—AND I WASN'T ALL THAT CRAZY ABOUT THE TOWN ITSELF.

STILL, I LAUGHED AT—AND KIND OF LIKED—THE WAY THAT LIFE HAD LED ME TO THE EXACT FATE I'D HOPED TO AVOID.

BESIDES US, THERE WERE ONLY FIVE PUNKS IN

ASHEVILLE, AND FOUR OF THEM HATED MY GUTS. THE FIFTH PUNK WAS NATHAN, AN ACTIVIST TRANSPLANT FROM GEORGIA WITH A SMALL HOUSE DOWNTOWN. TIRED OF THE FIVE-MILE WALK ALONG THE HIGHWAY, I MOVED IN WITH HIM.

NOW THAT I THINK ABOUT IT, THE WHOLE STORY IS TOO LONG TO TELL HERE. PERHAPS ANOTHER TIME. IN SHORT, CINDY AND I ENDED UP LIVING IN A WAREHOUSE WITH THE BAND THAT DESPISED ME. THEY'D HAD THE TEMERITY TO OPEN A PUNK CLUB DESPITE THE FACT THAT ASHEVILLE HAD NO PUNKS—A BIZARRE IDEA THAT TURNED OUT TO BE AN EXCELLENT ONE. BUILD IT AND THEY WILL COME! IT WAS LIKE THE PARASITIC JAPAN-ESE BEETLES AND MALAYSIAN BUNDLE BUGS THAT CAME TO THE FARM CINDY'S SISTER DID EVENTUALLY ESTABLISH. NO SOONER HAD THE SEEDLINGS BROKE THROUGH THE TOPSOIL, THE WEIRDEST AND RAREST OF PESTS ARRIVED ON THE SCENE.

MY HOUSEMATES AND UNWILLING COLLABORATORS HAD FOUNDED THE CLUB, BUT THEY WERE ODDLY INCAPABLE OF GETTING THE WORD OUT, EVEN AMONGST THEMSELVES. TOURING BANDS ARRIVED THAT NO ONE REMEMBERED BOOKING AND NO ONE WAS THERE TO SEE. CINDY AND I BEGAN MAKING FLIERS AND POSTING THEM AROUND TOWN. WE STARTED A MAILING LIST FOR FOLKS OUTSIDE OF ASHEVILLE BUT WITHIN REASONABLE DRIVING DISTANCE. THE NASCENT SCENE IN CHATTANOOGA WAS ESPECIALLY EXCITING, SO WE BORROWED FROM THEIR ENTHUSIASM AND INVITED THEIR BANDS TO PLAY. WE BEAT THE BUSH FOR WEIRDOS WHO'D ENDED UP IN ASHEVILLE FOLLOWING CAREERS, DOOMED RELATIONSHIPS, DRUG HABITS, OR SICK PARENTS—PEOPLE WHO LIVED AMONG US BUT IN ALMOST TOTAL ISOLATION. THEY WERE THE RAW MATERIAL FOR THE SCENE WE WERE TRYING TO BUILD, EVEN IF MOST OF THEM WERE INTENT ON ESCAPING RATHER THAN CREATING A TIGHT-KNIT COMMUNITY.

INSTEAD OF THE COP-OUT, DROP-OUT SCENARIO I'D EXPECTED FROM ASHEVILLE, RELOCATING THERE ENDED UP REJUVINATING ME. IT WAS A RENEWAL OF THE VOWS, A CONFIRMATION THAT THE THINGS I HELD DEAR WERE STILL EXCITING AND RELEVANT. ON THE WEST COAST, PUNK SEEMED UNWELL. THE WRITING WAS ON THE WALL: IT WAS TIME TO PACK IT UP, MOVE ON WITH LIFE, AND TRY SOMETHING ELSE. BUT IN ASHE-VILLE, PUNK STILL FELT FRESH. IT WASN'T PERFECT,

BUT IT WAS A DAMN GOOD TOOL TO WORK WITH. PLUS, IT FELT GOOD TO DANCE, AND PUNK WAS MUSIC ANYONE COULD PLAY. IT WAS EGALITARIAN.

I'D BEEN GOING TO SHOWS FOR YEARS, BUT HAD NEVER DEALT WITH ALL THE DRUDGEWORK INVOLVED WITH PUTTING THEM ON. IT WAS A COMPLETION OF THE CYCLE FOR ME AND CINDY, GOING FROM UNWITTING CONSUMERS TO BEHIND-THE-SCENES FACILITATORS. AS A WAY TO INCORPORATE OUR OTHER INTERESTS AND INCLUDE PEOPLE NOT IN BANDS, WE ADDED A SHORT LECTURE TO EVERY SHOW. CINDY SPOKE ON "EVERYTHING I KNOW ABOUT YUGOSLAVIA", BOB ON "WHY YOU SHOULDN'T GIVE UP HOPE."

LATE AT NIGHT, WHEN THE BANDS HAD BEEN PAID AND THE DEBRIS HAD BEEN SWEPT UP, WE JUMPED INTO CINDY'S TRUCK AND DROVE OUT TO THE FARM, WHERE WE HELPED HER SISTER HARVEST VEGETABLES BY THE LIGHT OF THE TRUCK'S HIGH BEAMS. WHEN SHE HEADED TO THE EARLY MORNING FARMER'S MARKET TO SELL HER CROPS, WE CRASHED OUT IN THE EMPTY CLUB.

CINDY AND I ENDED UP MORE OR LESS RUNNING THE PLACE. BY THE TIME EVICTION CAME, OUR HOUSEMATES HAD ALL BUT DROPPED OUT. THE SCENE WAS STEADILY GROWING, WITH NEW BANDS FORMING AND NEW PEOPLE ARRIVING EVERY WEEK. WE NEEDED A NEW PLACE TO HAVE SHOWS — AND FOR CINDY AND I TO SLEEP! MY FILES FROM THE TIME CONTAIN NOT ONLY THE NOW-USELESS KEYS FROM THE FIRST CLUB, "THE HEADQUARTERS," BUT ALSO THE PAPERWORK FROM THE VARIOUS LEADS WE FOLLOWED AS D-DAY APPROACHED, A LINE THROUGH EVERY LANDLORD WE SPOKE TO WHO SLAMMED THE DOOR IN OUR FACES. FINALLY, WE CON-VINCED AN ALREADY ESTABLISHED COMMUNAL HOUSE TO LET US TURN THEIR BASEMENT INTO A VENUE.

THAT'S WHERE COMETBUS 46½ PICKS UP. IT WAS AN ODD, IMPULSIVE, IN-BETWEEN ISSUE FREEBIE I DID TO DOCUMENT THE EXCITEMENT OF THAT ERA BEFORE IT DISAPPEARED. I'VE ALSO TACKED ON A FEW FLIERS THAT WEREN'T IN THE ORIGINAL EDITION, FROM SCENES I WAS ACTIVE IN LATER ON.

COMETBUS

#46½

→ FREE!

A PERSON WITH MONEY CAN PUT THEIR MESSAGE ON A BILLBOARD, A BUS STOP BENCH, OR EVEN A BLIMP. THEY CAN MAKE EVERY TELEVISION SET, EVERY RADIO, AND EVERY NEWSPAPER MOUTH THEIR WORDS. THEY CAN OPEN A BUSINESS AND PUT THEIR MESSAGE IN THE WINDOW. BUT THE PERSON WITH NO MONEY IS OUTSIDE. KEEP MOVING, SIR. KEEP MOVING, MISS. ONLY STOP TO SPEND AND THEN KINDLY MOVE ALONG. A PERSON WITH NO MONEY CAN ONLY PUT THEIR MESSAGE ON TELEPHONE POLES, AND WHEN THEY DO, WATCH OUT! THE PEOPLE WITH MONEY HAVE ALOTED THE PEOPLE WITH NO MONEY ONLY CERTAIN SPACES WHERE THEY ARE ALLOWED TO BE HEARD. THESE ARE CALLED "COMMUNITY" SPACES. THESE SPACES TOTAL ABOUT THIRTY FEET FOR AN ENTIRE CITY'S COMMUNAL NEEDS. THIRTY FEET FOR ALL THE LOST DOGS, LOST WALLETS, CHARITY RAFFLES, PUNK SHOWS, POLITICAL RALLIES, SUMMER SUBLETS, YARD SALES, RUNAWAY CHILDREN, ART, AND IDEAS. THE POSTERS PILE UP AND ARE TORN DOWN, COMPETING FOR THE TINY AMOUNT OF ALOTED SPACE. HOW CAN YOU COVER UP A POSTER FOR A CUTE LITTLE LOST PUPPY IN ORDER TO ADVERTISE YOUR CULTURAL EVENT? BUT HOW ELSE TO LET PEOPLE KNOW? WHAT IS PUBLIC SPACE FOR IF NOT FOR THE PUBLIC, THE WHOLE PUBLIC, NOT JUST ONE PART WITH A CERTAIN OPINION OR CERTAIN INCOME? WILL YOU CROSS THE LINE AND PUT YOUR POSTER ON THAT NEARBY EMPTY POLE? WELL, YOU JUST MADE A BIG MISTAKE. AS A MEMBER OF THE BUSINESS COMMUNITY, AS A TAXPAYER, AS A SWORN PROTECTOR OF LAW AND ORDER, AND FOR YOUR OWN GOOD, I'M GOING TO HAVE TO SEND YOU TO JAIL. BECAUSE, YOU'RE RIGHT! A PERSON WITH NO MONEY CAN'T AFFORD THAT HUGE FINE! HA HA HA! WHAT'S THAT? SOMETHING ABOUT THE FIRST AMENDMENT? YOU TRYING TO GET SMART WITH ME?? HOW FREE DO YOU THINK YOUR "FREE SPEECH" IS, ANYWAY? YOU'LL HAVE A LOT OF TIME TO THINK THAT OVER WHERE YOU'RE GOING. AND BY THE WAY, REMEMBER: KILL THE HIPPIES, ALLERGIC TO WHORES, DEAD THINGS, ONE REASON, AND CRAP FACTORY THIS THURSDAY NIGHT 6/15 AT OH MY. 201 BROADWAY, BACK DOOR.

UPCOMING SHOWS @
THE HEADQUARTERS

FRI: REEKS AND RECKS
12/11 WAR TORN BABIES

FRI 12/18: THE FRANTICS

SAT: RANDOM CONFLICT
12/19 PUGNACIOUS BASTARDS

TUE: THE BOILS
12/29 WAR TORN BABIES

SUN 1/3: THE MORONS

SAT 1/4: ULTIMATE DRAGONS

TUE 1/14: DAS KRIMINAL

ALL SHOWS CHEAP!
ALL AGES! 8:00 ISH!
504 MERRIMON AVE.

UPCOMING SHOWS AT
THE HEADQUARTERS

THU. JANUARY 14TH:
DAS KRIMINAL
CRAP FACTORY
ASTRID OTO

SAT. JANUARY 23RD:
SPAWN SACS
TUBE TOPS

THU. JANUARY 28TH:
HARBINGER
WAR TORN BABIES
BOBBY JOE EBOLA +
THE CHILDREN MACNUGGITS
CRAP FACTORY

SAT. JANUARY 30TH:
SPASMS
CHRIST FILTHY DOGS

504 MERRIMON AVE.

THE HEADQUARTERS HAS
FINALLY RELOCATED, WITH
A NEW NAME AND NEW
DARKER, SLEAZIER, SOGGIER
SPACE JUST ONE BLOCK
FROM DOWNTOWN!

WED: ANTI-PRODUCT, WAR TORN
6/23 BABIES, CHRIST FILTHY DOGS,
RAY GRADYS + SPEAKER: BOB

TUE: SHOTWELL, THE MORONS,
7/6 SPAWN SACS, FORCED
VENGEANCE, HO ON BORDEAUX
+ SPEAKER: LYNN "MY TRIP TO GUATEMALA"

SAT: FLESH EATING CREEPS, TBA
7/24

WED: RED MONKEYS, TBA,
8/4 THE 6 PARTS 7
TUE: KILL THE HIPPIES
8/10
WED: PANTY RAID, ASTRID OTO
8/18

OH MY! 201 BROADWAY

HEY, I DRANK TOO MUCH COFFEE AND DECIDED TO DO ANOTHER WEIRD HALF ISSUE. THESE ARE FLIERS I'VE DONE OVER THE PAST TWO YEARS, FROM TWO CLUBS WHICH I LIVED AT AND WAS INVOLVED IN. FROM "THE HEADQUARTERS", WHICH I ONLY ENTERED ON THE FRAY AND AT THE TAIL-END, TO "OH MY", WHICH CINDY + I BUILT AND HELPED RUN FROM BEGINNING TO END. ALSO, ONE OF THE FEW EVENTS IN BETWEEN THE TWO CLUBS, A READING/LECTURE AT "THE ACE OF SPADES" INFOSHOP.

THERE WERE MANY PEOPLE INVOLVED IN BOTH CLUBS, AND IN MANY LITTLE WAYS HELPING PUT ON, OR SABOTAGE, THE SHOWS AND SHOWSPACE. I HOPE SOME OF THEM WRITE ABOUT THE SHOWS THEMSELVES, DANCING IN THE DIM SWEATY BASEMENT WITH THE CREEK RUNNING THROUGH IT, OR DRUNK IN THE TORCH-LIT KUDZU-COVERED CHAOS OUT BACK. FOR MY ~~PART, I WANTED TO USE~~ PART, I WANTED TO USE PICTURES INSTEAD, TO TRACE AN OUTLINE AND TIMELINE OF BOTH CLUBS.

A GOOD FLIER IS AN INTEGRAL PART OF A GOOD SHOW

THE HEADQUARTERS

YET IN THIS CASE, THE FLIERS ALSO HAD A LIFE, AND A PURPOSE, OF THEIR OWN. AS THE CITY PASSED NEW LAWS AGAINST FLIERING, WE REDOUBLED OUR EFFORTS. WE EVEN DOUBLED AND TRIPLED THE SIZE OF OUR FLIERS, UNTIL MOST WERE HUGE 18"x 24" POSTERS. NATHAN AND I SCREENPRINTED THEM BY HAND, EACH ONE DRIPPING WITH THE LOUDEST, BOLDEST, BLOODIEST COLORS. RAISING THE ANTE NOT JUST AGAINST THE COPS, BUT FOR VIBRANT AND TRULY PUBLIC PUBLIC ART. AFTER A WHILE IT WAS A FULL-ON WAR. I'D STAND DOWNTOWN WAITING FOR TWO COPS TO PASS, GOING OPPOSITE DIRECTIONS. THEN, WHILE THEY WERE STILL SAFELY IN SIGHT BUT HEADING AWAY, I WALLPAPERED EVERY WALL I COULD FIND.

AGAIN, OTHER PEOPLE MADE FLIERS FOR BOTH CLUBS. THESE ARE ONLY MINE, ONLY ONE PART OF THE PICTURE, AND MAYBE OUT OF CONTEXT IN BLACK

AND WHITE, SHRUNK DOWN, AND OFF THE POLE.
YOU'LL JUST HAVE TO IMAGINE THE COLORS. IT WAS
THE FIRST TIME I'D EVER HAD A CHANCE TO
EXPERIMENT WITH COLOR, AND THE FIRST TIME
IN YEARS I WAS DRIVEN TO DO SO MUCH NEW ART.
SOMETHING INTOXICATING ABOUT THAT IMMEDIACY,
THAT URGENCY, THAT DIRECT HANDS-ON APPROACH
OF FLIERS, ESPECIALLY WHEN PRINTING THE FLIERS
BY HAND. AND THERE'S SOMETHING OF THE
MISSIONARY'S ZEAL IN GOING OUT TO PLASTER THEM
ACROSS THE WHOLE DAMN TOWN. SOME OF THE ART
I'VE SINCE RE-USED ON MAGAZINE AND RECORD
COVERS, I NEVER WOULD HAVE DONE WITHOUT THE
INITIAL URGENCY OF AN UPCOMING SHOW.

    THIS IS A LIMITED EDITION MONEY-LOSING
HALF ISSUE. NO MAILORDER. NO ADDRESS. NOTHING!
JUST A TELEPHONE POLE FELLED DOWNTOWN,
RUN THROUGH THE PAPER MILL AND THE XEROX
MACHINE. ENJOY!

AARON.

TIME FOR AN UPDATE ALREADY?
YUP. LOTS OF NEW BANDS, NEW
SHOWS, A COUPLE CHANGES
AND CANCELLATIONS:

TUE. JULY 6TH:
SHOTWELL, THE MORONS, SPAWN
SACS, FORCED VENGEANCE,
HO ON BORDEAUX, SOCIAL SCARE
+SPEAKER: B&B—"WHY YOU SHOULD KEEP UP HATE"

WED. JULY 21ST:
SETH TOBOCMAN AUTHOR OF
"YOU DON'T HAVE TO FUCK PEOPLE OVER TO SURVIVE"
WHITE COLLAR CRIME, PINK COLLAR
JOBS, ASTRID OTO

WED. AUG. 4TH:
RED MONKETS THE 6 PARTS 7

TUE. AUG. 10TH:
KILL THE HIPPIES, JACK PALANCE BAND,
CHRIST FILTHY DOGS, CRAP FACTORY

TUE. AUG. 17TH:
HIS HERO IS GONE, SOME SPANISH
BAND, PANTY RAID, ASTRID OTO

WED. AUG. 28TH:
OI POLLOI, WAR TORN BABIES

OH MY! 201 BROADWAY (IN BACK)

OH MY BACKYARD

SELLING OUT FOR CORPORATE $

HQ ƎH2O

504 merrimon

PAWNS OF SOCIETY

STRANGE ANTI-WOMEN RITUALS

old friends & family

YOU MUST! CHOOSE!

CLASS WAR

VS.

FIGHTING IMPERIALISM

EVICTION

saturday jan. 9 8:30 *the Punks*

JACK PALANCE BAND
SEGUE
CHATANOOGA 5
←MPLS
RICHMOND →
ULTIMATE DRAGONS

OI POLLOI

WAR TORN BABIES

MARK BRUBACK & SARAH O'DONNEL

OH MY!

201 BROADWAY
(IN BACK)

WED. JULY 28TH 8PM

A MULTI-MEDIA PRESENTATION
BY:
SETH TOBOCMAN
AUTHOR OF "YOU DON'T HAVE TO FUCK
PEOPLE OVER TO SURVIVE"; CO-FOUNDER
OF WORLD WAR THREE ILLUSTRATED

plus, from New York,
WHITE COLLAR CRIME
from Boone,
PINK COLLAR JOBS
and from upstairs,
ASTRID OTO

Gre
He
Sec

MILE MARKER

HARUM SCARUM

FROM PORTLAND

MARION

FOIL'N THE WORKS

THURSDAY, SEPTEMBER 2ND @ 8PM

OH MY 201 BROADWAY IN BACK

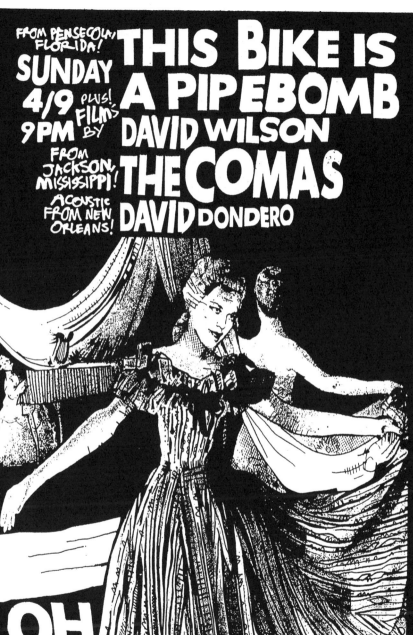

CLOVIS PRESS

welcomes springtime with our 1st annual

$40 BIKE SALE!!

BOOKS · **ZINES** · **DOGS** · **BIKES**

HISTORY WILL · ABSOLVE ME

That's right! 100 Bikes! $40 each!
Saturday 4/17 + Sunday 4/18/2004

229 BEDFORD · BROOKLYN.

COMETBUS

47

Lanky

$2

When I told Frank that Lanky was getting reprinted, he suggested including a glossary, since the thousand and one references in the text are hard to understand for those not from Berkeley and not around in the particular era in which the story is set. Rereading the book, I realized he was right. So, now, for the edification of the other ninety-nine percent, here's a quick guide to...

Who's Who & What's What in
"Lanky"

Albany—The shitty small town in the Eastbay, not the better known armpit of the far east. Before it became a city, Albany was the Berkeley dump.

The Avenue—Telegraph Avenue, the open wound left from where Berkeley's bleeding heart was removed. One might assume that the telegraph lines were removed too, but not so. They never ran on the Berkeley stretch of this street.

at work on Lanky

(A) State of Mind—The pride of the Bay Area's anarcho-punk scene, unfortunately their recordings never matched the excitement of their live shows.

Berkeley Farms—"Farms in Berkeley? Moo" is the slogan of this dairy, actually located in Hayward.

Black Hole, Dead Ted's, The Canterbury—Legendary LA punkhouses celebrated in story and song.

Blondie's, Fat Slice, La Val's—A three-way tie for worst pizza on the West Coast, a contest for which even the best wins no prize.

The Bubble Lady—Julia Vinograd, down-and-out poet laureate of People's Park, the only exception to Cafe Med's "no soliciting or dealing" rule.

Center and Shattuck—The main intersection of Berkeley's downtown, site of twin towers a whopping twelve stories high.

Cafe Milano—Hangout of the mods, before they got families and jobs.

The Campinile—Imagine the Bay Area as a house shared by four old phallic symbols who are always quarreling. The Oakland Tribune tower is broke and barely alive. Coit Tower is genteel and smug, while proudly touting its socialist past. It looks down on the Trans-America building which is rich but has no parrots or pedigree to boast of. Meanwhile, the Campinile bides its time. Soon UC Berkeley will acquire the deed to the property and evict the Campinile's annoying housemates. Then he'll finally have the place all to himself.

Co-op Kiddie Corral—The co-op grocery had eight different locations, plus a hardware store, pharmacy, bookstore, and travel agency. When the whole thing went belly-up in 1988, it was replaced by a high-end supermarket chain. The Eastbay has never been the same. The corral was the daycare center to stash your brats while you shopped.

Code of Honor—The Bay Area's best punk band, hands down, and if you want to fight about it, they are the perfect soundtrack.

Concord—A cultureless wasteland. The most stifling of all Eastbay suburbs.

Cyclotron—Other company towns have their mills that tear up steel or trees. Ours smashes atoms and is run by UCB.

NYC summer 2000

Czeslaw Milosz—Poland's most famous poet, though the vast majority of his life was spent in Berkeley. Personally, I prefer his prose; *The Seizure of Power* and *The Captive Mind* are both riveting.

Eschelman Hall—A UC Berkeley building where many student organizations are quartered. *Slingshot* had their office in Eschelman before leaving to "go among the people."

Fourth Street—A Telegraph alternative for those who prefer their shopping districts curated and controlled. Two guys own all the property and rent only to businesses that fit their Mayberry-as-mall aesthetic.

Glitterdoll graffiti—Frankie Glitterdoll was an unstoppable force in the glam-punk-junk whirlwind of 80s SF. His graffiti was *everywhere*. Reports of his untimely death were almost as common, though in the end true.

Greek Theatre—A stone, open air amphitheater in the classic style, with a stage graced by Desmond Tutu, the Go-Gos, the Grateful Dead, and me—when I walked across it in Berkeley High's commencement ceremony.

Hotel Carlton—R.K. Narayan wrote his worst—but best-known—novel at the Carlton while on a visit from India in the 50s. By the 80s it was an unrivaled palace of drugs and sleaze, and the only thing penned there was Neurosis's *Pain of Mind*.

Jake the Snake—The man to go to for fake acid, baby laxatives, and nickel bags of oregano. A fixture on the Avenue, he's probably now enjoying the view of the bay from the Big Q, San Quentin.

James Rector—a student/drifter shot dead in the People's Park riots of 1969, he became Berkeley's most famous martyr, though some grieved more for the promising artist standing next to Rector who was also hit. He lived, but was permanently blinded from the buckshot.

Lawrence Hall of Science and *Lawrence Berkeley Lab*—Other cities (like Albany) have a cross atop their highest hill. We have the bomb and a tribute to the men who made it.

Lemon Meringue—a street person who claimed, convincingly, to have been Joey Ramone's girlfriend in her younger days.

Licorice Pizza—a chain of Orange County record stores revered by the punks for the limited, live Black Flag single they released.

Lois the Pie Queen—a venerable Southern-style Oakland eatery.

Marin—Berkeley's steepest street. Stories of walking up it are long, stories of skating down it are not.

Mario Savio—Free Speech Movement figurehead and one of the greatest American orators of all time. In a just world, his speech about stopping the gears of the machine would replace the Pledge of Allegiance in our schools.

Martin Snapp—the "Eastbay Ear," Oakland Tribune's lighter and brighter version of the Chronicle's Herb Caen.

Middle Class—Out of vogue! The first-ever hardcore record was their 1978 EP.

Ms. Cat—A disturbed and disturbing woman who called Berkeley payphones but would only converse with men. For more details, seek out the 1984 *Cometbus* audio magazine, YCAM, on which she is interviewed.

Mongo Beti—One of the pioneers of modern African literature, his *Mission to Kala* (1957) is bitingly funny and pointedly harsh. In his later years he opened a bookstore while continuing to write novels of his own.

katie Glichberg

Mike Muir—Controversial singer of Suicidal Tendencies; a thug with a knack for uttering home truths.

Michael Delecour—One of People's Park's founding fathers. With his chiseled features and ponytail, he resembles a cigar store Indian.

Northside—the *other* side of campus, analogous to the dark side of the moon.

Peet's Coffee—Shell-shocked Vietnam vets and SSI recipients lined the bench outside this North Berkeley institution. At the time *Lanky* was written, Peet's had expanded to half a dozen locations but had yet to become a nationwide chain.

Perverts—A word I deeply regret using to describe the gay pick-up scene at the Berkeley waterfront. Kevin Army took me to task, writing a tender and explicit love song called "Aquatic Park" in response. Aggressive pick-up scenes make me uncomfortable, but I was ignorant and biased to demonize this one the way I did.

Pussycat Theater—A long-departed Telegraph porno palace.

Southside—The area around Telegraph Avenue, though the term has become antiquated. Once there were two sides of UC, now there are none. Cal students are too scared to set foot off campus, and the rest of us have no reason to cut across. Rather Ripped Records left Northside decades ago, and nothing sprung up to take its place.

Steve the Greek—The Avenue's least-loved restaurateur. Steve was openly ridiculed when his shop burned down, when not being blamed for starting the blaze.

First draft

Spirit of '29 Band—A streetcorner band who played "old-time music for the new depression."

Sproul Plaza—UC Berkeley's quad, birthplace of the Free Speech Movement and scene of the long struggle for divestment from South Africa. Phil Ochs played upper Sproul, the Fugs and Fang played down below. The Ramones too, but not Black Flag—they overslept and missed their noontime show. The Sproul fountain is dedicated to Ludwig von Shwarenburg, a much-loved and never tamed campus canine.

Stephen Lightfoot—Lightfoot is among the colorful but disturbing wingnut icons of the Lanky era who have recently resurfaced and returned to their old spots, making the novel timeless. Still on a mission to prove that Stephen King killed John Lennon, Lightfoot has called for a boycott of Moe's for selling Stephen King books. Reportedly, the author got a restraining order against Lightfoot—and who wouldn't? Incidentally, all quotes from Lightfoot and others in the scene reports are real.

Tim Yo—Yohannon, the godfather of punk. He could be found eating fries with Pushead in the McDonald's downtown.

TV20—A homespun local television station specializing in B-movies and schlocky 50s sitcoms.

UC, *UCB*, and *Cal*—the college which forms its own city-state within Berkeley's borders.

Walker's Rolling Museum—A rolling Civil Rights and Black History museum with an element of the lunatic fringe.

Wally George Show—Fanatical right-wing Orange County TV talk show that seemed amusing for its outrageousness; then came Fox News.

Watch the Gap—BART's slogan to remind passengers not to trip when exiting the train.

done!

Lanky

Aaron Cometbus

One

NATE AND AMANDA WERE AN ON-AGAIN OFF-AGAIN COUPLE AND I WAS ONE OF THOSE GUYS WHO WAIT ON THE SIDELINES TO SEE WHICH WAY THE WIND WILL BLOW. THE RELATIONSHIP VULTURE, LOWEST OF ALL LIFE FORMS.

BUT AMANDA WAS JUST AS BAD. AN OLDER, PUNKER GIRL FLYING CIRCLES OVER MY OWN FRAGILE RELATIONSHIP. SHE HAD MOVED TO BERKELEY FROM RENO AND ENDED UP WITH A JOB AT THE CHEESE SHOP RIGHT BY MY DAD'S HOUSE. IT WAS UNHEARD OF. PUNKS IN ALBANY? MOO.

WE SAT IN THE BRAND NEW PARK ON HER LUNCH BREAK, THE PARK WHICH USED TO BE THE PERALTA STREET TURNAROUND. THAT WAS A NEW IDEA IN ALBANY THEN, ACTUALLY FILLING IN SOME OF THE GREY WIDE OPEN STREETS WITH PARKS AND PEDESTRIANS. AMANDA AND I HAD OUR LITTLE PICNICS THERE, FEEDING ON TEMPTATION.

HOW OPEN IS AN "OPEN" RELATIONSHIP? THAT WAS THE QUESTION. IF A TREE FALLS IN THE FOREST, WHY WORRY? PERHAPS IT GOES DOWN WITH GREAT VIOLENCE AND NOISE, CRASHING AND CRUSHING ALL LIFE IN ITS PATH. BUT IF NO ONE IS THERE TO SEE IT FALL, THERE'S NO GUILT INVOLVED. WHY NOT LET NATURE TAKE ITS COURSE? BUT WE DREW OUT THE TEMPTATION, SAVORING IT, UNDRESSING EACH OTHER WITH OUR EYES ONLY, AND NOT OUR HANDS.

NATE AND AMANDA LIVED TOGETHER, AND I ALMOST MOVED IN NEXT DOOR. A GREAT APARTMENT RIGHT DOWNTOWN. CHEAP, BUT NO DOUBT EXPENSIVE EMOTIONALLY, AS THE WINDS AND WATERS WERE GETTING MORE AND MORE TURBULENT. HE AND I HAD THAT SAME ANIMAL ANIMOSITY, TWO GUYS GROWLING AND SOUNDING OUT

1

OUR TERRITORIES. WE WERE VERY MUCH ALIKE AND WOULD'VE BEEN GOOD FRIENDS, EXCEPT PART OF THE SIMILARITY WAS OUR TASTE IN WOMEN, AND, I FEAR, WOMEN'S TASTE IN US.

AS IT HAPPENED, THE WIND BLEW HIM AWAY. BUT NATE WAS NOT LONG GONE. HE CAME BACK IN WITH THE TIDE AND A WEDDING RING WHEN AMANDA FOUND OUT SHE WAS PREGNANT.

WELL, THERE ARE WORSE REASONS TO GET MARRIED.

Two

THREE OF THE MOTHERS I HAVE KNOWN, I TEND TO LUMP TOGETHER. NOT YOUNG MOTHERS LIKE AMANDA, BUT WISER, LARGER, AND MORE RUGGED OLDER SINGLE MOTHERS. ALL THREE WERE CRANKY AND MOODY, FUNNY AND A LITTLE CRUDE, WITH A STRENGTH AND STRENGTH OF CHARACTER WHICH I LIKED AND ADMIRED— A CHARACTER VERY DIFFERENT FROM THEIR DAUGHTERS, WHO ALL HAPPENED TO BE FRIENDS OF MINE. EXCEPT LARENKA, WHO WAS NOT SO MUCH A FRIEND AS A GIRLFRIEND.

THREE GIRLS, THREE MOTHERS. JO, MELODY, AND LARENKA. JO WOULD BE MAD TO HEAR ME COMPARE HER MOM TO MELODY'S, BECAUSE MELODY'S MOTHER ONCE CALLED JO UGLY. THAT'S HARD TO TAKE SERIOUSLY, ESPECIALLY IF YOU'VE SEEN JO, BUT WHO LIKES TO BE CALLED UGLY? I THOUGHT IT WAS SORT OF SWEET, MELODY'S MOTHER STEPPING IN TO DEFEND HER DAUGHTER AND WARD OFF POSSIBLE ENEMIES. BUT IT'S TRUE THAT OF THE THREE, MELODY'S MOM WAS A BIT OF A SNOB.

DID THE DAUGHTERS FEAR BECOMING THEIR MOTHERS, TAKING ON EXACTLY THE QUALITIES WHICH I ADMIRED? YES, THEY DID. THE MOTHERS WERE HANDSOME BUT NOT BEAUTIFUL. STRONG AND INDEPENDENT BUT WITHOUT MANY FRIENDS. SELF-AWARE IN WAYS THAT CONSTANTLY EMBARRASSED THE DAUGHTERS. YOU COULD SAY IT IS THE SAME FOR EVERYONE, THOUGH I'VE NEVER BEEN SCARED OF BECOMING EXACTLY LIKE MY MOTHER.

ALL THREE MOTHERS HAD MADE SACRIFICES TO RAISE THEIR DAUGHTERS WELL AND GIVE THEM A SENSE OF INDEPENDENCE. LARENKA'S MOTHER MOVED FROM A HOUSE TO A TINY APARTMENT, FROM A HICK-

TOWN TO DOWNTOWN BERKELEY, SO LARENKA COULD
FINISH SCHOOL WHERE THERE WERE MORE OPTIONS
AND MORE FREEDOM. THEY FOUND A PLACE ON THE
THIRD FLOOR OF A LARGE, DRAB APARTMENT BUILDING ON
CHANNING WAY, JUST ABOVE SHATTUCK. LANKY'S MOTHER
TOOK THE COUCH, AND LANKY GOT THE ONLY ROOM.

Three

OUR AGE DIFFERENCE WAS OF GREAT CONCERN
TO ME. AN UNBRIDGEABLE GAP OF UNDERSTANDING AND
EXPERIENCE. ONE YEAR. A RIDICULOUS JOKE NOW, BUT
AT THE TIME SOMETHING TO BROOD ABOUT.
LARENKA, MY YOUNG GIRLFRIEND. EVERY NIGHT I
WOULD COME TEARING OUT OF HER ROOM AT TOP SPEED,
PAST HER MOTHER SLEEPING ON THE COUCH, PAST MY
OLD ROTTING SOCKS UP IN THE APARTMENT BUILDING TREE,
AND OUT ONTO SHATTUCK AVENUE. EVERY NIGHT THE
GODDAMN 1:17 BUS, THE LAST BUS OF THE NIGHT, WOULD
PASS ME BEFORE I COULD MAKE IT TO THE STOP. THEN
I HAD AN HOUR WALK HOME, BROODING ABOUT HOW IT
WAS ALL ONE BIG MISTAKE.
IF I'M BAD NOW, I USED TO BE MUCH WORSE. THERE
WAS A HUGE MAGAZINE TO FINISH, AND ONLY ONE THING
WOULD GIVE ME THE EXTRA INSPIRATION AND ENERGY TO
COMPLETE IT IN TIME: LOVE. I ACTUALLY CALCULATED IT
OUT LIKE THAT, IN COLD BLOOD, THEN FOUND LARENKA
ON THE AVENUE.
POOR LARENKA, A RUSSIAN NAME MEANING DUMPLING
OR STRUDEL OR SOMETHING. WE HUNG OUT ON TELEGRAPH
OR FUCKED IN HER ROOM. THEN I WOULD GO HOME AND
PUT ALL MY TIME AND EMOTION INTO THE MAGAZINE.
A TERRIBLE, MANIPULATIVE THING TO DO TO SOMEONE,
I KNOW. BUT IT TURNED OUT TO BE THE BEST ISSUE YET.
AND NOT ONLY THAT. LIFE HAS A WAY SOMETIMES
OF TRICKING YOU INTO MAKING GOOD DECISIONS FOR
ALL THE WRONG REASONS.

Four

LANKY, ONE YEAR YOUNGER THAN ME AND THREE
YEARS YOUNGER THAN AMANDA. WE WERE HAPPY IN

SPITE OF IT ALL, AND IN SPITE OF SUSAN, THE VINDICTIVE
AND VICIOUS BEST FRIEND WHO ALWAYS REMOVED RAIL-
ROAD TIES FROM THE TRACKS, HOPING FOR A PILE-UP.

YES, BEFORE RISING TO FAME AS "SUSAN, THE JEWISH
NAZI SKINHEAD" AND "SUSAN, THE HUMAN PINCUSHION," SHE
WAS SIMPLY SUSAN, THE VINDICTIVE BEST FRIEND OF
LARENKA, MY GIRL. A SMALL ROLE WITH SUCH PREDICTABLE
LINES AS, "YOU COULD DO MUCH BETTER THAN HIM", AND,
"DON'T YOU THINK THAT GUY'S CUTE?"

SUSAN AND LARENKA WORKED TOGETHER ON
TELEGRAPH, HANDING OUT FLIERS FOR SHITTY PIZZA.
ONE WAS HIRED BY BLONDIE'S, THE OTHER BY FAT SLICE.
STATIONED ON SEPARATE CORNERS, THEY WERE SUPPOSED
TO COMPETE. BUT INSTEAD OF BECOMING RIVALS, THEY
JOINED FORCES, BECOMING CLOSE FRIENDS THE MINUTE
THEY MET.

THERE WAS A SUBCULTURE OF THE SOUTHSIDE
SUBCULTURE RESTRICTED TO PEOPLE WHO HANDED
OUT FLIERS. THEY HAD THEIR OWN HEROES AND HEROIN,
THEIR OWN GOSSIP GRAPEVINE, AND THEIR OWN SOCIAL
LADDER TO CLIMB. IF YOU WORKED HANDING OUT FLIERS
FOR BLONDIE'S, SHOULD YOU FUCK GUYS WHO WORKED FOR
BLONDIE'S OR GUYS WHO HANDED OUT FLIERS FOR FAT
SLICE? THE WHOLE THING WAS CONFUSING BUT EXCITING
FOR SUSAN.

BOB, A SMALL LAOTIAN GUY IN A PLASTIC A'S HAT
WAS BOSSMAN AND OVERLORD OF ALL THE FOLKS WHO
HANDED OUT FLIERS ON THE AVE. A REFEREE OF SORTS,
HE SENT SUSAN BACK TO HER CORNER. BUT SUSAN WAS
NOT ONE TO BE BOSSED.

LIKE ALL PEOPLE WHO TAKE MORE THAN THEY
GIVE, SHE SOON HAD MORE THAN SHE COULD TAKE. SHE
CRACKED. YOU SHOULD HAVE SEEN THE LOOK ON BOB'S
FACE. SUSAN CLIMBED UP TO THE HOTEL CARLETON
ROOF AND LET LOOSE WITH A WHOLE WEEK'S WORTH OF
HANDBILLS. THEY FILLED THE SKY ABOVE TELEGRAPH
LIKE THOUSANDS UPON THOUSANDS OF LITTLE BLUE AND
RED BIRDS, FLUTTERING IN THE WIND.

AS THE SIREN SONG BEGAN IN THE DISTANCE, EVERYONE
LOOKED UP TO SALUTE SUSAN. NOT JUST LANKY AND BOB'S
OTHER SLAVES. ALSO THE VENDORS, DEALERS, SANITATION
WORKERS, DRAG QUEENS, RIP-OFF ARTISTS, AND CAFE
DRAWING CREEPS. PERHAPS EVEN MICHAEL DELECOUR
LOOKED UP AND SHED A SINGLE TEAR.

I CRIED TOO. AS SUSAN WAS ENDING HER LAST
PAYING JOB, I WAS BEGINNING MY FIRST.

Five

CAMPUS COPY MART WAS A DINGY ROOM WITH FOUR XEROX MACHINES AND A LITTLE DESK. BEHIND THE DESK SAT A PIMPLY, SMELLY YOUNGSTER DRESSED IN RAGS. ME. I WAS LEANING AGAINST THE WALL WITH MY HEAD SLUMPED ON MY SHOULDER, VERY MUCH ASLEEP.

ONE OF THE REGULAR CUSTOMERS CAME IN AND SHOOK ME AWAKE. "I SAY", HE YELLED. "IS THIS PLACE UNDER NEW MANAGEMENT?"

"NO", I GRUMBLED. "SAME OWNERS. I'M JUST NEW HERE. AND YOU'RE THE FIFTH PERSON TO ASK THAT TODAY."

HE LOOKED ME OVER WITH NO ATTEMPT TO HIDE HIS DISGUST, THEN WATCHED ME OVER ONE SHOULDER WHILE COPYING HIS SOCIAL SECURITY FORM.

"THAT WILL BE FOUR CENTS, PLEASE", I SAID. HE KEPT HIS WALLET AT A SAFE DISTANCE, GOT A RECEIPT, AND DID NOT SAY THANKS.

AN UNGRATEFUL CUSTOMER IS THE LEAST OF YOUR WORRIES AT AN OVER-THE-COUNTER JOB, BUT I GOT THAT SAME TREATMENT ALL DAY LONG, EVERY DAY THE FIRST WEEK. GRUMPY SENIOR CITIZENS GIVING ME THE ONCE OVER TWICE. THE HAIRY EYEBALL. EVEN THE THIRD DEGREE, PREPARED TO CALL THE POLICE AND HAVE ME ARRESTED FOR TRESPASSING, BURGLARY, LARCENY, PROBABLY EVEN MURDER.

WHERE WAS PARVIZ AND NAHID, THEY ASKED. WHAT HAS BECOME OF THE NICE OLDER COUPLE WHO USED TO RUN THE PLACE? THE SWEET COUPLE WHO, THOUGH STRANGE IN THEIR WAYS, HAD BECOME PART OF THE NEIGHBORHOOD, PART OF THE DAILY ROUTINE?

THEY LOOKED ME OVER WITH MISTRUST AND FEAR, BLAMING ME FOR EVERY CHANGE IN THE WORLD OVER THE PAST FIFTY YEARS. FOR EVERY LITTLE FAMILIAR THING WHICH HAD SUDDENLY CEASED TO EXIST, THROWING THEM OFF BALANCE, LEAVING THEM MORE IN THE PAST THAN THE PRESENT.

I TRIED TO EXPLAIN. "NAHID AND PARVIZ STILL OWN THE PLACE", I SAID.

BUT NO ONE WOULD LISTEN. SOME CUSTOMERS EVEN THREATENED TO TAKE THEIR BUSINESS ELSEWHERE.

WHAT COULD I DO? I SHRUGGED AND POINTED TO ANOTHER COPY SHOP JUST DOWN THE STREET.

Six

CAMPUS COPY MART WAS RUN BY NAHID SOUFERIAN, A SHORT, FIERCE, INTENSE WOMAN WHO CHEWED NICOTINE GUM IN BETWEEN HER CIGARETTES. I WAS INSTRUCTED TO TELL CUSTOMERS THAT WE WERE "IN NO WAY CONNECTED TO ANY OTHER STORE OR PLACE OF BUSINESS", THOUGH THE CHARADE WAS RIDICULOUS. CAMPUS COPY CENTRE, THE "COMPETITION", WAS RUN BY NILOUFAR, NAHID'S TWIN SISTER, WHO WAS, IN FACT, IDENTICAL.

UNBELIEVABLE, I KNOW. BUT BELIEVE ME, IT WAS TRUE. I WORKED FOR THE SOUFERIANS FOR A YEAR AND A HALF AND STILL COULDN'T TELL THE TWO SISTERS APART EXCEPT FOR ONE DETAIL: NILOUFAR DIDN'T SMOKE.

DRIVING BACK AND FORTH BETWEEN THE TWO STORES WAS PARVIZ, NAHID'S HUSBAND, AN IMPOSING FIGURE, HEAD OF THE FAMILY AND KING OF THE CAMPUS COPY EMPIRE. THE CUSTOMERS WERE BEING DRIVEN BACK AND FORTH TOO, FROM ONE OF HIS STORES TO THE OTHER, IN AN ENDLESS CIRCLE. RIDICULOUS. BUT IT WORKED.

THE SOUFERIAN FAMILY WAS "FROM PERSIA", THEY TOLD ME. A CURIOUS EUPHEMISM, BUT AN UNDERSTAND-ABLE ONE. A WAY TO AVOID PERSECUTION AND BIAS, OR JUST AWKWARDNESS AND BAD JOKES. THE SAME REASON I DIDN'T WANT THEM TO KNOW I WAS JEWISH. SOME WORDS ARE BEST LEFT UNSAID.

Seven

SCIENTIFIC STREETS AND LITERARY WAYS, THAT'S HOW SOUTHSIDE IS SET UP. BANCROFT, CHANNING, AND DWIGHT WERE THE MEN OF LETTERS, BOWDITCH, ELLSWORTH, AND DANA THE MEN OF SCIENCE. ALSO CHOATE, WHOM TELEGRAPH AVENUE WAS NAMED AFTER BEFORE THE TELEGRAPH LINES CAME IN. BEFORE CHANGE SWEPT INTO TOWN, FOLLOWED CLOSELY BY PEOPLE ASKING FOR CHANGE, AND FOLLOWING THEM, THE WINGNUTS. THE

POLKA-DOT GUY AND STEVEN LIGHTFOOT. THE BUBBLE LADY AND LEMON MERINGUE. SOON THE FAMILIAR NAMES HAD CHANGED, AND THE FLAVOR AND CHARACTER OF THE AVENUE HAD MELDED AND MOLDED INTO SOMETHING NEW AND UNIQUE.

ONCE THE TOWN HAD FLOWED OUT FROM U.C.BERKELEY, BUT NOW U.C. BERKELEY FOUND ITSELF IN OFTEN HOSTILE TERRITORY, LOCKED IN A PERMANENT IDEOLOGICAL, CULTURAL, POLITICAL, AND REAL ESTATE BATTLE WITH THE COMMUNITY IT HAD HELPED CREATE. IN THIS SMALL CITY, A WAR RAGED WITH WORLDWIDE IMPLICATIONS. AS THE CHANCELLOR OF U.C. BERKELEY REFUSED TO DIVEST FUNDS FROM BUSINESSES INVOLVED IN SOUTH AFRICA, THE MAYOR OF BERKELEY WAS IN REBEL-CONTROLLED TERRITORY IN EL SALVADOR, DECLARING SAN ANTONIO LOS RANCHOS BERKELEY'S SISTER CITY. SHORTLY FOLLOWING THE PROCLAMATION, SAN ANTONIO LOS RANCHOS WAS NEARLY WIPED OUT OF EXISTENCE BY U.S. BOMBS.

THERE WAS A FEELING ON TELEGRAPH OF TIME SPENT INTENTLY, OF LIVES ACTIVELY LIVED OR EVEN SPENT, WASTED. LAYERS OF LIVES IN TRANSIT AND A FEW WHO STAYED. MELODY'S MOM TOLD ME ABOUT THE FIRST PANHANDLER SHE HAD SEEN, ARRIVING ON THE AVENUE IN 1966. THAT PANHANDLER WAS STILL THERE, BUT NOT MELODY'S MOTHER. LIKE MOST ADULTS WHO HAD SPENT THEIR YOUTH ON TELEGRAPH, SHE WAS SCARED OF IT NOW, AND DID HER BEST TO STAY AWAY. I HOPED THE SAME FATE DID NOT AWAIT ME.

I LOOKED AT THE OLD-TIMERS WITH RESPECT AND ADMIRATION, BOTH THE PEOPLE AND THE HANDFUL OF BUSINESSES HELD OVER FROM THE PRE-FREE-SPEECH MOVEMENT DAYS. BEFORE THE RIOTS, AND THE RISING PRICE OF BUSINESS INSURANCE BECAUSE OF BROKEN WINDOWS. BEFORE KEN SARACHAN, BERKELEY'S JUNK FOOD CZAR, WHOSE STORES AND COMPETITORS LITTERED SOUTHSIDE WITH NO LESS THAN FIVE PIZZA PARLORS, THREE COOKIE STORES, AND EIGHT ICE CREAM SHOPS, ALL WITHIN SIX CITY BLOCKS.

CHANGING TIMES. OF THE OLD-TIME STORES THERE REMAINED ONLY LAYTON'S, FOLEY'S DRUGS, THE MED, THE WESTERN STORE, AND LARRY BLAKE'S, IN FRONT OF WHICH WAS LANKY. THERE SHE STOOD, SMILING, HANDING OUT COUPONS FOR PIZZA, COOKIES, AND ICE CREAM.

Eight

SHE WAS A BOMBSHELL. ALMOND EYES, FULL BLOOD RED LIPS, LONG LASHES AND THAT CERTAIN MIX OF MISCHIEF AND CRUELTY, ALOOFNESS AND NATURAL BEAUTY THAT CASTS A SHADOW OVER YOUR HEART. EVERYONE ON THE STREET TURNED TO LOOK AT HER. AT LEAST, I IMAGINED THAT THEY DID. I KNOW MY EYES WERE NATURALLY DRAWN TO HER. MORE THAN ONCE I FOUND MYSELF CHECKING HER OUT FROM A BLOCK AWAY. "WHO'S THAT GIRL??", I'D SAY, THEN REALIZE WITH A SHOCK THAT IT WAS MY OWN GIRLFRIEND. THAT'S A GOOD FEELING, BUT ONE IMPOSSIBLE TO KEEP YOUR FOOT OUT OF YOUR MOUTH WHILE TRYING TO EXPLAIN.

UNLIKE A FEW GIRLS I'D HUNG AROUND IN THE PAST, LANKY DID NOT LOOK LIKE ME. NO, I WAS CHANGING. STILL SELF-INVOLVED, BUT AT LEAST NOW NOT JUST LOOKING FOR MY OWN REFLECTION. LANKY WAS TALL AND SKINNY LIKE ME, BUT HER FACE WAS TOTALLY DIFFERENT. OPEN WHERE MINE WAS CLOSED, SLANTED AND SHARP WHERE MINE WAS CURVED OR SMOOTH. A TOTALLY DIFFERENT FACE AND FEELING, AND A DIFFER-ENT BEARING. IT WAS FUNNY THE LONGER WE WERE TOGETHER BECAUSE, AS ALL COUPLES DO—WHETHER HUSBAND AND WIFE OR DOG AND DOGWALKER—WE BEGAN TO TAKE ON SOME OF EACH OTHERS MANNERISMS AND EXPRESSIONS. THE EFFECT WAS VERY STRANGE, AS OUR DIFFERENT MANNERS AND FACES WERE ILL-MATCHED.

SHE WAS SKINNY BUT STRONG, WITH FIRM MUSCLES AND A FIRM KISS, CHAPPED LIPS, SKIN NOT TOO SOFT. ILL-MATCHED OR NOT, WE HAD INCREDIBLY ROMANTIC SEX. STILL TOTALLY UNCOMFORTABLE AND ALIENATED FROM MY OWN BODY, I WAS ABLE TO BE COMFORTABLE WITH HERS INSTEAD. SHE HATED THE WAY I LAUGHED AT ALL THE WRONG TIMES, BUT I COULDN'T HELP IT. I WAS SO HAPPY.

Nine

A NEW GIRL, A NEW HAIR COLOR, A NEW YEAR: 5747, THE JEWISH NEW YEAR. ANY NEW START IS GREAT. BUT "ONE SWALLOW DOESN'T MAKE A SUMMER", AS

THEY SAY. WITH THE FALL LEAVES CAME SOMETHING ELSE TOO HORRIBLE TO FACE: HIGH SCHOOL.

YES, LANKY HAD TO GO BACK TO SCHOOL, TO BERKELEY HIGH, FOR HER SENIOR YEAR.

IF IT WAS EMBARRASSING TO STILL LIVE AT HOME AND HAVE A YOUNGER GIRLFRIEND, IT WAS INFINITELY MORE SO TO HAVE A GIRLFRIEND STILL IN HIGH SCHOOL. I WOULD RATHER EAT MY OWN PUKE, OR BE SEEN IN CAFE MILANO, THAN PICK HER UP AT THE PRISON FROM WHICH I'D JUST ESCAPED. I WAS A WORKING MAN NOW, BUT I STILL HAD NIGHTMARES OF CLASSROOMS AND BELLS AND NOT BEING ABLE TO GRADUATE. IT WAS DISGUSTING, REALLY. KISS ME, DARLING, BEFORE I RUN OFF TO CLASS. I DIDN'T LIKE TO DISCUSS IT. I WAS IN DENIAL.

THE CLOCK STRUCK 1:16. I CAME FLYING OUT OF LANKY'S DOOR AND STRAIGHT DOWN THE APARTMENT STAIRS, IN HOT PURSUIT OF THE EVER-ELUSIVE LAST BUS HOME. AT THE TOP OF THE SECOND FLIGHT, I TRIPPED, STUMBLED HEAD OVER HEELS, AND MANAGED TO SLIDE DOWN THE RAILING ON MY STOMACH. I ARRIVED FACE FIRST ON THE SIDEWALK IN TIME TO SEE THE LAST BUS PASS RIGHT BY. I YELLED, BUT THE DRIVER JUST HONKED AND WAVED. CURSES.

I LIKED TO WALK, BUT THE LONG WALK BACK FROM LANKY'S ALWAYS CAME WHEN I HAD ALREADY BEEN WALKING ALL DAY, OR WHEN THERE WAS WORK AT HOME WAITING, OR WHEN THERE WERE WORRIES ON MY MIND THAT I DIDN'T NEED TIME TO THINK ABOUT. THAT ONLY MADE THINGS WORSE.

NEWSPAPERS BLEW RIGHT DOWN THE MIDDLE OF SHATTUCK AVENUE. RATS CAME OUT OF THE CRACKS, RACOONS OUT OF THE SEWERS, AND EVEN DEER SOME-TIMES CAME DOWN FROM THE HILLS TO EAT OUT OF DUMPSTERS. IT WAS THAT DEAD AT NIGHT DOWNTOWN.

SOMEWHERE IN THE FAR DISTANCE, A SAXOPHONE PLAYED, SOUNDING LIKE SMOKE. I READ THE FLIERS, LOOKED AT PHOTOS IN THE PRESTO PRINT TRASH, SANG TO MYSELF. SOMEHOW IT TOOK HOURS TO MAKE IT HOME. SOMETIMES I CHANGED MY MIND AND WENT TO THE DONUT SHOP INSTEAD.

Ten

I LIVED WITH MY DAD, BUT WHAT'S THERE TO SAY ABOUT IT, REALLY? FOR THIS I MUST QUOTE JONATHIN

CHRIST FROM CODE OF HONOR: "I COULD NOT STAY AT HOME BUT I DID NOT HATE MY DAD, HE TRIED TO GIVE ME ALL THE THINGS THAT HE NEVER HAD".

YUP. THOUGH WE GOT ALONG, I WAS EMBARRASSED TO STILL BE LIVING AT HOME, AND OUR RELATIONSHIP WAS STRAINED. WHEN MY MOM HAD BEEN SICK, I HAD BEEN AROUND AS MUCH AS POSSIBLE TO HELP TAKE CARE OF HER AND THE HOUSE. WHEN SHE DIED, I HAD BEEN AROUND AS MUCH AS POSSIBLE TO HELP TAKE CARE OF HIM AND THE HOUSE. NOW I BADLY NEEDED A LITTLE SPACE OF MY OWN, BUT HAD TO FACE FACTS. THERE WAS NOWHERE FOR ME TO GO ANYWAY.

YOUR PARENTS TAKE CARE OF YOU FOR YEARS, AND THEN, INEVITABLY, THE ROLES SWITCH SOMEWHAT. A NATURAL FACT OF LIFE BUT STILL TRAGIC, AND IN BOUTS OF SELFISHNESS I CRIED MOST FOR THE FACT THAT I HAD TO GROW UP TOO SOON. MAYBE I NEEDED THE RESPONSIBILITY OF TAKING CARE OF MY DAD MORE THAN HE REALLY NEEDED TO BE TAKEN CARE OF, NEEDED TO FEEL LIKE I WAS DOING SOMETHING TO SOLVE A MOSTLY UNSOLVABLE SITUATION. BUT, WHATEVER. WE NEEDED EACH OTHER.

WE WOULD SIT AND TALK, IN THIS NEW RELATIONSHIP WE WERE BUILDING, THIS NEW FATHER AND SON BOND, BASED ON THE OLD BOND BUT WITH A NEW, MUTUAL RESPECT.

I WOULD SAY, "STOP INTERRUPTING ME! IF WE ARE GOING TO TALK, YOU ARE GOING TO HAVE TO REALLY LISTEN! THIS IS A CONVERSATION, NOT A LECTURE".

I FOUGHT TOOTH AND NAIL WITH HIM TO TREAT ME NOT LIKE ONE OF HIS STUDENTS, NOT EVEN NECESSARILY LIKE A SON, BUT LIKE A FRIEND. WE SAT AROUND IN THE EVENING DRINKING POT AFTER POT OF COFFEE AND DISCUSSING HISTORY. DEBATING. SOMETIMES ARGUING. TRYING TO KEEP HIM OCCUPIED, KEEP HIM FROM DROWNING HIS DEPRESSION IN ALCOHOL. TRYING TO KEEP MYSELF OCCUPIED AND KEEP FROM DROWNING MYSELF IN ALCOHOL, TOO, THOUGH I DIDN'T ADMIT IT AT THE TIME.

EVERY FRIDAY NIGHT WE WOULD MEET AT THE CAFE. A JAZZ GUITARIST PLAYED AND WE SAT AT MY REGULAR TABLE PLAYING CHESS AND EATING CAKE. IT WAS A NEW TRADITION I'D MADE AS A WAY TO GET HIM OUT OF THE HOUSE AND BACK A LITTLE BIT INTO THE STREAM OF LIFE. IT WAS NICE, BUT STRANGE, SINCE MY PARENTS HAD NEVER BEEN ONES TO GO OUT TO BE ENTERTAINED.

AN ODD PAIR, THIS SILVER HAIRED, BEAR-LIKE, BESPECTACLED AND LOST-LOOKING MAN WITH A YOUNG GUY WITH SPIKED HAIR AND HOLES IN HIS KNEES,

TOGETHER DRINKING AN OUTRAGEOUS AMOUNT OF COFFEE. THE MOTHER AND DAUGHTER DUOS AT OTHER TABLES EYED US WITH CURIOUS INTEREST. WHEN WE STOOD UP TO LEAVE, IT WAS OBVIOUS WE WERE FATHER AND SON. WE BOTH LURCHED FROM THE TABLE, MOVING IN FITS AND STARTS. BAD BALANCE, IT RUNS IN THE FAMILY. LUCKILY, SO DO BIG FEET.

Eleven

LIKE ANY COMMUNITY, BERKELEY HAS CERTAIN VALUES THAT ARE HANDED DOWN FROM GENERATION TO GENERATION, UNDERSTANDINGS WHICH KEEP THE MORAL FIBER INTACT AND GENTLY GUIDE YOU ON YOUR PATH THROUGH LIFE, FROM IMPRESSIONABLE YOUTH TO DYSFUNCTIONAL ADULT. FROM CO-OP KIDDIE CORRAL TO KENSINGTON CEMETARY.

WAR IS UNHEALTHY FOR CHILDREN AND ALL LIVING THINGS. VIOLENCE BEGETS VIOLENCE. DRUGS THAT WHITE PEOPLE DO ARE GOOD AND HEALTHY, DRUGS THAT BLACK PEOPLE DO ARE BAD AND EVIL. RIGHT WING CRIMINALS ARE GUILTY UNTIL PROVEN INNOCENT, LEFT WING CRIMINALS ARE ALL SIMPLY INNOCENT.

THESE PLATITUDES I KNEW WELL AND NEVER DOUBTED. I NEVER DECIDED FOR MYSELF. LIKE ALL ASSUMPTIONS, THEY WERE NOT MEANT TO BE LOOKED AT CLEARLY AND QUESTIONED.

I GREW UP, GOING THROUGH THE RITES OF PASSAGE, ON ACID, HOPING FOR A GOOD SHOT AT THE VICE-PRESIDENT WHEN HE TEMPTED FATE BY COMING TO VISIT BERKELEY ON HIS ANTI-DRUG CAMPAIGN. VIOLENCE AGAINST REAGAN AND BUSH, OF COURSE, WAS AN EXCEPTION TO THE RULE.

BUT EVEN MORE OF A CONFUSING MESS, MORE OF A BLOODBATH, MORE OF A RITUAL SLAUGHTER, WAS LEARNING MY LESSONS ABOUT LOVE.

IF YOU CAN'T BE WITH THE ONE YOU LOVE, LOVE THE ONE YOU'RE WITH. IF IT FEELS THIS GOOD, HOW CAN IT BE WRONG? ALL YOU NEED IS LOVE, NOT A BUNCH OF RULES.

THESE TOO WERE UNQUESTIONED BERKELEY ASSUMPTIONS. MONOGAMY, IN ABSENTIA, WAS FOUND GUILTY. NON-MONOGAMY, WITHOUT EXCEPTION, WAS THE RULE.

BUT NON-MONOGAMY WAS A TWO-WAY STREET

WITH MANY ACCIDENTS AND CASUALTIES, PLENTY OF PILE-UPS AND ROADKILL. MY YOUNG HEART WAS SHOT AT, STOMPED ON, AND RECYCLED. EVERY CHANCE OF A REALLY GOOD THING WAS DASHED AGAINST THE ROCKS OF FREEDOM AND UNDERSTANDING, USUALLY BY MY OWN BAD DECISIONS OR LACK OF EMPATHY.

WORSE, I'D NEVER REALLY LEARNED TO DRAW LINES. TO TREAT WOMEN AS FRIENDS, WITHOUT THAT SHADOW OF A DOUBT, THAT POSSIBILITY OF A MESSY, FRIENDSHIP-KILLING MISTAKE. I'D NEVER HAD CLEAR BOUNDARIES, NEVER BEEN IN A RELATIONSHIP THAT WASN'T "OPEN", AND NEVER QUESTIONED THOSE ASSUMPTIONS. NOT UNTIL LANKY.

Twelve

"ARE YOU DONE WITH THAT WHORE YET?", AMANDA ASKED ONE DAY.

"WHAT WHORE?" I SAID, INNOCENTLY.

"PERHAPS YOU MEAN, WHICH ONE?"

"YES", I SAID. "WHICH WHORE?"

"YOUR LITTLE HIGH SCHOOL GIRLFRIEND. THE ONE WHO WROTE ON YOUR BACK WITH MAGIC MARKER".

SILENCE SWEPT OVER THE PARK, THE PLAYGROUND, AND EVEN THE COP-FILLED 7-11 PARKING LOT ACROSS THE STREET. FINALLY I ASKED. "WHAT DID IT SAY?"

"NONE OF YOUR BUSINESS", SHE SAID, SQUINTING HER EYES AND LOOKING RIGHT THROUGH ME. "IT WASN'T WRITTEN TO YOU".

OUCH. BUT LOVE, LIKE I SAID, IS A TWO-WAY STREET, LIKE TELEGRAPH BEFORE 1972, WHEN THEY CHANGED IT TO DISCOURAGE CRUISING.

ONE NIGHT WHEN THE LIGHTS WERE OUT AND ONLY THE DIM GLOW OF THE PUSSYCAT THEATER'S NEON SIGN CAME THROUGH THE CRACKS IN THE CURTAINS, LANKY ASKED, "WHAT DOES 'PHEROMONIC' MEAN?"

"USE IT IN A SENTENCE".

"YOU MAKE ME PHEROMONIC".

"WHERE'D YOU COME ACROSS THAT?"

"I DUNNO. PROBABLY A BOOK I WAS READING".

"OR A LETTER, PERHAPS?"

"YEAH, I GUESS IT WAS A LETTER. FROM A FRIEND. HOW DID YOU KNOW?"

"LUCKY GUESS", I SAID. SOME FRIEND.

Thirteen

NATE, WHEN HE FIRST HEARD THAT AMANDA WAS PREGNANT, REPORTEDLY EXCLAIMED, "I'LL TEACH THE CHILD ALL ABOUT PUBLIC TRANSPORTATION! I'LL GET HIM MAPS FOR ALL THE LOCAL BUS ROUTES! WE'LL GO EVERYWHERE!"

OBVIOUSLY, THE MAN WAS OUT OF HIS MIND. AMANDA, ON THE OTHER END OF THE LINE OUTSIDE THE DOCTOR'S OFFICE, WAS SUDDENLY MORE WORRIED THAN AMUSED.

I FELT QUEASY TOO. A BABY. A FUTURE BART RIDER OR BUS DRIVER. FROM SCREAMING CHILD UP FRONT TO OLD DRUNK IN THE BACK, PISSING HIS PANTS. THAT WAS LIFE, AND HERE THESE TWO PEOPLE HAD DONE GONE AND MADE ANOTHER ONE. CONGRATULATIONS.

DON'T GET ME WRONG, KIDS ARE ALRIGHT, BUT DO YOU REALLY NEED TO MAKE ALL YOUR BODY FUNCTIONS PUBLIC AND TAKE THEM ON PUBLIC TRANSPORTATION? COME ON. AT ANY RATE, NATE NEVER DID GET THE CHANCE. SO, NOW, FOR THE SAKE OF THE CHILD, I'LL EXPLAIN IT MYSELF.

AC TRANSIT RUNS BUSES IN ALAMEDA COUNTY, HENCE THE NAME, WHILE BART (BAY AREA RAPID TRANSIT) RUNS TRAINS ALL OVER THE BAY AREA, INCLUDING THE SUBURBS. SIMPLE, EH? THERE'S ALSO MUNI, IN SAN FRANCISCO, THE CITY ACROSS THE BAY WHICH WE ENDEARINGLY CALL, "THE CITY".

THERE'S AN EASY WAY TO KEEP IT STRAIGHT. REMEMBER THIS: WHEN SUBURBAN BANDS GOT MAD, THEY SANG, "BART POLICE, YELLING AT ME, GET YOUR BOOTS OFF OF THE SEAT". BERKELEY BANDS, GETTING EXISTENTIAL, SANG, "RIDING ON THE BUS, I LOOKED OUTSIDE AND THOUGHT ABOUT DEATH". FRISCO BANDS, IN CONTRAST, TOOK LIFE IN THEIR OWN HANDS. "WHEN I STEP OUT OF THE HOUSE, STREETCAR TRIES TO RUN ME DOWN", SANG A YOUNG JONATHIN CHRIST. AND WHO COULD FORGET "LET'S KILL THE MUNI DRIVER"?

THERE ARE ALSO FERRIES WHICH RUN BACK AND FORTH ACROSS THE BAY, AND SOMETIMES HAVE LIVE BANDS, BUT NO SONGS I KNOW. FOR A SHORT TIME YOU COULD CATCH ONE RIGHT AT THE BERKELEY MARINA. DESPITE EFFORTS TO SAVE IT, INCLUDING A

"COUNTRY JOE AND THE FISH LIVE ON THE BERKELEY FERRY" EVENT, IT WAS SCUTTLED. APPARENTLY PEOPLE GOT "LIVE" (CARRYING ELECTRICAL CURRENT) CONFUSED WITH "LIVE" (TO RESIDE) AND SHRUGGED IT OFF AS NO GREAT SURPRISE. JUST ONE MORE REASON TO TAKE BART INSTEAD.

Fourteen

WE WERE TRUE BERKELEY KIDS. THE UNIVERSITY WAS OUR SANDBOX. WE PLAYED IN EVERY FREIGHT ELEVATOR, ON EVERY ROOF, IN EVERY UNLOCKED ROOM. WE KNEW THE PLACE INSIDE AND OUT GROWING UP, BUT NEVER REALLY SAW IT FOR WHAT IT WAS: A SCHOOL. WE WATCHED THE BANDS, WE RALLIED TO THE RALLIES, HELPED OCCUPY THE BUILDINGS, AND ONCE I SAW DIVINE AND JOHN WATERS SPEAK THERE IN PERSON. BUT A CLASS? A LECTURE? EVEN A FILM? NO WAY. AND THEY CLOSED THE LIBRARY FROM THE PUBLIC THE SAME YEAR I REALLY STARTED TO READ.

WE USED U.C. EVERY DAY, BUT COULDN'T SEE IT FROM THE SAME PERSPECTIVE AS A STUDENT, COULDN'T REALLY TAKE IT SERIOUSLY. WE FLEW PAPER AIRPLANES OFF THE TOP OF THE CAMPANILE. THE FACT THAT HALF OF OUR PARENTS WERE PROFESSORS DEAD SET ON SEEING US GO TO COLLEGE INSURED THAT NONE OF US EXCEPT MELODY EVEN APPLIED. JIMMY'S DAD, A HIGH SCHOOL TEACHER, WOULD HAVE BEEN HAPPY JUST TO SEE HIM WALK ACROSS THE GREEK THEATRE STAGE FOR BERKELEY HIGH GRADUATION. BUT THAT, TOO, WAS NOT TO BE.

WE RARELY EVEN MET A STUDENT, AND IT WASN'T FOR LACK OF TRYING. I USED TO STAND UP ON SPROUL EVERY FALL LOOKING FOR PUNKS AMONG THE NEW ARRIVALS, CHASING THEM DOWN AND LOADING THEM UP WITH FANZINES AND FLIERS FOR LOCAL SHOWS. TRYING TO SAVE THEM FROM BEING SUCKED IN, BUT I NEVER DID SUCCEED. CAL HAS A WAY OF CHEWING UP THE PEOPLE IT CAN'T SWALLOW WHOLE, AND THOSE WHO FAILED TO MAKE THE GRADE JUST WENT BACK FROM WHENCE THEY CAME.

HOW WELL DO YOU KNOW THE BACK OF YOUR HAND, REALLY? IT CAME AS A SHOCK TO FIND OUT AFTER THE FACT THAT THE OLD RADICALS AND UNDERGROUND PUBLISHERS I IDOLIZED WERE THE VERY SAME PROFESSORS THAT I SAT NEXT TO AT THE CAFE. THE AUTHORS AND POLISH POETS WHO I LOOKED TO FOR

INSPIRATION WERE THE SAME FACES LANKY WAS STICKING FLIERS IN FRONT OF ON THE AVENUE. TOWN AND GOWN MINGLED FREELY BUT DID NOT MEET.

WE FORGET NOW WHAT IT IS TO BE BERKELEY. WHO CAN BE PROUD OF IT ANYMORE WHEN IT'S IMPOSSIBLE TO GET IN THE DOOR? BUT SOME OF THE BEST THINGS, THE SAME OLD THINGS, ARE BEGGING TO BE REDISCOVERED, APPRECIATED, INHABITED. THE FIRE TRAILS, STRAWBERRY CREEK FLOWING UNDER SATHER GATE, EVEN THE STUPID MAYBECK HOUSES OR JUST ROOFTOPS AND WALKING AROUND THE CAMPUS LATE AT NIGHT. THE STUDENTS SUCK, BUT THAT SHOULDN'T KEEP US FROM MAKING GOOD USE OF THE PLACE. AND TELEGRAPH, POOR TELEGRAPH. WHO CAN REALLY STAND IT ANYMORE? BUT CAN WE AFFORD TO ABANDON IT?

IT'S A SUNNY DAY AND WE ARE SITTING WITH SOME OTHER SMELLY-LOOKING SOUTHSIDE TRASH GATHERED AROUND THAT FOUNTAIN DEDICATED TO A STRAY DOG. UPPER SPROUL. LANKY HAS BLONDE HAIR AND I HAVE ACNE. SHE IS LIZARD-LIKE, RESTING ON THE WARM ROCK WITH EYES HALF CLOSED, THE TIP OF HER TONGUE PEEKING OUT OF HER MOUTH AND INTO MINE. IN HER T-SHIRT AND FISHNETS SHE LOOKS SO THIN THAT I REMEMBER HOW I COULD FEEL HER BONES. LOOKING INTO HER LARGE NOSTRILS AND SLIGHTLY SUNKEN EYES, I WOULD SOME-TIMES IMAGINE WHILE HAVING SEX THAT I WAS FUCKING HER SKELETON. NOT MUCH OF A STRETCH OF IMAGINATION, OR ANYTHING GOTH. JUST A FACT, SHE WAS SKIN AND BONES.

THAT'S THE ONLY PICTURE I HAVE OF HER. SITTING AT THE FOUNTAIN ON A SUNNY DAY AMIDST A BUNCH OF PEOPLE, AND THERE WE ARE, ALL OVER EACH OTHER. IT'S EMBARRASSING, YET A KIND OF EMBARRASSMENT THAT FEELS GOOD. I HAVE A RULE, NEVER TAKE A PHOTO KISSING, BUT IN THIS CASE I'M HAPPY WE WERE CAUGHT UNAWARE. AMANDA TOOK THE PHOTO WHILE WE WEREN'T LOOKING, AND IT WASN'T UNTIL YEARS LATER, WHEN WE BEGAN TO COMPARE NOTES, THAT I GOT TO SEE IT AT ALL.

Fifteen

BERKELEY SCENE REPORT: LOTS OF NEWS THIS TIME. WILLIAM WOLBRINK, "THE POLKA-DOT MAN" WAS ARRESTED FOR BLOCKING A U.C. BERKELEY FIRE TRUCK. LAYING DOWN IN THE MIDDLE OF SPROUL PLAZA, PERHAPS IN HIS "UNDERWATER" MIME ROUTINE, HE "DID

NOT MOVE AND STARTED TO LAUGH", ACCORDING TO FIREFIGHTERS. CARRIED OFF BY THE COPS, WILLIAM BROKE HIS TWO-YEAR STRETCH OF NOT TALKING TO MEN WITH AN IMPROMPTU STATEMENT FOR THE PRESS. "SURE I'M A NUT, BUT I'M A CREATIVE NUT", HE SAID.

WHEN THEY HAULED WILLIAM AWAY, DID SPROUL GROW OMINOUSLY QUIET? OBSERVE, PERHAPS, A MOMENT OF SILENCE? NO, SIR. STREET PREACHERS, STREET SWEEPERS, AND SOAPBOX ORATORS RUSHED IN, COMPETING FOR THE CLEARING CROWD, CHASING AFTER NERVOUS HERDS OF OVERWORKED, OVERWHELMED UNDERGRADUATES. THE CONGA PLAYERS PLAYED ALONG, UCGLBA GAVE OUT CONDOMS, AND EVERY PAYPHONE RANG OFF THE HOOK THANKS TO SERIAL CALLER "MS. CAT". SHE PICKED UP THE POLKA-DOT MAN'S SLACK BY REFUSING TO SPEAK TO FEMALES.

J. J. CHIN STOOD ON A BUCKET BY THE KIOSKS, A LARGE SANDWICH BOARD WRAPPED AROUND HIM COVERED IN ILLEGIBLE SCRAWLINGS. "THIS IS NO FUN AT ALL", HE SAID IN BETWEEN SERMONS. "PEOPLE CALL YOU NUTS. THEY CALL YOU CRAZY. THEY MAKE FUN OF YOU". ONCE A CAMPUS VENDOR, HE'D JOINED THE FRINGE ARMY IN SUPPORT OF SHEEP HERDERS IN THE FALKLANDS, AND STAYED ON EVER SINCE.

IN A DIRECT CHALLENGE, STEPHEN LIGHTFOOT STOOD NEARBY, HOLDING A SIGN WHICH READ, "WHAT YOU SHOULD BE PROTESTING", REFERRING OF COURSE TO THE FRAME-UP OF MARK DAVID CHAPMAN. IN RESPONSE TO ACCUSATIONS OF BEING SPROUL PLAZA'S BIGGEST ASSHOLE, HE EXPLAINED, "WADING THROUGH SOCIETY'S APATHY CAN MAKE ANYONE BEHAVE LIKE A JERK AT TIMES". WORD. LIGHTFOOT SAID HE WAS ANXIOUS TO RESUME HIS QUEST AS A GOLF PRO, BUT FIRST, ONE SMALL TASK: PROVE THAT STEPHEN KING KILLED JOHN LENNON, AS ORDERED BY NIXON. IN THE MEANTIME, PLAY "ALL YOU NEED IS LOVE" VERY PAINFULLY OFF KEY, OVER AND OVER FOR YEARS.

YOU CAN'T PAINT A TRUE PICTURE USING ONLY THE BRIGHTEST, MOST VIBRANT COLORS, BUT THE PICTURE WITHOUT THEM WOULD BE LACKING THE LOCAL COLOR. AND WHY NOT PAINT WITH THE BRIGHTEST COLORS, ANYWAY?

NEXT ON MY LIST, OR PATH IF YOU FOLLOW, WAS BARRY, THE MYSTERIOUS MAN IN THE COURTYARD OF NORTHSIDE LA VAL'S. AS LONG AS ANYONE COULD REMEMBER, HE'D BEEN THERE WITH HIS TWO BOTTLES OF FANCY CHAMPAGNE, HIS PLASTIC BUCKET OF ICE, THE FAMILIAR RED SWEATPANTS AND PIGEON FEATHER IN HIS HAIR. MANY RUMORS HAD CIRCULATED ABOUT

HIM OVER THE YEARS, BUT THE TRUTH WAS MORE INCREDIBLE. HE WAS A SELF-TAUGHT SELF-DEFENSE TEACHER WHO TRAINED COPS AT THE SAN FRANCISCO POLICE ACADEMY. RECENTLY A STUDENT THERE HAD ACCIDENTALLY KICKED OUT BARRY'S TWO FRONT TEETH. "I BELIEVE IN MIRACLES", BARRY EXPLAINED, TURNING DOWN THE TRANSISTOR RADIO AND HIKING UP HIS RAINBOW SUSPENDERS TO EMPHASIZE THE POINT. "IF JESUS COMES THROUGH, I'LL BE ALRIGHT. IF HE DON'T, I'LL GO TO THE DENTIST".

THE POLKA-DOT MAN ENDED UP SURPRISING EVERY-ONE IN COURT. "I'M TRYING TO PROVE THAT A NOBODY, COMING FROM NOWHERE, CAN FACE INSTITUTIONS LIKE THE BERKELEY FIRE DEPARTMENT AND WIN", HE SAID. AND WIN HE DID.

BUT AT THE SECOND TRIAL, HE WAS NOT SO SUCCESSFUL. FINDING WILLIAM GUILTY, THE COURT SENTENCED HIM TO FIVE DAYS COMMUNITY SERVICE, STANDING ON SPROUL WEARING A SANDWICH BOARD INSTEAD OF HIS TRADEMARK DOTS, ADVERTISING THE U.C. NIGHT ESCORT SERVICE.

IT SEEMED REASONABLE ENOUGH, BUT WILLIAM NEVER QUITE SEEMED TO RECOVER FROM THE SHOCK. HE TOOK TO WEARING X'S INSTEAD OF O'S FOR A WHILE, BUT IN TIME GAVE THAT UP TOO. "I DECIDED ACTING WEIRD AND DRESSING WEIRD WAS REDUNDANT", HE SAID.

PERHAPS. BUT WHAT'S THE OTHER OPTION? WHERE HAVE YOU GONE, WILLIAM WOLBRINK? BERKELEY MISSES YOU.

Sixteen

I LIKED TO SPEND TIME WITH LANKY, BUT ALSO I LIKED TO SPEND TIME ALONE. "THAT SOLITUDE WHICH IS PAINFUL IN YOUTH BUT DELICIOUS IN THE YEARS OF MATURITY", AS EINSTEIN SAID. I WAS STILL A BIT OF A BABY BUT ALREADY SOMETHING OF AN OLD MAN, AND STARTING TO LIKE THE TASTE OF TIME ALONE, SOMETHING I'D ALWAYS HATED. STARTING TO MAKE PEACE WITH MYSELF AND MY OWN MIND, AND, EVENTUALLY, EVEN MY OWN BODY. STARTING TO UNDERSTAND MYSELF A LITTLE AND SOMETIMES LIKE WHAT I FOUND. AND SOMETIMES STRUGGLE TO CHANGE.

IT WASN'T EXACTLY SOLITUDE WHICH I LOVED BEST, BUT JUST A SENSE OF BEING BY MYSELF. MORE

OFTEN THAN NOT, MY PRIVATE TIME WAS SPENT IN PUBLIC. I LIKED TO BE AROUND PEOPLE OR PLACES WHERE I COULD FEEL THEIR PRESENCE, PLACES THAT FELT "LIVED IN". EMPTY STREETS, DOORWAYS, CAFES, ABANDONED BUILDINGS, BUSY BUSTLING AVENUES, BUSES, AND BART. RIDING PUBLIC TRANS- PORTATION, WALKING THE HILLS, SKATING AROUND, EXPLORING OR JUST SITTING ON THE ROCKS ON THE WATERFRONT. KEEPING MYSELF OPEN TO NEW IDEAS AND APPROACHABLE TO NEW PEOPLE. BUT MOST OF THE TIME, KEEPING SILENT.

WAS I LOOKING? HUNGRY? DESPERATE AND EAGER FOR SOMETHING I DIDN'T HAVE? MAYBE. MOSTLY I JUST LIKED TO WALK AND RIDE AROUND AND BE PART OF THE WORLD, A FINGERPRINT ON THE BIGGER PICTURE. I WAS SO HAPPY JUST TO FEEL A SENSE OF FREEDOM, TO MAKE MY OWN DECISIONS, TO HAVE MY OWN LIFE, EVEN IF THAT MEANT SITTING IN THE CAFE ALL DAY AND THE DONUT SHOP ALL NIGHT IF I WANTED TO. I WAS TROUBLED, BUT I WASN'T TRAPPED IN THEM. I COULD TAKE THEM WITH ME AND SORT THEM OUT OR JUST WEAR THEM DOWN. I COULD GO WHEREVER I WANTED, BUY WHAT I WANTED, AND NOT BE BOTHERED. IT WAS A LITTLE KID'S DREAM. I COULD REACH OVER THE COUNTER.

Seventeen

ALL THE OLD PEOPLE WHO CAME INTO CAMPUS COPY MART SANG THE SAME SAD SONG. "I'M OLD, I'M OUT OF TOUCH, I'M USELESS, I DON'T KNOW HOW ALL THESE FANCY NEWFANGLED MACHINES WORK".

"THERE'S NOTHING WRONG WITH BEING OUT OF TOUCH", I WINKED, "AS LONG AS YOU STILL GOT THAT HUMAN TOUCH". I TRIED TO EASE THEM UP, THEN TEACH THEM TO USE THE MACHINES WHICH WERE, FRANKLY, TEN YEARS OUTDATED THEMSELVES.

"STOP THAT!!" I SCREAMED, ALMOST GIVING THE POOR SENIORS A HEART ATTACK. BUT IT WASN'T THEM I WAS YELLING AT. IT WAS RIP, WHO THOUGHT IT WAS HILARIOUS TO RUN INTO THE STORE AND SNEAK UP BEHIND THE OLD FOLKS WHILE THEIR BACKS WERE TURNED.

"RIP! STOP SNEAKING UP ON THE CUSTOMERS!" I YELLED. "I TOLD YOU NOT TO SPIKE UP YOUR HAWK BEFORE VISITING ME AT WORK! GET OUT! YOU'RE GONNA GET ME IN BIG TROUBLE!"

NO USE TELLING THE PERSON WHO DOSED YOUR ENTIRE EIGHTEENTH BIRTHDAY PARTY THAT DANGER IS APPROACHING. HE STAYED TO WELCOME IT.

BUT YOU NEVER KNOW WHAT WILL BREAK THE ICE. AFTER A WHILE, THE CUSTOMERS STARTED SNEAKING UP ON RIP. ODDLY ENOUGH, OLD PEOPLE SEEM TO LOVE MOHAWKS. "CAN I TOUCH THAT?" THEY ASKED. "HOW DO YOU SLEEP?"

RIP SAID, "I DON'T". THEY NODDED. SENIORS, LIKE PUNKS, ARE KNOWN FOR DRINKING A LOT OF COFFEE AND NOT SLEEPING MUCH.

"I HAD A MOHAWK ONCE", ONE OLD MAN SAID. "IN THE FIFTIES". THAT MADE RIP FEEL PRETTY MOLDY. HE GROWLED, "I'LL GIVE YOU ONE AGAIN IF YOU HOLD STILL A MINUTE".

NEXT TO RIP, I LOOKED TAME AND REASONABLE, EVEN A LITTLE OLD FASHIONED. THE OLD FOLKS LOOKED AT ME WITH NEWFOUND RESPECT.

Eighteen

EVERYONE WAS RUSHING AROUND IN THAT PARTICULARLY EASTBAY WAY, DOING A MILLION LITTLE THINGS, PRETEND-ING THEY WERE ALL USEFUL AND NECESSARY. A FEW RUN-INS WITH FRIENDS, A FEW ERRANDS, A FREE FOOD HOOK-UP HERE AND A SENTIMENTAL BIT OF SIDEWALK GRAFFITI THERE. EVERYONE LOC'D OUT ON COFFEE AND LET LOOSE ON THE CITY STREETS, FOLLOWING HABITUAL ROUTES, RUNNING INTO EACH OTHER WHERE THEY CROSSED, WALKING OR RIDING ALONGSIDE FOR A WAYS TO TALK OR STOPPING MOMENTARILY TO SHARE A SMOKE.

SOMETHING WRONG WITH PEOPLE IN BERKELEY. NO ONE TALKS IN COMPLETE SENTENCES, NOTHING IS WEIRD TO ANYONE, AND CONVERSATIONS GO FROM ZERO TO EIGHTY IN POINT FIVE SECONDS. NO SOONER HAVE YOU SAID HELLO, THEY'RE TELLING YOU THEIR LIFE STORY, AND WHAT'S WEIRDER, YOU'RE FINISHING IT FOR THEM A MINUTE LATER. EVERYONE TALKS AS IF RESUMING AN OLD CONVERSATION WHERE IT LEFT OFF. EVEN PEOPLE WHO HAVE NEVER MET.

WORK PUT A BIG CRAMP IN MY STYLE, BUT IT WAS KIND OF NICE TO BE STATIONARY FOR A CHANGE, A STOPOVER FOR EVERYONE ELSE ON THEIR WAY ACROSS TOWN, A MESSAGE BOARD AND REST STOP FOR THE WEARY BERKELEY TRAVELERS. NO SOONER HAD NAHID STEPPED OUT THE DOOR, SOMEONE I KNEW WOULD STOP IN. USUALLY IT WAS RIP, LOOKING WIDE-EYED AND WILD.

"WHAT'S THE MOTHERFUCKING GLUE THAT HOLDS IT ALL TOGETHER?" HE ASKED AS I HELD OUT MY HAND.

I SAID, "WHAT ELSE?"

"THAT'S RIGHT", HE SAID. "PEET'S COFFEE. AND THE GIRL AT THE PEET'S BY THE CLAREMONT WHO KICKS DOWN FREE COFFEE COUPONS!"

"NO SHIT! I KNOW IT! SHE GIVES THEM TO ME TOO! I MEAN, IT'S ALWAYS NICE WHEN THERE'S A PUNK WORKING AND THEY GIVE IT TO YOU FREE, BUT YOU JUST NEVER KNOW! WITH COUPONS THERE'S NO MORE WORRIES!"

"WORD. AND NO MORE FUMBLING WITH BILLS TRYING TO FIGURE OUT WHETHER OR NOT THEY WANT YOU TO PAY".

WE DID A LITTLE PEET'S COFFEE DANCE, SHAKING HANDS AND EVERYTHING ELSE. AND THEN I ASKED, "SO WHAT ARE YOU UP TO TODAY?"

"OH, SAME AS ALWAYS. I WENT OUT TO THE CITY. SAT OUTSIDE THE PEET'S BY THE CASTRO, THEN RODE DOWN TO THE ONE ON MARKET, GOT ANOTHER CUP TO DRINK ON BART".

"AND THEN?"

"HOPPED THE GATE AT LAKE MERRITT STATION AND GOT A CUP AT THE PEET'S THERE. THEN, RODE UP TO THE CLAREMONT HOTEL."

"YOU FORGOT PIEDMONT".

THERE'S ONE IN PIEDMONT? OH SHIT. I DIDN'T KNOW. WELL, I STILL HAVE THREE MORE TO GO FROM HERE ANYWAY".

"SEVEN CUPS, IN ONE DAY?"

"EVERY DAY", HE SAID.

"UNTIL THE COUPONS RUN OUT".

"YES".

"GETTING ANY WRITING DONE?"

"BY THE TIME I COPY DOWN ALL THE NOTES ON MY ARMS AND HANDS", HE SAID, "IT'S TIME TO GO AGAIN".

"SO WHAT YOU'RE TRYING TO SAY IS..."

"RIGHT. DO YOU THINK I COULD USE THE BATHROOM?"

Nineteen

EVEN WITH OUR NEWFOUND BOND, ME AND MY DAD WERE VERY DIFFERENT CREATURES. I TENDED TO TAKE AFTER MY MOM, AT LEAST IN THE OBVIOUS WAYS. THE MAIN CONFLICT SHE'D HAD WITH MY DAD WAS THE SAME ONE I HELD, A GRUDGE OVER ORGANIZATION AND THE

STATE OF THE HOUSE. A BATTLE AGAINST HIS OBSESSIVE COLLECTING OF JUNK AND THE ELABORATE REASONS NOT TO LET EVEN ONE SCRAP BE SWEPT AWAY. IF ANYTHING, HE HAD GOTTEN WORSE AFTER MY MOM DIED. HE ATTACHED A MORBID SENTIMENTALITY TO IT ALL, A GRIEF-COLORED GLOSS THAT FENDED OFF ANY ATTACK.

I WAS SENTIMENTAL TOO, OF COURSE, BUT FEARED THAT THE GRIEF ITSELF WOULD BE A SECOND FUNERAL FOR US. PEOPLE ARE POSSESSIVE ABOUT GRIEF, AND POSSESSIVE ABOUT POSSESSIONS TOO, AND THE COMBINATION, AN UNQUESTIONABLE RIGHT TO BUILD UP AS MUCH OF BOTH AS POSSIBLE, WOULD SPELL OUT OUR DOOM. HE HAD A SENTIMENTAL ATTACHMENT FOR ALL MY MOM'S THINGS, PLUS HIS OWN THINGS FROM THEIR LIFE TOGETHER, INCLUDING MANY THINGS MY MOM HAD ALWAYS HATED. THIS WAS MY INHERITANCE. IT WAS HARD TO BE AT HOME.

JO AND RIP ALSO HAD PACKRAT PARENTS, AND WHEN WE WERE TOGETHER WE WOULD DISCUSS STRATEGY AND, I SUPPOSE, FIND SOLACE IN A SORT OF GROUP THERAPY. SADDLED AS WE ALL WERE WITH HOUSES FILLED TO THE BRIM WITH JUNK, I STILL CONSIDERED THEM LUCKY, FOR THEIR PARENTS' OBSESSIVENESS HAD TAKEN ON AN ACUTE, FOCUSED FORM. RIP'S DAD WAS AN ANTHROPOLOGIST SPECIALIZING IN FIELD RECORDINGS. JO'S MOM, A DOCUMENTER OF POLITICAL SPEECHES. BOTH HELD SACRED THE COLLECTING, AND CATALOGING, OF SOUND. JO AND RIP BOTH FOUGHT PILES OF DETERIORATING REEL-TO-REEL TAPES. I FOUGHT ALL SORTS OF ASSORTED TRASH AND MY DAD'S DUBIOUS EXCUSES. MOUNTAINS OF BOXES ("YOU NEVER KNOW WHEN YOU'LL NEED ONE"), STACKS OF COAT HANGERS ("GOOD FOR MAKING CERAMICS"), PILES OF PEET'S COFFEE BAGS ("YOUR MOM LIKED THE DESIGN"), STYROFOAM PEANUTS, POPSICLE STICKS, PLASTIC MILK JUGS, FABRIC SCRAPS, AND ON AND ON. WHAT RIP, JO, AND I HAD IN COMMON WAS THE BURDEN OF FIGURING OUT WHAT WAS REALLY WORTH SAVING AND WHY. THREE PARTS JANITOR, ONE PART ARCHIVIST. SHAKEN SLIGHTLY.

LIKE MY MOM, I HATED DISORGANIZATION AND NOT BEING ABLE TO QUICKLY FIND WHAT I WAS LOOKING FOR. LIKE HER, I HATED THE CLUTTER. BUT FOR ALL HER SHELVES AND FILE CABINETS, HER SYSTEMATIC AND LOGICAL SENSE OF ORDER, SHE TOO WAS A PACKRAT. THE AMOUNT OF CRAP SHE LEFT BEHIND WAS PHENOMENAL. AND I WAS THE ONE IN CHARGE OF CLEARING, CLEANING, AND SORTING IT ALL, THROWING OUT THE GARBAGE AND TRYING TO FIND A GOOD HOME OR GOOD CAUSE FOR THE REST, SOMETIMES BEHIND MY FATHER'S BACK. THE ALTERNATIVE WAS

PUTTING IT IN THE ATTIC WHERE IT QUICKLY BECAME A NEST FOR REAL RATS.

JO AND RIP WERE LUCKY. THEY COULD CONVERT THE DUSTY, BULKY ANALOG TO CONCISE, EASILY STORED DIGITAL TAPES. I WISH I COULD CONVERT THE MOUNTAINS OF SHREDS, SCRAPS, AND SPOOLS OF YARN AT MY HOUSE INTO SOMETHING SMALL AND USEFUL. I THOUGHT OF THE IRANIAN STUDENTS WHO TOOK OVER THE U.S. EMBASSY AND BROUGHT IN RUG WEAVERS TO PIECE TOGETHER ALL THE CLASSIFIED DOCUMENTS THE AMERICANS HAD SHRED. ONCE ASSEMBLED, THEY PUBLISHED IT AS A TWENTY VOLUME SET. MY MOM, A WEAVER HERSELF, HAD BEEN SO TAKEN BY THAT STORY, SHE TRACKED DOWN AND BOUGHT ONE OF THE BOOKS FOR ME. VERY COOL. BUT NOW I WAS STUCK WITH HER LOOM, TRYING TO MAKE SENSE OUT OF MY PARENTS' TRASH, AND I DIDN'T EVEN KNOW HOW TO WEAVE.

Twenty

THERE WAS A PILE OUTSIDE THE CESSPOOL, A GROWING TRASH HEAP. WHETHER A BOTTLE OR BLACK FLAG RECORD, OLD FOOD OR SHOES YOU'D JUST REMOVED TO SLEEP. WHATEVER IT WAS, IF JIMMY WAS BORED BY IT, HE THREW IT OUT THE WINDOW. THE PILE WAS NEARLY UP TO HIS SECOND FLOOR ROOM.

WHEN THEY GOT THE HOUSE, I WANTED TO LIVE THERE TOO. RIP, JIMMY, NOAH AND ME. WE HAD BEEN FRIENDS FOREVER. WE KNEW EACH OTHER WELL. THEY AGREED, AND WERE GLAD I UNDERSTOOD. THAT WAS EXACTLY WHY THEY HAD TO SAY NO.

I WAS HURT, BUT NOT TOO HURT TO LIVE ON THEIR COUCH EVERY WEEKEND RENT-FREE. I WOULD AWAKEN WITH A LIT CIGARETTE IN MY MOUTH AND JIMMY HOVERING OVER ME, POURING OUT WHOLE GARBAGE CANS FULL OF BOTTLES RIGHT NEXT TO MY HEAD. OR UZBEKO PLAYING HER FUCKING SAXOPHONE. SOMETHING WRONG WITH THAT GIRL.

ONE MORNING THERE WAS A MINIATURE OPERA AS RIP AND JIMMY'S BICKERING AND BANTER ERUPTED INTO A DUEL. FIRST WITH WORDS, THEN BOTTLES, BIKES, AND, WHEN THEIR SCREAMS AND CURSES REACHED A FEVERISH PITCH, A MELODIC CRESCENDO, A HARMONIC CONVERGENCE EVEN, JIMMY BROUGHT THE CURTAINS DOWN, LITERALLY, BY RIPPING RIP'S DOOR RIGHT OFF THE HINGES AND THROWING IT THROUGH THE FRONT WINDOW, INCHES FROM MY SLEEPY HEAD. THEN THEY KISSED AND POURED

EACH OTHER COFFEE. I USUALLY WAKE UP IN A GOOD, SILLY MOOD, BUT AT THE CESSPOOL I WOKE UP LAUGHING OUT LOUD.

CRUSTY-EYED AND BUMPING INTO THINGS, WE POOLED OUR FUNDS AND COOKED UP A HUGE FEAST. IT WAS THE BEST TIME OF DAY, CROWDING IN THE KITCHEN AND THEN LOUNGING ON THE PORCH. LISTENING TO THE GERMS FIRST 45, THE ONE RECORDED IN STEREO, VOCALS ON THE RIGHT SIDE AND MUSIC ON THE LEFT. SURE, LOTS OF PEOPLE LEARNED TO PLAY BASS LISTENING TO THE RAMONES FIRST ALBUM WITH ONE BROKEN SPEAKER, BUT HOW MANY PEOPLE LEARNED TO SING LISTENING TO DARBY CRASH A CAPPELLA? ONLY NOAH.

Twenty-one

THE CESSPOOL WAS LOCATED AT 41 BURL AVENUE, NEAR MACARTHUR BART. NEXT DOOR WAS 43 BURL, HOME OF THE NOTORIOUS VIOLENT YOUTH GANG, "43 BURL, FUCK THE WORLD". THOUGH IT WAS NOT UNCOMMON TO HEAR OF A GANG BASED OUT OF A PARTICULAR HOUSING PROJECT, IT WAS LESS COMMON TO HEAR ABOUT A GANG BASED OUT OF ONE LITTLE HOUSE, ESPECIALLY A SUBURBAN LOOKING FOURPLEX LIKE 43 BURL. PERHAPS SELF-CONSCIOUS ABOUT THE SUBURBAN APPEARANCE OF THEIR HOME TURF WITH ITS PINK TRIM AND TIDY PORCH, THE FOOT SOLDIERS OF 43 BURL, FTW STOOD GUARD ON THE SIDEWALK LOOKING GRIM AND MURDEROUS. A TRAIL OF "43 BURL, FTW" GRAFFITI LED FROM THEIR HOUSE TO THE CORNER LIQUOR STORE AND BACK.

IF WE SPRAYPAINTED, IT WAS ONLY ON THE LOWER NUMBERS. THE LIQUOR STORE, FALLING CLEARLY IN THEIR TERRITORY, WAS ALWAYS A TOUCHY ISSUE, AS WERE PARKING SPACES, AND RIP HAD TO REMIND ME AGAIN AND AGAIN NOT TO MAKE SO MANY HAND GESTURES, BECAUSE IN MY ANIMATED WAY OF TALKING I CAME CLOSE TO SETTING OFF A BURL STREET TURF WAR. I LOOKED LIKE I WAS "THROWING SIGNS".

LIVING IN THE SHADOW OF 43 BURL, IT WAS ONLY NATURAL THAT THE CESSPOOL WOULD FORM ITS OWN VIOLENT YOUTH GANG, MORE IN TRIBUTE THAN IN RESPONSE. THE CESSPOOL PUNKS, UNRULIEST OF ALL MOBS. COUNTING EVERYONE WHO CRASHED ON THE COUCH, WE HAD MORE STRENGTH IN NUMBERS THAN 43 BURL, FTW, THOUGH ANY ONE OF THEIR NUMBERS

COULD HAVE KICKED OUR COLLECTIVE ASS WITH ONE
HAND TIED BEHIND HIS BACK. WE WERE CAREFUL TO
KEEP ON GOOD TERMS THROUGH A SIMPLE, TACIT
UNDERSTANDING. WHEN OUR MOB HIT THE STREETS,
WE TOOK THE OPPOSITE DIRECTION.

WATCH OUT, CITY, THE FEARED AND REVERED CESSPOOL
PUNKS ARE HERE! LIKE A PACK OF FEROCIOUS LIONS,
THEY GROWL AND PROWL AROUND THE PAVEMENT LATE
AT NIGHT IN FRONT OF THE 'LECTRIC WASHHOUSE,
DOING THEIR LAUNDRY. THEY YAWN AND SCRATCH IN THE
MORNING, COOKING A BIG BREAKFAST, THEN STUMBLE
DOWN THE STAIRS AND DOWN THE LOW NUMBERS OF
BURL STREET TO STALK THEIR PREY.

DANGER LURKS AT THE LANEY FLEA MARKET! A
CLOUD OF SMOKE WITH BOOTS ON, PASSING FROM STALL
TO STALL WITH YELLOWY EYES! THEY STRIKE! ANOTHER
BOOK FROM THE HEINEMANN AFRICAN WRITERS SERIES
IS ADDED TO THE CESSPOOL LIBRARY! ANOTHER HOOPTY
BIKE! THEY STOP TO LIGHT ANOTHER SMOKE.

SOMETHING WONDERFUL ABOUT A POSSE OF PUNKS
WALKING DOWN THE STREET ON A SUNDAY SHUFFLING
THEIR FEET, PAUSING TO REST IN THE SHADE AND LOOK
AT THAT OTHER BRIGHT AND TIGHTLY PACKED BUNCH:
THE POND CARPS AT THE OAKLAND MUSEUM.

Twenty-two

RIP AND I HAD KNOWN EACH OTHER SINCE AGE SIX
AND SEVEN, RESPECTIVELY, LONG ENOUGH THAT THE
LINES BETWEEN US SOMETIMES BLURRED. VALUES OF
MINE HAD TAKEN ROOT IN HIS CHARACTER AND FOUND
MORE FERTILE GROUND THERE. IDEAS OF HIS, LONG
SINCE ABANDONED, HAD BECOME A WAY OF LIFE FOR ME.
WE WERE PART OF EACH OTHER ALMOST LITERALLY.

I COULD SEE PARTS OF MYSELF THAT I LIKED,
HATED, OR MISSED IN HIM. WAS THAT WHAT MADE US
GET ALONG? WOULDN'T THE PART OF HIM IN ME ALWAYS
SEE HIS SIDE? WOULDN'T IT PINE FOR HIM, WANTING TO
RETURN TO THE REST? OR WOULD IT BE THE PART THAT
ALWAYS CHALLENGED HIM AND GOT ALONG THE WORST?
SOMETIMES, I THINK, HAVING KNOWN EACH OTHER SO
WELL MADE IT HARD FOR US TO SEE WHO THE OTHER
PERSON REALLY WAS.

"ONE PERSON POSSESSES OF ANOTHER ONLY WHAT
ONE CAN CHANGE IN HIM". MALRAUX SAID THAT. BUT
LANKY DISAGREED. HER FRIENDS, SHE SAID, WERE THE

ONES SHE HAD CHANGED THE LEAST.

I THOUGHT, NO ONE REALLY NOTICES THE WAY THEY AFFECT THOSE AROUND THEM. DIDN'T LANKY SEE THE WAY SUSAN HAD TAKEN ON MANY OF HER CHARACTERISTICS, EVEN THE WAY SHE DID HER HAIR? PERHAPS YOUR BEST FRIENDS ARE THE ONES WHO IMITATE YOU THE MOST?

STRANGELY, THE WAY ALL THE GUYS IN OUR GROUP SPOKE WAS AN IMITATION OF RIP IMITATING ME. OR WAS IT AN IMITATION OF RIP IMITATING MY DAD, WHO YELLED WHEN HE ANSWERED THE PHONE AND HAD A STRANGE NONSEQUITUR OR "WORD SALAD" STYLE? OR AN IMITATION OF ME IMITATING RIP IMITATING MY DAD? WHEW! HOW-EVER IT HAD BEGUN, THERE WAS NO QUESTION THAT WE ALL SOUNDED THE SAME NOW, WERE REGULARLY MISTAKEN FOR EACH OTHER OVER THE PHONE, AND GOT ASKED ON THE STREET, "ARE YOU CANADIAN?"

YEARS AND MANY CHANGES LATER, I COULD STILL SEE GLIMPSES OF RIP IN JO, GESTURES OF SUSAN IN JIMMY, AND PARTS OF US ALL TRANSPOSED. WE'D BE TALKING AND A SINGLE PHRASE WOULD SLIP, OR SOME-THING ALL TOO FAMILIAR IN A MANNERISM OR WAY OF MOVING OR, DARE I SAY IT? A KISS.

A SHOCK OF RECOGNITION WOULD FOLLOW, BUT TOO EMBARRASSING OR TOO PAINFUL TO ACKNOWLEDGE. CRAZY. WE REALLY DO BECOME PART OF EACH OTHER IN ALL THIS PUSHING AND PULLING AND ROLLING AROUND.

Twenty-three

ONCE UPON A TIME TWO YOUNG PEOPLE MET AND BECAME LOVERS IN A LITTLE APARTMENT ON CHANNING WAY. JUST LIKE ME AND LANKY BUT A DECADE EARLIER AND A BLOCK DOWN. BUT THOSE TWO WENT ON TO KIDNAP PATTY HEARST AND ROB BANKS WITH THE S.L.A.! DAMN! MISGUIDED, PERHAPS, BUT A LOT MORE EXCITING THAN ANY OF OUR PROSPECTS.

FURTHER DOWN CHANNING WAS THE BLOCK THAT ONCE REMOVED ALL THE BACKYARD FENCES TO CREATE ONE LARGE YARD TO SHARE, EVEN SHARING CHILDCARE. WE WALKED BY AND WAVED. EVERY HOUSE HAD BRICK WALLS AND BARBED WIRE NOW. EVEN THE FENCES HAD FENCES.

IT WAS HARD TO BELIEVE THE NEIGHBORHOOD HAD ONCE BEEN A RADICAL HOTBED. NOW IT WAS SLEEPY, AND BARELY A NEIGHBORHOOD AT ALL. DESPITE BEING RIGHT DOWNTOWN, THERE WAS NOWHERE TO

GET COFFEE, AND NOWHERE FOR GROCERIES AFTER SEVEN AT NIGHT. IT WAS MORE DEAD THAN ALIVE.

WHAT HAPPENED? FROM WHAT I GATHER, HERRICK HOSPITAL EXPANDED, TAKING OUT THE HEART OF THE NEIGHBORHOOD WHEN IT DID, AND PUTTING IN A NEW WING AND A PARKING LOT IN ITS PLACE. NOT A LOT OF LAND INVOLVED, BUT ENOUGH TO BLOCK THE FLOW OF BLOOD.

I WONDERED WHAT IT HAD BEEN LIKE BEFORE. I DAYDREAMED, BUT DIDN'T COMPLAIN. AFTER ALL, SEASONS CHANGE. THE NEW WING BROUGHT NEW JOBS, AND NEW JOBS EVENTUALLY BROUGHT A NURSE FROM MADERA WHO WAS LOOKING FOR A PLACE TO MOVE WHERE LIFE WOULD BE BETTER FOR HER TEENAGE DAUGHTER.

WHO ELSE BUT MY BABY, LARENKA? "IF YOU COULD CALL THAT A LIFE," HER MOM SAID.

Twenty-four

NEXT DOOR TO LANKY LIVED SCOTT "RUSH" SHAW, "PARTY COORDINATOR" FOR LAAZ ROCKIT, ONE OF MANY LOCAL HAIR BANDS TRYING TO MAKE IT AT THE TIME. COMING HOME DRUNK ONE MORNING, SCOTT'S GIRLFRIEND CAME TO THE WRONG DOOR, AN EASY MISTAKE TO MAKE SINCE EVERY APARTMENT WAS IDENTICAL. BUT SO, IT TURNED OUT, WAS EVERY LOCK AND KEY. A LOT OF NEIGHBORS GRUMBLING WITH EACH OTHER AND THREATENING TO KILL THE LANDLORD THAT DAY.

WHO LIVED DOWNTOWN? BESIDES THE LANKY FAMILY, SCOTT "RUSH" SHAW, AND MELODY'S MOM? BESIDES NATE, AMANDA, AND THEIR CRAZY NEIGHBOR WHO'S APARTMENT I WAS SUPPOSED TO TAKE WHEN SHE GOT COMMITTED? WHO KNEW THAT SHE WOULD TURN OUT TO BE THE ONLY SANE ONE AFTER ALL? THE FEW PEOPLE WE SAW WERE STUDENTS, SINGLE MOTHERS, AND AN OCCASIONAL IMMIGRANT FAMILY. BUT THAT ACCOUNTED FOR LESS THAN HALF OF THE HOUSES AND APARTMENT BUILDING DOORS.

WHO LIVED BEHIND ALL THE YELLOW, BROKEN CURTAINS AND OVERGROWN GARDENS? THE OLD RADICALS, I ASSUME, GROWN OLDER. OR, RATHER, THOSE AMONG THE RADICALS WHO PACED THEMSELVES WHILE THE OTHERS BURNED OUT, WHO HELD ONTO THEIR PLACES

WHILE EVERYONE ELSE MOVED ON OR MOVED AWAY. A LOT OF SHUT-INS AND SECTION EIGHT CASES AND THOSE PEOPLE WHO'S LIVES CHANGED BUT COULDN'T BRING THEMSELVES TO GIVE UP AN AMAZINGLY CHEAP RENT-CONTROLLED PLACE.

SUSAN'S MOM COMES TO MIND. SHE HATED BERKELEY AND HIPPIES AND HELD A HIGH-PAYING JOB AS LOAN OFFICER AT A SUBURBAN BANK. BUT EVERY DAY SHE DROVE BACK FROM THE SUBURBS, PARKED IN THE PARKING LOT BEHIND TELEGRAPH, AND TOOK THE BACK ENTRANCE INTO HER APARTMENT. HER FRONT WINDOWS LOOKED OUT DIRECTLY ONTO THE AVENUE, BUT SHE KEPT THEM CLOSED AND BLOCKED BY HEAVY DRAPES, CHOOSING INSTEAD TO LOOK OUT THE SKYLIGHT, SIT ON THE FANCY COUCH, AND PRETEND SHE WAS SOMEWHERE ELSE.

WHY NOT JUST MOVE? BECAUSE, HER TELEGRAPH RENT-CONTROLLED APARTMENT WAS LARGE AND COST THE SAME AS WHEN SHE GOT IT BACK IN HER HIPPIE DAYS: SEVENTY BUCKS A MONTH. "THINK OF IT AS AN INVESTMENT", SHE LIKED TO SAY. HAVING ARRIVED ON TELEGRAPH TOO LATE TO REALLY MAKE THE HIPPIE SCENE, SHE HAD, HOWEVER, BEEN JUST IN TIME TO RELIEVE THE FIRST SHIFT.

"THESE PEOPLE COULD NOT HAVE ACHIEVED THE REVOLUTION", AS TROTSKY SAID, "BUT WERE PERFECTLY SUITED TO EXPLOIT IT".

Twenty-five

BUSINESS IS SELF-CONSCIOUS BY NATURE, ALWAYS STRIVING TO BE AS FAMILIAR AND UNTHREATENING AS POSSIBLE. MAYBE FOREIGN BUT NEVER ALIEN. WHICH IS REALLY JUST A MATTER OF PERCEPTION. AND APPEARANCES.

NEXT DOOR TO OUR COPY SHOP OWNED BY PEOPLE "FROM PERSIA" WAS THE "MEDITERRANEAN" RESTAURANT OWNED BY PALESTINIANS. NEXT TO THAT, THE YEMENITE PLACE NAMED AFTER A CITY 3,000 MILES FROM THE YEMEN BORDER: CASABLANCA. ON THE CORNER, THE KOREAN-OWNED DONUT SHOP STAFFED BY SKINHEADS. BUT THAT'S ANOTHER STORY.

MY BOSSES, THE SOUFERIANS, HAD EMIGRATED RIGHT AFTER REVOLUTION SWEPT THEIR COUNTRY. I WONDERED WHY THEY HAD LEFT. COULD THEY BE ROYALISTS? NATIONALISTS? COMMUNISTS? THEY HADN'T

EMIGRATED FOR PURELY ECONOMIC REASONS, THAT MUCH WAS CLEAR. I HYPOTHESIZED, AND READ UP ON THE SUBJECT ON THE SLY. BUT I DIDN'T PRY.

AS THE ONLY EMPLOYEE AT A FAMILY BUSINESS, I HAD QUICKLY BECOME ONE OF THE FAMILY. THAT MEANT, AS ONE OF THE FAMILY, I WAS OBLIGED TO BE THERE DAY IN AND OUT, ABOVE AND BEYOND THE CALL OF DUTY, RUSHING TO EVERY EMERGENCY. IF I FAILED, THEY TOOK IT PERSONALLY, AND I WAS MADE TO FEEL GUILTY INSTEAD OF REPRIMANDED. WHEN I WAS GOOD, I WAS A GOOD EMPLOYEE. WHEN I WAS BAD, I WAS A BAD SON.

DESPITE THE INCONSISTENCIES OR MAYBE IN SPITE OF THEM, WE GOT ALONG AND MISUNDERSTOOD EACH OTHER WELL, AND OUR DAILY BUSTLE TOOK ON THE TROUBLED BUT WACKY FLAVOR OF A SITUATION COMEDY. WHEN CUSTOMERS CAME IN, THOUGH, COMPLAINING ABOUT THE COPY STORE DOWN THE STREET "RUN BY CRAZY IRANIANS", I DIDN'T KNOW WHETHER OR NOT TO LAUGH.

Twenty-six

WHAT MADE MY JOB WORTHWHILE WAS THE REGULAR CUSTOMERS WHO CAME IN EVERY DAY AND, LITTLE BY LITTLE, WARMED UP TO ME. THEY'D TELL ME ABOUT THEIR SONS AND DAUGHTERS, THEIR GRAND-CHILDREN AND PETS. SOME WOULD TEACH ME A LITTLE LESSON EVERY DAY, OR TELL ME OF THEIR TRAVELS. SOME WOULD BRING A GIFT, A PIECE OF FRUIT OR A TAPE OF MUSIC THEY DIDN'T LIKE BUT THOUGHT MAYBE I WOULD. SOME DID NOT SPEAK ENGLISH BUT WOULD CONVERSE WITH ME A WHILE ANYWAY.

OF THEM ALL, MY FAVORITE WAS A LITTLE GUY WITH A GREEN TWEED HAT. IT WAS THE KIND OF HAT ALL THE OLD GUYS WORE BUT I COULD NEVER FIND. WHEN ASKED, "WHERE DO YOU GET A HAT LIKE THAT?", THEY ONLY THOUGHT I WAS MAKING FUN OF THEM.

"I SUPPOSE IT'S NOT IN STYLE ANYMORE", THEY'D SAY DEFENSIVELY, OR, "I'LL TELL YOU IF YOU TELL ME WHERE I CAN GET SOME HAIR". THE GUY WITH THE GREEN HAT JUST SHRUGGED, "SON, YOU WERE BORN TOO LATE. YOU HAD TO BE THERE WHEN THEY GAVE THEM OUT."

UNDERNEATH THE HAT, HE WAS FRIENDLY AND CHARMING AND HE JUMPED AROUND LIKE A LEPRECHAUN. HE ALWAYS MOVED A LITTLE LIKE HE WAS DANCING, LIKE IT

WAS THE FIRST DAY OF SPRING WITH THAT EXTRA KICK IN YOUR STEP. HE WOULD COME SHUFFLING INTO THE SHOP, EXCITED AND WITH A GLEAM IN HIS EYE. READY TO TALK, BUT QUIET AND THOUGHTFUL AT THE SAME TIME. HE WORKED FOR THE SOUTHERN PACIFIC RAILROAD, RESEARCHING THE HISTORY OF TRAINS. HE WAS WAY PAST RETIREMENT AGE, BUT SAID THERE WAS NO REASON TO STOP. HE LOVED HIS WORK.

I LOVED HIS WORK TOO. IT WAS MUCH MORE EXCITING THAN MINE, WHICH WAS, BASICALLY, MAKING COPIES FOR MY BOSS AND FANZINES AND FLIERS FOR THE SCENE. TALKING TO BANDS AND BOSSES ALL WEEK LONG, I GREW TIRED OF THE WHOLE BUSINESS. BUT THE OLD GUY SHOWED GENUINE INTEREST IN IT. THE RESPECT WAS MUTUAL, WHICH GAVE ME A MUCH-NEEDED BOOST. IT'S FUN, AND VERY RARE, TO EXPLAIN WHAT YOU DO TO SOMEONE OUTSIDE YOUR WORLD BUT GENUINELY CURIOUS.

HE TOLD ME HOW EXCITED HE WAS THAT HIS GRANDDAUGHTER WAS COMING SOON FOR A VISIT, AND PROMISED TO BRING HER ALONG TO MEET ME. SURE ENOUGH, HE WALKED IN ONE DAY WITH A TWELVE YEAR OLD GIRL IN TOW. BUT THERE WAS SOMETHING A LITTLE DIFFERENT IN HIS MANNER THEN. COULD HE BE SELF-CONSCIOUS? DIDN'T THAT GO AWAY WHEN YOU GREW UP?

HIS GRANDDAUGHTER WASN'T MAKING THINGS ANY EASIER. SHE WAS A SNOTTY, GUM-CHEWING, PRECOCIOUS PRE-TEEN, HIS POLAR OPPOSITE. HE INTRODUCED US, AND IT WAS THE SADDEST THING I'D EVER SEEN. YOU COULD TELL SHE THOUGHT HER GRANDDAD WAS THE MOST SENILE BORING OLD FART ON THE PLANET. HERE HE WAS, MAKING HER MEET HIS "FRIEND" AT THE COPY SHOP. SHE POLITELY SMILED, AS IF TO HUMOR THE OLD GUY IN HIS FINAL DAYS. BUT REALLY, I WAS HIS FRIEND.

IT HAD BEEN A WEEK OR TWO SINCE I'D SEEN THE MAN IN THE GREEN HAT. AN ELDERLY WOMAN CAME IN TO XEROX SOME SOCIAL SECURITY FORMS. SHE CAME TO THE REGISTER, FRUSTRATED, AND SAID, "COULD YOU PLEASE COPY THESE FORMS FOR ME? I'M DUMB. I JUST CAN'T FIGURE OUT HOW TO WORK THESE MACHINES."

I COULDN'T BELIEVE HOW OFTEN I STILL HEARD THAT LINE. LIKE EVERY OTHER TIME, I TOOK THE CUSTOMER ASIDE AND SHOWED, STEP BY STEP, HOW IT ALL WORKED. "IT'S THAT EASY?", SHE ASKED. YUP.

PAYING FOR HER COPIES AT THE COUNTER, SHE SAID, "MY HUSBAND USED TO COPY THESE FOR ME, BUT HE RECENTLY PASSED AWAY." SHE SEEMED AMAZINGLY STRONG ABOUT IT. "HE CAME IN PRETTY

OFTEN", SHE ADDED. "I THINK YOU KNEW HIM".
I SAID, "NOT THE SWEET GUY WITH THE GREEN HAT?"
SHE SAID,"YES."
IT WAS SAD BUT MOSTLY JUST STRANGE. HE'D
NEVER LOOKED OLD TO ME, OR SEEMED THE LEAST
BIT SICK.
I KNEW PEOPLE DIED, THAT IT HAPPENED SOONER
OR LATER TO EVERYONE. IT'S NATURAL, INEVITABLE, SO IT
SHOULDN'T REALLY BE SAD OR A SURPRISE, BUT SOMEHOW
IT ALWAYS IS ANYWAY. I GUESS THE SADDEST THING IS
WHEN YOU DON'T REALLY APPRECIATE SOMETHING OR
SOMEONE AND THEN ALL OF A SUDDEN THEY'RE GONE.
BUT THE MAN IN THE HAT, I REALLY DID APPRECIATE
WHEN HE WAS AROUND, AND THAT ONLY MADE IT
HARDER TO HEAR THE NEWS.
THEY SAY THAT PEOPLE NEVER REALLY DIE, THAT
THEY LIVE ON IN THE THOUGHTS OF US STILL ALIVE, BUT
I COULDN'T HELP FEELING LIKE ALL BUT A TINY
GLIMMER WAS GONE FOREVER. NOT JUST THIS ONE
MAN, BUT HIS WHOLE OLD WORLD STYLE, HIS QUIET
WISDOM, HIS VAST AND VARIED INTERESTS.
PEOPLE ALWAYS IDOLIZE THOSE WHO DIED YOUNG,
WHO DIED IN THEIR PRIME OR REALLY BEFORE THEIR
PRIME, BUT I IDOLIZED THOSE WHO FOUGHT IT THROUGH,
WHO LIVED A LONG, FULL LIFE AND ENDED UP ECCENTRIC,
INTERESTING OLD GUYS. SOMEDAY I HOPED TO BE ONE
OF THEM.

Twenty-seven

OLD MEN SAT IN THEIR CARS IN THE BRENNAN'S
PARKING LOT. PERVERTS? NO. THE PERVERTS PARKED
THEIR CARS A BLOCK AWAY, ON THE SOUTH SIDE OF
AQUATIC PARK. THESE OLD MEN FACING THE TRACKS
WERE PATIENTLY WAITING FOR SOMETHING ELSE:
TRAINS. SOME WERE ENGINEERS AND CONDUCTORS AND
BRAKEMEN, LONG RETIRED, BUT STILL DRIVEN TO THE
RAILS TO WAVE AT EACH PASSING BOXCAR. SOME WERE
OLD HOBOS AND HOBBYISTS WHO LOOKED THROUGH
BINOCULARS LIKE BIRDWATCHERS, NOTING EVERY
LITTLE DETAIL DOWN IN THEIR NOTEBOOKS, HOPING TO
SPOT A RELIC FROM RAILROAD'S GOLDEN AGE.
I SAW A HIPPIE IN RASPUTIN'S. HE'D BROUGHT IN
HIS ENTIRE RECORD COLLECTION TO SELL. RIDICULOUS,

I KNOW, BUT I ALMOST CRIED. HERE WAS THIS GUY LUGGING AROUND FIVE CRATES OF RECORDS, THE WELL-LOVED AND WELL-PLAYED COLLECTION OF A LIFETIME, AND ALL THE ASSHOLES AT RASPUTIN'S COULD DO WAS LAUGH. "WE'LL GIVE YOU TWENTY BUCKS IN TRADE FOR THIS PILE", THEY TOLD HIM. "THE REST IS TRASH".

BEHIND HIS BACK, THEY SNICKERED. "WHAT HOLE DID HE CRAWL OUT OF? YOU SEE PEOPLE LIKE THAT WHEN YOU WORK IN SAN LEANDRO, BUT NEVER HERE."

THOUGH NOT A LOVER OF HIPPIES MYSELF, I GREW DEFENSIVE. WHERE WERE THESE PEOPLE COMING FROM? CONCORD? COMING TO BERKELEY AND COMPLAINING ABOUT HIPPIES AND PEOPLE BEING OUT OF TOUCH? COME ON. WOULD I GET A JOB IN CONCORD AND THEN LAUGH AT EVERYONE FOR LOOKING THE SAME AND BEING LEMMING-LIKE CONFORMISTS WITH NO CULTURE OF THEIR OWN? NO. BECAUSE I'D GET KILLED. I ALREADY HAD A JOB, AND BESIDES, IT WAS CRUEL. WHY LAUGH AT SOMEONE FOR BEING OUT OF TOUCH OR BEHIND THE TIMES? ALL THAT PRESSURE TO "GET WITH THE PROGRAM" DIDN'T RECOGNIZE THE FACT THAT THERE WERE MANY DIFFERENT WAYS TO LIVE. BECAUSE OF THAT PRESSURE, A LOT OF PEOPLE FELT LIKE THEY EITHER HAD TO GIVE UP WHAT THEY LOVED OR GET LEFT BEHIND.

THE OLD WOMEN WHO CAME IN TO MY WORK, THE OLD MEN ON THE TRACKS, AND EVEN THE HIPPIE, NOT ALL THAT MUCH OLDER THAN MYSELF. THEY ALL HAD A SAD LOOK OF BEING PASSED BY AGAIN AND AGAIN. OF SEEING THE THING THEY LOVE BEING PHASED OUT OR DRIVEN INTO EXTINCTION. IF YOU DEVOTE YOUR LIFE AND MORTGAGE YOUR FUTURE ON ANY ONE WAY OR THING, YOU'RE ESPECIALLY VULNERABLE. OR ANY ONE PERSON, FOR THAT MATTER. BUT THAT'S WHAT COMMITMENT IS ALL ABOUT, ISN'T IT? CHOOSING YOUR SHIP TO GO DOWN WITH. WHICH MAY BE WHY PUNKS CAN ALWAYS BE FOUND HANGING OUT DOWN ON THE WATERFRONT.

Twenty-eight

IRANIAN MAGAZINE DISTRIBUTORS DOUBLE PARKED ON DURANT AND CAME IN TO CAMPUS COPY MART TO FILL THE RACKS WITH MAGAZINES. PAGE AFTER PAGE ADVERTISED LOCAL IRANIAN NIGHTCLUBS, THEATERS, MARKETS. OR RATHER, IRANIAN-AMERICAN, BECAUSE

AS AN EXILE COMMUNITY THEY HAD ADAPTED TO, AND ASSUMED, MANY TRAITS OF THE DOMINANT CULTURE, WHILE AT THE EXACT SAME TIME STRENGTHENING THEIR SENSE OF WHAT IT MEANT TO BE SEPARATE. PERSECUTION DOES THAT TO A PEOPLE.

IRANIAN MUSICIANS CAME IN TO MAKE FLIERS, IRANIAN FLORISTS DELIVERED FLOWERS, IRANIAN PLUMBERS CAME TO FIX THE DRAIN. I WAS JEALOUS. WHY COULDN'T THE PUNKS BE THIS SUPPORTIVE, THIS SELF-RELIANT? THIS STRONG? THE IRANIANS DIDN'T SUFFER OUR DOUBTS, OUR EXCUSES, OUR TENDENCY TO EMBRACE FAILURE. RIGHT IN THE MIDDLE OF HOSTILE TERRITORY, THEY HAD BUILT A FLOURISHING COMMUNITY, AND THEY VALUED IT DEARLY.

READING THE IRANIAN MAGAZINES WAS REFRESHING, BECAUSE PRESERVING YOUR CULTURE AND COMMUNITY ALWAYS CAME FIRST. ONLY THE PUNK MAGAZINES PUT ATTACKING YOUR COMMUNITY FIRST, FOLLOWED BY DISSECTING IT, DIVIDING IT, DISOWNING IT, AND RELEGATING IT TO A FAR-OFF DISTANT PAST. WHAT A NEUROTIC BUNCH. ALWAYS SQUABBLING.

I LIKED TO THINK OF CAMPUS COPY MART AS A SORT OF CROSS-CULTURAL BULWARK. THOUGH THE CULTURES THERE DID NOT EXACTLY MIX, THEY FLOURISHED WITH MUTUAL RESPECT, WORKING DIFFERENT SHIFTS. THOUGH I COULDN'T OFFICIALLY SUPPORT LOCAL FANZINES BY PUTTING THEM ON THE RACKS, I COULD UNOFFICIALLY SUPPORT THEM BY PRINTING EVERYTHING FOR FREE. SOON EVERY FANZINE SPORTED A FAMILIAR AD: CAMPUS COPY MART. GOOD FRIENDS, GOOD NEIGHBORS, GOOD COPIES.

Twenty-nine

PARVIZ INSTRUCTED ME TO ROLL PENNIES WHEN BUSINESS WAS SLOW. THERE WAS A HUGE BARREL OF THEM BEHIND THE COUNTER. FORLORN, UNCOUNTED, UNWANTED, NEARLY WORTHLESS, THE U.S. PENNY. POOR THINGS. AT FOUR CENTS A COPY, THEY JUST KEPT PILING UP. BUT AT FOUR-FIFTY AN HOUR, I WASN'T PAID ENOUGH TO KEEP THAT BUSY. NOT AT SOMEONE ELSE'S WORK.

I FIXED THE BROKEN MACHINES, BUT ONLY BECAUSE I LIKED FIXING BROKEN THINGS. I ALSO LIKED BREAKING THEM, WHICH I DID SYSTEMATICALLY,

SCIENTIFICALLY EVEN, IN A NEVER-ENDING CYCLE OF EXPERIMENTS. I RAN ALL SORTS OF THINGS THROUGH THEM, ADJUSTING THE RESULTS, PLAYING THEM LIKE AN INSTRUMENT, SOMETIMES LIKE A FRIEND, SOMETIMES AN OPPONENT. EACH HAD A DISTINCT PERSONALITY, EACH ITS OWN FLAWS AND LIMITATIONS. I RAN AROUND THE ROOM IN A CIRCLE, FEEDING A GRAPHIC OUT ONE MACHINE AND INTO THE NEXT, DARKENING, LIGHTENING, DISTORTING, ENLARGING, STRETCHING, AND BLURRING THE IMAGE AS IT WENT. I MUST HAVE LOOKED LIKE A MADMAN IN THERE DOING MY LITTLE DANCE, BUT DOESN'T EVERYONE LOOK LIKE A MADMAN DOING WHAT THEY TRULY LOVE? WHAT I LOVED WAS SEEING HOW MANY WAYS ONE PHOTO, ONE FACE, ONE LINE COULD BE ALTERED, HOW MANY DIFFERENT EMOTIONS IT COULD COME TO REPRESENT, AND HOW DIFFERENT EMOTIONS COULD BE WONDERFULLY MIXED.

I WORKED HARD FOR MY BOSSES WHEN THERE WAS WORK TO DO. I RAN THE JOBS, MOPPED THE FLOORS, CONVERSED WITH THE CUSTOMERS, OPENED AND CLOSED THE SHOP ON DIFFERENT DAYS. IT WAS PRETTY STRESSFUL, ACTUALLY, BUT I TOOK IT IN STRIDE AS LONG AS I WAS ABLE TO DO WHAT I WANTED ON MY DOWN TIME. READ THE IRANIAN MAGAZINES, WORK ON GRAPHICS, PUT LITTLE SUBLIMINAL MESSAGES ALL OVER THE SHOP IN THE LEAST LIKELY PLACES. I STRUCK A DEAL WITH THE VIETNAMESE RESTAURANT ON DWIGHT. I DESIGNED THEIR MENUS AND BUSINESS CARDS. THEY BROUGHT ME LUNCH. MMM. I CAN TASTE IT STILL.

AND WHILE I ATE, I ROLLED A FEW ROLLS OF PENNIES. ONE FOR PARVIZ, TWO FOR ME. THE LEVEL OF PENNIES IN THE BARREL NEVER SEEMED TO DEPLETE, NO MATTER HOW MANY I SPENT. PENNIES AT THE POST OFFICE, PENNIES AT THE CLUB, PENNIES ON THE BUS, AND OFTEN PEOPLE WOULD REFUSE THEM AND LET ME IN OR ON FOR FREE BECAUSE THEY HATED PENNIES SO MUCH. PENNIES AT THE LIQUOR STORE, PENNIES AT THE SUPERMARKET. PENNIES FOR EVERYTHING BUT BART.

Thirty

"LAST NIGHT I MET A MAN FROM CAMEROON ON THE BART TRAIN", I TOLD LANKY. "WE TALKED FOR A

LONG WHILE—WE TALKED ABOUT MONGO BETI! HE
GAVE ME HIS NUMBER TO CALL AND JOIN HIS FRIENDS
AND LEARN ABOUT CAMEROON".
   "WILL YOU CALL?"
   "ME? NO"
   "THAT'S JUST LIKE YOU, RIDE AROUND ON BART WITH
YOUR ATLAS AND YOUR OLD STAMP COLLECTION, BUT YOU
NEVER REALLY GO ANYWHERE OR GET TO KNOW ANYONE.
YOU'RE THE ULTIMATE TOURIST".
   "TODAY'S NOT THE END OF THE WORLD", I SAID, "SO
WHAT'S THE RUSH? EVEN IF IT WAS, SO WHAT? I CAN
ENJOY WHAT I DON'T KNOW ABOUT SOMEONE JUST AS
MUCH AS WHAT I DO".
   "THE ONLY THING YOU KNOW ABOUT HIM IS THAT
HE'S EXOTIC TO YOU. HE'S A STORY TO TELL".
   "IS THAT THE WORST THING? BETTER TO TALK ABOUT
A FOREIGN COUNTRY THAN ABOUT WHAT HAPPENED AT
WORK THIS MORNING".
   "WHAT HAPPENED AT WORK THIS MORNING?"
   "MAYBE I'LL SEE HIM EVERY YEAR ON THE
FREMONT LINE. MAYBE AFTER TWENTY YEARS WE'LL
EVEN BE FRIENDS. HE'LL INVITE ME TO HIS SON'S HIGH
SCHOOL GRADUATION. I'LL INVITE HIM TO... NO, MAYBE
YOU'RE RIGHT. I WOULDN'T INVITE HIM ANYWHERE.
OH, LIFE SUCKS".
   "DID YOU GET FIRED OR SOMETHING? IS SOMETHING
WRONG?"
   "DID I EVER TELL YOU ABOUT THAT GUY I MET ON
BART FROM TONGA? HE SAID..."
   "I KNOW, YOU TOLD ME".
   "HE SAID, 'IT'S A VERY SMALL PLACE...'"
   "AND YOU SAID, 'EVERYWHERE SEEMS BIG TO ME...'"
   "NO..."
   "BECAUSE I NEVER SEE ANYTHING EXCEPT THIS
BART CAR! HA HA HA!"

Thirty-one

   THE TRUTH IS, I WAS ALIENATED, AND WE WERE
ALL, ALL OF US, REALLY DEEPLY ALIENATED, AND ALL
MY TALK ABOUT THE FAMILY OF MAN AND TRUE MULTI-
CULTURALISM AND MUTUAL RESPECT AND COMMUNITY
DIDN'T KEEP IT FAR ENOUGH AWAY THAT YOU
COULDN'T FEEL IT AT ARM'S REACH, ALWAYS.

WHAT HELD SOCIETY TOGETHER, REALLY? WHAT WERE, AS JIMMY SAID, "THE STRINGS INSIDE THIS THING THAT 'KEEP THE WHEAT FIELDS FROM FLIGHT"? WHAT WAS THE FRAGILE THREAD THAT TIED US ALL TOGETHER, PASSING ON THE STREET AND THROUGH LIFE, AND FEELING EVEN A TINY BIT PART OF IT, AND PART OF EACH OTHER? THAT THREAD SEEMED DANGEROUSLY THIN.

ALL THE CLERKS AND COUNTER JOBS AND CROSSING GUARDS, THE BUS DRIVERS AND DONUT MAKERS AND SIDEWALK VENDORS, THESE WERE THE PEOPLE IN THE PUBLIC EYE, THE FACE THE REST OF SOCIETY HID BEHIND. THEY KEPT IT REAL. WHAT AN AWESOME RESPONSIBILITY! BUT HOW OFTEN FLAUNTED AND MISUSED! WHAT A FUCKING FACE TO FACE! ESPECIALLY IN THE MORNING! SAD TO SAY, MY THRESHOLD FOR ASSHOLES WAS LOW. ONE SNOTTY BUS DRIVER, RUDE CAFE WORKER, OR "POSTAL" POSTAL EMPLOYEE WAS ENOUGH TO TURN THE ALIENATION ON, AND FROM THERE IT WAS ONLY A MATTER OF THE USUAL YUPPIES, COPS, AND ANGRY DRIVERS TO PUSH ME INTO A CORNER, AND THEN SPARECHANGERS TO "SIR" ME RIGHT OVER THE EDGE. TO MAKE ME FEEL NOT ONLY NOT PART OF THE CITY, NOT PART OF SOCIETY, BUT LIKE I WASN'T EVEN PART OF THE WORLD.

IN TROUBLED TIMES LIKE THESE, I WOULD FEEL SO BAD, SO ALIENATED, I'D HAVE TO CALL THE CESSPOOL FOR REINFORCEMENTS.

"HELP ME!" I'D SCREAM. "I NEVER SHOULD HAVE GONE OUT IN THE WORLD TODAY! I SHOULD HAVE GONE STRAIGHT HOME FROM WORK, THOUGH OF COURSE THOSE ARE BOTH TRAPS TOO! OF COURSE! BUT GOD HELP ME, I'M ON FOURTH STREET! WHAT COULD BE WORSE! COME QUICK!! WHAT'S THAT? OH, SORRY, RIP. IT'S ME, AARON. FOURTH STREET. I KNOW! I KNOW!! THAT'S WHAT I'M TRYING TO TELL YOU!! YES! COME FAST!!"

RIP WAS THE TONIC FOR ME, THE SOLUTION TO ALIENATION, BECAUSE HE DIDN'T FIT INTO SOCIETY AT ALL AND NEVER HAD, AND ONE LOOK AT HIM COULD TELL YOU THAT, AND FILL YOUR HEART WITH JOY. IN A SLICK WORLD, WE WERE ROUGH EDGES. TOO ROUGH, PRIMITIVE, A THROWBACK TO A DIFFERENT TIME. OR ALIENS FROM ANOTHER PLANET, RIP SAID. FROM THE FUTURE. HE MADE ALIENATION INTO SOMETHING EXCITING. WE'D SNEAK ACROSS THE TRACKS TO SECOND STREET, WHERE THERE WAS DIRT INSTEAD OF CONCRETE, AND WORKERS WHO STILL USED THEIR HANDS. THEN DOWN TO THE WATERFRONT, WHICH NEVER FAILED TO

CHEER ME UP.

IF RIP WASN'T HOME, I'D TALK TO HIS HOUSEMATES. NOAH WOULD SAY IT WASN'T OUR WORLD AND NEVER HAD BEEN. JIMMY WOULD LAUGH AT MY WORRIES. AND IF I CALLED UP JO, SHE WOULD SAY IT WAS OUR WORLD AFTER ALL, AND WORTH FIGHTING FOR. ALL THREE PERSPECTIVES WERE COMFORTING AND REASSURING IN THEIR OWN WAY. THAT'S WHAT FRIENDS ARE FOR.

UNFORTUNATELY, LANKY WAS NO HELP WHEN I WAS IN ONE OF MY MOODS. DID SHE FEEL LIKE A STRANGER IN THE WORLD, REMOVED FROM THE STREAM OF LIFE? YEAH, SURE. DID THAT FEELING DISTURB HER? NOT IN THE LEAST. SHE ACCEPTED IT AS QUITE NATURAL AND NOT WORTH FUSSING ABOUT. SHE HAD HER FRIENDS AND WAS AT PEACE WITH HERSELF. WHAT MORE COULD YOU ASK FOR?

THE THINGS I WAS TORMENTED BY, AND IN LOVE WITH, WERE SIMPLY NOT PART OF HER PSYCHE. IF THEY ENTERED HER MIND, THEY DID NOT STAY LONG. BUT I BURNED INSIDE. WHAT MORE COULD YOU ASK FOR, INDEED! WHO'S WORLD WAS IT, ANYWAY? I WOULD HAVE TO LEAVE HER PLACE AND GO BACK OUT BURNING AND PACING THE STREETS.

Thirty-two

LANKY WAS THE BEST. NEARLY EVERYTHING A GIRLFRIEND COULD OR SHOULD BE. IN HINDSIGHT, BUT NOT AT THE TIME. AT THE TIME, I WAS MORE LOYAL TO RIP, JO, JIMMY, MELODY, AND NOAH. FRIENDSHIPS SHOULD ALWAYS COME BEFORE RELATIONSHIPS, THAT WAS ONE OF MY RULES. WHERE THAT, OR ANY OF MY THOUSAND OTHER ARBITRARY RULES CAME FROM, I DO NOT KNOW, BUT EIGHTEEN IS THE AGE FOR MAKING YOUR OWN RULES, WHETHER OR NOT THEY MAKE SENSE. AND SO, MY FRIENDSHIPS, NO MATTER HOW TENUOUS, CAME BEFORE LANKY. THEY TOOK PRIORITY.

RELATIONSHIPS HAVE A WAY OF TAKING OVER YOUR LIFE, SO IT'S GOOD TO TAKE PRECAUTIONS AGAINST THAT. BUT, LIKE MANY RULES, THE INTENTION WAS DIFFERENT THAN THE EFFECT. THE EFFECT WAS THAT I TREATED LANKY A LITTLE SHABBILY, AND TENDED TO FORGET THAT SHE COULD BE MY FRIEND TOO.

I EXPECTED MORE FROM HER THAN FROM MY FRIENDS, AND AT THE SAME TIME, WAS LESS UNDERSTANDING, LESS FORGIVING, AND MORE LIKELY TO DISMISS HER PROBLEMS AND OPINIONS. ALL OF US BOYS WERE LIKE THAT, WITH THE EXCEPTION OF JIMMY, WHO HAD THE SAME RULES FOR EVERYONE.

I SAY THIS PARTLY AS AN APOLOGY, AND PARTLY JUST BECAUSE, AS A RESULT, WE WERE ALL LOSING OUT A LITTLE BIT ON LIFE. NOW ON TO NOAH.

Thirty-three

WHEN I AM ANGRY, I GET A LITTLE BIT LIKE MY DAD. I CURL MY HAND INTO A FIST AND STAMP AROUND BITING MY THUMBNAIL. CRAZY UNREASONABLE AND PROUD, INDIGNANT ABOUT BEING RIGHT EVEN THOUGH I KNOW I'M WRONG. WATCH OUT, I'M WOUNDED. FAVORITE QUOTE: "I AM NOT YELLING!"

IF ALL GUYS GET A LITTLE LIKE THEIR FATHERS WHEN ANGRY, SHOULD WE SUPPOSE NOAH'S DAD WAS INCLINED TO FIND A MOB OF PUNKS AND TRAIL BEHIND THEM FOR MILES WHEN SOMEONE HURT HIS PRIDE? BECAUSE, THAT'S WHAT NOAH DID. HE WALKED A FULL BLOCK BEHIND THE REST OF OUR CREW. NOAH'S DAD WAS A CRAZED HUNTER NAMED "SNAP" WHO KEPT A FRIDGE FULL OF DEER PARTS. NOAH WAS DIFFERENT, EVEN A VEGETARIAN, AND YET, THERE WAS SOMETHING OF "SNAP" IN HIS EYES.

LIKE ALL GUYS, NOAH WAS A STRANGE GUY. THE CESSPOOL PUNKS WALKED DOWN THE STREET LAUGHING AND SMOKING AND SMASHING SHIT. BEHIND US, LIKE THE SETTING SUN, A LONG, LONE SHADOW LURKED WITH HANDS IN HIS TRENCHCOAT POCKETS: NOAH. SLOW DOWN AND HE WOULD ALSO SLOW DOWN. TRY TO TALK TO HIM, HE WOULD CROSS THE STREET. CHASE AFTER HIM, HE WOULD RUN.

WHAT WAS NOAH'S FUCKING PROBLEM? NO ONE EVER KNEW. MAYBE IT WAS NOAH TRYING TO AVOID CONFRONTATION, TRYING TO BE DIFFERENT THAN HIS ANGRY DAD. BUT, I DO NOT KNOW. FRIENDSHIP ISN'T ALWAYS ABOUT SEEING SOMEONE FROM ALL SIDES.

NOAH WAS NOT ALWAYS ANGRY. SOMETIMES HE WAS MOODY OR PENSIVE. HE DROVE HIS BOAT OF A CAR DOWN TO PIKE'S PEAK, A DECREPIT OLD DOCK IN

EMERYVILLE, AND SAT THERE WITH THE CLAMS DRINK-
ING MICKEY'S, STARING OUT, OR IN, AT THE GLOOM. HE
PARKED BY THE IRON WORKS WAREHOUSE LATE AT
NIGHT LOOKING OUT, OR IN, AT THE RAGING FIRE MELTING
EVERYTHING DOWN, DOWN, DOWN.

SUNDAY NIGHT AS THE NEW WEEK LOOMED NEAR
AND NOAH DROVE DOWN TO THE DOCK TO SIT HIGH ATOP
A MOUNTAIN OF EMPTIES, THE REST OF OUR CREW
DISPERSED TOO, EACH TO THEIR OWN PRISON OR POISON.
JO WENT TO WORK, MELODY TO HER AUNT'S BACK SHACK
TO GET SOME TIME ALONE, READING DEPRESSING POETRY.
JIMMY AND RIP RETURNED TO THE CESSPOOL, AND
LANKY TRIED TO DO A BIT OF SCHOOLWORK. I HAD TO
GO BACK TO MY DAD'S, THE OTHER HALF OF MY DOUBLE
LIFE, WHERE DISHES AND COOKING AND CLEANING WERE
WAITING TO BE DONE.

LANKY WAS WALKING ME HOME BEFORE GOING BACK
TO HER MOM'S PLACE. BUT WE RAN INTO SOMEONE
ALONG THE WAY. CASSIDY.

SHE WAS STANDING OUTSIDE A BREWPUB TOO
TERRIBLE TO BE NAMED, WAITING FOR THE CAB
SHE'D CALLED. LANKY GROWLED AND FUMED. CASSIDY
HAD A HABIT OF TALKING WITH HER HANDS. THEY
TOUCHED YOU FOR PUNCTUATION.

"JUST CHILL OUT, LANKY", I WHISPERED. "SHE'S
HARMLESS".

Thirty-four

A HUGE INFLUX OF WEST VIRGINIA PUNKS HAD
COME TO SETTLE IN THE BAY AREA. THEY ARRIVED
EN MASSE, AND MOST CONTINUED TO LIVE AND PLAY
TOGETHER IN ONE TIGHT UNIT, IN A HOUSE NAMED AFTER,
AND, STRANGELY ENOUGH, SHAPED LIKE THEIR STATE.
VERY PUNK, IF YOU KNOW WHAT HAND GESTURE WEST
VIRGINIA RESEMBLES.

BUT NOT CASSIDY. SHE HAD QUICKLY SEPARATED
HERSELF FROM THE PACK. IT WAS HARD TO BELIEVE
SHE HAD ONCE BEEN AN APPALACHIAN GIRL RUNNING
THROUGH THE FOREST CHASING AND BEING CHASED
BY KENNETH CUMBERLAND, BOTH NAKED AND LAUGHING
AND ROLLING AND PLAYING.

HOW COULD SOMEONE CHANGE SO MUCH IN SUCH A
SHORT TIME? ADAPT THEMSELF, REINVENT THEMSELF,
START ANEW? EVEN SOMEONE LIKE ME, TERRIFIED OF

CHANGE, HAD TO ADMIT CHANGE WAS BEAUTIFUL. IT WAS THE WELLSPRING OF LIFE. WHICH WAS FINE, AS LONG AS IT DIDN'T TOUCH MINE. AS LONG AS IT WAS KEPT AT A SAFE DISTANCE.

THE KENNETH I KNEW WAS GRUMPY AND A BIT OF A HICK. THE CASSIDY WAS ALL SOPHISTICATION AND CITY LIVING. I COULDN'T IMAGINE THEM AS A COUPLE, OR EVEN IMAGINE EITHER ONE RUNNING. NOW KENNETH JUST SAT AT THE CORNER BAR, AND CASSIDY WAS TOO FANCY TO MOVE ALL THAT MUCH.

WAS THIS REALLY THE SAME GIRL WHO BEAT UP THE MORGANTOWN SKINS WITH A BASEBALL BAT? I MARVELLED AT THE CHANGE, BUT SECRETLY WISHED I COULD CHANGE HER BACK, OR SOMEHOW HAVE BOTH. BUT IT WAS NICE TO KNOW, IF THESE TWO HAD ONCE BEEN ENGAGED, ANYTHING WAS POSSIBLE IN THE WORLD.

GO WALKING WITH CASSIDY AND SHE MIGHT FIND A PART FROM A SPACESHIP, A PIECE FROM A CRYSTAL BALL, A MASSIVE STATUE FROM THE WORLD OF MICROSCOPIC BEINGS. ANYONE ELSE WOULD HAVE SEEN ONLY ROCKS AND BROKEN GLASS. GO THROUGH YOUR POCKETS LATER AND THAT'S EXACTLY WHAT YOU'D FIND. HER ENTHUSIASM AND IMAGINATION WERE ATTRACTIVE, CONTAGIOUS, ENDEARING. BUT AFTER A WHILE, A LITTLE ANNOYING.

SHE BREATHED A BIT OF LIFE INTO A SOMEWHAT HOPELESS WORLD, AN INVITATION TO TRANSCEND ALL THE PETTINESS AND DRUDGERY ONE DAY OR ONE THEME PARTY AT A TIME. BUT TO CASSIDY, THERE WAS NO LINE BETWEEN FANTASY AND REALITY. EVERYTHING WAS FUN. EVERYTHING WAS MAKE-BELIEVE, NOT TO BE TAKEN SERIOUSLY. BUT NOW BACK TO NOAH.

Thirty-five

OF NOAH'S FAMILY, WE KNEW VERY LITTLE. HIS FATHER, SNAP, WHO WE MET WHEN NOAH MOVED IN, WAS INDEED A SCARY-LOOKING MAN. HIS MOTHER, DEAD LIKE MINE, HE MENTIONED ONLY ONCE. I RECALLED THE WAY MY MOM WENT BALLISTIC WHEN SHE CAUGHT ME AND MY BROTHER CALLING THE NEIGHBOR KID "EGGHEAD". "DON'T EVER, EVER MAKE FUN OF SOMEONE FOR BEING SMART", SHE SAID. NOAH SMILED. "MY MOM TOLD ME TO NEVER MAKE FUN OF SOMEONE FOR BEING STUPID". THE SAME PROBLEM SEEN FROM TWO DIFFER-

ENT ANGLES, OR TWO DIFFERENT OLD WOUNDS.

WE HAD A LITTLE GAME, RIP, JIMMY, AND I. WHILE NOAH WAS DOWN ON THE DOCKS SWIMMING IN HIS OWN SUFFERING, WE SOMETIMES SET OUT TO ALBANY SEARCHING FOR THE REST OF HIS FAMILY. ALL THE TIME WE HAD KNOWN NOAH, HE HAD NEVER BROUGHT US OVER TO HIS FATHER'S HOUSE, OR EVEN TOLD US WHERE IT WAS. BACK WHEN HE LIVED AT HOME, WE HAD TO MEET HIM AT WINCHELL'S INSTEAD. WHAT WAS HE SO EMBARRASSED OF? AS MDC SAID, "MY FAMILY'S A LITTLE WEIRD. ISN'T YOUR FAMILY A LITTLE WEIRD?" WE RESPECTED HIS PRIVACY, THOUGH THAT DIDN'T KEEP US FROM SEREPITITIOUSLY SNEAKING AROUND ALBANY TRYING TO SATISFY OUR CURIOUSITY. WE HAD IT WELL NARROWED DOWN, BUT NEVER KNEW FOR SURE.

ONE DAY A CHECK CAME IN THE MAIL FOR AN ALL-BERKELEY COMPILATION TAPE I'D PUT OUT. THEN AS NOW, I COULDN'T CASH CHECKS. NOTHING TO DO BUT RIP 'EM UP. CASH ONLY, FOLKS, LIKE THE SIGN SAYS. BUT THIS ONE HAD A BERKELEY ADDRESS AND PHONE NUMBER, SO I CALLED IT UP. AN ADULT ANSWERED THE PHONE. HE SAID HE'D SEEN THE AD IN MAXIMUM ROCK-N-ROLL. BEFORE TRYING AGAIN, THIS TIME WITH CASH, HE HAD ONE QUESTION TO ASK. WAS NOAH'S BAND ON THE TAPE?

HE SAID, "HOW DO I KNOW NOAH? WELL, WE'RE OLD FRIENDS, YOU COULD SAY. I'M HIS GRANDFATHER".

IN HIS PAINT-SPLATTERED CLOTHES, HE LOOKED A LOT MORE LIKE AN ARTIST THAN A HICK, OR SNAP. HE LOOKED UNCANNILY LIKE AN OLDER VERSION OF NOAH. I WAS SURPRISED I'D NEVER NOTICED HIM, SINCE WE HUNG OUT AT THE SAME CAFE. HE SAT ON THE BOTTOM FLOOR, WHERE I RARELY VENTURED, RESERVED AS IT WAS FOR PEOPLE WHO HAD BEEN THERE TWENTY FIVE YEARS OR MORE, OR STUDENTS TOO STUPID TO KNOW THE DIFFERENCE. I DELIVERED THE TAPE IN PERSON, BUT WAS CAREFUL TO KEEP IT A SECRET. HAD NOAH KNOWN, HE NEVER WOULD HAVE SPOKEN TO ME AGAIN.

I ACCOMPANIED NOAH ONE NIGHT ON A DRIVE DOWN TO PIKE'S PEAK, WHERE WE PARKED THE CAR BUT LEFT IT RUNNING, SITTING IN THE FRONT SEAT SMOKING WHILE RAIN HIT THE WINDOWS AND BANGED OUT A RHYTHM ON THE ROOF. HE SPOKE:

"I CAN'T SEE WHAT THE HELL I'M DOING WHEN I'M IN THE MIDDLE OF IT. I CAN'T EVEN SEE WHERE I AM. I MEAN, LITERALLY. I CAN'T EVEN SEE THE

CITY, OR FEEL ALIVE, UNLESS I LOOK AT IT FROM A DISTANCE. FROM OUTSIDE. TIME IS PASSING BY FAST AND I CAN'T EVEN TELL, I CAN ONLY FEEL IT WHEN IT STOPS. TICK, TICK, TICK. CAN YOU HEAR THAT?"

I HAVE A WAY OF DISAGREEING EVEN WHEN I AGREE. "I CAN HEAR IT", I SAID. "BUT I THINK IT'S A BOMB."

Thirty-six

NOAH HAD A BAND. EVERY SINGLE SONG WAS ABOUT HIS CRAZY, PREDICTABLE, LAME GIRLFRIEND. HE'D HAD MANY DIFFERENT GIRLFRIENDS OVER THE YEARS, BUT ONLY ONE SONG. GIRLS ARE CRAZY, THEY SUCK, THEY SCREW YOU OVER – SENTIMENTS ALL OF US HAVE FELT AT ONE TIME OR ANOTHER. BUT YEARS LIKE THAT, AND YOU START TO WONDER: WHAT IS MISSING FROM THIS PICTURE?

DEAR NOAH, WHY ARE YOU ALWAYS ATTRACTED TO CRAZY, PREDICTABLE, LAME GIRLS? WHY ARE THEY ATTRACTED TO YOU? WHAT MADE THEM SO CRAZY, AND WHAT CAN YOU DO TO SOLVE OR SOOTHE IT INSTEAD OF JUST LAY BLAME? MAYBE YOU SHOULD TRY A DIFFERENT APPROACH TO RELATIONSHIPS? NOAH, SON OF SNAP THE MAD HUNTER. MAYBE YOU SHOULD SEEK COUNSELING?

CASSIDY WAS LIKE A SONG, BUT NOT ONE OF NOAH'S. IMPULSIVE, UNPREDICTABLE, SHE OVERFLOWED WITH VIGOR AND THE JOY OF LIFE. SHE CARRIED YOU AWAY WITH HER IMAGINATION. BUT, SHE DID HAVE THE TENDENCY TO TAKE OUT EACH NEW BOY WITH THE MORNING TRASH.

IS THAT SO WRONG? MORALLY, ANYTHING CAN BE PROVEN TO BE RIGHT, BUT REALISTICALLY IT JUST ISN'T VERY NICE. RIP HAD TAKEN ME TO TASK ONCE FOR THAT SAME THING, SAYING IT WASN'T A MATTER OF BEING INDECISIVE BUT A MATTER OF BEING CALLOUS AND CARELESS WITH OTHER PEOPLE'S LIVES. BUT UNLIKE NOAH, CASSIDY WOULD NEVER CRITICIZE OR KISS AND TELL.

WHEN THEY COLLIDED, IT WAS NOT THE CRASH AND BURN YOU MIGHT EXPECT. IN FACT, THEY BALANCED EACH OTHER OUT NICELY. HE WAS THE QUIET, PREDICTABLE, SUBMISSIVE GUY THAT CASSIDY HAD WANTED ALL ALONG. SHE WAS THE UNPREDICTABLE, UNCONTROLLABLE GIRL NOAH HAD BEEN WAITING FOR. AHA!

Thirty-seven

WHAT WAS THE GLUE THAT HELD SOCIETY TOGETHER? WE WERE THE GLUE THAT HELD SOCIETY TOGETHER! THE PUNKS! NO SHIT! HUNTED, HATED, SHUNTED, PICKED ON AND ON THE RUN, PUNKS, FOR YOUR SPENDING DOLLAR, WERE STILL THE MOST CIVIC-MINDED PEOPLE AROUND. THE ONLY ONES LEFT TO EVEN TALK ABOUT SOCIETY, MUCH LESS SING ABOUT, GET BAD TATTOOS ABOUT, AND NAME THEIR PETS AFTER IT. WHERE COULD YOU FIND SOCIAL UNREST, VICTIMZ OF SOCIETY, SOCIETY SYSTEM DECONTROL, SOCIETY DOG, AND BAD POSTURE? IN THE NEWSPAPER? IN THE CORPORATE BOARD ROOM? NO. ONLY IN THE PIT.

"I'M NOT ANTI-SOCIETY", MIKE MUIR ONCE SAID. "SOCIETY IS ANTI-ME". WELL PUT. YET EVEN AS THE ORGANS OF SOCIETY ATTEMPTED TO BELITTLE US, NEUTRALIZE US, CO-OPT US AND EXPLAIN US AWAY, WE FOUGHT TIRELESSLY AGAINST SOCIAL DISINTEGRATION. AS THE WORLD BECAME A SLICK, SLIPPERY PLACE FILLED WITH PEOPLE WHO TUNED YOU OUT WHEN YOU ASKED FOR THE TIME, WHO WOULD HAVE RATHER DIED THAN SAID "HI" WHEN PASSING ON THE STREET, WHO COULDN'T EVER BE BOTHERED TO TAKE A MINUTE FOR A LOST TRAVELER OR STRAY PUPPY, THE PUNKS WERE A SHOUT OUT FOR HUMANITY, "A CRY FOR HELP IN A WORLD GONE MAD". ROUGH, UNPOLISHED, SOCIALLY INEPT, AND YET, WHAT ELSE WOULD YOU EXPECT? WHERE ELSE COULD YOU TURN FOR HELP? WHO ELSE KNEW THE STREETS AND THE CHEAP PLACES TO EAT?

EVERY DAY WALKING TO WORK AND EVERY NIGHT ON BART SOMEONE WOULD STOP ME TO ASK DIRECTIONS, ASK ADVICE, STRIKE UP A LITTLE CONVERSATION. LOOKING WEIRD, MAYBE PEOPLE THOUGHT THEY COULD TAKE THAT CHANCE. I HAD LESS OF A GUARD UP BECAUSE I HAD LESS TO LOSE, OR AT LEAST LESS TO PROTECT.

EVERY TIME I RODE MY BIKE AROUND, I'D HAVE TO STOP TO LOCK IT UP TO HELP PUSH A CAR STALLED IN TRAFFIC. WOULD THEY HAVE STOPPED TO HELP ME FIX A FLAT? HA! HA! HA! AND EVERY CHECKBOOK, WALLET, OR HOUND I FOUND WOULD BE SENT HOME WITH A NOTE, "FOUND BY THE PUNKS". DID I EVER GET A THANK YOU NOTE BACK? A REWARD? BEING

ALIVE AND IN LOVE AND A LITTLE PART OF HUMANITY
WAS REWARD ENOUGH.

IF THEY LAUGHED, WE LAUGHED BACK, OR GAVE
THEM SOMETHING TO LAUGH AT. IF THEY STARED,
WE LOOKED UP AT THE SKY, OR LOOKED INSIDE FOR
STRENGTH TO RISE ABOVE. AS FRANK MOORE,
BERKELEY'S ONLY QUADRIPLEGIC PERFORMANCE
ARTIST SEX CULT LEADER SAID, "PEOPLE ARE ALWAYS
LOOKING AT ME. SO WHY NOT LIKE IT?"

DID WE HELP OLD FOLKS CROSS THE STREET?
PUSH PEOPLE IN WHEELCHAIRS FOR MILES? ESCORT
WOMEN THROUGH SCARY NEIGHBORHOODS AT NIGHT?
OF COURSE. WE ALL DID. AND IT WAS NICE TO KNOW
THAT THOSE PEOPLE FELT MORE COMFORTABLE
ASKING THE PUNKS THAN ASKING SOME STRANGER
IN A SUIT. MAYBE IT WAS JUST BECAUSE WE WERE
THERE, ON THE STREET, WHILE EVERYONE ELSE
DROVE BY OR SAT IN THE SAFETY OF THEIR HOME.
BUT THAT TOO WAS PART OF THE PUNK CREDO. LIVE
YOUR LIFE IN PUBLIC, AVOID ISOLATION. BUT STILL,
WE FELT SO ISOLATED. WHY?

Thirty-eight

"WHAT IS PUNK?", THE REGULARS ASKED ME ONE
DAY AT WORK WHEN RIP WAS OUT OF SIGHT. ALWAYS
A HARD QUESTION TO ANSWER, BUT I DID MY BEST TO
EXPLAIN.

"PUNKS DON'T DRIVE CARS OR WATCH T.V.", I SAID.
"WE MAKE MOST OF OUR THINGS BY HAND, FOR THE
GOOD OF THE COMMUNITY RATHER THAN FOR FAME
OR FORTUNE".

"ON COMPUTERS", THEY SAID.

"NOPE. A LOT OF THE TIME WE DON'T EVEN HAVE
ELECTRICITY. AND WE PUT OUT CRANKY LITTLE NEWS-
LETTERS JUST LIKE I.F. STONE".

"IS THAT SO? YOU'RE PULLING OUR LEG!"

"IT'S THE TRUTH, FOLKS".

"SOUNDS VERY OLD FASHIONED", THEY SAID.

"YES" I SAID. "PUNKS ARE VERY OLD FASHIONED.
EVEN MORE THAN YOU!"

THEY GAWKED AND SHOOK THEIR HEADS. "NO!
COULDN'T BE!"

Thirty-nine

ALL THE GIRLS WERE SMOKING OR TALKING ON THE CORNERS OR RIDING BIKES WITH BELLS AND BIG BASKETS FULL OF GROCERIES. ALL THE THINGS GIRLS AND YOUNG WOMEN DO. BUT TO ME THEY ALL LOOKED VERY OLD.

I LIKED TO IMAGINE WHAT PEOPLE LOOKED LIKE AS CHILDREN AND WHAT THEY MIGHT LOOK LIKE AS SENIORS. BUT SUDDENLY, I LOOKED AT GIRLS AND THAT WAS ALL I COULD SEE. IT WASN'T JUST THE HORN RIM GLASSES AND VINTAGE DRESSES, EVERY LINE IN THEIR FACES AND CURVE OF THEIR BODIES SPOKE OF A FUTURE TIME WHEN THEY WOULD REACH REAL MATURITY. I COULD ONLY SEE THEM AS ROUGH DRAFTS, YOUNG SENIORS, FUTURE GRANDMAS. SOMETHING WAS WRONG WITH ME. I WAS NO LONGER ATTRACTED TO THEM, ONLY ENDEARED.

I THOUGHT EXPLAINING THIS TO LANKY WOULD MAKE HER HAPPY. WOULD EASE HER JEALOUSY. I WAS WRONG.

"WHY ARE YOU LOOKING AT THE GIRLS?", SHE DEMANDED.

"I LOOK AT EVERYONE", I SAID. "THE YOUNG AND OLD, MEN AND WOMEN, EVEN CRIPPLES AND BURN VICTIMS, THOUGH I ALWAYS FEEL BAD ABOUT THAT, LIKE THEY THINK I'M STARING AT THEM, OR TAKING PITY. BUT I DON'T WANT TO AVERT MY EYES AND SEEM UNNATURAL".

"LOOK AT ANYONE YOU WANT", SHE SAID, ICILY, "BUT NOT THE GIRLS".

"NO ONE LOOKS LIKE GRANDMAS", I SAID, EXCEPT THE YOUNG G'S. NOT EVEN THE GRANDMAS. THEY SEEM YOUTHFUL. IT'S FUNNY".

"FUNNY".

"FOR THE FIRST TIME I FEEL LIKE I CAN SEE A WHOLE PERSON IN A PERSON. I CAN SEE PARTS OF THEIR FACE, PARTS OF THEIR MANNER THAT SEEM SO YOUNG, LIKE STUBBORN, WORRIED KIDS. AND OTHER PARTS WHICH WILL SOMEDAY SETTLE INTO AN OLD AGE THAT'S NOT SO SELF-CONSCIOUS, NOT SO MANIC".

I WAITED FOR HER TO RESPOND OR ENCOURAGE ME TO GO ON. NO ENCOURAGEMENT FORTHCOMING, I PRODDED AROUND OTHER PARTS OF THE SUBJECT.

"I CAN SEE WHAT PARTS OF MY FRIENDS CAME FROM THEIR FATHER AND WHAT PARTS FROM THEIR MOTHER, AND HOW, WITH AGE, THOSE PARTS COME OUT MORE. FOR INSTANCE, THE WAY IN CERTAIN MOODS AND EXPRESSIONS, YOU LOOK A LITTLE LIKE YOUR MOM".

"I DO NOT LOOK LIKE MY CRAZY MOTHER!" SHE YELLED. "SHE'S CRAZY! SHE'S WEIRD LOOKING! I DON'T LOOK ANYTHING LIKE HER! I'M NOT LIKE HER!"

"YOU'RE MOM DOESN'T SEEM CRAZY TO ME. OR WEIRD LOOKING. I DIDN'T MEAN IT. YOU DON'T. PLEASE, LARENKA. DON'T CRY."

"SAY IT AGAIN", SHE SAID.

"YOU DON'T LOOK ANYTHING AT ALL LIKE YOUR MOM", I SAID.

"OKAY", SHE SAID. "FINE!"

Forty

LANKY WANTED ME TO GO WITH HER TO THE CITY TO LOOK AT ALL THE CHRISTMAS WINDOW DISPLAYS. COME ON, SHE SAID. PLEASE.

I SCOWLED. IN CASE SHE MIGHT THINK I WAS BEING UNREASONABLE, I ENUMERATED MY REASONS.

NUMBER ONE, I'M JEWISH. "THOU SHALT HAVE NO GODS BEFORE ME", AS IT IS SAID. NUMBER TWO, I'M AN ATHEIST, AGAINST ALL RELIGION AND MYSTICISM AND SUPERSTITION. NUMBER THREE, I'M A SOCIALIST AND HATE COMMERCIALISM AND BIG BUSINESS. NUMBER FOUR, FUCKING SANTA CLAUS, WINOS, DROOLING KIDS, HAPPY COUPLES, EGGNOG, SEASONAL DEPRESSION, AND SALVATION ARMY BELL RINGERS. NUMBER FIVE, I THINK I HAVE A RULE AGAINST IT.

WHAT A PAIN IN THE ASS IT MUST BE TO GO OUT WITH GUYS. NINE OUT OF TEN OF US ARE TOO CAUGHT UP IN OUR OWN REASONS OR RATIONALIZATIONS TO EVER HAVE FUN OR TRY SOMETHING NEW. HAD I EVER LOOKED AT CHRISTMAS WINDOW DISPLAYS BEFORE? NO. BUT AS A GUY, I WAS ALREADY SOMETHING OF AN AUTHORITY ON THE SUBJECT. DON'T TRY TO TELL ME ABOUT IT OR GET ME TO GO ALONG. I'M A GUY. I ALREADY KNOW.

LANKY GOT FLUSTERED, BUT WHAT COULD I DO? WE ALL MAKE OUR OWN CHOICES. WHY COULDN'T SHE

DO ANYTHING WITHOUT TELLING ME ABOUT IT, ASKING MY OPINION, OR BRINGING ME ALONG? THE WAY I FIGURED IT, THE MORE WE DID FOR OURSELVES AND KEPT FOR OURSELVES, THE STRONGER THE RELATIONSHIP WOULD BECOME. IT WAS GOOD TO LEAVE A LITTLE ROOM FOR MYSTERY. I WATCHED HER WALK AWAY TO CATCH THE BUS, AND JUST LET IT GO.

THEN I THOUGHT OF LANKY IN THE RAIN, GOING FROM WINDOW TO WINDOW WITH A LONGING LOOK IN HER EYE. SUDDENLY, MY SMUGNESS DISAPPEARED AND I FOUND MYSELF STANDING IN A LARGE DOGHOUSE.

DAMN. LOOKS LIKE I'D BLOWN IT. AGAIN.

IT WAS EXHAUSTING. THE MORE SURE OF YOURSELF ONE MINUTE, THE MORE LIKELY TO FIND YOURSELF A SECOND LATER DOUBLE-DIPPED IN SHIT. IN A RELATIONSHIP THERE WAS NEVER A DULL MOMENT, UNFORTUNATELY. I RAN STRAIGHT FOR THE BUS' STOP.

SHE WAS NOWHERE TO BE FOUND, BUT I CAUGHT THE FIRST TRANSBAY BUS THAT CAME ALONG. FOR ONCE I WOULD PROVE MY LOVE WITH A CHASE.

ON THE BUS I PLAYED OUT THE ARGUMENT IN MY HEAD LIKE A COURT CASE. "IS IT TRUE THAT THE ACCUSED ALWAYS COMPLAINS THAT HE HAS TO SET THE AGENDA FOR THE RELATIONSHIP, AND EVEN PLAN OUT THE DATES? BUT WHEN YOU COME TO HIM LOOKING FOR A LITTLE TOGETHERNESS, HE HAD THE GALL TO SAY NO TO YOU IN FIVE DIFFERENT WAYS? GUILTY! GUILTY! GUILTY!"

LOST IN FANTASY, I WAS SOON THINKING ABOUT OTHER THINGS, MOSTLY GET-RICH-QUICK SCHEMES, AND HAD COMPLETELY FORGOTTEN ABOUT LANKY AND OUR DIFFICULTIES. "WHAT WALKS ON FOUR FEET THEN TWO AND FINALLY THREE?", I PONDERED. "HUMANKIND, OF COURSE. BUT WHAT'S MORE PECULIAR IS HOW IT GOES FROM THE FRONT OF THE BUS TO THE BACK, THEN TO THE FRONT AGAIN. THAT, TRULY, IS THE MARCH OF LIFE. I WONDER HOW WELL 'REAGAN ON A CROSS' NECKLACES WOULD SELL? ELVIS ON A CROSS? RONALD McDONALD? JIM BAKKER? JERRY BROWN?" A WHOLE MARKETING LINE FLASHED BEFORE MY EYES. THIS WOULD BLOW THOSE DAMN DARWIN FISH RIGHT OUT OF THE WATER!

Forty-one

BART WAS ALWAYS QUIET, WITH EVERYONE'S HEAD IN A BOOK AND HALF THE PEOPLE FAST ASLEEP. ALL THE COMMUTERS IN A NURSERY-SCHOOL-LIKE SHARED NAPTIME, DREAMING THEIR DIFFERENT DREAMS TOGETHER. BUT THE BUS WAS NOT LIKE THAT AT ALL. THERE WAS SINGING, DRINKING, AND LOUD TALKING IN A FEW DIFFERENT LANGUAGES.

ON THIS PARTICULAR BUS, AGED ASIAN MEN IN INFANTRY HATS SAT WITH TALL ELDERLY BLACK MEN IN BASEBALL CAPS. THERE WAS A QUIET, STOIC INDIAN MAN IN A TURBAN, A STUDYING STUDENT, A GAGGLE OF HAUGHTY FILIPINO WOMEN. TEENAGERS BRAGGING, THREATENING, CUSSING, ARGUING, AND FLIRTING. A BOY WITH A BROKEN ARM IN A SLING. I STOOD UP TO SURRENDER MY SEAT TO AN OLD CHINESE WOMAN WITH THIRTY SHOPPING BAGS. "THE LAST OF THE GENTLEMEN" I THOUGHT, BUT THE YOUNG TEENAGERS JUST LAUGHED, POINTING AT THE HOLES IN MY PANTS.

I RECALLED THE TROLL-LIKE GUY I USED TO RUN INTO ON THE BUS HOME FROM HIGH SCHOOL. THE MAN WAS FANATICAL. EVERY WEEK HE HAD ANOTHER NEW YORK DOLLS BOOTLEG HE'D FOUND. HE RANTED AND RAVED ABOUT THE DOLLS, AND HOW THE DEAD BOYS WERE JUST SHIT ON THEIR HEELS. WE HAD A LIVELY, STEADY FEUD OF SORTS, AN ONGOING DEBATE. BUT THE OTHER PASSENGERS STARED IN HORROR. A KID AND AN OLD FAT GUY TALKING ABOUT DEAD BOYS AND DOLLS! UNBELIEVABLE! FREE SPEECH WAS ONE THING, BUT THIS WAS TOO MUCH! YOU NEVER KNOW WHAT KIND OF TRASH YOU'LL HAVE TO SIT NEXT TO WHEN YOU RIDE THE BUS!

THE BUS DID HAVE ONE SPECIAL ADVANTAGE. COMING OVER THE BAY BRIDGE, RIDING HIGHER UP THAN ALL THE CARS, YOU COULD SEE THE CITY SPREAD OUT IN FRONT OF YOU IN ALL ITS GLORY. IT SURPRISED ME EVERY TIME, JUST HOW BEAUTIFUL IT WAS. COMING INTO ANY CITY IS BREATHTAKING, BUT NONE WITH THE DRAWN OUT SUSPENSE OF SAN FRANCISCO, COMING INTO IT BY BRIDGE JUST AS THE SUN IS STARTING TO GO DOWN. BACK THEN THE SKYLINE WAS A LITTLE SPARSER. NOT THAT IT MATTERS SO MUCH, BUT YOU COULD REALLY TRACE ITS OUTLINE IN A RECOGNIZABLE SHAPE.

I RAN THROUGH THE STREETS FROM THE STATION TO UNION SQUARE LOOKING FOR THOSE FAMILIAR LONG LEGS AND SPIKEY BLONDE HAIR. I WEDGED MY WAY THROUGH THE CROWDS, CUT INTO LINES, CRANED MY NECK AROUND LOOKING FOR THE LANK. BUT NO LUCK. NOAH WAS RIGHT: YOU CAN ONLY SEE WHAT YOU NEED FROM A DISTANCE. I SLOWED DOWN TO LOOK AT ALL THE TOYS AND GINGERBREAD HOUSES AND MECHANIZED WINDOW DISPLAYS. AND THEN, AAUGH! I USED MY BROTHER'S I.D., BOUGHT A BOTTLE OF WHISKEY AND GOT DRUNK.

I GOT SAPPY AND SENTIMENTAL SEEING ALL THE CITY LIGHTS AND THE PEOPLE PILED HIGH WITH PRESENTS FOR THEIR LOVED ONES. I LOVE A CROWD. ALL THE SCURRYING LITTLE TYKES. THE TORTURED HORSES TETHERED TO FANCY CARRIAGES. THE "GLITTERDOLL" GRAFFITI. I BOUGHT A BAG OF ROASTED CHESTNUTS AND WENT UP THE ELEVATOR AT MACY'S TO DROP STUFF ON PEOPLE FROM THE ROOF.

ON THE TOP FLOOR THERE WAS AN EXHIBIT: SANTAS FROM DIFFERENT COUNTRIES AND DIFFERENT TIMES. SOME WERE SHORT AND EVIL LOOKING, SOME SKINNY AND STREAMLINED AND KIND. ONE WAS DRESSED IN BLACK! I LOOKED AROUND. NO ONE THERE BUT ME. SO, I CURLED UP IN THE SPACE BEHIND THE BLACK SANTA AND WENT TO SLEEP.

OH WELL. WHEN THERE'S NO ONE ELSE TO IMPRESS, SOMETIMES YOU HAVE TO TRY TO IMPRESS YOURSELF. I LAID THERE THINKING ABOUT LANKY, BUT NEVER DID TELL HER ABOUT IT.

Forty-two

THERE WAS THIS SKINHEAD DOWN AT THE DONUT SHOP. BUT ONLY BALD, NOT AN ACTUAL SKIN. HIS NAME WAS PEDRO, AND HE ALWAYS WORE THE SAME VICE SQUAD T-SHIRT TO WORK, WHICH I COVETED BUT NEVER GOT. HE WORKED ROUGHLY THE SAME HOURS AS MINE. IN BETWEEN CUSTOMERS, WE PACED IN THE ALLEY BETWEEN CHANNING AND DURANT, KEEPING AN EYE OUT FOR EITHER BOSS.

FOR MOST PUNKS, LEAVING THE FOLD IS A SLOW, GRADUAL PROCESS, BUT WITH PEDRO IT COULD BE TRACED TO HOURS, EVEN MINUTES. RELATIVELY NEW

IN TOWN, HE'D GONE TO SEE A SHOW AT THE NEW METHOD WAREHOUSE IN EMERYVILLE. OUT IN THE YARD HE GOT HIS ASS BEATEN FOR BEING A SKINHEAD. AND THAT WAS THE LAST SHOW HE EVER WENT TO.

POOR PEDRO, POOR ALL OF US WHO HAD TO LIVE THROUGH PUNK IN THE EIGHTIES. AND TO ANYONE WHO DIDN'T KILL THEMSELVES OR GET KILLED BACK THEN, OR MISSED IT ALL, GO DIE. I KNEW DEMPSEY AND MILES M, THE POOR FOOLS WHO BEAT UP PEDRO FOR BEING A SKINHEAD. WHY, PRAY TELL, DID THEY DO IT? BECAUSE THEY, TOO, WERE SKINHEADS.

BUT AS MDC SAID IN THEIR ONE GOOD SONG, "LIFE EVENS THE SCORE". ORIGINALLY, ON THE SEVEN INCH VERSION, THEY SAID, "GOD EVENS THE SCORE", BUT THEY REALIZED THAT LIFE WAS EVEN CRUELER THAN GOD BY THE TIME THEY GOT TO THEIR FIRST LP.

WHAT MDC MEANT WAS THAT THOSE SAME KNUCKLES WHICH SPELLED OUT "FUCK MODS" AND MADE SOUP OUT OF PEDRO'S FACE LATER COST MILES A PRETTY PENNY, WHEN HE BECAME A MOD AND HAD TO HAVE LASER SURGERY TO GET THE TATTOO REMOVED.

YOU'RE RIGHT, THAT STILL DOESN'T EVEN THINGS OUT. LASER SURGERY IS BETTER THAN STITCHES AND BONE GRAFTS. AND YOU KNOW WHY? BECAUSE LIFE ISN'T FAIR. IT NEVER EVENS THE SCORE, AND, IN FACT, YOU ALWAYS LOSE. SMALL COMFORT THAT PEOPLE LIKE MILES M ALSO LOSE, BECAUSE THEY STILL DON'T LOSE AS BADLY AS YOU. THAT'S WHY I'VE ALWAYS PREFERRED CODE OF HONOR TO MDC.

Forty-three

PEDRO WAS FROM ORANGE COUNTY. HE'D EVEN BEEN ON THE WALLY GEORGE SHOW ONCE. DUDE. NOT IN THE AUDIENCE, LIKE THE CIRCLE JERKS, BUT AS AN ACTUAL GUEST. I SWEAR TO YOU, I SAW THE VIDEO. DEE DEE, HIS GIRLFRIEND, WAS ALSO AN O.C. EX-PUNK. BACK IN FULLERTON SHE'D WORKED AT THE LEGENDARY LICORICE PIZZA WITH MIKE P. FROM MIDDLE CLASS. AGAIN, I MUST SAY: DUDE.

NOW THEY WERE GOING BACK TO VISIT FOR THE HOLIDAYS AND ASKED IF I WOULD BE WILLING TO WATCH OVER THEIR PETS. THAT MEANT A WHOLE APARTMENT TO MYSELF. FUCK YEAH.

HOWEVER, THE APARTMENT TURNED OUT TO BE A ZOO, AN EX-PUNK NOAH'S ARK FILLED TO THE BRIM WITH EVERY SPECIES OF SCREAMING PEST. SWARMS OF FISH, HERDS OF BIRDS, PILES OF SNAKES AND RABBITS AND GUINEA PIGS, PLUS A COUPLE CATS, FOR GOOD MEASURE. THIS JOB CALLED FOR A BOUNCER, AN ARMED GUARD, AND A ZOOKEEPER, ALL IN ONE. THAT I COULD FAKE, BUT IT ALSO CALLED FOR TEN HIPPIES, TO PROVIDE ROUND THE CLOCK AFFECTION AND LOVING CARE.

HOW COULD I FORGET? A MONKEY. THEY ALSO HAD A FUCKING MONKEY. RIP AND I LOCKED OURSELVES IN THAT APARTMENT TRYING TO FINISH THE NEW ISSUES OF OUR FANZINES. I HAD THOUGHT IT WOULD BE AN ARTISTS' RETREAT OF SORTS. "A STRATEGIC RETREAT", WE CALLED IT. A SILENT, PLACID ESCAPE. BUT FOR THREE DAYS, INCLUDING CHRISTMAS, WE PASTED AND CUT AND CRUMPLED UP HUGE STACKS OF PAPER WHILE THE FINCHES CHATTERED, THE PARROT BABBLED, THE MONKEY PLAYED WITH ITS LITTLE BELL. ONLY THE FISH WERE SILENT, WHICH MADE ME SUSPICIOUS.

Forty-four

I KNOW FISH. MY ONE AND ONLY STOOD BY MY SIDE SINCE I WAS A BABY, AND WHO ELSE COULD I SAY THAT ABOUT BESIDES MY BRO AND DAD? RIP CAME CLOSE, BUT HE HAD THE HABIT OF DISAPPEARING INTO THE WOODS FOR MONTHS AT A TIME.

FISH, THEY ARE STUBBORN CREATURES. EVEN MORE STUBBORN THAN MY DAD. THEY WILL HAPPILY DIE JUST TO PROVE A POINT, WHICH IS EXACTLY WHAT THEY BEGAN TO DO, AT A RAPID RATE, THE MINUTE RIP WALKED OUT THE DOOR. ALONE, I HAD TO FEND FOR MYSELF AGAINST THE MASS SUICIDE OF THE LITTLE MARTYRS.

I WANTED TO STRANGLE THEM. SLAP THEM AROUND AND DEMAND AN ANSWER. I SCREAMED AND POUNDED MY FISTS BUT THE COLD, FLAT, SLIMY CREATURES JUST LOOKED AT ME SILENTLY, MADE TERRIBLE FLAPPING AND GULPING NOISES, THEN DIED IN MY ARMS.

I HAD SAVED MY OWN GOLDFISH MANY TIMES WITH A QUICK SALTWATER BATH OR A BIT OF SODIUM BIPHOSPHATE IN THE WATER. BUT THESE WERE

TROPICAL FISH, A DIFFERENT SORT OF ANIMAL. NERVOUS, STUCK-UP, FRAGILE, AND GENERALLY SORT OF FRENCH. I CALLED THE ALBANY AQUARIUM, BUT IT WAS CLOSED FOR THE HOLIDAYS. I CALLED THE NUMBER PEDRO AND DEE DEE LEFT IN CASE OF EMERGENCY AND CRIED ONTO THE ANSWERING MACHINE.

THERE WERE DIFFERENT AQUARIUMS MIXED WITH DIFFERENT VARIETIES AT DIFFERENT TEMPERATURES. I COULDN'T JUST COMBINE THEM, YET ONE HAD FISH KEELING OVER AND THE OTHER WAS LEAKING! ALL THE ANIMALS SENSED MY PANIC AND WENT INTO HYSTERICS AND GYMNASTICS.

POOR FISH, DROPPING LIKE FLIES. POOR PEDRO AND DEE DEE, IN LOS ANGELES' PUNK HEARTLAND WHILE I KILLED THEIR KIDS. POOR LARENKA, WHO WOULD BE HURT BY WHAT SHE DIDN'T KNOW. MOST OF ALL, POOR ME, WINNER OF THE BLACK, CLOUD-SHAPED TROPHY. KNEE-DEEP IN THE BLOOD OF INNOCENTS, I WAS ALSO MISSING A VERY HOT DATE.

A SIX FOOT FLAME IN A SLEEVELESS SHIRT AND CATHOLIC SCHOOL MINISKIRT STOOD LEANING AGAINST THE NEWSPAPER MACHINES AT BERKELEY BART WAITING FOR ME WHILE MILES AWAY I WAS PACING AROUND PEDRO'S FUMBLING WITH THE SUPERGLUE, FEELING LIKE THE LITTLE BOY WITH HIS FINGER STUCK IN THE DYKE. I WAS ALREADY LATE. HOW LONG WOULD SHE WAIT?

Forty-five

I CALLED NATE AND AMANDA. NOT TO SAY HELLO, BUT TO SWEAT PANIC-STRICKEN OVER THE PHONE, SCREAMING ABOUT DEAD PETS AND ANGRY GIRLFRIENDS. AFTER ALL, THEY LIVED DOWNTOWN. ALL I NEEDED WAS A LITTLE FAVOR, A MESSAGE DELIVERED ACROSS THE STREET. WHY NOT? IT WAS WATER UNDER THE BRIDGE WITH US, OFFICIALLY. BUT WHEN IS IT EVER, REALLY? THEY WERE BUSY, NATE SAID. WATCHING T.V..

LANKY STOOD AT CENTER AND SHATTUCK GETTING ANGRIER EVERY MINUTE, UNAWARE OF MY PREDICAMENT. WHAT MADE IT WORSE WAS THAT WE'D BEEN FIGHTING, FOLLOWED BY MY THREE-DAY SILENT TREATMENT TRYING TO FLUSH THAT FEVER OUT. I HADN'T EVEN GIVEN HER THE NUMBER AT PEDRO'S PLACE. NOW HER ANGER GAVE WAY TO WORRY AND IMAGINING THE WORST. THE EVE

OF OUR ANTICIPATED REUNION, AND I WAS NOWHERE TO BE FOUND.

THEN I REMEMBERED A TRICK FROM LONG AGO, WHEN THE PUNKS PRACTICALLY LIVED DOWNTOWN. A LOCAL BAND HAD GOTTEN THEIR NAME FROM THE CENTER AND SHATTUCK PAYPHONE. I DIALED THEIR NAME, HOPING THE NUMBER HADN'T BEEN CHANGED.

SURE ENOUGH, A VOICE CAME ON THE LINE WHICH I RECOGNIZED. ONE OF THE DOWNTOWN DRUG DEALERS. "WHAT DO YOU NEED?", HE ASKED.

HE SAID, "LANKY? WHAT THE HELL IS THAT?"

BUT IN A MINUTE, I HAD HIM YELLING IT OUT LOUD.

Forty-six

EVERY DAY I THOUGHT ABOUT MY FRIENDS AND WAS SO THANKFUL THEY WERE MY FRIENDS. IT COULD BE WORSE: THEY COULD BE MY ENEMIES. WORSE YET, MY BOYFRIENDS AND GIRLFRIENDS. YES, IT WAS SCARY TO SEE THEM START TO GO OUT WITH EACH OTHER. BUT I WAS HAPPY FOR THEM, BECAUSE AT LEAST IT WASN'T ME.

I LIKED NOAH, THOUGH IT WAS TIME HE WROTE A SONG ABOUT HIMSELF. I LIKED CASSIDY, THOUGH SHE TURNED OUT TO BE THE CRAZIEST ONE YET. BIRDS OF A FEATHER, THEY BELONGED TOGETHER. LET NATE AND AMANDA MAKE THEIR BABIES, IT WAS THE LABORS OF A DIFFERENT COUPLE I WAS REALLY LOOKING FORWARD TO. WHEN NOAH'S NEXT ALBUM CAME OUT, WE WERE ALL GOING TO HAVE A GOOD ASS TIME SINGING ALONG. SPECULATION OF FUTURE SONG TITLES RAN HIGH. PERHAPS A DOUBLE L.P. WAS ALREADY IN THE WORKS?

CASSIDY AND NOAH, OUT ON A DATE AT THE OLD-TIME MOVIES. THE PARAMOUNT THEATER, NEWLY RENOVATED, THE GLEAM IN DOWNTOWN OAKLAND'S EYE. A FANCY, BOURGIE DRESS-UP AFFAIR, BUT CHEAP. CASSIDY AND NOAH SAT UP FRONT. AND ME AND LANKY? WE WERE FIVE ROWS BACK, OUT ON OUR BIG MAKEUP DATE, AND NOT ABOUT TO GIVE OURSELVES AWAY. HAPPY TO BE TOGETHER AGAIN AFTER THE SEPARATION AND ALL THE STRESS AND DEAD PETS AND WORRYING AND WAIT. SOMETIMES YOU CAN'T HELP HOLDING HANDS.

ONSTAGE, THE ORGANIST BEGAN, A LITTLE PRE-SHOW

TUNE TO SET THE MOOD, A BIT OF FANFARE AND FOREPLAY. SOON THE FABULOUS MISS VICKI WOULD APPEAR TO SPIN THE ROULETTE WHEEL. KEEP YOUR TICKET STUBS READY, LADIES AND GENTLEMEN. WHO HOLDS THE LUCKY NUMBER, WINNER OF A WEIGHT LOSS PLAN OR LUNCH FOR TWO AT LOIS THE PIE QUEEN? PERHAPS A DATE WITH "EASTBAY EAR" MARTIN SNAPP?

ANTICIPATION RIPPLED THROUGH THE AUDIENCE. AND THEN A CHEER! THE FABULOUS MISS VICKI STALKED ONSTAGE! BUT ONE VOICE ROSE ABOVE THE REST: CASSIDY. SHE STOOD UP SCREAMING AND HOLDING A BANNER. MISS VICKI BLUSHED AND SQUIRMED. HAD CASSIDY REALLY GONE SO FAR AS TO GUESS HER MEASUREMENTS, MAKE TWO MATCHING SEQUINED DRESSES, AND SEND ONE TO MISS VICKI BACKSTAGE? YUP. WHO ELSE?

DURING INTERMISSION, I WALKED LANKY TO THE LADIES ROOM DOWNSTAIRS. NOAH WAS IN THE LOBBY. THE SMOKING ROOM, ONCE UPON A TIME. HE LOOKED TIRED.

"SOMETIMES", HE SAID, "A GUY WISHES HE HAD A GIRLFRIEND HE COULD GO TO THE MOVIES WITH. AND JUST SIT THERE, LIKE EVERYBODY ELSE".

Forty-seven

PEDRO AND DEE DEE RETURNED HOME. "LOOKS JUST THE WAY WE LEFT IT", THEY SMILED. I GRITTED MY TEETH AND TAPPED THE TABLE NERVOUSLY. "YOU DID A GREAT JOB, AARON! THANKS SO MUCH!! HERE'S A LITTLE SOMETHING FOR YOUR TROUBLES".

I PUT MY ARMS OUT, HOPING TO SLIDE INTO PEDRO'S MUCH-COVETED VICE SQUAD T-SHIRT. I'D BEEN WEARING IT FOR TWO WEEKS, FROM THE MINUTE AFTER THEY STEPPED OUT THE DOOR TO A MOMENT BEFORE THEY WALKED BACK IN. NOW RESTING IN THE CLOSET WITH THE REST OF THEIR CLOTHES, IT WAS PROBABLY STILL WARM, WHICH WAS MORE THAN YOU COULD SAY FOR THE SCHOOL OF FISH I HAD SLAUGHTERED.

INSTEAD, HE HANDED ME A HUNDRED BUCKS. I BEAMED. THAT COVERED THE SUPERGLUE, ALL THE FISH I'D HAD TO REPLACE, THE LAMP I HAD TO HAVE REPAIRED, THE RUG I HAD TO HAVE STEAM CLEANED, PLUS ENOUGH LEFTOVER FOR A BOTTLE OF WHISKEY AND

A COUPLE EGG ROLLS AT "HUNGER PANG". WHAT A RELIEF.

THE PETS ALL HOWLED, SWAM AROUND, AND FLEW ABOUT IN A FRENZY. THEY WANTED TO TELL ON ME, OR AT LEAST POINT AN ACCUSING FINGER. BUT SADLY, THEY HADN'T EVOLVED ENOUGH YET, POOR CREATURES. I WAVED GOODBYE. WELCOME BACK, GUYS.

IMAGINE MY SURPRISE WHEN I RAN INTO PEDRO AND DEE DEE DOWNTOWN TWO NIGHTS LATER. WHAT WERE THEY DOING CARRYING HUGE SUITCASES? WASN'T IT SOON TO BE LEAVING AGAIN? AND WHO WERE THEIR SUITCASE CARRYING FRIENDS?

WHEN THEY GOT CLOSER, I RUBBED MY EYES. IT WAS NONE OTHER THAN BOB THE LAOTIAN, THE WINGNUT WHO LOOKS LIKE LENIN, AND A CHILDHOOD FRIEND OF MINE I KNOW ONLY AS "FIVE".

"HEY, THIRTEEN", HE SAID. OUR ROLL CALL NUMBERS FROM FOURTH GRADE GYM.

"I DIDN'T KNOW YOU ALL KNEW EACH OTHER", I SAID, STUPEFIED. THEY ALL SMILED A CONSPIRATORIAL SMILE.

"GOING ON A TRIP?" I ASKED, BUT THEY SHOOK THEIR HEADS AND SMILED AGAIN. I WAS GETTING PRETTY TIRED OF THIS GAME.

"WELL THEN WHAT THE FUCK ARE YOU DOING", I SAID, "WALKING AROUND TOWN WITH SUITCASES AT THREE A.M.??"

THEY PICKED UP THEIR SUITCASES AND SHOOK THEM. IT WAS A BEAUTIFUL SOUND, SOMETHING LIKE A SALSA BAND. HUNDREDS OF COLORS OF SPRAYPAINT CANS RATTLING ALL AT ONCE. TAGGERS.

NOW I SMILED. NO MATTER HOW MUCH YOU KNOW ANYONE, THERE'S SO MUCH YOU NEVER REALLY KNOW.

Forty-eight

LIKE ME, JO STILL LIVED AT HOME, BUT SHE WAS WORKING AT THE MENTAL WARD AT ST. MARY'S, SAVING UP TO GET A PLACE OF HER OWN. AS NIGHT ATTENDANT AT THE NUT HUT, I DIDN'T GET TO SEE HER MUCH ANYMORE, BEING STUCK ON THE DAYSHIFT MYSELF. I WAS MORE LIKELY TO SEE HER MOM, SITTING AS SHE DID SOMETIMES AT HER OWN TABLE AT THE CAFE, DRINKING ESPRESSO. I SAT AT A TABLE IN THE OPPOSITE CORNER, READING THE PAPER AND DOING THE CROSSWORD

PUZZLE. IF JO'S MOM WERE TWENTY YEARS YOUNGER, IT WOULD HAVE BEEN MY DREAM DATE. IF ONLY YOUNG GIRLS WERE THAT SOLITARY AND SELF-COMPOSED.

THE CAFE CLOSED AT ELEVEN, BUT THE DONUT SHOP NEVER CLOSED, AND ACTUALLY SEEMED TO OPEN UP MORE AND MORE WITH THE DARKNESS, LIKE A MOONFLOWER. A LONG COUNTER FACED THE WINDOW, PERFECT FOR COLLATING FANZINES WHILE WATCHING THE STREET LIFE DIE. A FEW TIMES JO FOUND ME THERE, UNBEARABLY EARLY IN THE MORNING ON HER WAY HOME FROM WORK. HEAD DOWN ON THE COUNTER, IN A MESS OF XEROXED PAGES AND IN FULL VIEW OF THE PASSING CARS, I WAS FAST ASLEEP.

IT WAS NICE THAT THE DONUT SHOP WORKERS DIDN'T MIND PEOPLE SLEEPING IN THEIR STORE, BUT IN MY CASE IT WOULD HAVE BEEN BETTER TO GET WOKEN UP. I'D FALL ASLEEP THERE FOR HOURS AT A TIME. NO ONE TOLD ME THE ORANGE POT WAS DECAF.

Forty-nine

"GUESS WHAT HAPPENED TO ME TODAY AT WORK", JO SAID.

I SAID, "YOU KNOW I DON'T LIKE TO TALK ABOUT THINGS THAT HAPPENED TODAY, NOR ABOUT THINGS THAT HAPPENED AT WORK".

SHE SAID, "FIRST OFF, THIS WOMAN CAME INTO THE OFFICE EVERY HALF HOUR FREAKING OUT, SAYING SHE WAS GOING TO DIE. I HAD TO CALM HER DOWN. NO, YOU'RE FINE, I SAID. YOUR MEDICAL REPORT IS FINE. I'M PRETTY SURE YOU'RE NOT GOING TO DIE. SHE'D LEAVE, BUT THEN COME RIGHT BACK AGAIN. FINALLY SHE CAME BACK ALL HAPPY AND RELIEVED. I'M NOT GOING TO DIE, SHE SAID. I FOUND OUT WHAT THE PROBLEM WAS AFTER ALL. MY TONGUE IS PREGNANT WITH A NINE YEAR OLD BOY"

THOUGH IT BROKE HALF MY RULES, IT WAS NICE TO HEAR JO'S STORIES FROM WORK. HEARING OTHER PEOPLE'S IRRATIONAL FEARS MADE ME REALIZE MINE WEREN'T SO RATIONAL EITHER, NOR WAS MY SELF-DIAGNOSIS MUCH BETTER. THEY MADE ME SEE THE HUMOR OF THE STRUGGLE OF LIFE, IN BETWEEN THE TEARS.

"I HAD TO ASK ANOTHER PATIENT SOME QUESTIONS

FOR A QUESTIONAIRE", SHE SAID. "I ASKED IF HE HAD
ANY ISSUES WITH AGING. HE SAID, ISSUES WITH AGING?
NONE AT ALL. IN FACT, IN THE LAST WEEK I'VE HAD
SEX WITH FIVE WOMEN OVER A HUNDRED YEARS OLD".
    "BUT HE KEPT ASKING, ARE YOU TRYING TO GET
INFORMATION ON MY COLON? HE SAID THE POLICE HAD
SURROUNDED HIS HOUSE AND, OVER THE COURSE OF A
WEEK, REMOVED HIS COLON EIGHT TIMES".
    I SAID, "THAT'S GOTTA SUCK"
    JO SAID, "YEAH, AND YOU THOUGHT YOU HAD A BAD
WEEK".

Fifty

    LARENKA, MELODY, AND JO. THREE GIRLS, THREE
MOTHERS. A SLIGHT REFRAIN, IF I MAY.
    MOTHER NUMBER ONE, A NURSE WITH A VERY DRY
SENSE OF HUMOR, LIVING ON A COUCH WHILE HER
TEENAGE DAUGHTER TOOK THE ONLY ROOM.
    MOTHER NUMBER TWO, A PRESS OPERATOR KNOWN
FOR AVOIDING TELEGRAPH ALTOGETHER AND CALLING JO
UGLY, THOUGH THAT'S HARD TO TAKE SERIOUSLY IF YOU'VE
EVER SEEN JO.
    MOTHER NUMBER THREE, A SOLITARY FIGURE
DRINKING ESPRESSO IN THE DARK CORNER OF THE CAFE,
TEACHING ETHICS AT THE UNIVERSITY BY DAY AND
LIVING BY NIGHT IN A NETHERWORLD OF OLD REEL TO
REEL TAPES, GATHERING DUST.
    THERE WAS ALSO SUSAN'S MOTHER, THE STALIN OF
RENT CONTROL, WHO BROUGHT THE REVOLUTION TO THE
BANK, LITERALLY, PLUS AMANDA, DOWNTOWN BERKELEY'S
OWN MOTHER-TO-BE. ACK! TOO MANY MOTHERS TO
KEEP TRACK OF. PLUS, ONE AUNT: MELODY'S.
    BACK IN THE DAY, MELODY'S MOM MOVED TO
BERKELEY FROM REDDING. SHE GOT AN APARTMENT
DOWNTOWN, RIGHT ABOVE HINK'S DEPARTMENT STORE.
ARRIVING TEN YEARS EARLIER THAN SUSAN'S MOM THE
LOAN OFFICER, SHE STILL FOUND HERSELF TOO LATE.
TOO LATE TO BE A BEATNIK, TOO GRIM AND DETERMINED
TO BE A HIPPIE. SHE SAT AROUND THE GREY APARTMENT
READING POETRY AND BEING DEPRESSED AND LONELY.
    MELODY'S AUNT, HOWEVER, HAD NO SUCH HANG-UPS.
CAREFREE AND LIGHTHEARTED, THE ARCHETYPICAL
SECOND CHILD, SHE HAD MISSED OUT ON MOST OF THEIR

PARENTS' SEVERITY AND ANXIETY. WHILE MELODY'S MOM WAS DRINKING BITTER WINE AND TRYING TO MAKE SENSE OF SEYMOUR KRIM, MELODY'S AUNT WAS HITCHHIKING ALL AROUND THE COUNTRY WEARING NOTHING BUT A PAIR OF OVERALLS.

CURSE THE SECOND CHILD! OVERNIGHT, SHE HAD TURNED FROM ALL-AMERICAN CHEERLEADER TO HITCH-HIKING HIPPIE SCUM. EVEN YEARS LATER, WHEN MELODY'S MOM AND AUNT WERE BOTH OLD AND SETTLED, THE OLD SCARS STILL STUNG.

POOR MELODY'S MOTHER, WITH HER STEELY EYES AND JUTTING JAW, HER RAKES AND HOES, TRYING TO KEEP HER LITTLE PLOT AT THE COMMUNITY GARDEN CLEAN AND STRAIGHT AND BRING UP A YOUNG GIRL THE SAME WAY. BEHIND HER BACK, SHE WAS BETRAYED. WHEN IT CAME TIME FOR MELODY TO LEAVE THE NEST, MELODY HEADED STRAIGHT FOR HER MOM'S OLD NEMESIS. BOO! HISS! MELODY'S AUNT.

MELODY RUBBED SALT IN THE OLD WOUNDS WHEN SHE DECIDED TO MOVE INTO THE ENEMY CAMP. BUT WHO COULD BLAME HER? IT MUST SUCK TO BE A MOTHER. MELODY'S MOM STILL HAD THE SAME APARTMENT DOWNTOWN. MELODY'S AUNT HAD A NICE PLACE BY GILMAN WITH A BIG GARDEN AND A BACK SHACK WITH MEL'S NAME WRITTEN ALL OVER IT.

Fifty-one

GROWING UP CLOSE TO CAMPUS, MELODY'S MOM CAUTIONED HER NOT TO GO TO PARTIES AT THE NEARBY U.C. BERKELEY FRAT HOUSES. GO TO PARTIES AT U.C. BERKELEY INTERNATIONAL HOUSE INSTEAD. FIND A NICE FOREIGN GUY WITH SOME EDUCATION. GOOD ADVICE, EXCEPT MELODY ALWAYS WOUND UP IN LONG-TERM, LONG-DISTANCE RELATIONSHIPS WITH GUYS WHO, MOST OF THE YEAR, LIVED IN COUNTRIES TOO FAR AWAY TO EVEN BE ABLE TO AFFORD TO CALL.

SHE WAS THE ONLY ONE OF OUR CREW TO REALLY USE BERKELEY'S VARIED RESOURCES. SHE LEARNED SWAHILI, AND HOW TO KICKBOX. NOT ONLY DID SHE CHECK BOOKS AND PAINTINGS OUT OF THE MAIN LIBRARY, SHE BORROWED PIPE CUTTERS AND POLE PRUNERS FROM THE TOOL LIBRARY AND GOT MUSHROOM COMPOST FROM THE COMPOST LIBRARY. I RAN INTO HER THERE ONCE. I'D

COME TO BE ALONE, SIT ON BIG PILES OF SHIT, GET DRUNK, AND FORGET EVERYTHING I KNEW. SHE'D COME TO JOIN OTHER PEOPLE WITH SIMILAR INTERESTS, A V.C. EXTENSION COURSE LEARNING ABOUT WORMS. "SEE, EVEN A BIG PILE OF SHIT HAS A LOT OF LIFE IN IT," SHE SAID.

THERE WAS A PARK NEAR HER AUNT'S PLACE WHERE I SPENT MANY MEMORABLE MOMENTS OF MY LIFE. I'D BEEN THERE WITH MELODY, PLAYING BASKETBALL. I'D BEEN THERE WITH JO, MAKING OUT. I'D PLAYED THERE ON THE SWINGS AS A LITTLE KID, AND SAT THERE ON THE SWINGS WITH NOAH ONCE, LATE AT NIGHT, WHEN HE TOLD ME HE WAS GOING TO HAVE A KID. I WAITED, BUT NO KID EVER CAME, AND THE SUBJECT WAS NEVER BROUGHT UP AGAIN. TALK ABOUT AWKWARD. IT WAS FINE WITH ME EITHER WAY, BUT AT LEAST HE COULD HAVE LET ME KNOW THAT THEY HAD CHANGED THEIR PLAN.

PLACES GET STACKED WITH MEMORIES WHEN YOU LIVE IN ONE PLACE TOO LONG AND TRY TO CRAM AS MUCH LIFE AS POSSIBLE INTO A SHORT TIME, GETTING OLD TOO SOON. YOU CAN'T TAKE A STROLL IN THE PARK WITHOUT WALKING DOWN MEMORY LANE. IT'S DANGEROUS. YOU GET POTHOLES IN THE TREADMILL OF YOUR MIND.

Fifty-two

LANKY HAD A WAY OF DISARMING ANY NEW OPPONENT, AND THAT MEANT ANY GIRL WHO ARRIVED AND GAVE ME SO MUCH AS A GLANCE. THERE WAS NO NEED, BECAUSE BY THAT TIME I WAS HERS, MORE THAN I EVER THOUGHT POSSIBLE. WE'D GONE FROM "DON'T ASK, DON'T TELL" TO "LOOK BUT DON'T TOUCH", AND NOW TO MY SURPRISE I FOUND THAT I DIDN'T EVEN LOOK MUCH ANYMORE. BUT SHE PERSISTED.

SHE CO-OPTED THEM. USUALLY IN A SUBTLE WAY IMPOSSIBLE FOR ME TO PIN DOWN, SHE WOULD STEAL A BIT OF THEIR STYLE OR MANNER OR MANNERISM. JUST A TRACE, ALMOST AS IF TO ENTRAP ME. I HAD TO PRETEND NOT TO NOTICE OR RECOGNIZE IT. IF I DID, THAT ADMISSION ALONE WOULD BE PROOF I'D PAID CLOSE ATTENTION TO SOMEONE ELSE.

SHE WOULD ASK TRICK QUESTIONS, TESTING ME.

SHE'D EVEN LITERALLY BORROW AN ITEM OF CLOTHING FROM AN IMAGINED ENEMY. SHOULD I SAY THE BORROWED CLOTHES LOOKED GOOD? OR BAD? WHO KNEW? BUT PULLING ANOTHER GIRL'S PANTS OFF YOUR GIRLFRIEND IS ENOUGH TO CROSS THE WIRES AND HOPELESSLY CONFUSE THE SIGNALS IN YOUR HEAD.

SHE WOULD BEFRIEND THESE GIRLS, BRINGING THEM CLOSE ENOUGH IN SO THAT THEY WERE NO LONGER AN OUTSIDE THREAT. THEY COULD BE KEPT TABS ON. PERHAPS SHE EXTRACTED A BIT OF KNOWLEGE OR PERSONAL FEAR FROM A RIVAL WHICH COULD BE USED AS AN EMOTIONAL CROWBAR IN CASE OF EMERGENCY. THEN SHE WOULD "NORMALIZE" THE SITUATION. PUT US ALL TOGETHER WHERE IT WOULD BE SO AWKWARD THAT ANY POSSIBLE FANTASY WAS SHOT, OR SO NORMAL AND BORING THAT ANY ROMANTIC SPARK WAS EXTINGUISHED.

IN THIS METHOD, OR MADNESS, I FOUND MYSELF GOING OUT WITH EVERY GIRL IN THE WORLD. ALWAYS SOMETHING NEW, ALWAYS SOMETHING TO WORRY ABOUT AND WONDER ABOUT AND MAYBE EVEN FANTASIZE ABOUT. BUT ALWAYS LANKY. THOUGH I WISHED SHE WOULDN'T WORRY, THINGS COULD HAVE BEEN WORSE.

MELODY SAW THINGS A LITTLE DIFFERENTLY.

"YOU IDIOT", SHE SAID. "JUST BECAUSE SHE'S LOOKING UP TO AND IMITATING THESE OTHER GIRLS DOESN'T MEAN SHE'S DOING IT FOR YOUR SAKE. MAYBE SHE'S CRUSHED OUT ON THEM, SO SHE'S JEALOUS OF YOU GETTING THEIR ATTENTION. MAYBE THEY'RE CRUSHED OUT ON HER, SO THEY'RE JEALOUS OF YOU GETTING HER ATTENTION. BUT PROBABLY, IT'S NOT ABOUT YOU AT ALL. YOU'RE JUST IN THE WAY EITHER WAY."

Fifty-three

BERKELEY IS FULL OF UNLIKELY PEOPLE GIVING EACH OTHER HUGE HUGS, STRANGE SPONTANEOUS REUNIONS LIKE TINY LITTLE EXPLOSIONS ON EVERY CORNER WHICH LEAVE PASSERBY SCRATCHING THEIR HEADS. WHERE ON EARTH COULD THESE PEOPLE KNOW EACH OTHER FROM?

ONE SAYS, "HOW LONG HAS IT BEEN? TEN YEARS?"

"YOU LOOK GREAT!" THE OTHER SAYS, AND A LOT OF TIMES IT'S ACTUALLY TRUE.

LANKY

IN A PUNK SCENE FULL OF PROFESSOR PARENTS, MINE WAS STRICTLY THIRD RUNG. HE TAUGHT MACRO-ECONOMICS AT A LOUSY STATE SCHOOL IN THE SOUTHBAY, AND BARELY HAD TENURE. BUT I WAS PROUD. HIS STUDENTS, MOSTLY REFUGEES FROM THIRD WORLD COMMUNIST REGIMES, WERE EVERYWHERE, AND IT WAS RARE THAT WE WENT OUT TO SHOP OR EAT WITHOUT RUNNING INTO ONE AND TAKING PART IN A LITTLE JOYFUL REUNION OF OUR OWN. HIS JOB KIND OF SUCKED, I GATHERED, BUT THIS FRINGE BENEFIT WAS A NICE ONE WHICH I TOO, COULD ENJOY. THAT AND, OF COURSE, FREE OFFICE SUPPLIES.

I'D GROWN TALLER THAN MY DAD IN TIME, BUT THERE WAS NO CHANCE OF KNOWING MORE, NO MATTER HOW MUCH I READ. HE RETAINED THE "DAD" GRANDEUR AND AWE-INSPIRING COOL ON THAT COURT, THOUGH I KEPT TESTING HIM. WHEN I STUMPED HIM THE FIRST TIME, OVER THE FAILED 1905 RUSSIAN REVOLUTION, I WAS SO PROUD THAT I HAD MY OWN PARADE. HA! FACE! MOM CLAIMED IT WAS ONLY THAT HE WAS TIRED, OR I'D MISUNDERSTOOD, BUT I KNEW BETTER. WE'D DISCUSS OR ARGUE ABOUT EVERYTHING, AND EVEN OUT SHOPPING I WOULD LEARN A NEW THING OR TWO FROM HIS STUDENTS. FOR INSTANCE, MOST OF BERKELEY'S INDIAN BUSINESS OWNERS AREN'T FROM INDIA AT ALL, BUT THE INDIAN COMMUNITY IN SOUTH AFRICA. WHO KNEW?

JIMMY TELLS A RELATED STORY. THIS IS THE SHORT VERSION: JIMMY IS A YOUNG PUNK. JIMMY'S DAD, THE HIGH SCHOOL ENGLISH TEACHER WELL KNOWN (AND SECRETLY LOVED) FOR BEING A KOOK, TAKES YOUNG JIM OUT SHOPPING FOR PUNK RECORDS. ON THE HORIZON, A MASSIVE FIGURE APPROACHES. IT IS NONE OTHER THAN XAVIER X, LEGENDARY KING OF THE EASTBAY PUNKS, TWO HUNDRED AND EIGHTY POUNDS OF SOLID STEEL WITH A TOOTHACHE AND A BAD HANGOVER, WHO HAS WORKED SECURITY AT THE LOCAL RECORD STORE SINCE APPROXIMATELY 35 B.C..

JIMMY'S LIFE IS RUINED. SPOTTED SHOPPING FOR PUNK RECORDS WITH HIS DAD BY THE LEGENDARY XAVIER X, HE BEGINS TO DIE OF EMBARRASSMENT.

BUT, IT GETS WORSE. COULD IT BE? XAVIER HOVERS ABOVE JIMMY'S DAD AS IF TO STRIKE! JIMMY TRIES TO WARN HIM, TRIES TO SCREAM, BUT IS ROOTED TO THE SPOT, PARALYZED BY FEAR. THE NEXT THING HE KNOWS, XAVIER HAS HIS FATHER IN A HEADLOCK. XAVIER SPINS JIMMY'S DAD AROUND, AND WITH MASSIVE, TATTOOED ARMS, BEGINS TO SQUEEZE THE VERY LIFE OUT OF HIM.

IT IS TOO GHASTLY TO BEHOLD. JIMMY COVERS HIS EYES.

BUT WHAT'S THIS? A STRUGGLE? NO. WHEN JIMMY LOOKS AGAIN THEY ARE SMILING AND PATTING EACH OTHER ON THE BACK! IT IS QUITE A SIGHT. THE BURLY XAVIER X IS LOOKING AT THE GAWKY, GAP-TOOTHED TEACHER WITH PUPPY EYES.

IT SEEMS THAT XAVIER WAS ONCE IN JIMMY'S FATHER'S REMEDIAL ENGLISH CLASS. HE SAT IN THE VERY BACK, LOOKING AT WAR COMIC BOOKS. HE WAS FUNCTIONALLY ILLITERATE. EVIDENTLY ALL THE TEACHERS IN THE PAST HAD BEEN TOO SCARED OF XAVIER TO TEACH HIM, OR EVEN APPROACH HIM AND TRY.

JIMMY'S DAD SAID, "NOW XAVIER, IF I BRING YOU A BOOK ABOUT WAR, IF I HELP YOU THROUGH IT, WILL YOU READ IT?

XAVIER SAID YES, AND THOUGH IT WAS A STRUGGLE, HE KEPT HIS PROMISE, MAKING IT ALL THE WAY THROUGH, AND LEARNING TO READ IN THE PROCESS. THE BOOK? YOU GUESSED IT: WAR AND PEACE.

Fifty-four

MY DAD STARTED NEW HOME IMPROVEMENTS OR SELF-IMPROVEMENTS EVERY WEEK, BUT HE HAD NO INTENTION OF COMPLETING THE TASKS. HE GREW FOND OF THE HALF-FINISHED WORK, THE FAMILIAR EXCUSES, THE PROCRASTINATION. HE TOOK COMFORT IN BEING IN THE MIDDLE OF A WEB OF HIS OWN MAKING WHICH NO ONE COULD UNDO.

MY BROTHER WAS WISE, REMAINING A PART OF THE FAMILY BUT ABANDONING THE HOUSE COMPLETELY. FOOLISHLY, I STAYED ON, FALLING FOR EVERY NEW PROJECT MY DAD SUGGESTED. IF NOTHING ELSE, IT WAS A CHANCE TO BOND. BUT THAT BOND WAS TURNING TO BITTERNESS AS I SAW MY PRECIOUS WORK GO TO WASTE. LEAVE FOR ONE WEEKEND AND HE WOULD FILL IN ANY SPACE I HAD CLEARED AND LOSE ANYTHING I HAD SAVED. LEAVE FOR TWO WEEKS AND A YEAR'S WORTH OF WORK WAS THROWN AWAY. IT WAS A SORT OF TERRITORIAL PISSING, A WRENCH IN THE WORKS TO PREVENT PROGRESS AND CHANGE.

HE TALKED UP PLANS TO CLEAR AND FIX UP THE HOUSE SO WE COULD RENT OUT ROOMS TO STUDENTS AS

A WAY TO MAKE THE MORTGAGE PAYMENTS, BUT WHEN IT CAME DOWN TO IT HE COULDN'T BEAR TO SEE THE PLACE SLIP EVEN ONE BIT OUT OF HIS CONTROL. HE WANTED TO FEEL LIKE WE WERE DOING SOMETHING TO SOLVE THE PROBLEM, YET MADE SURE TO PREVENT ANY SOLUTION. AND THE PROBLEM REMAINED: A MASSIVE BALLOON PAYMENT LOOMED OMINOUSLY AT THE END OF A SECOND MORTGAGE, ARRIVING SOON, AND MEANWHILE HE'D TAKEN OUT A THIRD ON THE SIDE. ONLY EIGHTEEN AND I WAS ALREADY IN MIDDLE-AGE, MIDDLE CLASS HELL.

MUCH AS HE LOVED THE CLUTTERED, UNORGANIZED, UNFINISHED MESS, I HAD GROWN UP HATING IT, AND WAS OBSESSIVE IN MY DESIRE TO KEEP THINGS STRAIGHT AND GET THINGS DONE. GROWING UP IN A STY, I WAS FILTHY AS A PIG, BUT I WAS THE MOST ORGANIZED PIG ON EARTH, A PIG WITH ALPHABETIZED AND NUMBERED FILES, SCHEDULES, CALENDARS, AND LISTS. I'D DRINK COFFEE AND MAKE LISTS OF FILES, LISTS OF SCHEDULES, LISTS OF CALENDARS, AND LISTS OF LISTS.

OBSESSIVENESS, IT TAKES ON MANY FORMS, BUT THEY'RE ALL CUT FROM THE SAME CLOTH. "AN APPLE DOESN'T FALL FAR FROM THE TREE", AS THEY SAY. BUT ALSO, "A MAN WHO SITS UNDER A TREE TOO LONG WILL FIND THE BIRDS SHITTING ON HIS HEAD."

I THREW UP MY HANDS AND TORE AT MY HAIR, GROANING, STORMING THROUGH A HOUSE FILLED WITH JUNK, ORGANIZED AND DISORGANIZED, FINISHED AND UNFINISHED, MY DAD'S AND MINE. I RACED AROUND LIKE A MADMAN, BITING MY NAILS, PACING A PATH THROUGH THE TRASH, FOLLOWING A TRAIL OF OLD, CROSSED-OFF LISTS. ALAS, A LIST IS MADE TO BE LOST.

MEANWHILE, SOMEONE ELSE WAS FOLLOWING A TRAIL OF MISPLACED, HALF-EMPTY CUPS OF COFFEE, LOOKING FOR THE ONE JUST POURED, STILL WARM. WE BUMPED HEADS.

DAD.
SON.

Fifty-five

MY DAD HAD AN OLD FRIEND, JOEY, WHO HE MET AT HIS FIRST JOB UPON ARRIVING IN CALIFORNIA WITH

MY MOM. IT WAS AT A FACTORY IN LOS ANGELES.
ON HIS FIRST DAY OF WORK, DAD WAS BROKE AND
HELLA HUNGRY. HE TURNED TO THE GUY NEXT TO HIM
AND ASKED TO BORROW FIVE BUCKS. LIKE FATHER,
LIKE SON YOU MIGHT SAY, BUT THE FRIENDSHIP OF
A LIFETIME WAS BORN.

MY MOM AND DAD MOVED TO BERKELEY AND
JOEY STAYED IN LOS ANGELES, MARRYING A GIRL
NAMED LILY. HE DIDN'T STAY LONG AT THE FACTORY,
BUT DID STAY WITH THE UNION, EVENTUALLY BECOMING
A HIGH-LEVEL NEGOTIATOR FOR THE TEAMSTERS.
LIKE MY PARENTS, JOEY AND LILY HAD TWO CHILDREN.
BUT GROWING UP FAR APART, ME AND MY BRO BARELY
KNEW THEM.

MY MOM AND DAD HAD MANY FRIENDS, BUT THEY
WERE MY MOM'S FRIENDS ORIGINALLY. MY DAD NEVER
REALLY HAD CLOSE FRIENDS OF HIS OWN. "OLD"
FRIENDS, BUT NOT CLOSE ONES. I VOWED NEVER TO
LET THAT HAPPEN IN MY OWN LIFE, THOUGH SADLY,
I NOW SEE IT AS SOMEWHAT INEVITABLE. JOEY WAS
PERHAPS MY DAD'S CLOSEST FRIEND, AND THE SAD
THING WAS, HE LIVED FOUR HUNDRED MILES AWAY.
WE RARELY HAD TIME OR A GOOD REASON TO VISIT.
WHAT REASONS ARE THERE, REALLY, THAT BRING
PEOPLE TOGETHER, EXCEPT WEDDINGS AND FUNERALS?
AGAIN, THERE ARE WORSE REASONS TO GET MARRIED.

THE CEREMONY AND CELEBRATION WERE LIKE
NOTHING I'D EVER SEEN. OF COURSE, BECAUSE I'D
NEVER BEEN TO AN IRANIAN WEDDING BEFORE.
BUT I'D BEEN TO A LOT OF WILD SHOWS AND NEVER
SEEN SUCH JUBILANT, RAUCOUS DANCING. ZHALEH,
JOEY AND LILY'S ELDEST DAUGHTER, WAS THE BLUSHING,
GLOWING BRIDE.

AS ALWAYS, I WAS AWKWARD IN FORMAL ATTIRE
AND HIDING IN A CORNER. BUT I SUDDENLY BECAME
AWARE THAT EVERYONE WAS CALLING MY NAME.

"AARON, AARON, THE BRIDE IS LOOKING FOR YOU",
THEY SAID, AND SURE ENOUGH, BEFORE I COULD
GATHER MY SENSES AND RUN, ZHALEH WAS BEFORE
ME, WHISPERING IN MY EAR, BLUSHING, IT SEEMED,
EVEN MORE THAN BEFORE.

"I NEED A SAFETY PIN!!" SHE SAID. "MY DRESS,
IT'S FALLING OFF!!"

EVEN IN A SUIT AND TIE, I HAD A FEW WITHIN
EASY REACH. MY BRACELETS, A JUNGLE OF KEEPSAKES
AND CHARMS, WERE HELD TOGETHER WITH THEM.

"OH THANK YOU! THANKS SO MUCH!" SHE GUSHED.
"YOU SAVED ME! I KNEW YOU WOULD HAVE ONE", THEN

SHE LAUGHED AND RAN BACK TO JOIN THE DANCING.

I TOLD THE STORY TO NAHID, MY BOSS. SHE DID NOT LAUGH, BUT INSTEAD NODDED, THEN CALLED HER HUSBAND PARVIZ AT THE OTHER SHOP. HE DROVE UP NOT FIVE MINUTES LATER.

PARVIZ HANDED ME A STACK OF COPIES WHICH A DISGRUNTLED CUSTOMER HAD BROUGHT INTO THE STORE, COMPLAINING ABOUT "THOSE PUNKS UP THE STREET AND THEIR BROKEN MACHINES". THERE WERE LINES ALL ACROSS THE PAGE, SCRATCHES I COULDN'T EXPLAIN. NOT THE PRODUCT OF ONE OF MY EXPERIMENTS, THOUGH IT WAS A NICE EFFECT. I WAS CURIOUS ABOUT THE TECHNIQUE. PARVIZ OPENED UP THE BIG XEROX 1065 MACHINE.

"THIS IS THE XEROX DRUM", HE SAID.

"YEAH, YEAH", I SAID. "I KNOW. THAT'S WHERE I REMOVE THE PAPER WHEN IT JAMS".

"YES", HE SAID. HE POINTED TO THE SCRATCHES ON THE COPIES AND THEN TO MY BRACELETS. I COULD SEE, AFTER ALL, A CERTAIN RESEMBLANCE.

"OKAY, OKAY, I GET IT", I SAID. THEN HE LEFT AND I TOOK OFF THE TRINKETS AND KEEPSAKES AND SAFETY PINS ONE BY ONE.

Fifty-six

I WAS WALKING THE BACKSTREETS BACK FROM THE MARINA, FEELING MORE A PART OF THE WORLD THAN USUAL, WHEN I CAME ACROSS A MAN LOCKED OUT OF HIS CAR. A BUSINESSMAN. OTHER DRIVERS SLOWED DOWN TO LOOK AND A FEW STOPPED TO SIGH AND TALK ABOUT THE TIME THEY WERE LOCKED OUT. "RELATING", THE MODERN SUBSTITUTE FOR SYMPATHY, EMPATHY, OR GENUINE SUPPORT. TO MY SURPRISE, THE BUSINESSMAN WAS CALLING OUT FOR A SAFETY PIN.

"A SAFETY PIN? I HAVE A SAFETY PIN!" I SAID, STEPPING FORWARD AND REACHING DOWN MY PANTS.

SEE, PUNKS REALLY ARE THE GLUE THAT HOLDS SOCIETY TOGETHER. WHO ELSE WOULD HAVE A SAFETY PIN? NO ONE BUT A BABY IN DIAPERS. I STARTED TO TELL THE BUSINESSMAN TO REMEMBER THAT NEXT TIME HE WAS SITTING AT HIS DESK ABOUT TO FORE-CLOSE ON MY HOUSE. REMEMBER WHO SAVED YOU WHEN YOU WERE LOCKED OUT?

BUT HE INTERRUPTED ME.

"NOT A SAFETY PIN", HE SAID. "A PEN. I NEED A PEN".

"YES! I HAVE THAT TOO!" I SAID. "NOT ONLY AM I A PUNK, BUT ALSO A WRITER! PENS AND SAFETY PINS, THAT'S LIKE MY COAT OF ARMS! MY LANCE AND SHIELD! MY CREAM AND SUGAR!"

THE CAR WINDOW WAS OPEN JUST ENOUGH TO FIT HIS HAND IN, AND THE PEN WAS JUST LONG ENOUGH TO FLIP THE LOCK.

I SAID, "GLAD TO HELP A BROTHER IN NEED.... WE'RE ALL IN THE SAME GANG.... CAN'T DO THAT WITH A COMPUTER, SIR".

BUT HE DID NOT RESPOND. HE JUST GOT IN HIS CAR AND DROVE AWAY. HE DIDN'T EVEN SAY THANKS.

"HEY! WAIT!" I YELLED. "THAT GUY STOLE MY PEN!"

Fifty-seven

RIP, JIMMY, LARENKA, SUSAN, NOAH, CASSIDY, JO, MELODY, THAD, UZBEKO, AND ME. WE ALL HAD NICK-NAMES, AND MOST OF THEM WERE SELF-DEPRECATORY. TAKE YOUR WORST QUALITY OR MOST EMBARRASSING MOMENT AND HOLD IT UP FOR EVERYONE TO SEE. PROUDLY. A NEW NAME, A CHANCE FOR A NEW START. EVEN TELEGRAPH HAD AN OLD NAME IT HAD OUTGROWN WHEN IT REALLY CAME INTO ITS OWN. NICKNAMES WERE EMPOWERING. THEY ALSO TENDED TO ENCOURAGE SPLIT PERSONALITIES, THOUGH THAT WASN'T APPARENT UNTIL YEARS LATER, WHEN SUSAN, WHO WE CALLED "STEAKNIFE", TURNED OUT TO HAVE YET ANOTHER NAME AND ANOTHER SECRET LIFE. FUNNY, WHILE "RIP" WAS RIP'S REAL NAME, "SUSAN" TURNED OUT TO BE FAKE. HER REAL NAME, "NEL", LIKE THE STORY OF HER LIFE BEFORE WE MET, MADE US SHUDDER. THE THINGS SHE HAD DONE IN HER PAST, WE WOULD NEVER HAVE GUESSED. BUT I DIGRESS.

SLIP, ITCHY, LANKY, STEAKNIFE, TUMOR, SLITHER, AXEFACE, MELODRAMA, OOPS!, ROBO, AND ME, WHO'S EMBARRASSING NICKNAME I SEEM TO HAVE FORGOTTEN. TOGETHER, THE GALLANT KNIGHTS OF CESSPOOL PLUS GUESTS, WE GATHERED IN THE "LIVING" ROOM TO PREPARE FOR OUR DANGEROUS MISSION: A JOUST TO THE DEATH. HIDDEN DEEP WITHIN THE CASTLE LAIR OF THE CHRIST-IANS, HIGH UPON THE HILL, STEEPED ATOP THE HIGHEST PEAK, WAS THE LEGENDARY CROSS-SHAPED HEDGE. THE

TWO THINGS WE HATED MOST, TOGETHER! MUST AVENGE! MUST SMASH THE CROSS-SHAPED HEDGE! MUST SHRED, BLEND, PULVERIZE, MIX, CHOP, MASSACRE, AND TENDERLY ANNIHILATE THE CROSS-SHAPED HEDGE!

WE LEFT BEHIND A FEW SOLDIERS TO HOLD DOWN THE FORT. OOPS! BEGGED TO COME ALONG, BUT WE WOULDN'T LET HIM. NO, OOPS! NO, ROBO. YOU CAN'T COME. YOU CAN'T WALK WITH US ALL THE WAY UP MARIN. YOU DON'T WANT TO.

WHY WOULD OOPS! AND ROBO BEG TO COME ALONG? WOULD YOU JUMP OFF A CLIFF IF ALL YOUR FRIENDS DID? OF COURSE! BECAUSE MOST OF US ARE JUST DYING TO JUMP OFF A CLIFF, AND CONFORMITY WOULD OFFER A CONVENIENT EXCUSE. BUT THEY WERE DENIED, AND WHY? BECAUSE TOO MANY COOKS IS EVEN WORSE WITH NO FOOD.

THERE IS A PARTICULARLY FULFILLING FEELING OF DIVING INTO A HEDGE. OF LOSING YOURSELF IN IT, DEEP AMONG THE LEAVES AND DUSTY DEBRIS, SWIMMING, LOSING YOUR HAT IN IT USUALLY TOO AND GETTING PULLED OUT BY YOUR CREW JUST IN TIME FOR A MAD DASH FROM THE ANGRY NEIGHBORS AND NEIGHBORHOOD WATCHERS.

IT'S AN ADDICTIVE FEELING NOT UNLIKE THE BEST DANCING, WHEN YOU LOSE ALL SENSE OF UP AND DOWN. YOU EVEN LOSE TRACK OF THE DISTINCTION BETWEEN YOUR BODY AND OTHER BODIES—OR WALLS, FLOORS, AND DRUMSETS.

BUT A GOOD HEDGE HAS EVEN MORE OF AN ANTI-GRAVITY EFFECT. FIRM, YET PLIANT. GENTLE AND LOVING, YET BRUTAL AND UNFORGIVING. AT ONCE FAMILIAR AND FULL OF SURPRISES; SURPRISES CONSISTING OF, BUT NOT LIMITED TO: BROKEN BOTTLES, OLD TOYS, SHARP STICKS, BRICKS, THORNS, AND OUR FAVORITE, METAL FENCES. MANY A NIGHT WE WERE IMPALED, NAY, FLAYED, BY AN ERRANT HEDGE. NIGHTS FOR WHICH WE STILL BEAR THE SCARS.

WE ALL SAT TOGETHER, GROUPED LIKE A LIST OF AFFLICTIONS OR SYNONYMS FOR SUFFERING. GATHERED IN FRONT OF THE RESERVOIR IN THE EARLY MORNING MIST, STILL SOAKED FROM THE RAIN AND SORE FROM THE BATTLE, LICKING OUR WOUNDS. DID I MENTION IT WAS MY BIRTHDAY PARTY?

19. THE YEARS, THEY PASS SO FAST.

Fifty-eight

"ISN'T THAT THE PRESENT YOU GAVE ME FOR MY BIRTHDAY OUT IN THE TRASHHEAP?"

"YES, AARON, I DECIDED TO SMASH IT INTO TINY, JOYFUL BITS."

THAT WAS JIMMY. TERRIBLY SELF-RIGHTEOUS, WITH ABSOLUTELY NO REGARD FOR THE FEELINGS OF OTHERS. TERRIBLE BECAUSE JIMMY'S ARMOR MADE HIM IMMUNE TO MY FAMILIAR GUILT TRIPS. HE WAS THE ONLY ONE I COULDN'T CONVINCE TO WAKE UP TO TALK OR STAY UP AND WALK ALL THE WAY UP MARIN, EVEN FOR MY ANNUAL BIRTHDAY CELEBRATION. WHILE UZBEKO AND THAD WERE TOLD TO STAY, I BEGGED JIMMY TO COME ALONG.

"JIMMY!" I SAID. "THERE IS TIME TO SLEEP LATER! TEN YEARS FROM NOW WHEN WE LOOK BACK ON THIS NIGHT, YOU WON'T REMEMBER BEING ASLEEP. BUT COME WITH ME, AND IT WILL BE A NIGHT YOU WILL NEVER FORGET. REGRET, YES. BUT NOT FORGET."

"AARON", HE SAID, SLOWLY, SURELY, UNCONDITIONALLY. "I CHOOSE NOT TO GO".

IT WAS ALWAYS LIKE THAT WITH HIM.

"JIMMY! HOW COULD YOU THROW AWAY MY BACKPACK? HOW COULD YOU FLAKE ON ME WHEN WE HAD PLANS TO MEET? WHERE IS THE TEN DOLLARS YOU BORROWED?"

"AARON", HE WOULD SAY, WITH THE SAME SELF-ASSURED GRIN. "I HATED YOUR BACKPACK. I DECIDED TO FLAKE ON YOU. YOUR TEN DOLLARS I SPENT ON SPEED, AND IT WAS DELICIOUS".

NOW I RAN INTO HIS ROOM ON MY BIRTHDAY, THE MORNING AFTER THE PARTY, IN A MAD PANIC. JIMMY WAS JUST GETTING UP.

"JIMMY, WHERE ARE MY KEYS? I LEFT THEM ON THE 'LIVING' ROOM TABLE FIVE MINUTES AGO".

JIMMY SAID, "I DON'T BELIEVE IN KEYS".

"JIMMY! I DON'T CARE! I NEED THOSE KEYS! I NEED TO BE AT WORK IN FIVE MINUTES TO OPEN THE SHOP!"

HE WAS UNFAZED.

"JIMMY! WHERE ARE THEY?"

"YOUR KEYS? I THREW THEM IN THE TOILET. THEN,

I TOOK A HUGE SHIT. BUT YOU COULD PROBABLY STILL FISH THEM OUT. I DIDN'T FLUSH".

AT CAMPUS COPY MART, CUSTOMERS WERE ALREADY LINED UP OUTSIDE THE DOOR. DAMN SENIOR CITIZENS. MUCH AS I HATED THE STUDENTS, THEY AT LEAST SLEPT IN.

I WAS ON THE PAYPHONE IN THE ALLEY TALKING TO PARVIZ, ATTEMPTING ONE EXCUSE OR ANOTHER. UNLIKE JIMMY, I WAS AFFECTED BY GUILT, AND PARVIZ NEVER LET UP.

"WE HAVE SMALL BUSINESS. WE TREAT YOU LIKE SON. I MUST ONCE AGAIN CLOSE MY STORE TO DRIVE THERE AND LET YOU IN? I DO NOT UNDERSTAND. PLEASE EXPLAIN AGAIN".

Fifty-nine

SENIOR CITIZENS, PUNKS, AND IRANIANS WERE NOT MY ONLY CUSTOMERS. EVERYONE NEEDED SOMETHING COPIED, AND FOR ONE REASON OR ANOTHER, MANY PASSED UP THE NEARBY CORPORATE GIANT TO COME TO ONE OF OUR HOLE-IN-THE-WALL SHOPS. MAYBE BECAUSE THEY WERE CHEAPSKATES, OR THEY WANTED TO SUPPORT SMALL, LOCAL BUSINESSES. OR MAYBE BECAUSE WE WERE FRIENDLY BUT DIDN'T ASK QUESTIONS. AT "MY" STORE, YOU COULD COPY COPYRIGHTED MATERIAL. YOU COULD ALSO COPY YOUR GUN OR YOUR BREASTS, AND STRANGERS CAME IN TO DO BOTH.

LIKE EVERYONE ELSE, I HAD A LITTLE BUSINESS GOING ON THE SIDE. A LITTLE OF THIS AND A LITTLE OF THAT. I DESIGNED WEDDING INVITATIONS, BIRTHDAY CARDS, MENUS AND LOGOS. I FORGED TICKETS AND COUPONS. I GOT TO KNOW THE OTHER TELEGRAPH-AREA BUSINESSES, LARGE AND SMALL, LEGAL AND OTHERWISE. FROM STEVE THE GREEK TO JAKE THE SNAKE.

ONE OF THE MOST EXCITING WAS "THE CAVE", A TINY THEATER WITH AN OFF-THE-WALL, SOMETIMES OFF-THE-CUFF APPROACH. A VERY NICE LAD NAMED FAROUK, A FORMER EMPLOYEE OF THE TELEGRAPH REPERTORY CINEMA, HAD BOUGHT THE PLACE WHEN, AFTER TEN YEARS BARELY STAYING AFLOAT, IT FINALLY WENT UNDER. FAROUK BROUGHT IN NEW BLOOD AND A FRESH APPROACH, WITH COUCHES AND LATENIGHT CULT FLICKS AND FOUR DOLLAR TRIPLE FEATURES,

A CINEPHILE'S DREAM.

BERKELEY ISN'T ONE OF THOSE PLACES WHERE YOUNG PEOPLE OWN THEIR OWN BUSINESSES. THE CITY IS FIRMLY IN THE HANDS OF THE BABY BOOMERS, AND WILL BE UNTIL THEY MEET THEIR EARLY GRAVE. AND THAT'S OKAY. JUST ONE DAY IN SEATTLE WILL SHOW YOU WHY NOT TO TURN YOUR TOWN OVER TO TWENTY-SOMETHINGS. BUT IT WAS NICE TO HAVE JUST ONE LITTLE CAVE.

UP THE STAIRS NEXT TO FRED'S MARKET, UNDER THE ROOF WHERE RIOT POLICE SHOT JAMES RECTOR, WAS THE DARK, STICKY THEATER. IT WAS SOMEPLACE I COULD TAKE LANKY, AND I DON'T MEAN "TAKE" THE SAME AS WHEN I TALK ABOUT THE TWO OF US GOING TO LA LOMA PARK, THE BOTANICAL GARDENS, THE BATHROOM AT MY WORK, THE CROSS-SHAPED HEDGE, OR THE ROOF OF THE DURANT PARKING GARAGE. BECAUSE, I'M TOO SHY TO EVEN KISS IN A MOVIE THEATER. BUT I HAD A STACK OF FREE PASSES, AND WHERE ELSE COULD YOU SEE "DON'T LOOK BACK", HEAR THE SPIRIT OF '29 BAND PLAY, AND VISIT AN ALL-JELLO SNACKBAR ALL IN ONE NIGHT? IT WAS LIKE THREE DATES AT ONCE, WHICH, I HOPED, MADE UP FOR LOST TIME. I EVEN INVITED SUSAN, MY SELF-APPOINTED IN-LAW, ALONG ONCE OR TWICE TO TRY TO MAKE PEACE. BUT, THERE ARE EASIER THINGS TO MAKE. FINALLY I SUCCEEDED IN A SORT OF TRUCE, SETTING HER UP WITH JIMMY. WITH THOSE TWO GOING OUT AT LEAST OUR MUTUAL DISLIKE WAS A FAMILY MATTER. YOU CAN DISLIKE YOUR NOSE, BUT WHAT TO DO? IT'S STILL PART OF YOUR FACE.

ONE DAY I WAS RECORD SHOPPING, USING FAKE COUPONS I HAD MADE, WHEN I GOT A HEAVY TAP ON THE SHOULDER. I TURNED AROUND EXPECTING TO FIND AN ANGRY EMPLOYEE, BUT INSTEAD FOUND MY EMPLOYER ALONG WITH HIS ENTIRE FAMILY. PARVIZ, NAHID, NILOUFAR, HER HUSBAND, AND THEIR THREE KIDS IN TOW. THE WHOLE CAVALCADE.

WERE THEY UNCOMFORTABLE IN THE PUNK SECTION OF THE RECORD STORE? UNHAPPY IN THIS UNFAMILIAR SETTING? NOT AT ALL. I WAS UNCOMFORTABLE AND SHRINKING IN TERROR. THEY WERE AT EASE AND PLEASED TO RUN INTO ME UNEXPECTEDLY, GRINNING AND LAUGHING GOOD-NATUREDLY AT MY DISCOMFORT. JUST LIKE IN NINTH GRADE WHEN MY BIOLOGY TEACHER SHOWED UP TO CLUB FOOT TO SEE Ⓐ STATE OF MIND, I WAS IN SHOCK. I'D NEVER SEEN THEM OUTSIDE THE COPY SHOP, NEVER EVEN THOUGHT ABOUT THEM REALLY LIVING OUTSIDE THE ROLES I KNEW.

Sixty

ONCE I WAS AT A ROCK AGAINST RACISM SHOW AT DOLORES PARK. YIPPIES HAD GARBAGE BAGS FULL OF JOINTS, THROWING THEM OUT INTO THE AUDIENCE. THE DEAD KENNEDYS WERE ON STAGE. NOT A BIG DK'S FAN, I HEADED UP THE HILL IN SEARCH OF SOME AIR. FURTHER AND FURTHER I CLIMBED, THROUGH A DENSE CLOUD OF DUST, DOGS, PUNKS, AND WEED. I SCALED THE HIGHEST PEAK AND, FINALLY EMERGING FROM THE GREEN CLOUD, I COLLAPSED, TRYING TO CATCH MY BREATH.

"WHY, HELLO", A VOICE SAID.

"FRANCO!" I EXCLAIMED.

AT THE VERY TOP OF THE HILL, COMPLETELY OBLIVIOUS TO HIS SURROUNDINGS YET AT THE SAME TIME PERFECTLY IN TUNE WITH THEM, SITTING LIKE A GURU, WAS FRANCO FROM MDC. HE APPEARED TO BE DRINKING HIS OWN PUKE.

LIKE ALL THE OLDER PUNKS IN TOWN, FRANCO HAD LONG AGO GROWN USED TO MY PESTERING QUESTIONS. WILLINGLY OR NOT, THE SCENE ELDERS HAD ASSUMED RESPONSIBILITY FOR THE EDUCATION AND MORAL GUIDANCE OF US YOUNG PUNKS. YOU WOULD NEVER HAVE THOUGHT TO BRING YOUR QUESTIONS OR PROBLEMS TO PARENTS, TEACHERS, OR RABBIS, BUT WITH SOMEONE LIKE FRANCO OR TIM YO, YOU KNEW YOU COULD ASK THEM ANYTHING. "FRANCO", I ASKED. "WHAT THE HELL IS THAT?"

"THIS", HE SAID, PAUSING MEDITATIVELY, "IS CALLED SPIRULINA".

"IT LOOKS GROSS AS HELL, DUDE".

FRANCO PONDERED MY POINT, STROKING HIS BEARD. "YOU CAN LOOK AT IT TWO WAYS", HE SAID. "AS A PUKE-LIKE, LUMPY BEVERAGE THAT TASTES LIKE DIRT. HMMM".

HE SMILED AND TOOK A SIP.

"OR AS ALGAE GROWING PEACEFULLY IN ALKALINE LAKES, BLANKETED IN DROPLETS OF MORNING DEW, BLENDED INTO A NATURAL, AND WONDERFUL, HEALTHY DRINK".

"GIMME SOME", I SAID.

HE WAS RIGHT ON BOTH COUNTS. IT TASTED LIKE WHAT IT WAS: POND SCUM. YET WITH THE PROPER ATTITUDE ANYTHING COULD BE REFRESHING.

YEARS LATER FRANCO BECAME A TRAVEL AGENT, BUT MAINTAINED MUCH THE SAME PHILOSOPHICAL

APPROACH. "IT'S REWARDING", HE SAID, "HELPING PEOPLE GET WHERE THEY NEED TO GO". SOTHIRA FROM CRUCIFIX, LATER AN INSURANCE SALESMAN, MIGHT HAVE A HARDER TIME RECONCILING THE DIFFERENT LIVES AND DIFFERENT TIMES.

BUT MAYBE NOT. EVERYONE THINKS THEY'RE THE ONE WHO HASN'T CHANGED.

Sixty-one

WHAT WAS THE GLUE THAT HELD US TOGETHER? WHAT KEPT US FROM SPLITTING UP INTO A MILLION SPLINTER GROUPS? WHAT KEPT US FROM BREAKING INTO FRACTALS, OR FRAGMENTS, OR GETTING SMASHED IN HALF BY THE CYCLOTRON? WHAT HAPPENED IF YOU THREW YOURSELF UPON THE GEARS OF THE MACHINE, AS MARIO SAVIO SUGGESTED, BUT THE MACHINE REFUSED TO STOP? WHAT THEN? WAS THERE A BACKUP PLAN? DOES TIME HEAL ALL WOUNDS? NO!

WE USED TO YELL "NO PASARAN!", THE SLOGAN FROM THE SPANISH CIVIL WAR. BUT "THEY SHALL NOT PASS" WAS WISHFUL THINKING IN 1939 MADRID AS WELL AS BERKELEY 1984. THE BATTLE CRY OF DEFEAT, OR AT LEAST DENIAL. "NO BACKUP PLAN!", "WATCH THE GAP", OR "OUCH!!" WOULD HAVE BEEN MORE HONEST. BUT IS IT ALWAYS BETTER TO BE REALISTIC? WHO'S WORLD IS IT? THEIR WORLD!

WHAT ARE WE MARCHING FOR? CAN WE REACH CONSENSUS? PROCESS! PROCESS! WHO'S IN CHARGE OF THIS UNRULY MOB? WHAT DO WE HAVE IN COMMON? HOW CAN WE FIGHT AGAINST AN ENEMY WE CAN'T EVEN SEE? WHAT DO WE WANT? THE WORLD! WHEN DO WE GET IT? NEVER!

WHAT IS PUNK? HOW OPEN IS AN "OPEN" RELATION-SHIP? WHAT IS THE DIFFERENCE BETWEEN SPIRULINA AND SEWAGE? HOW CAN YOU BE FROM A COUNTRY THAT LONG AGO OFFICIALLY CEASED TO EXIST?

MAYBE IT WAS MORE ABOUT CHOOSING YOUR OWN LABELS THAN IT WAS ABOUT PLEASING THE CUSTOMER AFTER ALL. DEFINING AND INCLUDING YOURSELF. IF WE CALLED IT OUR WORLD AND ADOPTED IT, WOULD IT LEARN TO LOVE US AND ANSWER WHEN WE CALL?

Sixty-two

I LIED, TWICE. TO SIMPLIFY THINGS, AND BECAUSE IT'S ALWAYS EASIER TO DISMISS PEOPLE AND TRIVIALIZE THEM WITH GENERALIZATIONS THAN IT IS TO TELL THE WHOLE TRUTH.

FIRST OFF, MDC HAD A BUNCH OF GOOD SONGS, NOT JUST ONE. AND I LOVED THEM. NOT FOR THEIR MUSIC, BUT FOR LIVING THEIR POLITICS AND PASSIONS, FOR LIVING STRANGE, INTERESTING LIVES, AND FOR PUTTING BACK ENERGY AND LOVE INTO THE SCENE WE WERE ALL PART OF. BASICALLY, FOR BEING A BUNCH OF WEIRD-ASS QUEER SKINHEADS FROM TEXAS LIVING IN AN ABANDONED BREWERY IN S.F. AND SURVIVING SELLING WEED. THAT DIDN'T SEEM STRANGE AT ALL AT THE TIME. THAT WAS SAN FRANCISCO IN A NUTSHELL. BUT THE MOST FASCINATING THINGS ARE USUALLY WHAT WE ACCEPT FIRST AT FACE VALUE.

MDC WERE, TO ME, A PERFECT EXAMPLE OF TAKING THE IDEAS OF PUNK LITERALLY, MUCH MORE LITERALLY THAN ITS CREATORS HAD IMAGINED. BECAUSE IF PUNK IS ABOUT ANYTHING, IT'S ABOUT SAVING YOUR OWN LIFE AND RE-DEFINING IT ALONG THE LINES YOU CHOOSE— AND HELPING OTHERS DO THE SAME. I LOVED THE PISTOLS, BUT THEY WEREN'T ABOUT BASEMENT SHOWS, FANZINES, TRAVELING, MOHAWKS, GOOD COOKING, AND CREATING COUNTER-INSTITUTIONS. I LOVED THE RAMONES, BUT THEY DIDN'T MAKE SQUATS, BIKES, BAD TATTOOS, ACTIVISM, LIBRARIES, OR PUNKHOUSES. OUR EVERYDAY LIFE HAD LITTLE TO DO WITH THE BURNED OUT, SOLD OUT, STRUNG OUT AND LEFT-FOR-DEAD SCENE THE FIRST PUNKS LEFT BEHIND.

I LOVED THE CLASH, BUT THE BANDS I LOVED BEST NOT ONLY PLAYED SHOWS, THEY HELPED PUT THEM ON. AND ONCE I CAUGHT DAVE MDC TRYING TO SNEAK INTO A SHOW. HE WAS COPYING THE STAMP FROM SOMEONE'S HAND OUTSIDE CLUB FOOT. SHAME ON YOU, DAVE! BUT REALLY, IT MADE ME VERY HAPPY.

HE CAUGHT ME ONCE TOO, GETTING INTO THE CAR AT THE "AROUND THE CORNER FROM THE CLUB GETTING PICKED UP BY YOUR PARENTS" SPOT. DAVE JUST HAD TO INTRODUCE HIMSELF TO MY MOM AND DAD, TELL THEM ABOUT HIS BAND, ABOUT THE SCENE, ABOUT HOW PROUD THEY SHOULD BE OF ME, AND HOW MUCH HE

LIKED MY FANZINE. THE SURROGATE PARENTS MEET THE OFFICIAL PARENTS, IT WAS VERY EMBARRASSING. ESPECIALLY SINCE THEY DIDN'T KNOW I DID A FANZINE, OR WHAT THAT WAS.

BUT NOWHERE NEAR AS EMBARRASSING AS THE TIME I WAS AT TEMPLE WITH MY WHOLE FAMILY FOR THE HIGH HOLIDAYS. WHO SHOULD BE IN THE NEXT AISLE OVER? NONE OTHER THAN THE "NEW YORK DOLLS ARE BETTER THAN THE DEAD BOYS" TROLL-LIKE F BUS GUY. I TRIED TO HIDE, BUT TO NO AVAIL. HE WAS PROUD OF ME, HE TOLD MY PARENTS. I WANTED TO DIE.

Sixty-three

THE SECOND LIE WAS ALSO ABOUT SONGS. NOAH, MY FRIEND WITH THE ENDLESS MISOGYNIST REPERTOIRE, WHOSE SETLISTS READ LIKE A RAYMOND CHANDLER INTRO ("ANOTHER BLONDE", "CRAZY EYES", "SMEARED LIPSTICK", "SHE PACKS A .38") ACTUALLY HAD ONE NON-GIRL SONG. IT WAS CALLED "SMALL STAGE", AND IT SEEMED TO SUM UP SO MUCH OF THE FUTILITY OF OUR EXISTENCE IN JUST A FEW LINES. I LOVED THAT SONG.

"IT'S A SMALL STAGE. SOMETIMES TOO SMALL. SOMETIMES I WONDER IF IT'S A STAGE AT ALL."

WELL, LYRICS NEVER REALLY TRANSLATE SO WELL WITHOUT MUSIC, MUCH AS PEOPLE TRY. AND MUSIC WITHOUT LYRICS? NOTHING AT ALL. HOW TWO THINGS SO DIFFERENT CAN NEED EACH OTHER SO BADLY, I'LL NEVER KNOW.

THE CESSPOOL WAS EVENTUALLY THE SUBJECT OF THREE DIFFERENT SONGS. THOUGH I DIDN'T OFFICIALLY LIVE THERE, I WAS PROUD AS COULD BE. IT WAS STUNNING TO FEEL YOURSELF AND YOUR FRIENDS BECOME PART OF THE FOLKLORE, TO HAVE SOMETHING YOU'VE DONE BECOME PART OF THE HISTORY—OR EVEN THE SCENERY— OF THE SCENE. PART OF THE LANGUAGE, SONG, AND TEMPER OF THE TIMES. IT WASN'T A PUNKHOUSE UNTIL IT GOT THANKED ON A RECORD OR IMMORTALIZED IN SONG, THAT WAS ANOTHER RULE. BUT IT WAS STILL A SHOCK TO HAVE IT COME TRUE.

THE CESSPOOL, RIGHT UP THERE WITH THE BLACK HOLE, DEAD TED'S, THE CANTERBURY. THE FIRST SONG DESCRIBED IT AS A DUMP, THE SECOND AS A PRISON,

AND THE THIRD, A PETTING ZOO. PERFECT. THERE SURE WAS A LOT OF PETTING GOING ON.

Sixty-four

EVERY MORNING WHEN NOAH WENT TO WORK, HE'D FIRST HAVE TO WAKE UP THE HOMELESS GUY WHO SLEPT IN THE BACK OF HIS CAR. ONE TIME THE GUY CRAWLED UNDERNEATH ALL THE TRASH THAT HAD COLLECTED IN THE BACKSEAT, AND NOAH DIDN'T NOTICE HIM THERE UNTIL HALFWAY TO WEST BERKELEY. WHEN THE GUY SPRANG UP LIKE A HUGE, RAGGED JACK-IN-THE-BOX, NOAH SWERVED AND SCREAMED.

"WHAT THE FUCK?" THE GUY GROWLED. "WHY YOU GOTTA SCREAM LIKE THAT? WHOA, NELLY! WHERE THE HELL YOU GOING? YOU'D BETTER TAKE ME BACK HOME!"

NOAH SAID, "NO WAY, DUDE! I'M ALREADY LATE! YOU CAN GET OUT RIGHT HERE."

THE GUY STARTED SCREAMING THEN. IT ALMOST TURNED INTO A FIGHT RIGHT THERE, AND WOULD HAVE IF NOAH HADN'T THOUGHT FAST.

"TAKE IT EASY", HE SAID, "AND GET A LITTLE EXTRA SLEEP. I'LL BE DRIVING BACK IN EIGHT HOURS".

IN A WORLD OF INSECURITIES AND HALF-TRUTHS, THERE WAS SOMETHING REFRESHING ABOUT JIMMY'S CERTAINTY, EVEN WHEN HIS HONESTY HURT. HE ACCEPTED EVERYTHING, INCLUDING THE GAP TOOTH AND MALE PATTERN BALDNESS PASSED ON FROM HIS FATHER, AND HE ACCEPTED THEM WITH PRIDE. THERE WAS NO TOILET PAPER AT THE CESSPOOL, EVER, SO JIMMY TOOK SHOWERS INSTEAD AFTER HIS MORNING SHIT. THERE'S SOMETHING TO LEARN FROM EVERYBODY, AND ALTHOUGH THAT WASN'T IT, I DID ADMIRE HIS RESOURCEFULNESS. JIMMY NEVER COMPLAINED.

RIP WAS TELLING ME ABOUT THE FIRST TIME HE HAD SEX, HOW HE ACCIDENTALLY BIT HIS TONGUE. THERE WAS SUDDENLY BLOOD EVERYWHERE, AND AT FIRST THEY DIDN'T KNOW WHERE IT WAS COMING FROM.

"I FELT LIKE GENE SIMMONS", HE SAID.

"I KNOW, I KNOW" I SAID.

"WHAT DO YOU MEAN, I KNOW, I KNOW?", RIP YELLED. "HOW CAN YOU KNOW? HOW CAN YOU UNDERSTAND? FOR

ALL YOU KNOW I FELT LIKE RICHARD SIMMONS! I HATE IT HOW EVERYONE SAYS THAT! WHY DON'T YOU JUST LISTEN FOR ONCE WITHOUT HAVING TO BE PART OF THE ACTION? WITHOUT TAKING IT OVER AND ACTING LIKE YOU WERE THERE?"

"I WAS THERE", I SAID.

"DON'T TELL ME THAT WAS YOU!"

"NO", I LAUGHED. "BUT IT MIGHT AS WELL HAVE BEEN. I WAS IN THE NEXT ROOM".

Sixty-five

JO AND I SAT UP ON THE HILL BY MY OLD HEBREW SCHOOL, EATING ICE CREAM. THAT WAS OUR LITTLE RITUAL WHICH WE ALWAYS RETURNED TO, SOONER OR LATER, WHEN WE GOT THE CHANCE. WARM SUMMER NIGHTS WITH SHOES OFF AND FIREFLIES, EVEN IF IT WAS WINTER AND WE HAD TO PRETEND.

SHE HAD A DEEP, THROATY, SCRATCHY VOICE, THE KIND STRIPPERS AND BLUES SINGERS AFFECT, BUT IN JO'S CASE IT WAS NEITHER NATURAL NOR AFFECTED, BUT CAUSED BY A DEGENERATIVE THROAT DISEASE. AS ALWAYS, I STARTED TO SAY, "I HOPE THE ICE CREAM MAKES YOUR THROAT FEEL BETTER", BUT CAUGHT MYSELF QUICK. JO WASN'T SELF-CONSCIOUS ABOUT HER CONDITION, BUT IT WAS DEPRESSING AND SHE WAS TIRED OF HAVING TO EXPLAIN: SOMETHING CAN BE BROKEN AND STILL NOT HURT.

THE VIEW AND ALTITUDE LENT A SENSE OF DISTANCE AND DETACHMENT, A FEELING OF RISING ABOVE. WE LOOKED DOWN ON THE RIVER OF OUR TROUBLED LIVES, SHATTUCK AVENUE. JO'S VOICE PUT ME IN A TRANQUIL, TRANCE-LIKE STATE, THE LOW, SOOTHING SOUND OF A SOUL SONG. OF ALL MY FRIENDS, SHE WAS THE BIGGEST DREAMER, AND OUR CONVERSATIONS ROOTED MORE IN VAGUE HOPES THAN SPECIFIC, EVERYDAY FEARS.

"IT'S LIKE A SMALL TOWN THIS LATE", I SAID.

"HERE AT FOUR A.M. IS LIKE ARCATA ON A FRIDAY NIGHT", SHE SAID. "IT'S NICE"

"IT'S EASIER TO FOCUS AND DECIDE WHAT TO DO. LESS OPTIONS. WE SHOULD GIVE UP THE DAYTIME ALTOGETHER".

SHE LAUGHED, "I ALREADY DID, LONG AGO", BUT THEN TIGHTENED UP, A LITTLE OUT OF CHARACTER I THOUGHT.

"HEY", SHE SAID. "I HAVE SOMETHING TO TELL YOU".
MY HEART WAS UNSURE WHETHER TO SWELL AND RISE OR CURL UP AND DIE. I HELD MY BREATH.
"I'M IN LOVE WITH ONE OF YOUR FRIENDS".
MY MIND RACED THROUGH INNUMERABLE POSSIB-ILITIES, COMBINATIONS, AND CATASTROPHES. "I'M SCARED TO ASK".
"RIP", SHE SAID.
"RIP?" I SIGHED, SMILED, LET OUT MY BREATH FOR WHAT SEEMED LIKE FIVE MINUTES. I POINTED AT HER AND LAUGHED.
"WHAT'S SO FUNNY?" SHE ASKED. WORRIED.
"WHAT A RELIEF!" WAS ALL I COULD SAY.

Sixty-six

IT WAS EARLY SUNDAY MORNING, EASY JAZZ AND INTERVIEWS ON THE RADIO, TAGGERS OUT COVERING THE TOWN IN GRAFFITI ON THE ONE SHIFT COPS SKIPPED. THE DEADEST OF THE DOWN TIMES. PEACEFUL AND QUIET, REFRESHING, EXCEPT, AS OFTEN HAPPENED WHEN MY DAYS OFF ROLLED AROUND, I'D BEEN UP FOR TWO AND A HALF DAYS STRAIGHT, MOSTLY ON ACID. COMING DOWN, I ALSO CAME HOME TO LANKY.
"YOU SHOW UP", SHE SAID, "NOW THAT EVERYONE ELSE HAS GONE TO SLEEP". SHE RUBBED HER EYES AND FROWNED AT MY FACE. "YOU LOOK LIKE HELL AND YOU'RE HALF DEAD. YOU GIVE EVERYONE ELSE YOUR BEST, AND WHAT DO I GET?"
"I SAVE THE BEST FOR LAST", I SAID, AND IT WAS TRUE. SUNDAY MORNING WAS MY BEST. ONLY AFTER THAT BEAUTIFUL FIFTY-HOUR MARK OF SLEEP DEPRIVATION DID I SLOW DOWN AND FIND A BIT OF INNER PEACE. ONLY THEN COULD I REALLY EMBRACE THE PRESENT INSTEAD OF MISSING THE PAST OR FEARING FOR THE FUTURE. ONLY THEN COULD I REALLY GET OUT OF MY OWN HEAD AND LOVE SOMEONE ELSE.
"LANKY", I SAID. "FOR YOU, THE WHOLE WORLD. IT'S SUNDAY MORNING! OUT OF THE BEDROOMS AND INTO THE STREETS—WE'RE GOING TO HAVE A PICNIC".
THERE ARE CERTAIN PLACES YOU CAN ONLY FIND BY ACCIDENT OR ON ACID, AND IT'S NEXT TO IMPOSSIBLE TO FIND THEM AGAIN. HOW ELSE WOULD WE HAVE FOUND THE CROSS-SHAPED HEDGE, THE REPLICA OF THE

EIGHTEENTH CENTURY MOORISH CASTLE, AND THE TREE WITH THE HIDDEN BOX OF KEYS? NOW I RETRACED MY LATEST STEPS WITH LANKY FOLLOWING MY LEAD. OVER FENCES, ACROSS CREEKS, UP AND DOWN THE GREEN EMPTY FIELDS SHADOWED BY LAWRENCE HALL OF SCIENCE, AND HIDDEN UNDERNEATH. THOSE HILLS BY THE CYCLOTRON ARE AN EXPLORER'S PARADISE, WITH UNMARKED, UNMAPPED AREAS AND EVEN EMPTY BUILDINGS, WITH SOME HIGHLY SENSITIVE, HIGHLY SECRETIVE, HIGH-SECURITY AREAS IN BETWEEN, JUST TO KEEP THINGS INTERESTING.

"YOU'VE GOT TO BE CRAZY TO HAVE FOUND THIS PLACE", LANKY SAID, WARMING HER LEGS IN THE SUN, COOLING HER FEET IN THE WATER. "BUT I'M GLAD YOU'RE CRAZY. THIS IS THE NICEST PLACE I'VE EVER BEEN. A WATER-FALL, RIGHT HERE IN BERKELEY. WHO'D HAVE THUNK IT?"

DRAGONFLIES BUZZED AROUND BUTTERFLIES AND IN THE SUN AND SHADE WE SPLASHED ABOUT. YES. AND LINGERED, LETTING THE SUN LICK THE WATER FROM OUR SKIN.

"I THINK I'M LYING ON TOP OF A DYING ANIMAL", SHE SAID. IT'S ALWAYS A LITTLE AWKWARD, THE FIRST THING YOU SAY AFTER HAVING SEX. MIGHT AS WELL JUST EMBRACE THAT AWKWARDNESS AND HAVE FUN WITH IT. BUT WHATEVER IT WAS UNDER LANKY, IT WAS NO LONGER ALIVE, IF IT HAD EVER BEEN, AND IT PEELED RIGHT OFF. NATURE SURE IS GROSS, BUT THERE'S NO USE PRETENDING WE'RE NOT A PART OF IT.

"DIDN'T YOU SAY THIS WAS A PICNIC?", SHE ASKED. "WHERE'S THE FOOD?"

Sixty-seven

RIP CAME BY MY WORK LOOKING DISTURBED. "GUESS WHAT JUST HAPPENED TO ME", HE SAID.

"YOU GOT TOGETHER WITH JO?"

"NO. I MEAN YES. FUCK! THAT'S NOT THE POINT! HOW DID YOU KNOW? THE POINT IS, I WAS WALKING HERE JUST MINDING MY OWN BUSINESS, AND THIS FUCKING WACKO NEW-AGE FUCK COMES OUT OF THE KARMA-DHARMA PLACE ON COLLEGE AND STARTS SCREAMING AT ME!"

"OBVIOUSLY UPSET ABOUT YOUR FINALLY GETTING A GIRLFRIEND".

"NO. NOT AT ALL. SHUT UP. HE WAS SCREAMING AT ME

SAYING I BROKE HIS FUCKING WINDOW. WHAT THE HELL? I DIDN'T BREAK YOUR FUCKING WINDOW, ASSHOLE, I SAID, EXCEPT ACTUALLY I SAID IT NICER. I SAID, YOU ARE MISTAKEN, YA DAMN GURU WEIRDO, SO STOP YAPPING AT ME".

"HA HA HA".

"YOU THINK IT'S FUNNY? NO. HE STARTS SCREAMING IN MY FACE. A FAT FUCK WEARING ALL ORANGE, PROBABLY A HIPPIE ONCE. SANDALS AND BEADS. YOU'D THINK HE'D BE SCARED OF ME, BUT NO. IT'S EMBARRASSING. PEOPLE ARE PASSING BY. GIRLS. BUT HE GETS RIGHT IN MY FACE AND SAYS, DON'T TRY TO DENY IT. I KNOW IT WAS YOU".

"HOW DID HE KNOW?"

"THAT'S WHAT I SAID! HE SAID, I KNOW IT WAS YOU. I CAN TELL BY YOUR AURA. WAIT RIGHT HERE, HE SAID. I'M CALLING THE COPS. FUCKING BERKELEY. SOME DAYS, I DUNNO".

Sixty-eight

BERKELEY SCENE REPORT. CHEAP FOOD IN B-TOWN? YOU BET. THE ALL-NIGHT DONUT SHOP IN THE SATHER GATE CENTER NOW SERVES SUSHI. AND YOU CAN JOIN THE REGULARS AND THE SKINHEAD STAFF IN A GAME OF WINGNUT JEOPARDY WHILE YOU DINE....IF YOU'RE UP EARLY, HEAD TO THE HEIDELBERG, TELEGRAPH'S ONLY ASIAN-RUN GERMAN HOFBRAU. SAURKRAUT WITH THOSE POTSTICKERS, MAAAN? THE DEAD ANIMAL DECOR ALONE IS ENOUGH TO TURN YOUR STOMACH, BUT THE FOOD IS DIRT CHEAP, AND WITH FREE REFILL COFFEE AT ONLY 45¢, HOW CAN YOU LOSE? WHY WIN WHEN YOU COULD SIT HERE INSTEAD?.....MANUEL'S, THE DURANT CENTER RESTAURANT, IS CHEAP, YES, BUT NOT FREE AND EASY. THEY SHOULD USE THE CIRCLE JERKS QUOTE AS THEIR MOTTO. AFTER A RECENT VISIT, THE JERKS STUMBLED ONSTAGE IN S.F. AND ANNOUNCED, "NEVER EAT MEXICAN FOOD IN BERKELEY". NOW THAT LA VILLA HERMOSA HAS CLOSED, I CAN ONLY SAY, "HOW TRUE".

THE DURANT CENTER MERCHANTS KEEP TALKING ABOUT REMODELING, A THINLY VEILED THREAT TO GET RID OF "UNDESIRABLES" WHO CONGREGATE THERE. BUT WHO ARE THE UNDESIRABLES? ONE SELF-ACKNOWLEGED DRUG DEALER HAD THIS TO SAY: "I'VE LIVED IN BERKELEY

ALL MY LIFE AND THESE GEEKS FROM OHIO RIDE THEIR MOPEDS DOWN TO MANUEL'S AND GET ROWDY. A COUPLE WEEKS AGO I SAW THE COLLEGE GUYS RIP OUT A STOP SIGN AND THE COPS DIDN'T NOTICE A THING. THE COPS WILL GET US EVERY TIME FOR LOITERING AND WILL DRIVE BY A RIPPED OUT STOP SIGN AS IF NOTHING HAPPENED". YUP. ALREADY THE MERCHANTS HAVE PUT A LOCK ON THE FAMED DURANT CENTER "ENTER THE DOOM" BATHROOM, IMMORTALIZED IN THE CRUCIFIX SONG, "STEEL CASE ENCLOSURE". WHAT WILL BE NEXT? A LOCK ON THE BENCHES? A COP IN THE DUMPSTER? WHERE ARE ALL THE OLD DURANT AVENUE GANGS WHEN WE NEED THEM TO STAKE THEIR CLAIM? "DURANT MOB RULES", THE ALL-GIRL TERROR OF THE EARLY EIGHTIES, COULD THEY BE LURED OUT OF EARLY RETIREMENT? EVEN A "RED ROCKETS" REUNION OF THE STREET TUFFS FROM THE SEVENTIES WOULD BE ENOUGH TO SCARE OFF THE NEW DURANT CENTER SECURITY GUARD.

MUSIC EVERYWHERE: NEVER MIND THE CLUBS AND THE MOTHERFUCKIN' BREWPUBS, THE REAL NOISE IS ON THE STREET AT NIGHT. A SYNTHESIZER BAND WITH THE HAUNTING NAME "FISH OF DEATH" PLAY ONLY IN PARKING GARAGES. A BALD MAN WITH A WALRUS MOUSTACHE, STANDING ON ONE LEG FOR HOURS, PLAYS SAXOPHONE NEAR THE HIDDEN CHESS TABLES BY UCB'S EVANS HALL. BY ESCHELMAN, A PIANIST BANGS ON HIS KEYS FROM THE BACK OF HIS '59 CHEVY PICKUP. "BERKELEY ALLOWS ME TO DO WHAT I WANT", HE SAYS. "A MUSICIAN NEEDS A CITY".... ESKIMO, THE ACOUSTIC STREET BAND REMINISCENT OF THE VIOLENT FEMMES, TOOK THINGS A STEP FURTHER RECENTLY BY MOVING AN ENTIRE PARTY OUT OF A HOUSE AND INTO THE GREEK THEATRE LATE ONE NIGHT, SETTING UP CANDLES ON THE STAGE AND PLAYING A GREAT SET, INCLUDING THE TV20 JINGLE.... FREE RADIO BERKELEY, DENIED AN AMPLIFIED SOUND PERMIT FOR A RALLY, SOLVED THE PROBLEM BY BRINGING NEW MEANING TO B.Y.O.B.: BRING YOUR OWN BOOMBOX. WITH EACH ONE TUNED INTO FREE RADIO BERKELEY, AND BLARING...

ARGH! URG! UGH! FUCKING ART CARS! EVERYWHERE YOU GO! YOU CAN'T GET AWAY FROM THEM! HOWEVER, "WALKER'S ROLLING MUSEUM" IS A NOTABLE EXCEPTION. CHECK IT OUT! RELICS FROM THE CIVIL RIGHTS STRUGGLE MIXED WITH ELVIS, LAST SUPPER, AND MICHAEL JACKSON PARAPHERNALIA, PLUS STUFFED DOLLS, SMURFS, JOHN F. KENNEDY AND PEE WEE HERMAN. ONE BUCK GETS YOU IN....

DURING A RECENT SHOWING OF THE 1964 MOVIE "THE T.A.M.I. SHOW" AT THE U.C. THEATER, THE BERKELEY

MODS CAUSED A STIR BY GETTING UP EN MASSE AND HUFFILY WALKING OUT WHEN LESLIE GORE APPEARED ON SCREEN TO SING "YOU DON'T OWN ME". IT'S GOOD TO HAVE MODS AROUND SOMETIMES BECAUSE THEY MAKE PUNKS SEEM RELEVANT AND REASONABLE. THANKS, GUYS! WHEN THEY FILED BACK INTO THE THEATER IN TIME FOR JAMES BROWN DOING "I'M A MAN", THEY SEEMED RELIEVED. GUESS IT WAS A LITTLE HOT OUT ON THE STREET WITH ALL THOSE PARKAS ON....

ALBANY DECIDED TO ENTER THE TWENTIETH CENTURY RECENTLY, AND, AS PART OF THE PLAN, PUT IN BIKE RACKS ON EVERY BLOCK! PERHAPS THEIR CONSULTANTS SHOULD HAVE STEPPED OUTSIDE TO FIND OUT WHAT EVERYONE ON SOLANO ALREADY KNOWS: NO ONE RIDES BIKES IN ALBANY. THEY WENT UNUSED, BECOMING BIRD RACKS INSTEAD. THEN THE CITY PLANTED TREES, BUT FORGOT TO LEAVE ROOM FOR THE ROOTS TO GROW, AND, OF COURSE, THEY DIED. POOR CITY PLANNERS, AT LEAST THEY TRIED. WHEN ALL THE TREES WERE REMOVED FROM TELEGRAPH LAST YEAR EVERYONE TALKED ABOUT STATE CONTROL AND F.B.I. PLOTS, BUT REALLY IT WAS THE SAME THING: BAD PLANNING. ONE FROST AND THEY ALL DROPPED LIKE FLIES....LASTLY, THERE MAY SOON BE A NEW SISTER CITY FOR BERKELEY: JABALIYA, GAZA! JABALIYA, COME MEET OUR OTHER SISTERS: GAO, MALI! LEON, NICARAGUA! MATHOPESTAD, SOUTH AFRICA! AND THE BURNING, SMOLDERING RUINS OF SAN ANTONIO LOS RANCHOS, EL SALVADOR! WELCOME TO THE FAMILY, AND GOOD LUCK! YOU'LL NEED IT!

Sixty-nine

A SUCKY THING ABOUT RELATIONSHIPS IS HAVING TO EXPLAIN EVERYTHING. YOU FEEL LIKE A LITTLE KID, OR AN INVALID.

I NEED FOOD NOW. I'M GOING TO THE BATHROOM NOW. I NEED YOU TO HOLD ME NOW.

HAVING TO VOCALIZE EVERYTHING IS GOOD BECAUSE IT MAKES YOU MORE ARTICULATE, BUT BAD BECAUSE, IN EXPLAINING, YOU HAVE TO SIMPLIFY WHAT YOU'RE SAYING, BOIL ANY FEELING DOWN TO ITS MOST EASILY UNDER-STOOD, MOST DIGESTABLE FORM—THE LOWEST COMMON DENOMINATOR.

I'M HAPPY NOW. I'M SAD NOW. I FEEL HURT.

BUT REALLY, EMOTIONS ARE NOT SO EASILY EXPLAINED. WHEN LANKY HIT A GRATE IN THE ROAD AND FELL OFF THE SKATEBOARD RIGHT ONTO HER FACE, I WAS VERY CONCERNED. BUT, TO TELL THE TRUTH, I WAS ONLY HALF CONCERNED. THE OTHER HALF WAS A MIXTURE OF LOVE, DISGUST, VICARIOUS PAIN, AND SEXUAL EXCITEMENT.

WHEN WE PARTED WAYS, EVEN JUST FOR A DAY, WE ACTED LIKE CHARACTERS IN A SHAKESPEAREAN TRAGEDY. BUT UPON CLOSER EXAMINATION YOU WOULD FIND SOMETHING OTHER THAN BEING AWAY FROM MY BELOVED ON MY MIND. TEN PERCENT OF ME WAS BUMMED AT HAVING TO BE APART. ANOTHER TEN WAS JUST BORED. THE OTHER EIGHTY, FRANKLY, WAS RELIEVED. I'M NOT ONE FOR LENGTHY GOODBYES.

THE FACT IS, YOU JUST CAN'T SHOW ALL THE MIXED EMOTIONS ON YOUR MIND WITHOUT HURTING SOMEONE'S FEELINGS. AND SO, YOU CHOOSE ONE PART TO PUT UP FRONT.

YOU'RE RESPONSIBLE FOR YOUR FACE AFTER A CERTAIN AGE. THIRTY? THIRTY FIVE? IT BEGINS TO TELL THE STORY OF YOUR LIFE BY ITSELF, NO MATTER WHAT YOU TRY TO MAKE IT SAY. BUT UNDER TWENTY, TWENTY-FIVE, YOUR FACE IS STILL UP FOR GRABS TO A CERTAIN EXTENT. A MASK. OR AT LEAST, IT'S HARDER TO READ.

LANKY HAD THE ANNOYING HABIT, LEFT OVER FROM JUNIOR HIGH DRAMA CLUB, OF EXAGGERATING EVERY EXPRESSION. SHE CONTORTED HER FEATURES SO THEY COULD BE EASILY SEEN AND UNDERSTOOD BY AN AUDIENCE A HUNDRED FEET AWAY. IT DROVE ME CRAZY. WHEN SHE WAS HAPPY SHE LOOKED HAPPY, HAPPY, HAPPY LIKE A CLOWN. WHEN SHE WAS SAD, SHE WAS SAD LIKE ONE OF THOSE DAMN SAD CLOWNS. BUT WHAT WAS REALLY GOING ON INSIDE?

ALL THOSE IDEAS THAT YOU RUIN TRYING TO EXPLAIN. ALL THOSE THOUGHTS THAT GET LOST IN TRANSLATION. ALL THOSE WAYS YOU CHANGE AND SIMPLIFY THE THINGS YOU SAY IN ORDER TO GET THE REACTION YOU NEED. AND THEN, YOU NEVER DO GET THE REACTION YOU REALLY NEED, DO YOU?

SOMETIMES I HATE BEING IN LOVE.

Seventy

"A SERIES OF ABSURDITIES, OF STUPIDITIES, OF MISTAKES, WERE BECOMING APPARENT. THE REVOLUTION

LANKY

WAS BEING SIDETRACKED FROM ITS MAIN TRUNK LINE
AND IT WAS TRAVELING ALONG A SPUR LINE. IT IS AS
IF THE TRAIN FROM HAVANA TO ORIENTE, BECAUSE
OF A WRONGLY SET SWITCH IN SANTA CLARA OR IN
MATANZAS, GOES OFF ONTO A SIDE TRACK AND ENDS
UP IN THE ZAPATA SWAMP. TRAVELING THE LINE WE
WERE ON, WE WERE HEADED FOR THE ZAPATA SWAMP,
BECAUSE WE HAD TAKEN A COMPLETELY WRONG
SPUR LINE". —FIDEL CASTRO

AN ANONYMOUS LETTER ARRIVED IN THE MAIL.
"ANONYMOUS", THAT IS. EVEN BEFORE OPENING IT I
COULD TELL IT WAS FROM LANKY, AND I HAD SOME IDEA
OF WHAT WAS INSIDE. THERE WAS SOMETHING PRE-
DICTABLE IN THIS ATTEMPT AT BEING UNPREDICTABLE,
WHICH MADE ME SAD.
    "MEET ME AT THE MAIN LIBRARY AT NOON ON SUNDAY",
IT SAID, AND ALLUDED TO A ROMANTIC RENDEZVOUS.
    ALL WEEK LANKY TRIED TO TEST ME TO SEE IF
I KNEW, BUT I PLAYED IT STRAIGHT-FACED. SHE WENT
SO FAR AS TO PESTER ME ON SATURDAY NIGHT ASKING
WHAT MY PLANS WERE FOR TOMORROW. WHAT COULD
I DO BUT LIE? I DIDN'T WANT TO RUIN HER SURPRISE.
    SHE HAD GOTTEN IT INTO HER HEAD THAT I WANTED
A GIRLFRIEND WHO WAS MORE MYSTERIOUS AND UNPREDICT-
ABLE. A GIRLFRIEND WHO WOULD IMPRESS AND INSPIRE
ME. SURE, WHO DOESN'T? BUT THIS WAS JUST SORT OF DE-
PRESSING. IT'S RARE THAT ANYONE STRIKES A GOOD BALANCE
BETWEEN BEING THEMSELF AND IMPRESSING SOMEONE
ELSE, ESPECIALLY AT THE TAIL-END OF A RELATIONSHIP.
    I WOULD HAVE LOVED TO SLEEP IN ON SUNDAY, BUT I
ROUSED MYSELF AND DOUSED MYSELF WITH BOILING HOT
COFFEE. I SOAPED MY HAIR AND TRIED TO LOOK NICE.
THEN I HOPPED ON MY BIKE.
    LANKY WAS THERE WAITING. SHE LOOKED GREAT.
    "YOU DIDN'T KNOW IT WAS ME", SHE LAUGHED,
BITTERLY. "YOU THOUGHT IT WAS SOME OTHER GIRL YOU
WERE COMING TO MEET. SO, ARE YOU DISAPPOINTED?"
    WE LOCKED THE BIKES AND HIKED UP THE DWIGHT-
DERBY TRAILS TO SKYLINE BOULEVARD, THEN FOR MILES
ALONG GRIZZLY PEAK, ARGUING THE WHOLE WAY. SO
MUCH FOR WALKING IT OFF.
    "STOP THAT!!" SHE SCREAMED. "HOW CAN I FIGHT WITH
YOU IF YOU KEEP STOPPING TO SMELL THE ROSES?"
    "MAYBE IT JUST ISN'T GOING TO WORK OUT BETWEEN
US", I SAID. I MEANT, "PLEASE TELL ME IT WILL, PLEASE
SAY ANYTHING", BUT WAS TOO STUPID AND TOO PROUD TO

SAY IT THAT WAY, AND SHE WASN'T LISTENING BETWEEN THE LINES.

SHE GOT ANGRY AND HURT AND DEFENSIVE. SHE SAID, "WHY DO YOU HAVE TO BE SO MEAN?"

I SAID, "WHY DO YOU HAVE TO GET DEFENSIVE AND TAKE EVERYTHING SO PERSONALLY EVERY TIME WE TALK?"

IMMEDIATELY, SHE STARTED CRYING. LIKE A DAM BURSTING, TEARS FLEW EVERYWHERE. THEY ACTUALLY CAUGHT AIR.

CONGRATULATIONS, YOU HAVE HIT THE JACKPOT BY GUESSING THE WORST POSSIBLE WORD OR PHRASE TO USE. EVERYONE HAS A FEW. THOSE CODE WORDS WHICH PUSH THE BUTTONS AND SET OFF THE INSTINCTUAL, IRRATIONAL REACTION WHICH AUTOMATICALLY ENDS ANY CONVERSATION. IN LANKY'S CASE, THESE INCLUDED "SKINNY", "CRAZY", "WINGNUT", "YOUR MOM", AND THE SEEMINGLY HARMLESS "EVERY TIME", WHICH HER EARS HEARD AS, "YOU DO IT WRONG EVERY TIME".

"PLEASE, LANKY, DON'T CRY", I SAID, TRYING TO HOLD HER. "I DIDN'T MEAN IT THAT WAY".

YES, THE DAYS WHEN YOU GET ALONG ARE GREAT.

Seventy-one

I WAS IN THE MUNI UNDERGROUND, IN THE BUZZING YELLOWY LIGHT AND ECHOING SOUNDS OF THE POWELL STREET STATION. A LITTLE CHANGE OF PACE FROM BART.

ALMOST PREHISTORIC DOWN THERE, CAVE-LIKE AND CAVERNOUS WITH STALACTITES AND WATER DRIPPING, EVEN AN OCCASIONAL BAT. BUT ON ALL SIDES, THE WHITE WALLS RISE UP. TO REASSURE YOU, TO CHALLENGE THE PRIMORDIAL CHAOS, OR AT LEAST COVER IT UP. AN END-LESSLY REPEATING PATTERN OF CIRCULAR TILES, COOL AND PLEASING TO THE TOUCH. A SIXTIES-ERA STAR TREK MOTIF. NOT AS SCARY AS THE FUTURE, NOT AS OUTDATED AS THE PAST, BUT SOMETHING IN BETWEEN. THE MOST SENTIMENTAL OF ALL THINGS: THE FUTURE THAT NEVER CAME. BECAUSE, ISN'T THAT WHAT WE MISS THE MOST?

SOMETHING ALWAYS DRAWS ME TO THOSE TILES, TO TOUCH AND BRUSH AGAINST THEM, HAPPY AND CHILDLIKE, ALL THE WHILE OF COURSE PRETENDING TO BE ANNOYED AND IMPATIENT FOR MY TRAIN TO COME. TRACING THEM WITH MY GRIMY HANDS, COUNTING THEM, AND TRYING TO

LOOK CLOSE FOR MY REFLECTION. HALF THE TIME I'M NOT WAITING FOR THE TRAIN AT ALL, OR EVEN SURE WHICH DIRECTION I'M GOING.

THIS TIME I FOLLOWED THEM ALONG, AND WHAT SHOULD I FIND? OR RATHER, WHO? NONE OTHER THAN JONATHIN CHRIST HIMSELF.

JONATHIN CHRIST, THE SINGER OF CODE OF HONOR. THE MAN WHO USED THE WORD "FIGHT" 42 TIMES ON ONE SIDE OF A RECORD. THERE HE STOOD, LOOKING SMART, SHARP, BORED, TOUGH, AND RESTLESS. LOOKING, LIKE HE ALWAYS DID, LIKE HE WAS POSING FOR A PHOTO. "WITH ONE FOOT PROPPED UP AGAINST THE WALL, TRYING TO LOOK LIKE LOU REED", AS THEY USED TO SAY.

WE SAID HELLO AND HAD A LITTLE CHAT. I HAD TO HOLD ON TO MY HAT. THERE WAS A STORM BREAKING DOWN THERE. OCEAN BREEZE TORE ACROSS THE AVENUES AND INTO THE MUNI TUNNELS WHERE IT PASSED FROM STATION TO STATION, GATHERING STEAM. WAY DOWN UNDERGROUND, WHERE DAY AND NIGHT DIDN'T MATTER, THERE WAS STILL SOME SERIOUS WEATHER TO BE RECKONED WITH. I PROPPED MY LEG AGAINST THE WALL TOO AS I TALKED TO JONATHIN AND WISHED I COULD SMOKE.

I KNEW HIM AS I KNEW MANY OF THE OLDER PUNKS, ON A FIRST NAME BASIS BUT NOT AS FRIENDS. WITH THE FAMILIARITY OF HAVING BEEN AT ALL THE SAME SHOWS BUT NOT THE INTIMACY OF HAVING HAD ALL THE SAME LOVERS. THROUGH HIS BAND AND MY FANZINE, BUT NONE OF THE LITTLE RITES THAT MAKE UP DAILY LIFE.

RUNNING INTO HIM NOW WAS A SORT OF REVELATION. PART OF IT WAS THAT PUNK IS GOOD BECAUSE, INSTEAD OF MOVIE STAR IDOLS, YOU GET REAL-LIFE ROLE MODELS YOU CAN LOOK UP TO AND MAYBE EVEN RUN INTO, TROUBLED LIKE YOU, IN THE SUBWAY STATION. BUT WHEN YOU DO, WHEN YOU DO FIND YOURSELF IN THE SAME LITTLE LIFE AS THE PEOPLE YOU LOOK UP TO, USUALLY IT MEANS IT'S TIME FOR THEM TO LEAVE. SAD BUT TRUE, JONATHIN DEPARTED THE SCENE SOON AFTER.

HOW COULD I EVER HOPE TO FILL HIS SHOES? I COULD NEVER GET MY CHEEKS THAT HOLLOW, OR PANTS PEGGED THAT TIGHT. MY FUCKING FEET WERE JUST TOO BIG. I WANTED TO BE LIKE HIM AND HIS SONGS: SHARP, TIGHT, BLACK AND WHITE, WITHOUT AMBIGUITIES. BUT TRY AS I MIGHT, THE PROFESSOR'S KID IN ME ALWAYS CAME OUT, RIPPING THE PEGGED PANTS, SCREAMING FOR BOOKS AND GLASSES. I WANTED TO SING, OR AT LEAST BE ABLE TO CONVERSE LIKE A NORMAL HUMAN BEING.

INSTEAD I EITHER LECTURED OR TOOK NOTES. ABSENT-MINDED, I LEFT THE STOVE ON. CHALK STAINS APPEARED ON MY BAGGY PANTS THOUGH I NEVER CAME WITHIN A MILE OF A CLASSROOM. JONATHIN CHRIST NEVER WORE A GODDAMN BACKPACK!!

WHAT TO DO? I WAS LESS LIKELY TO FIGHT THAN TO GO HOME AND WRITE ABOUT IT. BUT FOR A SHORT TIME, WE STOOD TOGETHER, WAITING FOR THE NEXT TRAIN.

Seventy-two

SPRING WAS UPON US, AND IT WASN'T JUST THE UGLY DUCKLINGS AND CZESLAW MILOSZ AT AQUATIC PARK THAT TIPPED ME OFF. I WAS UNDER THE FREEWAY, IN FACT, WHEN I SPOTTED JON VON OUTSIDE SPENGER'S. "AHA!" HE SAID AS I WALKED UP. "I SEE THEY GOT YOU TOO!"

HMM. I RAISED MY EYEBROWS AT HIM.

"YOU DIDN'T COME HERE FOR THE BUZZCOCKS SHOW?," HE ASKED.

I SHOOK MY HEAD. HE SHOOK HIS, TOO, SADLY. POOR JON. HE SHOWED ME THE ANNOUNCEMENT IN "THE LIST" CONCERT GUIDE. THE BUZZCOCKS, THE ZERO BOYS, AND CRIME AT SPENGER'S FISH GROTTO. APRIL FIRST.

YES, SPRING WAS UPON US, WHICH COULD ONLY MEAN ONE THING: TIME FOR PASSOVER, THE JEWISH FESTIVAL OF SUFFERING, SOMBER REFLECTION, AND SELF-DENIAL. NO, JUST KIDDING. PASSOVER, THE BLACK SHEEP OF JEWISH HOLIDAYS, IS FESTIVE. WE CELEBRATE THE BLOODY SLAUGHTER OF THE EGYPTIANS WITH A LONG, DRUNKEN FEAST, RETELLING THE STORY AND REVELING IN ALL THE GORY DETAILS.

OH, I ALMOST FORGOT. FOR THE GOYIM IN THE AUDIENCE, THERE'S ANOTHER HOLIDAY. AND TO CELEBRATE THAT YEAR, SCOTT "RUSH" SHAW, "PARTY COORDINATOR" FOR LAAZ ROCKIT, FINALLY MADE GOOD ON HIS PROMISE TO TIE HIMSELF TO THE HUGE CROSS UP ON TOP OF ALBANY HILL.

AS THE ALBANY POLICE FORCE PLAYED THE PART OF THE ROMANS, DRAGGING SCOTT "RUSH" SHAW THROUGH THE THORNS AND BEATING HIM MERCILESSLY, A VERY DIFFERENT SCENE WAS UNFOLDING DOWN IN THE VALLEY BELOW. IN THE DIM AIRLESS DIN OF CAMPUS COPY MART, I WAS WORKING UP THE COURAGE TO CONFRONT MY BOSS.

AT FIRST I ASKED NICELY. "I NEED TWO DAYS OFF", I SAID.

BUT I KNEW TIME OFF WAS NOT GOING TO COME EASILY. NOT WITHOUT A STRUGGLE, AS MY HISTORY OF SERVITUDE FOR THE SOUFERIAN FAMILY CLEARLY SHOWED. ON MY BIRTHDAY, THEY HAD MADE ME WORK. SICK WITH A FEVER OF ONE HUNDRED AND ONE, THEY HAD MADE ME WORK. ONLY WHEN MY TEMPERATURE HAD REACHED ONE HUNDRED AND TWO HAD I REFUSED, A LIBERTY THEY STILL HADN'T FORGIVEN ME FOR. IN EIGHT MONTHS AT CAMPUS COPY MART, THAT HAD BEEN MY ONE DAY OFF.

EACH TIME I BROACHED THE SUBJECT WITH NAHID, SHE BRUSHED ME OFF. "THERE IS ONLY US TWO AT THE SHOP", SHE SAID. "IF YOU LEAVE FOR A DAY, WHAT CAN I DO? ALREADY SIX DAYS A WEEK I WORK. THERE IS NOTHING TO DO BUT LOCK THE DOORS AND TURN BUSINESS AWAY. THIS IS WHAT YOU WANT?"

I WAS PERSISTENT. SHE RECONSIDERED, BUT THEN CHECKED THE CALENDAR AND SAID THERE WAS NO WAY. PARVIZ HAD PLANS ON THOSE VERY SAME DAYS. NAHID WOULD HAVE TO RUN CAMPUS COPY CENTRE WITH HER SISTER WHILE I RAN CAMPUS COPY MART BY MYSELF. NOT ONLY WAS IT IMPOSSIBLE TO GIVE ME THOSE TWO DAYS OFF, I WOULD HAVE TO WORK A DOUBLE SHIFT.

IT WAS THE FIRST TIME I FELT PAINTED INTO THAT PARTICULAR CORNER. I DIDN'T WANT TO MENTION MY JUDAISM, BUT HOW ELSE COULD I EXPLAIN THE IMPORTANCE OF TAKING TIME OFF FOR PASSOVER? JUDAISM WAS A BIG PART OF MY LIFE, AND THE MAIN THREAD THAT BROUGHT MY FAMILY TOGETHER. IT WAS ALSO SOMETHING I HAD NEVER MENTIONED TO MY BOSSES FOR FEAR OF SEEING A SIDE OF THEM I COULDN'T LIVE WITH. AFTER ALL, IRANIANS WERE NOTORIOUSLY ANTI-SEMITIC. JEWS THERE HAD BEEN PERSECUTED FROM ANCIENT TIMES ALL THE WAY UP TO THE PRESENT REGIME, WHEN IT REACHED A FEVERED PITCH.

I DIDN'T WANT TO FORCE THE ISSUE AND RISK A FIGHT, BUT I COULDN'T FIND ANY OTHER WAY. EVERYONE ELSE GOT THEIR RELIGIOUS HOLIDAYS OFF FROM WORK, SO WHY DID I HAVE TO DEMAND MINE? IT WAS IRONIC. PASSOVER IS THE CELEBRATION OF JUDAISM'S LIBERATION FROM BONDAGE AND OUR DELIVERANCE INTO FREEDOM. FORTY YEARS IN THE DESERT CAME NEXT, BUT WHO'S COUNTING? AT LEAST WE WERE FREE.

"I REALLY NEED THOSE DAYS OFF", I TOLD HER. "IT'S A HOLIDAY. I NEED TO SPEND IT WITH MY FAMILY".

SHE FROWNED. "A HOLIDAY? WHAT HOLIDAY?"

"MY RELIGION. A RELIGIOUS HOLIDAY. IT'S CALLED 'PASSOVER'. IT'S, UH, A JEWISH HOLIDAY. I'M JEWISH".
"YOU'RE JEWISH??" SHE SAID.
AS HER EYES SCRUTINIZED ME, THEY BEGAN TO GLOSS OVER. SHE LOOKED AT ME, STARED THEN SMILED.
"PARVIZ IS JEWISH", SHE SAID.
AND THEN, SHE STARTED TO CRY.

Seventy-three

THERE WERE ERAS THAT DULLED THE SENSES AND ERAS THAT SHARPENED THEM. PEOPLE TOO. LANKY WAS LIKE THAT. SHE HIGHLIGHTED THAT ERA SO MUCH THAT SHE BECAME SYNONYMOUS WITH IT. JUST MAKING ME MORE AWARE, BRINGING EVERYTHING INTO FOCUS. SHE WASN'T THE MAIN PICTURE, NOT MY MAIN FOCUS, NOT PERHAPS AS IMPORTANT TO ME THEN AS SHE IS NOW, LOOKING BACK.

A LOT OF PEOPLE PASS THROUGH YOUR HANDS LIKE WATER, BUT NOT LARENKA. AND NOT JUST BECAUSE SHE WAS MY FIRST REAL GIRLFRIEND, BUT BECAUSE OF WHAT THAT MEANS: SHE WAS THE FIRST PERSON I HAD TO STRUGGLE TO TRY TO UNDERSTAND IN THAT DESPERATE WAY THAT WE ALL GO THROUGH IN TRYING TO GO OUT. TRYING TO REALLY SEE ANOTHER PERSON FOR WHO THEY ARE, SEPARATE FROM YOU AND YOUR NEEDS, STRUGGLING SO HARD BECAUSE YOU NEED TO FIGURE OUT HOW TO BE TOGETHER. CONFUSING? YES. TRYING TO SEE THE WORLD THROUGH THEIR EYES, OR SEE BOTH OF YOUR LIVES FROM THE OUTSIDE.

NEVER MIND. IT'S JUST, I STILL HAVEN'T TOLD YOU MUCH ABOUT WHO SHE IS. I CAN'T. I NEVER REALLY KNEW. I LOOKED, BUT WAS NOT VERY GOOD AT LISTENING. ALL I CAN SAY NOW IS THAT SHE WAS A BIG PART OF MY LIFE FOR A RELATIVELY SHORT TIME. AND THOUGH OUR STORY DOESN'T REALLY SHOW IT, SHE OPENED MY HEART UP AND MADE LIFE SEEM LARGER AND MORE ALIVE, SOMETHING TO CHASE AFTER AND PURSUE AND ENGAGE, INSTEAD OF JUST MAKE YOUR WAY THROUGH.

Seventy-four

I NEEDED A LAUNDROMAT. THE GOOD ONE UNDER THE HOTEL NASH WAS CLOSED. I LOOKED THROUGH THE DIRTY GLASS LONGINGLY, STARING AT THE STAR TREK PINBALL MACHINE. WEIRD TIMES, BREAKING UP TIMES ARE CRUEL BECAUSE YOU FEEL ALMOST AS IF YOU'RE FALLING IN LOVE. YOU LOSE YOURSELF THINKING FONDLY ABOUT YOUR GIRL AND THEN SUDDENLY YOU REALIZE YOU JUST KISSED HER GOODBYE. YOU WANT TO RUN BACK AND FIX THINGS, BUT HOW FAR BACK DO YOU HAVE TO RUN? WEEKS? MONTHS? YEARS? AND RUNNING THROUGH IT ALL IN YOUR MIND, ALL THE PAINFUL THINGS ALSO RETURN AND RISE UP TO THE SURFACE.

ON MY BACK WAS A PILE OF OLD, MOLDY, RIPPED UP BITS OF PUNK STUFF THAT NEEDED SOAKING. CLOTHES MOSTLY, PLUS A FEW BOOKS AND MAGAZINES. I'D CLEARED MY THINGS OUT OF HER ROOM. I COULD SMELL HER, THOUGH, STILL, ON SHATTUCK AVENUE, SOAKED INTO MY CLOTHES. I LOVED THAT SMELL, DEEP AND LUSTY LIKE A CAMPFIRE AND ROASTING COFFEE. BUT I HAD TO WASH IT OUT OR MY HEART WOULD BREAK RIGHT THERE ON THE STREET AND I'D CRY INTO A BIG PILE OF DIRTY SOCKS. IT'S THE OFF THINGS THAT GET YOU. THE ART CARS THAT DRIVE BY ALL WACKY WHEN YOU'RE TRYING TO FIGHT. THE CAMERA CAR DRIVES PAST AND TAKES YOUR PICTURE. LIFE IS CRUEL.

"BETTER TO LIVE IN A BIRDLESS COUNTRY WITH NO SUN THAN TO GO YOUR OWN WAY ALWAYS". ROD McKUEN, SAPPIEST OF ALL SEVENTIES POETS SAID THAT. HE ALSO SAID THIS:

"IT'S EASIER TO REMEMBER
THE STREETS WHERE IT HAPPENED
THAN THE NAMES
AND WHO WAS THE ONE ON CHANNING WAY".

Seventy-five

THERE ARE ALL KINDS OF COOL COMBINATION BUSINESSES. BUT A LAUNDROMAT/BAR IS NOT ONE OF THEM. AT LEAST, IT'S NOT ON MY LIST. ONE HAD OPENED UP ANYWAY, UNFORTUNATELY, IN NORTH BERKELEY, WITHOUT BOTHERING TO FIRST ASK MY PERMISSION. AS A MATTER OF FACT, I WAS AGAINST IT. BUT, I FIGURED, AT LEAST IT WOULD BE OPEN LATE.

I WALKED IN, STAGGERING UNDER MY LOAD, REALIZING A LITTLE TOO LATE THAT OTHER PEOPLE'S DIRTY LAUNDRY IS CLEANER THAN MINE, TO SAY THE LEAST. YOU'D THINK THE ONE PLACE PEOPLE WOULD NOT COMPLAIN ABOUT DIRTY, STINKY CLOTHES IS A LAUNDROMAT, BUT ALAS, THIS WAS A LITTLE ON THE FANCY SIDE. AN "UPSCALE" LAUNDROMAT, BELIEVE IT OR NOT.

I MADE MY WAY QUICKLY PAST ALL THE BAR STOOLS AND BETTY PAGE CLONES HOLDING THEIR NOSES. I THREW MY PILE OF FILTH INTO A SPEED QUEEN IN THE BACK. NO SOONER HAD I PUT IN MY FOUR QUARTERS, I GOT A TAP ON THE SHOULDER. FUCKING CHRIST, WHO COULD IT BE THIS TIME?

I TURNED AROUND AND LOOKED RIGHT INTO TWO PAIRS OF EYES. EYES SMILING AND SWIMMING IN ALCOHOL. IT WAS NATE AND AMANDA, BOTH QUITE DRUNK.

THEY WERE CELEBRATING. ALL THROUGH PREGNANCY AMANDA COULDN'T SMOKE OR DRINK. NOW SHE'D BEEN MAKING UP FOR LOST TIME BY PARTYING ALL WEEK. DIDN'T I HAVE ANYTHING TO SAY? CAT GOT YOUR TONGUE?

I WAS STUNNED. I STAMMERED OUT A FEW WORDS. "CONGRATULATIONS?"

"YAY!!". SHE HUGGED ME. NATE LOOKED ON AS STERNLY AS YOU CAN AFTER TEN STRAIGHT WHISKEYS. TRYING TO SNEER, HE LEERED INSTEAD. I STEPPED BACK.

"I WAS JUST TELLING NATE HERE THE OTHER DAY", SHE SAID, "I WONDER WHAT HAPPENED TO THAT CUTE BOY I USED TO HAVE A HUGE CRUSH ON".

MARRIED OR UNMARRIED, IT'S NEVER SAFE TO SPEAK THOSE WORDS, AND AS THE CASE WAS FOR NATE AND AMANDA, THEY WERE SOON UNMARRIED. OR SEPARATED, AT BEST. THE DAY AFTER LANKY TURNED EIGHTEEN, SHE DISAPPEARED. AND SO DID NATE.

Seventy-six

AMANDA KEPT THE APARTMENT, AND EVERY OTHER WEEK, ON SUNDAY, IN THE EARLY AFTERNOON, I VISITED HER THERE. A MAN OF ROUTINE, SOME THINGS NEVER CHANGE, YEAR AFTER YEAR. WE SAT ON HER BED WHILE SHE SMOKED, TALKING ABOUT THE GOOD TIMES WE'D HAD AS THEY RECEDED FARTHER AND FARTHER INTO THE DISTANCE.

AS SOON AS HER SON COULD WALK, HE CAME IN THE ROOM AND WEDGED HIMSELF BETWEEN US TO KEEP US APART. CUTE. THIS TOO BECAME PART OF THE ROUTINE, WITH HIM POUNDING INSISTENTLY ON THE DOOR IF IT WAS LOCKED.

ONE DAY THE PHONE RANG. AMANDA REACHED OVER AND PICKED IT UP. IT WAS NATE.

"NATE", SHE TEASED. "YOU'LL NEVER GUESS WHO'S HERE WITH ME".

THIS WAS A DANGEROUS GAME, AND ONE I WANTED NO PART OF. I WAVED MY ARMS AND SHOOK MY HEAD.

"HOW DID YOU GUESS?" SHE SAID. "IT'S JUST LIKE OLD TIMES".

I COULD FEEL THE HEAT FROM THE OTHER END END OF THE LINE AS HE BURNED UP WITH JEALOUSY. PERHAPS HE WONDERED. AFTER ALL, THE KID DID LOOK MORE LIKE ME.

BUT NATE, I NEVER EVEN KISSED HER.

COMETBUS

#48

$2

BACK TO
THE LAND

part

1

THE
KIDS

WHY "BACK TO THE LAND"?

BECAUSE I HEARD MANY PEOPLE SAYING THE SAME THINGS: THE CITIES ARE GETTING WORSE. CRIME IS ON THE RISE. CAN'T TRUST ANYONE ANYMORE. GOTTA GET SOME LAND AND MAKE A REAL LIFE AWAY FROM ALL THIS MISERY, ALL THIS CAPITALISM. GOTTA SPLIT THE CITY SO I CAN CLEAN UP MY ACT. THERE'S NOTHING LEFT FOR US HERE ANYMORE.

EVERYONE SEEMED TO AGREE, OR JUST ACCEPT THESE CLICHES AS FACT. A COMMON UNDER-STANDING. I WANTED TO TAKE A CLOSER LOOK. NOT TO DISMISS THESE IDEAS, BUT AT LEAST QUESTION THEM, LOOK INTO THE REASONS BEHIND THEM AND THE POSSIBLE RESULTS. THE BEST WAY I COULD FIGURE WAS TO LISTEN TO PEOPLE WHO ARE, YOU COULD SAY, A DIRECT PRODUCT OF THESE IDEAS: CHILDREN OF THE BACK-TO-THE-LANDERS A GENERATION AGO.

IT'S TRUE I HAVE A BIAS. BUT AS OFTEN AS NOT, MY LEADING QUESTIONS LED SOMEWHERE I DIDN'T EXPECT, AND MY OWN ASSUMPTIONS WERE PROVEN WRONG.

JOIN ME, IF YOU WILL, AS WE BEGIN.

YAEL, 30, IS A WRITER. SO IS ALMOST EVERYONE I KNOW, BUT FOR YAEL IT IS HIS MAIN OCCUPATION AND LIVELIHOOD. HE IS ALSO THE PROUD FATHER OF TWO KIDS. WE TALKED IN A BOWLING ALLEY AND WHEN THAT GOT TOO LOUD, CROSSED THE STREET TO THE BEACH.

YAEL

WHEN DID YOUR PARENTS MOVE TO THE LAND?

In the early 80's.

NOT TIL THEN?

Yeah, 1980.

WHERE HAD THEY BEEN ALL THROUGH THE SEVENTIES?

In Southern California. But my dad, he went to Vietnam. And after that, he couldn't really hang so much. So he went to Alaska a lot. He was working in Alaska nine months out of the year, and coming back, and not really digging the city.

WHAT WAS HE NOT DIGGING ABOUT IT?

Just people, I guess. Maybe it was just the 70's. He was just like, Fuck this, I want to do it all for myself. You know, be self-sufficient, grow weed, and get out of the tax bracket, or whatever. I don't know if it was the economics that was tripping him out, or if it was just society, people in general, the hustle and bustle. He had trouble trusting people in business. He just wanted to trust himself, I guess.

For my sister though, she was just starting to go to high school. She was cutting school and going to the beach, and she had tons of friends. Life was good for a teenage girl at that time and at that place too, and then it's like, BOOM! Up to the top of a mountain in the middle of nowhere.

IS IT A CONFLICT, A PARENT'S NEED TO BE SELF-SUFFICIENT, AND YOUR NEEDS AS A KID? I DON'T THINK KIDS WOULD RANK SELF-SUFFICIENCY REAL HIGH UP ON THEIR LIST.

No, not at all. No, they want to be, I wanted to be at school or go with friends, and stuff like that, but just didn't have time because we lived so far away from town. It was like, get up early, drive an hour and a half to school. Go to school, go back home, kind of do a little homework.

DID YOU REMEMBER THE CITY?

I was just a little ass kid. I was like, preschool. We came up first for a while and tried to build a house and stuff, started to build our house. We had a teepee and an army tent. And then one storm wiped out our army tent, so we had to go back. I was living with my grandmother down in Southern California for almost a year.

WHILE THEY BUILT THE HOUSE?

Well, we came back and the house wasn't built yet. But they had one of those trailers that you can put in the back of your pick-up truck to make your pick-up truck a camper, they had one of those up on blocks for me and my sister. And they were in the tent, another tent. The house was being framed and stuff. But I was there when they built it.

HOW MANY ACRES WAS IT?

36.

THAT'S TWICE WHAT THE WHITE HOUSE HAS.

Hmm.

DID YOUR PARENTS ADJUST WELL TO LEAVING THE CITY?

The hardest thing was learning how to grow weed. The first year we only got an ounce. For the whole year. Maybe two. And I'm sure my dad smoked more than that, you know, So it wasn't a cash business until the third year, we finally got enough to pay for sheetrock and visqueen. We had visqueen on our windows for a long time.

WHAT'S THAT?

The plastic stapled to the window holes. "Hippie glass", they called it. And "hippie shingles" is tarpaper.

ON THAT MOUNTAIN, WERE THERE A LOT OF PEOPLE WHOSE FAMILIES WERE NATIVE TO IT, OR WAS IT ALMOST ALL BACK-TO-THE-LANDERS?

There was maybe one or two families who had been there for very long. And then there's the ranch families up on there, and they're old school, like third generation. And they had nothing to do with pot farming. Supposedly.

WAS THE FACT THAT YOU WERE SMALL FARMERS, DID THAT EVENTUALLY CROSS SOCIAL AND CULTURAL LINES SO THAT YOU GOT ALONG WITH OTHER FARMERS' FAMILIES WHO HAD REGULAR CROPS?

There are no regular crops up there. The only other kind of farmers are like ranchers, there's a couple cattle ranchers. There seems to be a lot of hicks but not a lot of farms. Just hicks living in trailers, living the same as the hippies, they just don't like the hippies. The only ones that crossed to both were the bikers. The bikers had friends in every single faction, from the hicks to the hippies to the Native Americans. They knew all the people in the cities too.

DID THOSE BARRIERS REACH DOWN TO THE KIDS TOO, OR DID THE KIDS START TO GET ALONG MORE?

Well, everyone went to the same school. My parents didn't have any friends that were different, but I did, growing up. Everyone was in the same school no matter what your parents did. There was a pretty incredible amount of respect, actually. Because, the main thing is, your kid isn't supposed to lie. That's the weird thing about doing something illegal for a living as a family. Like, I feared cops. I feared authority. Still, if a cop gets behind me when I'm driving, my knees start shaking. A helicopter, you hear a helicopter, you hit the trees. It's just the way it is.

DO YOU FIND YOURSELF STUCK WITH SOME OF THESE FEARS THAT ARE A LITTLE OUT OF PLACE NOW?

Yeah, and I think lying about what you do for a living too, it can't be that good for you in your growth as a person. It's like, some lies are cool, some lies aren't right. All the pot farmer kids, they shut the fuck up. They didn't talk about it. Everyone kind of knew who was the pot farmers and tried to keep it a secret.

WHAT WOULD YOU SAY YOUR FAMILY DID?

Carpenters, There's more carpenters in that town than anywhere else. Everyone's a carpenter.

AS THE WEED GROWING BECOMES MORE SUCCESSFUL, ARE THERE CLASS DISTINCTIONS?

Of pot farmers? Oh yeah. Who grows the best weed.

NO, I MEAN, DON'T THE HIPPIES EVENTUALLY BECOME RICHER THAN THE PEOPLE WHO'D BEEN ON THE LAND BEFORE, AND THERE'S RESENTMENT TOWARDS THAT?

No, but you see some people that grow for their families, and maybe have a good crop, and you see they get a new truck, or they finish their house, or they get a T.V. or something like that.

But that's normal. Everyone wants everyone to do well, you know. It's not like you're in direct competition. There's only so many people that buy the stuff.

BUT WHAT ABOUT THE PEOPLE WHO DON'T GROW WEED? THE RANCHERS AND STUFF. THE RANCHERS SEE YOUR DAD'S HOUSE GO FROM HIPPIE SHINGLES TO THE REAL THING.

They don't see that. They never come anywhere near us, they never come up there. Only the people that even get in the gate, through the driveway, is friends. Only thing is, you can't get fancy cars, and you can't have nice clothes. That's the thing. Living where you are, you can't have a fancy car anyway. Just a good truck is all you need. Or a Subaru.

WHAT DO YOU THINK ARE SOME OF THE GOOD THINGS AND SOME OF THE DRAWBACKS OF HAVING A CLOSED COMMUNITY? MOST OF THE PEOPLE IN THAT AREA WERE TRANSPLANTED...

M-hm.

SO YOU GET THIS TRANSPLANTED CULTURE AND IT'S SORT OF INSULAR. OUT OF NECESSITY. BECAUSE YOU COULDN'T HAVE OUTSIDERS TOO MUCH. SO DOES IT BECOME XENOPHOBIC? DOES IT BECOME, LIKE YOU DON'T GET NEW BLOOD IN?

Well, when you're a kid you don't really realize any difference because you don't really see a difference, there's nothing to compare it to. But, you know, it's boring as fuck. There's the same kids, you know what kids there are that you can play with when you're growing up. And they're always a few miles away, so either you gotta walk, minimum 3 miles, or 15 miles, whatever.

BUT I MEAN LIKE, WITH THE ADULTS, DO YOU NOTICE THAT THERE'S NOT DIFFERENT CULTURES COMING AROUND, THERE'S NOT NEW PEOPLE, A NEW INFLUX...

There's a lot of cultures. There's people from all over the place on the same mountain that all have the same sort of bond. It's like self-sufficiency, and weed I guess.

I WAS JUST WONDERING IF AS PEOPLE GREW OLDER, AS THE RELATIONSHIPS CHANGED, THE CULTURE KEPT REINVIGORATING ITSELF, OR IF IT STARTED TO GET KIND OF MOLDY AND FREAKY.

Yeah, I don't know. I don't think it reinvigorated itself. It definitely fizzled out and did its own thing. It wasn't like there was ever a sense of permanence with anyone there. Everyone was kind of like, "I'm doing this for a while". But the community wasn't really a community, it was like different families. It was like tribal, more. We were up there, we had cousins, aunts, my mom's family moved up there, so all her brothers and sisters were there. So it's like real tribal, cousins and things, their family, our family, and you know who belongs to what family.

DID YOU LIKE THAT?

No, I hated it. It fucking drove me crazy. I hated it. I wanted new people every day. I wanted freaks and, experience and, you know, interaction with people. I really wanted to meet some girls, man.

DATING MUST BE KIND OF ROUGH ON THE MOUNTAIN.

Oh yeah, it's impossible.

THAT IDEA OF SELF-SUFFICIENCY, IN A WAY, IF YOU'RE GROWING WEED AND YOU'RE SELLING IT TO OTHER PEOPLE, YOU'RE NOT EXACTLY SELF-SUFFICIENT. YOU'RE PART OF SOCIETY. YOU'RE DOING SOMETHING WHICH NEEDS OTHER PEOPLE.

See, that was a contradiction that I realized early on, like "This is kind of bullshit, you know?" I knew it was bullshit. I knew that like everything serves a purpose and everybody's using everyone else one way or another. And I just wanted to be on the right side of that, I didn't want to be the one that's getting the boot stomped on my ass every fucking day. I wanted to be somebody that was either doing the stomping or just floating free, away from all that.

YOU THINK THAT'S WHAT SOCIETY IS?

Society is completely a web of entangled favors, deals, ripoffs. There's a consequence for everything in society, no matter what it is. And somebody always gets the short end of the stick.

DON'T YOU THINK IT'S SOMETIMES BASED ON MUTUAL BENEFITS?

There's not always benefits, though. It's like, I'm fucked this way or I'm fucked this way. Which way am I fucked less?

DO YOU HAVE MORE OF A DESIRE TO BE PART OF IT THAN YOUR DAD DID?

Maybe I just accept it more. I didn't go through anything really horrible early on to freak me out, like my dad did. He's seen something that I've never seen, so his view is different. He was shipped off to fight some crazy war. And he felt totally taken advantage of, put in a position he never wanted to be put in. And me, I have nothing like that.

BUT DO YOU STILL SORT OF HAVE HIS VIEW FROM GROWING UP AS HIS SON?

I think it's more like, it's a reaction that I had. I didn't want to be like my dad, I didn't want to be on a pot farm, I never wanted to grow pot, I never wanted to be there.

IT SEEMS LIKE, OKAY, PEOPLE ESCAPED FROM MAINSTREAM CULTURE, AND USUALLY THEY HAD THE MONEY TO ESCAPE. BUT THEN THEIR KIDS AREN'T ABLE TO ESCAPE, SOMETIMES. MAYBE LIKE DRUG USE, WHERE IT'S EASIER TO GET IN THAN OUT, YOU KNOW WHAT I'M SAYING? IT'S EASIER TO GO INTO VOLUNTARY POVERTY, OR VOLUNTARY ISOLATION, THAN TO COME BACK IN.

Coming in is definitely difficult, but not dropping out, I see what you're saying. I think it's harder to come out of that than to go into it, definitely. And it's harder to come into society if you've never been in it.

DO YOU KNOW IF YOUR PARENTS WENT TO THE LAND IN ORDER TO RAISE KIDS, OR WAS IT MORE THEIR OWN THING?

Um, I think it's both. But in our case it's more my dad. He was the main one. But it's weird, my uncle, and my dad, all them motherfuckers at the same time, it's like, Let's get out! Let's go here, in the middle of nowhere. It's weird.

I WALKED ACROSS THE MIDWEST LAST SUMMER, AND THIS GUY FROM CHICO PICKED ME UP HITCHHIKING. HE SAID HE WAS ONE OF THIRTY PEOPLE FROM CHICO WHO MOVED TO THAT ONE LITTLE RURAL AREA OF KANSAS BACK IN 1970, AND THEY'RE ALL STILL THERE.

That just tells you, if you're planning on going to Chico, that Kansas is better than Chico. Okay? Way better. So don't go to Chico.

BUT IT'S STRANGE THAT THESE IDEAS CAN JUST SPREAD LIKE A FLU THROUGH A WHOLE GROUP OF PEOPLE.

It's true. And it's probably happening right now too. Probably whole families are leaving the Bay Area, or Orange County, or wherever they're at. Especially now.

WHAT ABOUT DRUG CULTURE? GROWING UP, IS IT JUST LIKE ANYTHING ELSE AFTER A WHILE?

Well you see, when I grew up, pot wasn't a drug. For us, weed wasn't a drug. You can't tell anyone we do it, but it's fine. Beer and pot and wine, those are the three things you see all the time. And occasionally the parents would do some mushrooms, and get all wacky. But you'd never see like coke, you'd never see anybody doing that stuff, but people all around my life were doing it.

Well, naked people. I know if I think my kids were going over to
somebody's house and their parents are going to be naked the whole
time, now I'd kind of trip out. But back then, when I grew up, we'd
always laugh about them, make up names about them and stuff. Cuz
they're naked hippies. It's like, you know, your parents are fucking naked hippies. But what are you gonna do? I'm gonna come over,
you know, we're still gonna hang out, but your parents are some
naked hippies. I've got the crazy Nam vet dad, but you've got the
naked hippie parents.

WHAT ABOUT YOUR PARENTS' ABILITY TO CHANGE? TO
CHANGE WITH THE TIME, AS THE CULTURE BECOMES
A LITTLE DIFFERENT?

I think now they look back at those years and they don't really
talk about them that much. They talk about them, but they don't talk
about them with other people. Still, that tribal thing carried on.
Like the people in our family, we talk about it with and they bullshit about the old days. But now they have new sets of friends and
a new way of life. Less stoned. Getting old.

YOUR PARENTS HAVE KIND OF A NICE HOUSE NOW, NO?
WHEN I VISITED I REMEMBER THEY SEEMED ALL
PROUD LIKE, "WE'RE SET UP NOW." LIKE THEY'D SUCCEEDED,
KIND OF.

Well, getting out of it was the main thing. Because we had a
great crop and sold the land and got out of it, and then moved to
the town. And with the money we bought a cheap house in town and
my dad bought a big rig, and then he was trucking. He was doing
that. He was making money there, but not really that great. But
yeah, we had it going on kinda. The main thing was that it didn't
get busted, it didn't get ripped off.

WAS THAT PRETTY COMMON, TO GET RIPPED OFF?

Yeah.

WHO'D BE DOING THE RIPPING OFF? OTHER KIDS, OR
PEOPLE FROM OUT OF TOWN?

Assholes. People from out of town, people from in town, different
part of town, different mountains.

DOES IT GET SORT OF PARAMILITARY STYLE OUT THERE?

Sometimes, yeah. People got murdered on the mountain. More than
once. People got killed. But that's just because they were doing it
wrong. You do it enough to sustain your family and get by until the
next year. Those people didn't really get knocked off. You get

people that had fucking plantations, 300 acre ranches with just tons of weed. And people that were doing other things, heroin, coke, and stuff like that. Those people are getting shot. You know, some of the motorcycle gangs would be involved with some things.

WHAT DO YOU MEAN, "SOME OF THE MOTORCYCLE GANGS"?? SEE, THAT'S THE KIND OF THING THAT SEEMS NORMAL TO YOU, BUT NOT TO ME.

You know.

YOU MEAN THEY'D BE INVOLVED IN MURDERS.

Yeah, yeah. And there'd be asshole growers, and they'd get ripped off by the gangs.

ABOUT HOW MANY PEOPLE WERE ON THE MOUNTAIN YOU LIVED ON? WAS IT A DISTINCT COMMUNITY WHERE IT'S LIKE, "HERE IS OUR MOUNTAIN"?

Well, you know every single person on the mountain.

WE'RE TALKING TWO HUNDRED? THREE HUNDRED?

One hundred.

AND MORE THAN A COUPLE PEOPLE GOT MURDERED ON THAT MOUNTAIN?

Yeah. M-hm. They were the assholes though. Every time. There'd be people that just grew stupid. And that would piss us off, you know, because most of the people on that mountain were family-oriented. And there'd be just a handful you never knew. Those are the ones who didn't show up at the road association meetings. The ones who didn't show up at the barbecues and the big hippie parties. Everyone else knew each other. And there's only a couple stores. You can only buy dog food at one place.

WHAT ABOUT PEOPLE WHO FELL OUT OF FAVOR NOT BECAUSE THEY WERE GROWING BAD, BUT OUT OF PERSONAL REASONS AND DIFFERENCES? DON'T YOU GET SHUNNED BY THE MOUNTAIN?

Yeah. Certain people do things, they want favors. Certain people try and flex, you know. Yeah, you can get mountain shun if you fuck up. Definitely.

FOR EXAMPLE?

There was this one guy, he was a junkie or something. He had a tick in his belly button and he was all paranoid, he thought he had cancer. So he sold everything he owned, pretty much, except for his land. He had a trailer and some land. He sold all his guns. He sold all his crop hella cheap. He got a stack of money, he went down to San Francisco and spent it. Lived the rest of his life doing smack and fucking hookers, right?

That's what he did, except he ran out of money before he died. And the tick got bigger and bigger, he thought he had cancer. And then he ended up at the free clinic all wasted one day, "Aaaugh, how come I'm not dead?"

"Because you have a tick, asshole!"

And then he came crawling back up to the mountain, and he burned it down.

BURNED DOWN THE MOUNTAIN?

Uh-huh. I guess he was trying to get money from insurance or something.

OH, BURNED DOWN HIS LAND?

But it burned down the whole mountain. Not the whole mountain, but hella people lost their houses. He got some mountain shun out of that. You get mountain shun if you burn the mountain.

I was stuck on the other side of that fire too. It was like a loop up there, and I was below the loop, staying at a friend's house. It was night and we're trying to drive out of the fire on this dirt road. There's fire right in front of us. Went up the backside, on this other guy's road I'd never been on. And waited. And then it got put out.

ARE THERE OTHER KINDS OF DISASTERS LIKE THAT?

Forest fires.

FOREST FIRES, BIKER GANGS, PEOPLE RUNNING AROUND WITH GUNS. ISN'T THAT A LITTLE ALARMING AS A CHILD?

Not really. Because it was so boring that anything interesting was cool. A fire. Yeah! Woo!

There was this guy who was always naked, except he'd wear combat boots and a holster with a fucking '38 in it. And a cowboy hat. And he'd just run around. And he'd come by, like after school, he knew my sister would be coming up the mountain. He'd always come and wait for her so that she'd see him naked. See him on the road. He started meeting her at the bus stop and shit. And say, "I'll give you ten dollars if you come up and wash my dishes in my house."

She was like 15. "Ugh, gross! Get away".

"Come on, man. Come up and do my dishes". Crazy shit.

ACROPOLIS WAS INTERVIEWED IN HIS BERKELEY APARTMENT. HE IS 28 YEARS OLD AND WORKS AS A CAMERA GRIP FILMING COMMERCIALS. IN THE TEN YEARS I'VE KNOWN HIM, HE'S MENTIONED HIS PARENTS MAYBE TWICE.

ACROPOLIS

SO WHERE DID YOUR PARENTS MEET?

San Francisco State.

M-HM. WERE THEY CITY PEOPLE?

Yeah, Oakland and San Francisco.

DO YOU KNOW WHEN THEY DECIDED TO MOVE TO THE LAND AND WHY?

They moved in '65. My father was teaching at U.C. Berkeley, and about then they figured things were going down, it'd be better to move North.

WHAT DID THEY THINK WAS GOING DOWN?

Well, that's sort of why a lot of people moved away, they thought there was going to be a major breakdown here.

FOR INSTANCE...

Possibly a revolution, possibly an economic crisis. And, I think my father was a bit paranoid. But they felt like they would have a better life if they lived in a smaller environment, and be closer to some kind of Earth that people don't believe is in the city.

WAS IT A LARGER CULTURAL BELIEF OR WAS IT THEIR OWN?

They probably thought it was a larger cultural belief. I think there was some spiritual reasons involved too. But I don't want to get into it, you know what I mean?

IF THEY THOUGHT THERE WAS GOING TO BE A REVOLUTION, DID THEY WANT TO BE SAFE FROM IT,

OR WANTED TO START CREATING A NEW SOCIETY, OR?

They wanted to create a new society. A couple times they
threatened us with living in Eugene, in a Sufi community. I'm
really happy we didn't. Unfortunately, I did have to visit friends
of theirs there.

**DO YOU KNOW WHAT THE FUTURE WAS THAT THEY SAW?
IF THEY HAD A FIVE YEAR PLAN, OR A THIRTY YEAR PLAN?**

My father predicted an apocalypse, and through some epiphany,
after being up for three days, assumed heavy meditation and being
outside of the city would be a bigger and better life.

WHEN WAS HE EXPECTING IT?

He was expecting it, I think, in the early 70's.

SO HE HAD MADE PLANS ACCORDINGLY?

I think so.

DID YOU COME BEFORE THE APOCALYPSE OR AFTER IT?

Probably at the head of it.

**DON'T YOU THINK SOMEONE PROBABLY WOULDN'T HAVE
A KID IF THEY THOUGHT THAT THE WORLD WAS GONNA
END? OR FIGURED, WHAT THE HELL?**

I really have no idea.

**DID HE TALK ABOUT THE APOCALYPSE THING TO YOU
LATER ON?**

He never did, but I found out through other family members.

**GROWING UP, DID YOU HAVE A FEELING THAT YOUR
PARENTS WERE DIFFERENT THAN OTHER PEOPLE?**

I assumed everybody was like my parents. Which I discovered after
a while was not the case. Which threw me off quite a bit.

BECAUSE OF CULTURAL THINGS OR IDEAS OR...

Being a vegetarian, having rice cakes for lunch. The health food
consciousness wasn't as popular. Nor was tofu, and I was usually
laughed at.

YOU HAD TOFU IN YOUR BAG LUNCH?

Yeah, and it didn't quite go over well at the elementary school.
The kid with the diet".

LET'S BACK UP. THEY DIDN'T GET ACREAGE, YOU SAID.

THEY GOT A HOUSE?

They lived in a van for a bit, and toured the country. Followed a guru or something. I've never told anyone this.

CONSIDER IT A PUBLIC SERVICE ANNOUNCEMENT. DID THEY TALK TO YOU ABOUT THE CITY WHEN YOU WERE GROWING UP?

Sometimes my mom would take me to Sufi things in San Francisco, I'd be forced to go along. I got forced to go, when I was about ten, to EST training. That's where I met Kyle, actually. We became EST buddies, out of thousands of kids we picked each other. We wrote each other's addresses down, but we never wrote.

We met again through punk rock. Me and Kyle were both having to move out when we were 16, out of our moms' houses, things weren't so good for either of us. His mom found the address and said, "Why don't you write this guy? Here's a friend".

It was my old address from EST training.

KYLE, 28, WAS INTERVIEWED IN HIS OFFICE AT THE COMPANY HE OWNS AND DIRECTS. GOLDFISH SWAM IN THE TANK, PEOPLE SWARMED BY ON THE STREETS BELOW. LIKE ALL THE KIDS IN PART ONE, KYLE SPENT HIS FORMATIVE YEARS IN NORTHERN CALIFORNIA'S HUMBOLDT COUNTY.

SO, YOU MET ACROPOLIS AT EST TRAINING?

Yes. In San Jose. When we were both eleven. He was the first vegetarian I'd ever met.

WHAT WAS EST TRAINING LIKE, FOR PEOPLE WHO DON'T KNOW? BECAUSE A LOT OF PEOPLE HAVE NOT HEARD OF IT.

That's hard to explain to people who don't know. Basically, there were a whole slew of weird self-help sort of pseudo-Zen "programs" you could do in the late 70's, early 80's, and this is the one my mom fell in with, ran by this guy Werner Erhard in San Francisco who later I think ran off because he was being charged with molesting his stepdaughters. Then EST changed and became some sort of business seminar. But at the time it was all basically about narcissism, how you were the only person in the world, and life was just your dream, and, uh, how god thinks you're an asshole.

DID YOU HAVE TO DO THAT THING WHERE EVERYONE SITS AROUND IN A CIRCLE AND EACH PERSON YELLS, "I AM AN ASSHOLE"?

That was in the adult one, but not in the kid's one. There were all these processes, but that one wasn't part of it.

HOW DID YOU FEEL ABOUT YOUR MOM BRINGING YOU TO THAT? AS PARENTS ARE TRYING TO FIGURE OUT WHAT'S BEST FOR THEMSELVES AND WHAT'S BEST FOR THEIR KIDS, YOU END UP IN SOME KIND OF STRANGE PLACES.

Well, it was early on, for me. I did EST twice, I did it once when I was six, and then when I was eleven. And I took it as pretty normal. I didn't really realize yet how flaky my mom was, or at least there was only a few things I was aware of her being flaky about. It was later that I sort of lost all belief and hope in the things that she endeavored for us to do.

YOU'D COME FROM THE CITY TO THE HILLS.

Yes.

WAS IT A ROUGH TRANSITION?

Yeah, I really thought I was going back in time, that's how I imagined it. I didn't want to go at all, and the first year was really horrible. Jed was the only person who kind of related to me. I didn't like it at all. But it turned out to be excellent, actually.

HOW SO?

Well, I had never done anything. I guess there's not a lot of stuff you're supposed to do when you're young, but I was afraid of doing anything. And living in a really small community, you kind of are unable to escape being noticed, so even if you have an interest in something and you're too afraid or shy to try, you maybe end up doing it anyway, because you catch someone else's attention.

Like I'd wanted to try out for a play, and there were tryouts. I made it as far as outside the door of the playhouse, and then I gave up. Two weeks later somebody had to get a job and leave the show. And my friend who was in the play suggested me to take over the part. So I got a role, without even having to try out, and I ended up being in a lot of plays when I was young.

Just that sort of thing, where if you have an inkling of an idea, the reverberations are a lot more massive than, say, in the suburbs, where I'd been previously.

WHAT ABOUT GETTING INVOLVED IN RADIO UP THERE? IS IT FAIR TO ASK THE NAME OF YOUR OLD SHOW?

Yes. "Wild in the Streets".

WASN'T THERE ONLY ONE REAL STREET?

Exactly. Wild in the Street. That would have been more accurate.

RADIO SEEMED REALLY IMPORTANT IN THAT COMMUNITY, BECAUSE PEOPLE WERE SPREAD APART. IT HAD A WHOLE DIFFERENT FUNCTION.

Absolutely. There was no television, really. You couldn't get anything unless you had some kind of high-fangled satellite. There was no cable, and the stations were all in cities miles and miles away, so they didn't really come in. So, yeah, radio played a bigger part, and I always had to respond to people who had heard my show who didn't listen for the music, but listened because there weren't a lot of radio stations, and it was supposed to be representative of the community.

I remember once there was a cassette of German soccer chants we played just as a joke. And some dreadlocked German guy cornered me in front of the supermarket and called me a fascist. He's all, "I left Germany to get away from that stuff, and you bring it to my new community". He was really mad. It was pretty frightening. And I just kept thinking, why are you listening to my show anyway?

YOUR LITTLE BROTHER IS STILL UP THERE, RIGHT?

Yes.

WHAT IS IT LIKE HAVING LEFT THERE, AND KNOWING THAT HE'S GROWING UP THERE, AND SEEING THAT FROM A DISTANCE?

That's a good question. One of the things that's weird is how marijuana has totally different social connotations. And my little brother has had his run-ins with it already, and he's only eleven years old. And that, to me, living here and being really separate from it, is really kind of alarming. But at the time, being young, I remember younger kids with whom it was totally socially acceptable, their parents would let them smoke pot, and it was part of the whole culture.

And so, to me, I don't really know what opinion to have on it, my brother interacting with that kind of scene. Although it does worry me, because I didn't really have any experience like that when I was eleven. So I don't know.

DOES IT CREATE A WEIRD IMBALANCE TO HAVE LEFT THERE, AND TO HAVE BECOME A SUCCESSFUL BUSINESS OWNER? COMPARED TO THERE, WHERE IT SEEMS LIKE NOT MUCH MONEY COMES IN EXCEPT THROUGH MARIJUANA?

Right. No, that is weird, that is a really weird thing. But it's like, a lot of my friends who aren't growing pot, that's what they did. They had to leave. Because, I mean, I couldn't even get a summer job to save my life when I was there and I was young.

COMETBUS READERS SHOULD ALREADY BE FAMILIAR WITH JED, A LONGTIME FRIEND AND FIVE-TIME ROOMMATE OF MINE. AS ALWAYS, WE WALKED WHILE WE TALKED, FROM BAY FARM ISLAND TO ALAMEDA, FROM ALAMEDA TO DOWNTOWN OAKLAND, AND THEN ON BART TO S.F.

JED

WHEN DID YOU MEET KYLE?

When I was thirteen. In the eigth grade. And it was pretty cool because we had both come from the same background, different parts of the Southbay.

GROWING UP IN THE CITY AND THEN HAVING TO MOVE TO THE LAND WITH YOUR MOM.

Yeah, like, I don't know if I should say this, but his mom had some problems and he was always talking about her having fucked up parties and stuff like that. I was like, yeah I know. My mom was always having fucked-up parties too. Or was always drunk all the time and throwing shit.

I don't know, it was pretty cool, you know, because we had something in common. I was like, yeah, I hate this place. There's no cool people here, no punks. He was like, yup. I know.

Because, I'd already been there for a year and a half. And the only other cool people I could think of were Maya, and I don't know, a couple other people. The heshers had just gotten meaner and the hicks had just gotten meaner.

DID YOUR MOM LIVE DIFFERENTLY IN THE COUNTRY THAN SHE HAD IN THE CITY?

Yeah, I mean, my whole family did. My mom, and my grandpa and grandma and everybody. My grandma started a huge garden and stuff. And my brother, me and my brother digging holes and piling up wood and stuff.

DID YOU LIKE THAT?

It was pretty fun, for a while.

Yeah, totally. She stopped drinking and got all healthy. And I was totally happy. It was the first place I lived where there was some kind of solitude, not just a bunch of crazy people running around all the time, It was the first year I was able to do any real homework. I actually passed one grade, it was the only grade I ever passed. With an A. It was pretty cool.

DID YOU LIKE THE SOLITUDE?

I loved it. Then. After a while I didn't like it. I started fucking up in school more. Everything started pretty much going downhill.

WHY WAS THAT?

Why? Because I didn't really have anyone to help me with my homework anymore. My mom was always taking off. She started doing weird drugs again. Not drinking, but doing speed and acid and stuff like that.

IS IT HARD HAVING THAT FEELING OF SOLITUDE AND QUIETNESS AND PEACE JUST FOR A WHILE GROWING UP, THEN TO NOT HAVE THAT NOW?

Yeah, it's almost impossible. I totally miss it. I liked it. I could spend years and years just sitting in my room listening to music and like, playing drums. I don't know, doing whatever I wanted to. Reading. Not talk to anybody, that would be fine. Doing my homework.

I got pretty distraught sometimes, thinking about the fact that I wasn't hanging out with anybody. But I always knew there were other people in the other hills all around me that were doing the same thing.

The only thing that really held me together for a while was our band. That was really important.

YOU FORMED A PUNK BAND JUST OUT OF THE KIDS IN IN THE HILLS? THE HILLS?

Yeah. Me and Kyle and Scott.

DID YOU HAVE A MOHAWK?

Yeah.

FUCK YEAH.

And then we realized there were other punks in other parts of

the county and in other counties a little ways over. It was prett
cool. Then I started to feel better about kind of being a future
dropout. I didn't care anymore. I don't know if you'd call it
growing up, but not really caring about the stuff you used to car
about. My family didn't really matter as much. I wasn't just like
thinking about going out and playing basketball with my grandpa
anymore, or anything dumb like that. Sports. I didn't care. Diffe
ent world.

YOU MEAN YOU DIDN'T WORRY ABOUT THOSE THINGS ANYMORE, OR YOU DIDN'T CARE?

I just didn't care. I mean, I cared a little bit. But things
like Christmastime didn't matter as much. It matters now, but I
don't know, I didn't worry about it as much.

YOUR MOM LIVES ON THE LAND STILL, RIGHT?

Yeah, totally.

AND WHEN YOU GO BACK AND STAY WITH HER, DO YOU LIKE THAT?

Yeah, I love it. It's great. Totally.

COULD YOU SEE LIVING THERE YOURSELF FOR A LONG TIME?

No. Hell no. Of course not. No. I mean, I like it because I can
go back there and detach myself for a while. Get healthy and get
my strength back, I don't have to talk to anybody. It's not
really fast-paced. Here, you have to be all fast-paced. It just
takes me away from all the pressure and stuff like that.

DO YOU HAVE A DIFFERENT PERSPECTIVE THAN PEOPLE YOU KNOW WHO GREW UP ENTIRELY IN THE CITY?

Different perspective? Yeah. I have more acceptance of a lot of
things that people in the city don't like. Like hippies. There's
just a different community in the country that you have to accept
Getting along with everybody. Freaks and losers and everybody.

HOW MUCH DID THE WHOLE POT GROWING SCENE AFFECT LIFE WITH PEOPLE YOU KNEW?

Affect them?

WHEN THEIR FAMILIES WERE INVOLVED IN GROWING.

Well, our next door neighbors grew 200 plants on their front
porch. I don't know. I know I was pretty paranoid. We had plants

for a little while but my mom freaked out one day and destroyed all the plants because some helicopters flew over the house.

WAS EVERYONE TOTALLY PARANOID ABOUT HELICOPTERS ALL THE TIME?

Yeah. Pretty much. Kind of like it is here, but for a different reason.

DO YOU THINK THAT PARANOIA SEEPS INTO YOU, FROM GROWING UP WORRYING ABOUT THAT? FROM GROWING UP WITH A BUNCH OF PEOPLE WHO WERE SMOKING TOO MUCH WEED?

I've never really worried about it much, to tell you the truth. I mean, there were people with machine guns running around the woods. Growers and stuff. I used to worry about my brother sometimes because he'd take off and just run around in the woods. I thought he'd get shot, or something like that. But I never saw too many pot farms. I saw one once. I mean, I clipped pot plants.

HOW MUCH DID YOU GET PAID?

Like five dollars an hour (laughs).

YOU CAN'T REALLY GET THAT FUCKING SMELL OFF YOU FOR WEEKS, HUH?

No. Not really.

ISN'T IT BAD, LIKE YOU GO TO SCHOOL THE NEXT DAY AND EVERYONE CAN SMELL IT STILL?

Yeah, the smell of pot in class was pretty strong. I didn't know what it was when I first got there. I just had to get used to it.

BECAUSE THE KIDS WERE HARVESTING IT OR SMOKING SO MUCH?

Both.

EVERYONE UP THERE KNOWS WHEN IT'S HARVEST SEASON, DON'T THEY?

Yeah, pretty much. I would always wish that my mom was growing more pot whenever I would go over to anyone else's house around there, you know? Big huge houses, giant mansions out in the middle of the hills. Huge floors and big ass swimming pools and stuff like that. And I'd be like, "Man, why are we living in a shitty fucked-up house with holes in the walls?"

part

2

THE
ADULTS

EVERYONE HOPES THEIR DECISIONS ARE THE RIGHT ONES, HOPES THEIR PLANS WORK OUT. OF COURSE THEY HARDLY EVER ARE, THEY HARDLY EVER DO. WHAT'S AMAZING TO ME IN THESE INTERVIEWS IS PEOPLE'S RESILIENCE. THEIR ABILITY TO REBOUND, RECOVER, AND START ANEW. TO TAKE LEMONS AND MAKE LEMONADE.

EVERYONE THINKS THEIR DECISIONS ARE PERSONAL ONES. MAYBE ONLY IN HINDSIGHT CAN THE LARGER SOCIAL FORCES BE SEEN, THE PREVAILING IDEAS OF THE TIME, THE MORALS AND GUIDELINES IN WHICH YOU FRAME YOUR DECISIONS AND BUILD YOUR LIFE. IDEAS OF WHAT'S RIGHT AND WRONG, WHAT'S PERMISS-ABLE AND WHAT'S NOT. IN YOUR SUBCULTURE AND IN THE MAINSTREAM. THIRTY YEARS AGO OR TODAY.

I DON'T WANT TO BLAME ANYONE FOR DECISIONS THEY MADE. BUT WE HAVE OURSELVES TO BLAME IF WE DON'T LEARN FROM OTHERS' EXPERIENCE, OR AT LEAST TRY. FROM THEIR STRUGGLES, THEIR SUCCESSES AS WELL AS THEIR MISGIVINGS.

NOW THE ADULTS, TO GIVE SOME HISTORICAL PERSPECTIVE. THESE TWO MOVED TO THE SAME AREA AND AT THE SAME TIME AS THE KIDS, BUT WERE A FULL GENERATION OLDER. MORE IMPORTANTLY, THEY MADE THE DECISION OF THEIR OWN ACCORD.

(NOTE: LINDA "FITZPOO" FITZPATRICK AND JAMES "GROOVY" HUTCHINSON WERE TWO YOUNG HIPPIES MURDERED BY NEW YORK CITY DRUG DEALERS IN 1967. "THE PINK PALACE" WAS A NOTORIOUS HIGH RISE HOUSING PROJECT IN SAN FRANCISCO'S WESTERN ADDITION THAT BECAME SYNONYMOUS WITH CRIME, URBAN BLIGHT, AND FAILED HOUSING POLICIES.)

MURRAY IS ANOTHER OLD FRIEND OF MINE, AND WAS

INCREDIBLY PATIENT AS MY CRITICAL, INQUISITIVE QUESTIONS TURNED INTO INTERROGATION AT TIMES. THE PEACEFUL LATE-NIGHT AT THE MARINA HELPED BALANCE THE MOOD.

MURRAY IS 52.

MURRAY

WHO WERE THE FIRST BACK-TO-THE-LANDERS YOU KNEW? WHEN WAS THE FIRST TIME YOU STARTED TO HEAR ABOUT THOSE CURRENTS?

'68 in New York City, there was a group called "Up Against the Wall, Motherfuckers". They were sort of anarchist thug street organizers that used to start riots on a regular basis. A significant group of them all split to New Mexico in, must have been '68 or '69, when things got too hairy in the city. And some people from Ann Arbor, from the White Panthers, joined up with them there. We never saw them again, but we heard stories and saw occasional photos of them running around on horses, sort of reverted back to nature.

REVERTED?

Well, I mean, they were playing Cowboys and Indians and Revolutionaries. I suppose it wasn't that different than what they were doing in the city. Being revolutionaries, but a different context, different tools.

AND THE FIRST PEOPLE THAT YOU KNEW PERSONALLY?

I knew a few of them. Not like best buddies or anything, but to talk to them in the streets. And some of the Ann Arbor people from the Panthers, I knew a few of them. If you want someone I knew intimately, that would probably be a guy I used to live with in Berkeley. He and his girlfriend split up to the Sierra around 1971 or '72. I went up to visit them once and he had corn growing out of his ears already, and there was machines all over the place, tractor pieces. There was a whole culture gap that opened up between us in the space of a couple years.

WHAT DO YOU MEAN?

Just, we'd lived together in Berkeley and in Ann Arbor. We'd been to Woodstock together. We'd known each other for quite a few years. Here he'd been gone to the Sierra for about two years, and there was no longer that much to talk about. He was babbling about spring planting, and I was talking about parties and clothes and stuff from down in Berkeley. And, I never saw him again.

WHEN DID IT GAIN MOMENTUM? BECOME MORE OF A NORM?

If you're talking personally, I did not know personally a lot of back-to-the-landers until I went to the country myself. But it was a dominant theme in the culture as far back as the end of the '60's. Basically when things started going really wrong in the Haight and in the Lower East Side, when a lot of people started getting killed and overdosing and stuff, and people were saying the dream was over, we're gonna split to the country. Like Abbie Hoffman says in his book, "The hippies were always going to split to the country." But at that point, a lot of them did. There were always communes out in Marin, which was basically at that time the country, as early as the mid to late '60's. And some of those people just headed farther north as Marin started getting more settled.

WHERE DID THE ASSUMPTION COME FROM TO GO BACK TO THE COUNTRY IN THE FIRST PLACE?

Well, you know, the hippies were a lot about nature and being natural. It kind of made sense. I could tie that in to my own crystallizing moment when I decided to go, when my girlfriend and I got chased around San Francisco by this gang. This was already 1981. But it was a really terrifying experience, these guys chasing us with two by fours. We came very close to being seriously beaten or maybe worse. And I said, "Fuck this! Fuck this city! I'm going to go out and start my own city somewhere else!"

And I think that really was the sentiment that the hippies were having way back to the Sixties. A lot of what they were trying to do, the city is a pretty harsh environment to try to do it. And there was this kind of childlike, wistful dream that "out there in nature, no one would be there to fuck with us". We could just "do our own thing" and, you know, all the animals would be our friends, and help us.

DIDN'T YOU EVENTUALLY HAVE TO GET SOME GUNS TO KEEP THE ANIMALS AWAY?

That's part of the rude awakening that befell a lot of people. No, I don't think most of the hippies thought in terms of problems. Their conception of nature was largely derived from Disney movies. Seeing all the animals smiling and singing in the forests that were always neat and clean.

Within a year or two of arriving in the country, a lot of people were telling the same story. "Well, we came here, and the next thing we knew, there were rednecks picking on us. We couldn't get jobs, and the crops died. The weather was lousy, the soil was lousy, the animals came and ate all our seeds."

You know, that kind of thing.

LET ME PULL THINGS BACK A BIT. WHEN YOU SHOWED UP IN NEW YORK AND YOU SHOWED UP IN BERKELEY, HADN'T A LOT OF PEOPLE ALREADY LEFT? WASN'T THERE A SENSE THAT "THE REAL THING" HAD GONE ALREADY?

That's true, yeah. That's true for both places. I didn't get to the Haight until June of '68, and I vividly remember the first person we ran into that we knew was this guy from Ohio, and he'd been a real hippy-dippy love child, but now he was dressed kind of seedy gangster style, carrying a briefcase that was full of drugs and a gun. And he's like, "All the hippies are all gone, man. You got here too late. You gotta split. There's nothing but violence and death and hate here."

And that was my introduction to the Haight.

As far as New York, I'd been there a bit earlier. The scene sort of died away that same year because there was a really sensational murder on my block. It was on the cover of Newsweek.

"GROOVY"?

Yeah, "Groovy" and his girlfriend. But the Lower East Side was a pretty hellish place even at the most fantastic of times. The love dream never fully got off the ground in New York anyway, and people were always a lot more edgy and cynical and hard-nosed. They laughed at California-type hippies.

WAS THERE A SENSE THAT THE CULTURE WAS ELSEWHERE, AND DID YOU HEAR REPORTS BACK FROM VERMONT AND MENDOCINO?

I don't know, I mean, those of us who were actually on the streets in New York or San Francisco or Berkeley did tend to have kind of a sarcastic attitude about the hippies who went up to the country. Like they just couldn't take it, couldn't cut the mustard.

I remember, I might have told you about this before, the summer of '70, this was a crystallizing force in the Back-to-the-Land movement too. There was a festival up in Washington, at a place called "Sky River", and the concept of it was that your ticket to the festival was a partial deed to the land. The money that they got from ticket sales was used to buy the land on which the festival was, and at the end of the festival everyone was gonna stay and build a city.

WOW.

And you know, I was one of the people that stayed. So was that guy who ended up in the Sierra.

DID YOU KEEP THE DEED?

Oh, I still have it, yeah.

YOU'VE NEVER GONE BACK TO LOOK?

No, we stayed. We stayed at the end of the festival. It was in September, and we started digging foundations for houses and digging wells, and basically trying to have a hippie, anarchist-ically-run city. What we of course weren't prepared for is, about that time of year the rains come, and in Washington it rains horrendously. And here we are out there getting hepatitis and flu and everything else. And getting rained on about twenty-two hours a day.

But still, we were gonna stick it out.

And then, after about two weeks, the sheriff came with a whole bunch of deputies and just threw us off.

We said, "No, look, we own this property", and he said, "I don't care. Get off. Tell someone else."

And that was the end of that particular dream.

WAS THERE A CLEAR LINE DRAWN BETWEEN THE PEOPLE WHO WANTED TO STAY IN THE CITIES AND THOSE WHO WANTED TO LEAVE? WAS THERE A CLEAR LINE, LIKE THE CULTURAL RADICALS WANTING TO LEAVE, AND THE POLITICAL RADICALS WANTING TO STAY? SAN FRANCISCO VERSUS BERKELEY?

Definitely there would be a line between the political and the cultural people. There always was. That was only bridged temporarily during the height of the war and the so-called revolution at the end of the Sixties, where the apolitical hippies and the very political New Leftists sort of found enough common cause to do things together. But it didn't last long. By Kent State or shortly thereafter, the hippies said, "Wait a minute! I didn't know they were going to shoot at us! That's not mellow!"

And the leftists got more and more extreme to where they started planting bombs and talking about killing the policeman, and so on.

SO WHICH ONES LEFT?

Most of the people who left were the cultural rebels, although there's certainly a strong streak of political values, to this day, in Humboldt and Mendocino. There's a high political consciousness, but it tends to be more around environmental and land use issues than like, "Let's overthrow the government." It's sort of a general anti-authoritarianism.

RATHER THAN REVOLUTIONARY?

Well, there's some people that would consider themselves
revolutionary and consider that they're waging cultural guerrilla
war by creating free territories, or autonomous territories. But
generally, the more political people would sneer at the hippies
who went off to stare at their navels and grow flowers and
vegetables.

WAS THERE ANY VOCAL SPLIT AT THE TIME? DID ANYONE SAY, "THESE ARE OUR CITIES, THESE ARE OUR SCHOOLS, THESE ARE OUR BATTLES AND WE HAVE TO TAKE RESPONSIBILITY FOR THEM"?

Just focus on the prime ethos of the hippie movement, "drop out".
We don't have schools, we don't need schools, everything's gonna
be free. There was a notion that nobody should have to go to school
if they didn't want to. There was a notion that the government was
completely useless. You should just ignore it and it would go away.
That would probably be the hippie way of looking at it as opposed
to the leftist way, which would be let's get involved, get control
of it, or let's overthrow it.

I remember getting annoyed at some of the people who'd gone to
the communes up in Marin sneering at us who were still in the city
as being slow, we hadn't figured it out yet. Or we were only
interested in partying and taking drugs. We were gonna miss the
boat. When the big clampdown came, we'd still be stuck there and
get rounded up in the concentration camps, and they'd be up there
free in the country.

WERE PEOPLE PRETTY SURE IT WAS GETTING WORSE?

You need to remember that in 1968 there were a lot of people
who genuinely believed the revolution was imminent, that the
whole system was coming down. So, obviously, a certain number of
people who went to the country saw themselves probably as refugees
from the impending chaos. Certainly the riots that followed Martin
Luther King's assassination in April of '68 gave that impression.
There were riots simultaneously in over a hundred American cities.
It was pretty intense. I was living in a black neighborhood in
Akron, Ohio at that time, sitting in my room watching it on T.V.
and at the same time outside hearing the sirens and seeing the
flames. Add some psychedelic drugs to that mix and it's easy to
believe that society is not gonna be around for long.

DO YOU THINK THERE'S SOMETHING APOCALYPTICAL, RELIGIOUS ALMOST, ABOUT A DOOMSDAY MENTALITY LIKE THAT?

When you bear in mind that probably 98% of the people involved
in this movement were either christian or jewish, and they both

tend to traffic in the same kind of imagery, yeah. I mean, most of the kids thought that they had left that all behind, but you don't do it that easily. I myself, of course, didn't do it either. I had a very strong streak of that morality even though I was ostensibly an atheist.

SO YOU HAVE PEOPLE MAKING DECISIONS BASED ON THE WORLD ENDING...

I made decisions based on that. I can't speak for a lot of others. I didn't go to the country at that point, but I dropped out of everything and abandoned all responsibility. For instance, I was wanted by the police. I was in some serious trouble, and I was thinking, all I've got to do is stay loose for a year or two and then it's not gonna matter anymore. Same with going to school or working or any of that stuff.

ON ONE HAND, PEOPLE WERE MAKING DECISIONS BASED ON THE IDEA THAT THERE WASN'T GOING TO BE A FUTURE, TO AN EXTENT. AND THEN AT THE SAME TIME, PEOPLE WERE HAVING KIDS.

Yeah, I always thought that was crazy. But I'd say probably the people who were oriented towards families would be much more likely to go to the country, because it was hard to see how there'd be much of a future for raising little children in some of the cities. I mean, there was a family across the street from me in the Lower East Side, and I was always astounded at them. They had everywhere from a fourteen year old down to a one year old, and a bunch of kids in between. And our block, it was just a nightmare. I was terrified all the time. And these kids just played in it as if it was a yard in the suburbs. Nothing touched them. But that was unusual. There wasn't a whole lot of hippie children in the cities. I was at the age where I wouldn't even consider having children.

WHAT DID HIPPIES' PARENTS THINK ABOUT THEIR KIDS GOING BACK TO THE COUNTRY?

I'll tell you, if they had yet invented the concept of "deprogrammers" yet, they would have done a great business.

THERE'S THIS IDEA OF "BACK" TO THE LAND. "BACK" IN QUOTES. BECAUSE MOST OF THE PEOPLE HADN'T COME FROM THE LAND.

Well, actually, you might be forgetting that a lot of them had, but maybe a generation or two earlier. For instance, my parents had always lived in cities, but their parents had lived on farms, either in Europe or America. And to them, it was a big progress that they had gotten to the city and got jobs and proper houses and electricity and plumbing. And to them it was like, "We have arrived." So it was crazy to see their children giving all that up. My parents were always very contemptuous of the country, they just thought, "Why the hell would you want to live there for? It's just a bunch of hicks. A miserable, hard life."

I COULDN'T TELL IF IT WAS MORE A MYTHICAL, YOU KNOW, THE GERMAN-ARYAN MYSTICAL IDEA OF "BACK TO THE LAND".

The Twenties movement? I was going to bring that up just now, but I thought it might be ranging too far afield.

NOT AT ALL.

The Wandervogel. It was a response to social dislocation.

AND THE YOUTH GROUP?

Well, some of them turned into the Hitler Youth, but that was later on.

DO YOU SEE SOME OF THAT OLD GERMAN MYSTIC IDEA OF "THE LAND" WITH ITS HEALING POWERS AND "PURENESS" CREEPING IN?

Yeah, I long ago drew the analogy and said, geez, the hippies and these people back in the Twenties have a lot in common, and similarly, there's a danger of it going the same way as those German kids did when things went wrong, when the economy crashed and their dreams were shown to be very unrealistic, some of them reacted very badly to that. Yeah, there's a mystical and almost fascistic streak to the hippies as well. It's not the predominant characteristic, but it's there. There's a religious aspect to it. A lot of the hippies, especially the Back-to-the-Landers, got into pagan mythologies and Earth worship and goddess worship and magical amulets and stones and circles and all that stuff.

WHAT DISTINGUISHES THE BACK-TO-THE-LANDERS FROM THE "WHITE FLIGHT" OF THE FIFTIES AND SIXTIES?

That's a good question. I hadn't really thought about it much, but my immediate answer would be that the people who split to the suburbs were not trying to make any great break from the old society, but rather, trying to replicate what they had left in safer, cleaner conditions.

I THINK THE SUBURBS HAVE A PARASITIC RELATIONSHIP TO THE CITY. IT'S LIKE, "WE CAN LIVE HERE AND PAY

That's a question that really grabbed a hold of me as soon as I moved to the country because I saw this complete alienation between the two. And part of my mission became trying to bridge that gap, because I saw that the two cultures had a lot to offer each other.

WHEN YOU MOVED UP THERE, WHAT WAS YOUR PLAN?

I think my plan, even though I was about ten or fifteen years too late, my plan was remarkably similar to those of the hippies: "I'm just going to go there and it will be groovy". You know, the land was beautiful, though I did happen to see it first at a time when everything was green and fresh. I didn't know what it was like it mid-summer when it was all baked dry.

I thought I was gonna, you know, commune with the trees and be inspired to write books and music and stories and wander around in the fields. It wasn't thought through too thoroughly, I must admit.

DIDN'T YOUR SISTER LIVE UP THERE TOO?

That's how I ended up there. Her boyfriend got in trouble back East and wasn't allowed to leave the state. So I got into looking after their house, their land. This is when I was always on drugs and partying down in the Bay Area, and it was a way to sort of clean up and clear my head, by sitting up there for a few days in the woods. And I had this one really intense experience that probably set me on that path. One time in around March I went up there, and I come around the bend, and the moon had just come out from behind some of those dark, brooding stormy clouds that they have in the late Winter. There was patches of snow all over the mountain, it dominated the horizon and it just chilled me right to the soul. I was like, "God, you could just die up here if you didn't know what you were doing." And suddenly I had this really deep hunger. Everything in the city was like partying, fun and games and dress up, and I was like, "This is real. This is real life." I said, "I want to do something like that in my life where it matters what you do."

So, it was another year or two before I moved up there, but I think that's when the die was cast. I had to go.

BRUCE ANDERSON IS THE PUBLISHER OF THE ANDERSON VALLEY ADVERTISER, PERHAPS THE BEST AND MOST VITAL NEWSPAPER IN THE COUNTRY, A GREAT COMBINATION OF INTERNATIONAL AND VERY LOCAL NEWS, ALL OPINIONATED AND INFORMED.

BRUCE

BRUCE IS 62.

WOULD YOU CONSIDER YOURSELF PART OF THE BACK-TO-THE-LAND MOVEMENT?

Yeah, in a way, an odd sort of way. Ling and I had become foster parents, we'd started that in '68. We had some pretty tough kids, mostly black kids, living with us in San Francisco, usually two, three kids at a time. But once they were out the door, it was difficult to supervise them, to keep them out of trouble, so we thought, well, we'll move to the country and work with juvenile delinquents there. The theory being that they would be less delinquent in the country than in the city, which was of course totally delusional. So that's how it happened. I'm not really a country person. I didn't want to move to the country and have chickens and gardens, that sort of thing, or homestead a parcel of land. I just wanted to work with delinquents out of a city context. So my brother Ken and I drove around up north, and we found a place in Boonville that was for lease, so we moved up there.

THAT WAS 1970, 1971?

1970.

SO, RIGHT AT THE VERY BEGINNING OF THE REAL BIG INFLUX OF HIPPIES?

Right. I was always lumped in with the hippies because they didn't know quite where to place me, but since I hung out with so-called hippies...

SO YOU WERE WELL PLACED TO OBSERVE THE WHOLE HIPPIES IN THE COUNTRY PHENOMENON?

Yeah. But we were running, or at least trying to run a very straight operation, a structured sort of operation.

There was a lot of conflict. I remember going to a meeting in '71 or so because a group in Boonville calling themselves Cold Steel was picking up hippies or so-called hippies hitchhiking and cutting their hair, beating them up, stuff like that. People were getting assualted in downtown Boonville, and the hippies, so-called, or people who were new in the area, were quite concerned, so they called a meeting to try and deal with it. And I said, "Well, why don't we start by shoving some cold steel right up their ass and see how they like it?" And they said, "But we're nonviolent," and I said, "Well, I'm not!" I was thinking, you don't want to let yourselves be pushed around, and I'd already had a lot of clashes with local people, just over the fact that we were primarily a black operation. One black kid who lived with me - who went on to become a professional hit man for the Black Guerrilla Family, who kills people in jail, not a liberally oriented person as a child or an adult - wanted to take auto mechanics at Boonville High School. Otherwise, we were mostly home schooling. So, he had a big afro then, and I take him down to school and the superintendent says, "Well, if he's going to come to school here, he's got to get a haircut." I said, "No, he doesn't." It's already 1971, it's already been to the Supreme Court.

And he said, "Well, we run our school district differently here, you newcomers blah blah blah, you're not going to tell us what to do." So I told him, "Well, if you touch him, or try to cut his hair, there's going to be some serious... you're going to have trouble." He says, "Well, we'll see about that. You come to the school board meeting and make your case."

I had to come back to this school board meeting, where I get up and introduce myself. I'm trying to be reasonable, right? "I'm Bruce Anderson, and the superintendent has told me that my foster son here will have to have his hair cut." And the school board, they were sort of peering back at me, and as I was talking, there's a packed house, you know, forty people, and some guys in back of me were saying, "Sit down, shut up." I look around and I could tell the whole town was fired up, they were going to draw the line. There was obvious racism at work, too. I said, "Well, if you touch him you'll be sued," and so forth. They said, "Are you threatening us?" It went back and forth like that for a while.

When I walked out - no kids were with me or anything - I walk out the door by myself, and a guy slugs me! I'll never forget that. So he slugs me, I slug him back. I got the best of him, and we wound up rolling around on the grass there.

And that was the end of it. The kid took the auto shop class, and had no problem.

You know, as soon as the so-called liberals - hippies, liberals, up-from-hippies, whatever they were - here in Anderson Valley captured control of the school board, it got a lot worse. Architecturally, where they hauled in "temporary structures" - you can see them, we still have a couple - that were like medium security style prisons. The schools actually became much more authoritarian, in a friendly fascist sort of way, and there was sort of a general swing to the right. There was nothing going on in the curriculum. I sort of assumed that once the "good people" took over from these terrible rednecks, some interesting things would happen, but it actually got worse.

IT SOUNDS LIKE, FROM WHAT YOU'RE SAYING, THAT YOU HAD AN INITIAL SYMPATHY FOR THE HIPPIES, THE BACK-TO-THE-LANDERS, EVEN IF YOU DIDN'T AGREE WITH THEM ON EVERYTHING, THAT THEY WERE BASICALLY "THE GOOD GUYS".

Yeah. We were McGovern headquarters in '72, worked side by side with a lot of them...

WHAT WERE YOUR HOPES FOR WHAT THE BACK-TO-THE-LAND MOVEMENT COULD TURN INTO?

I thought we could have a little more humane, forward-looking local government. But that certainly hasn't worked out, because what happened was that the so-called hippies, after several years of self-indulgence, basically recaptured middle class privileges of education, so forth, and moved right into the power slots, at least at the local county level. And they've been just as repressive and reactionary and backwards as the people they came to oppose.

ONE THING I WAS ASKED TO GET YOU TO COMMENT ON WAS THE IDEA THAT THIS WHOLE BACK-TO-THE-LAND THING WAS JUST AN EXAGGERATED FORM OF "WHITE FLIGHT" OR SUBURBANIZATION.

In retrospect, I think there was a definite element of that.

OR ESCAPISM...

Yeah, I think so. But I've never really identified with it, and the nature of our business, what we were doing, didn't really leave any time for going to counterculture functions.

AND AS TIME WENT ON, YOU TOOK OVER THE LOCAL NEWSPAPER AS WELL.

Right, and my assuming control of the newspaper was not met with... Well, the liberals were much more apprehensive and upset about it.

WHAT YEAR DID YOU TAKE OVER THE NEWSPAPER?

In 1984.

OH, THAT LATE? SO BY THAT TIME YOU'D PROBABLY ALREADY SUCCEEDED IN ALIENATING YOURSELF FROM A SIGNIFICANT PART OF THE COMMUNITY?

Yeah, from many people here. I was always complaining about the school board and the county schools, it was practically a full time occupation. Besides being responsible for dependent kids, I was always having trouble with the schools. And with social workers, social services type of people, who ordinarily would be considered liberals.

SO WOULD YOU SAY THAT BY THE TIME YOU'D TAKEN OVER THE PAPER, YOU'D PRETTY MUCH LOST FAITH IN ANYTHING HOPEFUL ABOUT THE...

About the counterculture? Oh yeah, absolutely. I always saw it as pretty much class-based anyway. You know yourself, hippies were pretty much securely middle class people. They knew that in a pinch they could phone home, get a financial bailout. There were very few working class hippies.

WOULD YOU SAY THAT WAS AT THE HEART OF A LOT OF THE ANIMOSITY BETWEEN THE HIPPIES AND THE REDNECKS?

Yeah, because the rednecks, they saw - and I think fairly accurately - the whole hippie phenomenon as a great big "Fuck you" to them. Here they are, paying their mortgages, going out to work and everything, and they're confronted with all these people who are in some kind of position where they don't have to do that, so their whole way of living is kind of a sneer at the conventional ways of doing things. And later on, I think we saw that big time with Judi Bari. I used to have arguments with her all the time. I'd say, look, you can't be a hippie in the hills and then ride out and organize, say, mill workers in Fort Bragg. People who were born and raised together, gone to school together, and have this shitty job that they need in order to do what they have to do. You can't. You'd have to go to work in the mill, you'd have to knock off the whole hippie bullshit angle if you're going to make any kind of so-called environmentalist-logger alliance. That was our biggest bone of contention, really.

I ALWAYS THOUGHT THERE WAS THIS KIND OF ATTITUDE IN THE ENVIRONMENTAL MOVEMENT THAT REEKED OF, "WELL, WE KNOW BETTER THAN YOU BACKWARD PEOPLE, YOU'RE KILLING THE FORESTS AND WE'RE TRYING TO SAVE THEM, WE'RE MORE SENSITIVE THAN YOU ARE, WE'RE BETTER HUMAN BEINGS..."

Right. And that's not a good organizing principle.

IT DIDN'T SEEM TO WORK TOO WELL.

No, it didn't. And look what's happened to the environment.
This is supposed to be ground zero, ecotopia... Christ, and it's
just massive devastation. And now that the wineries are picking
up steam, which to my mind are much more destuctive than timber
companies. And here's where the class angle comes into play.
There's very little visible opposition to what the wine industry
is doing. And that's a totally bad industry. It depends entirely
on Mexican poverty, sucks up water, destroys the natural environment, uses a lot of chemicals... What could be worse?

CAN YOU THINK OF ANYTHING POSITIVE TO SAY ABOUT THE BACK-TO-THE-LAND MOVEMENT?

No. Frankly, I can't. Well, let's see. What would be a good
thing? I think that it's probably made the area a little more
diverse. But that's another thing that was wrong with it. One of
the worst things that came out of the Back-to-the-Land movement
was, if you look at the events calendars of all these local papers
up here, you've got like this round of basically urban-style
activity. So if you want to live in the country, why do you have
to have concerts, "boogies", this constant round of frenetic
activity. Why do you need a public radio station? Why do you need
any of this shit if you're living up in the country? This is all
an outgrowth of the groovy people, the wonderful people, and I
think what they've done, largely, is just sort of urbanized,
suburbanized the whole area north of Cloverdale.

YOU'VE REMARKED A FEW TIMES IN THE PAST ABOUT HOW SOME OF THE HIPPIES DEALT WITH THEIR CHILDREN..

There was a sort of gross irresponsibility that just seems to
me like moral, ethical cowardice. A lot of kids ended up, it seems
to me, semi-abandoned while their parents behaved in an adolescent
way. Children aren't a joke. You're going to fuck up your kid if
you do that. If you have a kid, you've got to take care of him.
It's a life sentence. You shouldn't have them in the first place
if you're not going to provide some measure of stability and
three meals a day. There was a lot of irresponsibility and I think
a lot of children were harmed. So you see a funny thing happening
up and down the North Coast, where children did this about-face on
their parents' "alternative" lifestyle. They'd immediately move to
the city and get a conventional job and become totally conventional, ambitious, burgeoning capitalists. You saw a lot of that.

And then the Tree Frog Johnson case, that was probably the most
extreme case. Here's a guy who's molesting children in Anderson
Valley for a long time, and the counterculture types are saying,
"Oh, he's so good with kids, he always likes to take our kids
camping," and then, when he's found out, instead of busting his
ass, calling the cops on him, he's just shunned. So then he goes
up to the Whale School in Albion and harms children for another
year or so. He finally ends up kidnapping a kid, completely

destroying the little boy he was with, made the kid into a kidnapper. The kid's still locked up. It was very unfair. Alex Cabarga. I remember him very distinctly when they were in Boonville, because you would see them all the time.

IT SEEMS LIKE A LOT OF THAT HAPPENED UP HERE, MAYBE NOT ON SUCH AN EXTREME SCALE, BUT SOME OF THE HIPPIES SEEMED TO TREAT THEIR CHILDREN MUCH THE WAY THEY DID THEIR DOGS AND CATS, LIKE LETTING THEM LOOSE WHEN THEY GOT BORED WITH THEM, SAYING, "OH, THEY CAN GO BACK TO NATURE".

Yeah, I think they did. I think it was very painful. It's too bad we haven't had any good memoirs yet. A lot of young people still aren't talking about that, but it definitely happened.

WHAT ABOUT JIM JONES'S PEOPLE'S TEMPLE BEING ABLE TO RECRUIT RATHER EASILY?

They tried to recruit us, actually.

THEY WERE PRETTY SUCCESSFUL UP HERE, WEREN'T THEY?

Yeah, but they imported most of their congregation. Jim Jones practically ran Mendocino at one time. He was chairman of the Grand Jury, the media naturally were at his feet. He was kind of off our screen, too, but one of the women who died with him, who's described as his mistress, she came out to see us one night. They saw us and thought, "Oh, interracial couple, all these black kids, natural People's Temple recruits." People were always trying to get us to go to that church, but we never had any interest in it. I knew a lot of the people who got killed, though.

BUT JONES NEVER CAME AROUND HERE?

Jones taught school in Boonville, but that was just before I arrived. He left Anderson Valley in '68, before that he taught at the elementary school.

I WONDER HOW THIS FITS INTO PEOPLE'S UNWILLINGNESS TO SAY NO, THAT'S NOT GOOD, WE'RE NOT GOING TO TOLERATE THAT, LET'S JUST BE GROOVY AND OPEN...

He was an early player of the race card. He would fake events. I remember once when he erected a gun tower at his People's Temple property over in Redwood Valley, and he said he needed a 24-hour watch because the rednecks were doing drive-bys, threatening to burn him out because it was an interracial church. But there was no proof those episodes ever took place. But he would always use that. Any sort of criticism of him - and I don't think there was much - and he'd say, "You're just doing this because you resent the interracial harmony we've created."

SO THERE WAS THIS GENERAL TENDENCY, THOUGH, TO BE UNCRITICAL, WHETHER OF A FANATIC LIKE JIM JONES, OR A CHILD MOLESTER, OR JUST THE RANDOM ABUSE OR NEGLECT OF CHILDREN.

There was this whole feeling of "The Man", the cops being the enemy, that whole Blue Meanie mentality, which I think still prevails. I mean, anybody who came out of the Sixties knew that if you got arrested, you also got beat up, that was part of the package. Police departments are much more sophisticated now, they're more wary. They can revert, of course, at any time, but they're much more wary of lawsuits. But yeah, there'd been brutality, so certainly people were wary of the police.

I THINK IT GOES BEYOND JUST BEING UNWILLING TO COOPERATE WITH POLICE. THERE'S THIS ATTITUDE OF, "OH, HE'S JUST DOING HIS OWN THING, MAN..."

There was a lot of that. That was just outrageous. I'll give you an example. One day, at this place we were leasing, we had a pond. So I pull up with a carload of delinquents, and we were going to go swimming. There was a bunch of so-called hippies at the pond, and they were all nude. It was mostly women, actually, walking around nude. And the delinquents, of course, they were sixteen, seventeen year old boys, and they just started practically salivating. So I said to the women, "Look, you've got to cover up here a little bit, these guys might misunderstand nudity. Someone could get hurt here, I can't watch all of them every minute." We had some pretty tough kids.

But I get this earful of, "Man, the human body is beautiful, blah blah blah..." I always felt like saying, "Well, yours isn't. Would you mind covering up?" We'd get stupid disputes like that all the time. Or a guy would buy one of our kids a couple fifths of whiskey. We were dealing with kids who would drink the whole fifth and maybe die, who had no sense of proportion or restraint. I remember one time, grabbing a guy coming out of the Boonville Lodge with a whole case of liquor. My delinquents had pooled their money. I just grabbed the stuff and started pouring it out. The guy must have thought I was some kind of temperance fanatic. He said, "Hey, weren't you a kid once, man? Didn't somebody buy for you?" I said, "Yeah, but these guys are a little different, you know what I mean? You're not going to have to stay up with them all night when they fight and start breaking shit."

We had a lot of conflicts like that. Because I was dealing with guys who'd come out of the inner city, in some ways like hippie kids, just totally abandoned, who'd grown up in situations where they were accustomed to using force and violence, or at least the

threat of it, to get what they wanted. Completely undisciplined.
But that's what we were dealing with. It was naive, what we were
doing, futile in almost all cases. But we couldn't operate in
that loosey-goosey sort of social circumstance.

I'M ALSO GETTING THE IMPRESSION THAT YOU FELT SOME OF YOUR IDEALISTIC THEORIES ABOUT THE BENEFITS OF COUNTRY LIVING FOR TROUBLED INNER CITY YOUTH DIDN'T QUITE WORK OUT?

Well, the whole system is wrong, which I quickly discovered,
because when the state, the authorities, finally get around to
intervening in a kid's life, it's way too late. So by the time
a kid gets to be ten, even younger, he's already got sort of a
psychopathic way of operating.

HOW MANY KIDS CAME THROUGH YOUR GROUP HOME?

Over the years, probably 100, maybe up to 150. I run into black
kids all the time in San Francisco who I know from Boonville,
who've either been in my home or another group home here in
Boonville.

HOW MANY OF THEM WOULD YOU CONSIDER TO BE SUCCESS STORIES?

It's hard to say. A lot of them just disappeared after they
left us. Quite a few of them went right on into the adult penal
system. Like this kid I mentioned earlier, the Black Guerilla
Family enforcer, I picked up a San Francisco Examiner one day,
maybe three or four years ago, and there was a horrifying story
about him, how he had reached through the bars of the Oakland
City jail and strangled to death an inmate passing by. They'd
had to use five cops to get him off this guy. He was that strong.
At the time he was awaiting trial for a series of murders he'd
committed in jail.

AND YOU WERE HIS FOSTER DAD?

Yeah.

HOW DO YOU FEEL ABOUT THAT?

Uh... I got him into weights, so I'm sure it made him a better
enforcer... But looking back, even when I knew him as a twelve
to fourteen year old... Of course, the brilliant decision was
made to re-unite him with his family, which was non-existent,
basically. He was dangerous, he'd do dangerous things, like if
he got a younger, weaker kid alone he'd beat him up. You always
had to keep an eye on him. A lot of kids were like that. You
could see it coming in a lot of ways. We had constant episodes
of fire starting, animal torture, you know, all the psycho signs.

WOULD YOU SAY THAT ANY OF THE KIDS BENEFITED FROM COMING OUT HERE TO BOONVILLE?

Oh yeah, I get letters from guys, phone calls, all the time, telling me how they really liked it up here, how they knew I tried to help them. Just the stability, just the peacefulness of it. You get three meals, you get a regular routine, which was all new. Kids relate to that, especially kids from chaotic backgrounds.

SO AGAIN, HOW MANY WOULD YOU CONSIDER "SUCCESS STORIES"?

In what sense?

THEY STAYED OUT OF PRISON...

Probably a third. But they might have stayed out of prison anyway, you never know. It's really a crapshoot, when you look back on it. One kid, for example, who still comes up for holidays, married now, a very conventional guy, he grew up in the Pink Palace in San Francisco. Remember the Pink Palace? His family was so bad they got kicked out of there. That's how bad they were. His sisters were prostitutes, there were always pimps hanging out there, always tough guys. Cops would only go in there four to six at a time. It was completely out of control. I'd go up to his family's apartment. It was scary for me going there, the elevator never worked, I'd have to hike all the way up twelve floors, go into his house, everything smelled like urine, it was completely fucked up, mattresses on the floor, that was the home he grew up in, and he's fine. Somehow, emotionally, from his mother, I think - who went off the tracks, too, was involved in a lot of criminal activity - but somehow he got what he needed emotionally. He's a very mellow guy, always was, even when he was a little kid. Well, he'd pulled a knife on somebody in some kind of a fight. That was just the kind of shitty scene that went on around there. But he was never violent, and he lived up here for eight or nine years. Went to college and got a job, married and doing fine.

ON THE OTHER SIDE OF THE COIN, I'VE SEEN EXAMPLES UP HERE OF VERY MIDDLE CLASS WHITE GUYS WHO GO UP TO THE WOODS AND KIND OF GO FERAL, START RUNNING AROUND WITH GUNS AND KNIVES, SHOOTING EACH OTHER'S HORSES OR WIVES OR EACH OTHER OVER SEEMINGLY PETTY SQUABBLES. IT SEEMS AS THOUGH COUNTRY LIFE HAD JUST THE OPPOSITE EFFECT ON THEM, KIND OF BROUGHT OUT THE "LORD OF THE FLIES" INSTINCT.

I don't know where that came from. It always mystified me.

OKAY, I'M GOING TO ASK YOU NOW TO SUM UP WHAT IT ALL CAME TO.

I bought the newspaper. I mortgaged my house to do so, a miracle of capitalism, you might say. We bought this house for $23,500, right, with $1,000 down, and suddenly it's worth $180,000 or something by 1984, so I was able to mortgage it and buy the paper for $20,000. And it was an existing, legally adjudicated paper, which means it had a postal permit, qualified to run legal ads.

Obviously I took it in a completely opposite direction. Most of the advertising fled immediately, so I knew I'd have to make it interesting enough to a wider range of people since I'd have to rely on stand sales and subscriptions to support myself. And it's worked out. It's gotten a lot better over the years.

But I bought it as a political weapon. I wanted to destroy the school system, and I wanted to destroy the County Office of Education, so I used the paper basically to culminate about a fifteen year war against the County Office of Education. Finally, you know, the superintendent went to jail, and then another guy just went to jail recently, and that was very gratifying.

So that was my main thing, and it really grew out of the foster home, because I was always clashing with the judges, the fucking social workers, and the school people. So the paper, I was going to use it as something to beat them over the head with on a weekly basis. And I did. As well as a lot of other people and institutions over the years.

SO HERE YOU ARE SOME THIRTY YEARS LATER, YOU'RE PART OF THE LOCAL ESTABLISHMENT.

Not really.

WELL, IN A SENSE...

Well, I'm here, they kind of have to deal with me, but I'm certainly not part of anything.

NOBODY ELSE IS GOING TO BE ABLE TO SET UP A SUCCESSFUL COMPETING NEWSPAPER IN THE AREA.

They tried. Boycotts and everything.

AND YOU'RE OBVIOUSLY NOT GOING AWAY. SO IN THAT SENSE YOU'VE PUT DOWN DEEP ROOTS IN THE COMMUNITY, WHETHER PEOPLE LIKE IT OR NOT, WHETHER YOU LIKE IT OR NOT.

Well, I have a lot of criminal in me too, in my psychological makeup. My attitude has always been, "I'll take it one step farther." I think people sense that in the paper.

SO YOU'RE PROBABLY HEADED FOR FAME AND FORTUNE THEN. AS BALZAC SAID, "BEHIND EVERY GREAT FORTUNE LIES A CRIME..."

Yeah, but I don't have the fortune part. There's a lot of crime, but no fortune so far.

Yeah, for better or worse. In sort of an odd way... I just wrote a long story this week based in Fort Bragg, a murder case. A lot of people over the years have come to depend on the paper. It's the court of last resort. Actually, it's the way papers are supposed to function, idealistically.

IT'S THE WAY PAPERS DID FUNCTION 100, 200 YEARS AGO.

I think they did. But around here they haven't functioned that way, probably ever. People call here all the time and say, "Hey, nobody else is interested, will you listen to my story?" And that's very gratifying, in a way. So I find myself obligated to keep on doing it. There's always somebody out there who needs to have his story heard. Otherwise they're just completely shut out of the media.

I WANT TO WRAP THIS UP WITH A DEFINITIVE COMMENT ABOUT WHAT IT ALL ADDED UP TO.

My experience?

YEAH, YOUR EXPERIENCE, THE WHOLE COUNTERCULTURE, BACK-TO-THE-LAND THING... I MEAN, HERE WE ARE, YOU'RE NOW AN ELDER STATESMAN OF SORTS, WHAT DID IT ALL MEAN TO YOU?

Um, nothing at all, really. It suburbanized the North Coast, and made it, I think, a little worse.

SO ARE YOU SORRY YOU CAME?

To Boonville? No, not really. It's an ideal climate here in Anderson Valley, probably one of the best climates in the world, you're two hours from at least the possibility of art and stimulation in the Bay Area. No, I feel very fortunate, really, because people will never have a deal like this again, do you think it's going to happen again, where people can buy forty acres of land for, say, $18,000? That was possible in Boonville right up till about 1975. Those days are definitely gone.

SO, ANOTHER VERSION OF THE FRONTIER CLOSING, LIKE AT THE END OF THE NINETEENTH CENTURY, THE END OF THE WILD WEST?

Yeah, just like the genocidal attack on Mendocino County Native Americans in the middle of the 19th century. You had the attack of the counterculture, and they sort of mopped it up. It was a hundred, hundred and fifty year process, and the hippies finished

part 3

3

BACK TO THE LAND

WHO OF US DOESN'T NEED AN ESCAPE?

AS DAN B. SAID TO CINDY, "I'D THINK AARON
WOULD LIKE THE IDEA OF GETTING SOME LAND.
AFTER ALL, HE'S ALWAYS GRUMPY AND COM-
PLAINING ABOUT HOW THERE'S TOO MUCH NOISE
AND TOO MANY PEOPLE AROUND".

IT WAS TRUE. WHEN I FIRST DECIDED TO
DO THIS PROJECT, I WAS LIVING IN A CITY
WHERE EVERYONE CAME TO "ESCAPE THE CITY
AND LOOK FOR LAND TO BUY". AN ENDLESS
SUCCESSION OF PEOPLE SHOWED UP, STAYING
FOR MONTHS AT A TIME, SLEEPING ON OUR
PORCH WHILE THEY OSTENSIBLY LOOKED FOR
JOBS IN ORDER TO SAVE UP MONEY AND BUY
LAND. OF COURSE, NO ONE BOUGHT LAND, BUT
NEITHER DID THEY CONTRIBUTE TO OUR SCENE
THERE IN THE CITY WHICH THEY LOOKED DOWN
ON, ALL THE WHILE USING UP ITS RESOURCES.
I WAS OUT OF MY MIND FROM ALL THE PERM-
ANENT HOUSEGUESTS ALL TALKING ABOUT
BUYING LAND AND BEING SELF-SUFFICIENT.

WHICH BRINGS US TO THE SECRET AGENDA
AND MAIN REASON FOR THESE INTERVIEWS.
A LOT OF PEOPLE ARE TALKING ABOUT GETTING
LAND. A LOT OF PEOPLE ARE THINKING ABOUT
HAVING KIDS, WHETHER OR NOT THEY TALK
ABOUT IT. I HAPPEN TO BE AGAINST BOTH, BUT
THAT DOESN'T MEAN I'M IMMUNE TO THE
URGES. IF WE'RE MAKING A LIST, I'M ALSO
AGAINST SELF-SUFFICIENCY, BUT THAT TOO IS
A PERSONAL CHOICE. IT'S JUST THE ASSUMPTIONS,
AND THE LACK OF OPEN DISCUSSION WHICH MAKES
ME NERVOUS. I WANTED EVERY PERSON WHO
TALKED ABOUT HOW THE CITY WAS NO PLACE TO
RAISE A KID TO HEAR THE OTHER SIDE OF THE
STORY. I WANTED TO MAKE THE POINT THAT

NEITHER ONE IS MORE PURE, MORE PERFECT, MORE "REAL". I WANTED TO REMIND EVERYONE THAT THE CRIME RATE HAS BEEN DROPPING STEADILY FOR YEARS, AND AN INCREASED FEELING OF VULNERABILITY PROBABLY HAS MORE TO DO WITH GETTING OLDER, AND MEDIA SENSATIONALISM, THAN BECAUSE "THE CITIES ARE GETTING WORSE".

OF COURSE, I HAD MY OWN ASSUMPTIONS. I THOUGHT ONLY PEOPLE WHO GREW UP IN THE CITIES AND SUBURBS WANTED TO BUY LAND. ONLY THOSE WHO KNEW NOTHING ABOUT THE DRAWBACKS AND HARDSHIPS. AGAIN, I WAS WRONG. THESE LAST FOUR INTERVIEWS ARE PEOPLE WHO LITERALLY WANT TO GO "BACK".

AT ANY RATE, IT'S IMPORTANT TO LOOK AT WHAT CHILDREN NEED TO GROW AND BE HEALTHY AND HAPPY AND WELL-ADJUSTED. BECAUSE, AS ADULTS, WE NEED MANY OF THE SAME THINGS, AND NEED TO PROVIDE THEM FOR EACH OTHER.

WE DO NEED TO BE IDEALISTIC, TO TRY NEW THINGS, CHASE OUR DREAMS, AND BUILD OUR OWN COMMUNITIES. BUT WE NEED TO DO IT SERIOUSLY, WITHOUT ILLUSIONS OR ASSUMPTIONS.

LET US PLAN OUR FUTURES WISELY. OUR DECISIONS TODAY, OR LACK OF DECISION, AFFECT MORE THAN JUST OUR OWN LIVES.

MAYA

JED TOLD YOU WHAT??.

That you were interviewing children of hippies.

NO, NO.

Right, but it made me think how people tend to assume that back-to-the-landers and hippies are the same thing. Where if your parents were hippies then you grew up in the country and lived off the land. And in most cases that's probably how it is. But my parents didn't like hippies.

HAD THEY GONE UP EARLIER?

Actually, I only found out recently, talking to my dad about it. He said he didn't know about this "back to the land" movement. And if he'd known about it, he wouldn't have done it. I mean, it seems like if you really wanted to do something, it wouldn't matter that all these people you don't like are doing the same thing.

My mom felt some of this too, but my mom was more extreme in feeling that hippies in general were lazy. And they didn't like the whole drug thing. My dad came out of being in the Navy for 13 years. Coming from that background, and it wasn't like he was drafted. He chose to go in there, and he stuck with it. My mom was teaching high school English in the late 60's. She just said she didn't like all the drugs. Which is understandable. Yeah, my dad said he wouldn't have done it if he knew all these people were doing the same thing.

WHICH WAS WHAT?

Well, they were totally into living in the country and making all their own stuff, that's what they wanted to do. My dad wore a beard because he didn't like his chin. But he was always afraid that people would think he was a hippie because of that. And if he got broken down by the side of the road, he didn't want people to not help us because they'd think we were hippies, so he'd tell me and my sister to make sure we looked really nice. Be very respectable. Because he thought hippies weren't respectable. That kind of thing.

I don't know how self-sufficient my parents hoped to be. They were very realistic, and took it very seriously, and read a lot about how to do it. So they may well have known that they might not be able to pull it off as much as they'd liked.

YOUR DAD BUILT THE HOUSE, NO?

My dad's still working on the house. His passion is woodworking, and he's spent twenty-five years on the house already. It's quite a work of art. Unfortunately, our bathroom didn't have doors or walls until I was thirteen, and I didn't have bedroom walls or doors until I was sixteen. And my bedroom was tiny because when he first arranged it he kind of pictured us staying little girls forever, our little furniture.

The house is really nice now that only two people are living in it. Yeah, it was hard not having walls. The second summer we didn't have a roof, and that summer it really rained a lot. He was redoing the roof, so everything was covered in tarps. We were living in tents. Me and my sister had a tent, my parents had a tent.

That reminds me of something else. They didn't raise us with a TV. My dad always said that the TV didn't work, after they moved it up from the city it wouldn't work. Suddenly when I was fifteen he got out the TV and got it working. So I was kind of suspicious, but by that time I was glad to have not had a TV. They said it got damaged when we had no roof and it rained, but I don't know.

WERE YOU HOMESCHOOLED?

No. I really wanted to be. But you see, my mom is a teacher and really into supporting public schools. They weren't so much into retreating from traditional society. They respected the way things were, the way things had been traditionally as far as education. They weren't trying to do things differently in that regard. They just wanted to live in the country and make their own food, that kind of thing. But they had us do 4-H.

Yeah. I didn't want to do 4-H and I did want to be homeschooled. I wanted to go in the other direction. They finally let me do Independent Study my last couple years, which was an option up there because so many kids lived way out. It wasn't home school-ing, but close enough. But it took me two years to persuade them to let me do that.

I wanted to take the proficiency test, leave school early and go to the community college, but they wouldn't let me do that. They were so afraid of me doing something different and it not working out. They wanted me to do the proven path. Even though they had taken quite a risk moving to the country, beyond that they weren't risk takers and they didn't encourage me or my sister to be. In fact they discouraged us.

My parents were very concerned about what kind of judgement others would have of them. Especially people they respected. My dad would complain, he wanted me to wear white tennis shoes, jeans, and a white t-shirt. To look very normal. And they were very frustrated with me in my attempts to do things differently. Not so much that it bothered them, I think they were worried about what other people thought.

A LOT OF PEOPLE ARE LOOKING TO BUY LAND NOW. I GUESS THAT'S MY REASON FOR INTERVIEWING PEOPLE WHO GREW UP ON THE LAND. A LOT OF PEOPLE WHO GREW UP IN THE CITY ARE HAVING SOME OF THE SAME DREAMS, BUT MAYBE DON'T KNOW PEOPLE WHO GREW UP ON THE LAND. AND I GUESS THEY'RE STARTING TO THINK ABOUT HAVING KIDS, WHETHER THEY ADMIT IT OR NOT. HAVE YOU SEEN THAT? WHAT ADVICE WOULD YOU GIVE TO PEOPLE THINKING ABOUT IT?

Well, I've met people a lot younger than me. In their early Twenties. People who I think really don't realize what it takes both financially and in other ways. I definitely encourage people to do it if they're realistic about it and they have a lot of money to do it. But these days, homesteading, I think it's for wealthy people. I certainly can't afford to buy land. And you have to be able to make a living in some way to support yourself while you're on the land, because you can't be totally self-sufficient for a long period of time.

I would love to do it myself, actually. I garden and I can food and preserve food and make my own ice cream and make my own root beer and do all that stuff my parents were doing. But, I don't live in the country. I do what I can living in the city.

DO YOU SEE PEOPLE ENTERTAINING CERTAIN DELUSIONS? OR MAKING THE SAME MISTAKES?

Yeah. People think they'll sew clothes for a living. Go into

town and sell jewelry they make, or something. Maybe I'm discouraged, but I just don't think that works. Very rarely. It can
work for a year, and then you're out of money. There's land
taxes, property taxes, healthcare. Especially if you have kids.
Gas, car maintenance. All these things that can cost a lot of
money.

People I've encountered are too dreamy about how they can make
a living. Then again, I could be biased because that's something
my parents drilled into me. You know, you can't make a living
doing this, you really have to be part of society.

So I've always worried about money. And other people don't
worry about money.

OTHER PEOPLE HAVE RICH PARENTS.

(laughs)

PINKY GREW UP IN
MINNESOTA.

SHE IS 23.

PINKY

FIRST OF ALL, YOU DIDN'T SPEND VERY MUCH TIME, ONLY SIX YEARS ON THE LAND?

M-hm.

DO YOU FEEL LIKE IT WAS A FORMATIVE TIME, LIKE IT AFFECTED YOUR PERCEPTION OF THINGS? LIKE IT AFFECTED YOUR VALUES MUCH?

Definitely. We learned a lot of things right away. Like fear of cops. And stuff like that. A lot of other people in the town looked at us right away. My sister was three years older than I was too, she picked up on stuff a lot more.

DID THAT FEAR OF COPS, AND FEELING OF BEING DIFFERENT, DID THAT TRICKLE DOWN FROM YOUR PARENTS, OR DID YOU LEARN IT YOURSELF?

It was probably from my dad. The fear of cops thing came because the police came and beat the shit out of my dad, right in front of all of us.

FOR WHAT?

Because they knew he was selling drugs. This threatening thing, it was really fucked up. It had to do with the bikers in the town who sold speed, they somehow got the cops to go beat him up.

DON'T YOU NEED TO BE KIND OF NEAR THE CITY TO SELL DRUGS?

No. Not in rural Minnesota. Everyone smoked weed. Everybody, constantly. I don't think my parents went up to the city, ever.

Both of them had a huge fear of the city. They thought it was really corrupt and bad.

DID THEY THINK IT WAS GETTING WORSE?

Definitely worse. My mom used to live in Minneapolis, but she wouldn't go back there. She wouldn't trust anybody and would lock her car. Be afraid of certain neighborhoods, and things like that.

THE BACK-TO-THE-LAND THING SEEMS A LITTLE DIFFERENT IN MINNESOTA BECAUSE THE LAND IS PRETTY CLOSE, NOT JUST A MYTHICAL IDEA.

Most people in that part of Minnesota worked on various farms. I did. If you're in high school or junior high and you want to make some kind of money, you work on farms. My dad worked on all kinds of farms. His grandparents, both sets, had farms.

WAS HE TRYING TO FOLLOW THEIR FOOTSTEPS OR GO FOR SOMETHING FURTHER BACK?

I just think he wanted to be not reliant on money. Even though he sold weed. He always taught me, he used to always say, "We have all the time in the world, we have all the money in the world, we just have to know how to get it and use it". I think that was the main motivation for him.

I remember my dad when I was little, all the time telling me I didn't have to work, and telling me we had all the time in the world. My mom would want to hurry up and go do something. He'd say, "We have all the time in the world, we don't have to go now." He was just really laid back.

THE FARMLAND WHERE YOU LIVED, WAS IT FARMED?

There was projects, you know. We had huge gardens, and we'd all do the canning. A lot of the food we ate came from there. There was a huge sweet corn patch. And fruit trees also. But there would be a project where one person decided he was going to grow all sorts of beans, and had no idea how to do it. There'd be things like that. Every once in a while someone would try to clear a bit of field. There were fields that were totally over-grown, but they were farmable fields. The people who moved there however many years later, we went back there and the people who had bought the land were farming it. They had cleared down most of the forest and were farming that too.

SOME TRADITIONAL FARMERS HAD BOUGHT IT.

Yeah, commercial farmers. I went to school with the daughters of the people who had it, so they'd tell me about it sometimes.

But they didn't live in the house, they lived somewhere else and just bought it for the land and left the house standing. Tore the barn down and the outbuildings.

YOU LIVED WITH A WHOLE GROUP OF PEOPLE, RIGHT? WHEN YOUR PARENTS LEFT THE LAND, DID THAT HOUSE FALL APART? DID THE REST OF THE PEOPLE STAY?

There's a big part of that part of my life that I don't remember at all, from the divorce I guess, and I had to see all these psychiatrists and all this stuff. And there's a huge section of my memory missing so I really don't know, but I'm pretty sure that there were still people living there after my parents moved into town. My memory is really hazy between when I was six and when I started going to school in town. This big missing piece.

THAT'S PRETTY YOUNG FOR MUCH MEMORIES AT ALL.

I have a lot of vivid memories from living there. A lot of things were really really clear. One of my earliest memories was when I was two and we were out there. It was something my sister remembered too.

SOMETHING INTERESTING, OR JUST A PERSONAL THING?

Well, we were in a field, with all these people on acid. And my sister was trying to explain to me, and I was just really, really little. She was five and trying to explain to me what was going on. It was just this crazy thing. And there was sunflowers everywhere.

THAT'S NOT YOUR FIRST MEMORY?!

Yeah, as near as I can tell, that's my oldest memory. All of the adults were crazy, and me and my sister were just like, da-da-da. Now looking back, like what the fuck? A bunch of people on acid and two little kids running around a field, that could be really bad. And acid was a lot different then, a lot stronger. It seems really irresponsible now, but you can't do anything about that. Obviously nothing happened.

WAS IT STRANGE COMING OFF THE LAND AND GOING TO SCHOOL IN TOWN FOR THE FIRST TIME?

It was really strange. It was a lot bigger, it scared me a lot. I was really, really, really shy and I didn't talk to anybody for a long time. And I had hand-me-down and second-hand clothes, and in Freeborn that hadn't mattered because everyone else was

farmer's kids and it wasn't a big deal. But in town it was.
Everyone had their name brand clothes. I felt really weird about
that, and everyone thought I was really weird. My hair was always
all matted up too, the teachers would try to comb my hair out.

IS IT A HANDICAP OR A GOOD THING TO NOT BE PREPARED FOR THE BAD THINGS YOU ARE GOING TO FACE?

I think it was definitely a good thing, a lot just because
later on when I stopped trying to make myself like the normal
people and I realized that being an individual and doing individual things, like dressing how I want, that it was a lot easier
because I'd seen everyone else do that before. And I knew that
was okay, and people, adults, you know, could do that, so that I
could do it. And in junior high I found myself doing a lot of the
things that the women who lived there used to do, like I did
beaded jewelry, and embroidery, and quilted. And I found I had a
lot of interest in that, and I already knew a lot about it. I
could make my own clothes already, and stuff like that.

ARE YOU DRAWN BACK TO THE LAND? OR DOING THE SAME SORTS OF THINGS?

Yeah, I'm caught up in that. I was living on this land in
New Mexico for a long time, a year anyway, a year and a half,
I was on my friend's land, and tried different projects on
different friends' lands across the country. And I was gonna buy
land in Taos.

EXPENSIVE, ISN'T IT?

No, it's really, really cheap.

JUST CAN'T DRINK THE WATER.

Yeah, there is no water. That's why it's cheap. I don't know.
It was definitely something I intended to do, until the people we
were going to buy land with got into this really bad situation.
So now I've saved more money and my life's changed and I have
different plans, but the money I've saved is for buying land
eventually. So I guess I am drawn to that.

HOW CAN YOU GET IT WITH A BUNCH OF PEOPLE AND AVOID THE KINDS OF PROBLEMS YOUR PARENTS HAD?

I'm not getting land with a bunch of people. That's what I
learned in Taos.

BECAUSE?

Because it's something that I want to keep for a while, even if I don't use it all the time. It's something I could keep and, you know, pay taxes on, for potentially a long time. And you never know, people change. I don't want it to be like in fifteen years one of the people I bought land with is an asshole that I don't want to talk to...

TRY SIX MONTHS.

Yeah, exactly. Or anything. They go back to the city and they're a junkie or something, and they want to sell the land to some asshole. I don't want to have to deal with that. That's what I learned, is if I just buy it myself, my friends can stay there, people I choose. I want things to just be my own.

IS THERE A WAY TO MAKE LONGTERM PLANS WITH YOUR FRIENDS, HOW TO GROW OLD TOGETHER AND HAVE A PLACE TO GO, WITHOUT HAVING TO TOTALLY BE IN CHARGE OF IT YOURSELF? IS THERE A WAY AROUND IT?

I think there is, depending on the right people, and as long as a serious agreement is made at the beginning about what happens if everyone starts to hate each other.

WHEN.

Yeah, when. I mean, it's the same thing when my parents got divorced. They thought they'd be together forever, they had a kid, they were married for however many years, maybe ten. And that's a long time to spend with someone. And they got divorced, things fell apart. It's something that happens.

IS IT BETTER TO GO INTO THESE SHARED THINGS AND FACE THE EVENTUAL DESTRUCTION AND BITTERNESS, OR JUST KEEP THINGS ON YOUR OWN TERMS?

That's something I've been thinking about a lot with, like, one other person. That I think I could live with. We have been living together for so long. And I think that probably it would be alright. We've been talking about buying land together but having it divided from the start. Or else buy land that adjoins each other, but that's a really rare thing to find, two separate plots of land that are touching.

That's something that I've been thinking about, although the main rule was that I'd get it by myself. And not go in on it with somebody. But I feel like now I can maybe make an exception. Because he's such a reasonable person. I'd worry more about me being the asshole. Me being the one who would fuck everything up.

UDO IS STUDYING TO BECOME A RABBI. I INTERVIEWED HIM IN A PARKING LOT IN ALAMEDA. UDO IS 28.

UDO

WHAT MADE YOUR PARENTS DECIDE TO GO "BACK TO THE LAND"? WAS IT A CONSCIOUS CHOICE?

I think so. First of all, I strongly get the impression from my mother that she never liked Los Angeles and never liked that part of California. And my father had left Southern California on a scholarship as an art student. He had left L.A. to go to the Bay Area, he was really into the beatnik thing. As a painter. And he apparently was a talented painter. But, he was young, things didn't work out, and he was going to get drafted because he couldn't stay in school for financial reasons, and so he wound up going to Vietnam. And after that, he came back, and that's when he met my mother. He was like this artist guy, my mom was this girl, you know, and from there they went traveling, hitchhiking around. Hitchhiking up in Seattle, and living around Seattle. And then they wound up moving into Humboldt County so my father could finish school at Humboldt State.

DO YOU KNOW WHY THEY CHOSE TO GET TO A SMALLER PLACE?

I think it was everything. For the art, for the kids. I think they were trying to meet some kind of ideal. In my baby book my dad has these notes I can only paraphrase, but it kind of gives you a sense of, you know, I was born in '73, and it gives me a sense that freedom and freeness, or whatever, was kind of coming to an end. And a way to hold out a little longer was to maybe live in this kind of a situation. That's the opinion I get, and it was not so much of a survivalist mentality, but really like a way of keeping, yeah, keeping... Well, maybe it was a little bit of a survivalist mentality. But not paranoid survivalist. A progressive survivalist thing, of trying to keep continuity.

WHAT DO YOU THINK ABOUT THAT?

I think it's noble. There's a side of me at this point in my life where I kind of want to do it. I have a sense where I want to move back. I'm finishing college right now. It took me a while to go back and do it, but I had to go through a lot of things in my life. And I kind of want to move back, in a sense I want to go back to Humboldt State and live that lifestyle. But more self-reliant. Like Thoreau, Emerson.

BUT WERE YOUR PARENTS LIKE THOREAU AND EMERSON?

I don't think they were. I think they lived within their own guidelines. Their own guidelines which they continuously changed. Which is so human, human beings have these guidelines which they set up and then continually break them. That's the thing that religion offers, if you're going to join a cult or join a religion, is religion offers set guidelines which are very definitive, which you do not break. They are guidelines like anything else, but the idea is that they are supposed to have more meaning to them than just guidelines that you set up which you break.

BUT IF IT'S A NOBLE IDEAL...

Yeah, it is noble.

BUT IS IT REALISTIC? IS THE PROBLEM WITH THE FACT THAT IT'S A NOBLE IDEAL BUT THE WAY IT GETS TRANSLATED INTO REALITY OR YOUR LIFE IS FLAWED?

Yeah. Yeah, there are problems. I think the isolation that they ultimately set themselves in was pretty serious. Especially when it came to... Well, there was a baby that was born before me. There was a baby before me that came that didn't make it. And that's to me the antithesis of how things failed. For whatever reason, it kind of made my parents' relationship fall apart. Even though they had two kids after that. And it kind of showed how, maybe it was the time where they lived or maybe it was the fact that they were young and they didn't know better. Maybe it was the fact that they were so isolated from their parents or people that could really help them out in other ways. Again, how isolated they truly were. A series of events occured, and, you know, the baby didn't make it.

IS IT FAIR TO ASK ABOUT THAT? OR BETTER NOT TO PRY?

Well, I don't know. I mean, I think what happened was, they were in this rural setting. And they had a dispute with the landlord, who was some elderly man. My dad's a 'Nam vet, he was a Marine in

Vietnam, right? So he pulls out a gun, he's gonna kill the guy.
Because the guy's gonna evict them because he says they didn't pay
rent. They paid rent, but they never kept receipts because he's
this old man. You know, this elderly man.

So my dad just all of a sudden tasted blood. It was only two or
three years ago he was in the bush killing people. He pulled out a
gun, he was gonna blow the guy's head off. My mom is like six or
seven months pregnant, she's fighting with my dad not to shoot him.
Meanwhile there's this old man outside. There's this young couple
fighting over whether or not to shoot him. From there they packed
up the whole house, and then my mom went into labor. And then the
baby didn't make it. And it just sparked off this whole thing that
was really unfortunate. And I don't know how, somehow me and my
brother were born. And not too long after that, things dissolved.
Dad left, and he went back to the city to be an artist, he realized he couldn't just be an artist in the middle of nowhere. And
my mom stayed because she felt there was no need to go anywhere,
you know. And that was it.

JONAH WAS INTERVIEWED IN MY ROOM, A KUDZU-COVERED SHACK IN THE BACK OF A BIG PUNKHOUSE WHERE AS WE SPOKE, A SWEATY BASEMENT SHOW ENSUED. WE ATE SOUP. JONAH IS 23.

JONAH

ALL BUT ONE OF THE KIDS I'VE INTERVIEWED GREW UP IN NORTHERN CALIFORNIA. YOUR PARENTS WERE FROM THERE, RIGHT?

One of my parents. My mom was from California. She's from Orange County. My dad was from Vancouver.

HOW DID YOUR MOM END UP IN CANADA?

My mom went up with some of her friends who were dodging the draft in '70 or '69. She met my dad who was involved in this mass exodus, who went to Nelson.

NOW SLOW DOWN. A MASS EXODUS FROM WHERE?

From Vancouver, and from the cities on the West Coast mostly. Heading into the interior. A lot of draft dodgers went up into the interior too, because it was easier to get across the border, and they were into the small towns anyways. So Nelson was a hot spot.

WHERE IS NELSON?

In the Eastern interior of B.C. It's right above Spokane.

AND THE HIPPIES HEADING WEST FROM THE COAST AND THE DRAFT DODGERS HEADING NORTH CONVERGED?

Yeah. That's how my parents met. My dad, I believe he was teepee-sitting for some of his friends who were also my mom's friends. And my mom's records were stored at his teepee. And they got eaten by the dog that lived there. So that was it.

WERE THERE WORRIES ABOUT YOUR MOM GETTING DEPORTED?

No. I mean my mom was sent back a couple different times, taken from Nelson and sent back, but that was before I was born. At some point she got residency status as a legal alien.

YOU TOLD ME YOUR DAD MOVED TO THE LAND, BUT WASN'T A BACK-TO-THE-LANDER?

He knew there was a movement at the time, he said that everyone around him at the time was going "back to the land", or whatever. Everybody was doing it. But he felt that's what he'd been wanting to do his whole entire life. That it was an individual choice as well as a social movement that he was influenced by.

BUT HE WAS A FOLLOWER, OR A FAN, OF THE GUY WHO STARTED "THE FARM", RIGHT? HAD HE HEARD ABOUT IT, OR READ ABOUT IT, OR WHAT?

"The Farm" in Tennessee? He'd gone there at one point. He was influenced by the Farm, and by Stephen Gaskin, its founder.

DIDN'T YOUR DAD CHANGE HIS NAME?

Let me tell you, he was born Patrick Henry. Then he changed his name when he decided to go back to the land, he changed his name to Dharma. I grew up calling him Dharma until I was eight. Then he changed his name to Stephen, because of Stephen Gaskin, who was a huge influence to him. And he thought that that was also a very respectable name, instead of Dharma. So now he's Stephen Dharma Patrick Henry Cannon.

AND YOU ARE?

Jonah Laser Cannon.

SO WHAT WAS NELSON LIKE?

Where they moved it was very mountainous, just on the edge of the Rockies. Intense, rugged land. Everybody was selling their farms. All the real farmers were selling their farms.

BECAUSE?

Because, I don't know. Economics? They were all moving to the city or something.

DID YOUR PARENTS INTEND TO FARM THERE? HOW DID THEY INTEND TO EARN A LIVING?

I think he had an idea of going to be self-sufficient.

DID THAT HAPPEN?

They had a big garden, I don't know if they were self-sufficient. I don't think they were.

HOW DID THEY MAKE MONEY TO SURVIVE?

Well, part of it was that my parents bought a section of land with a group of other people. And my dad built a house there. And in order to build the house he also had to be doing construction and intensive labor jobs in nearby, sort of nearby, cities. And he would go away for a week or two at a time and come back for the weekends. And he worked on dams. Yeah, to save up money. And to pay for additions to the house.

HOW MANY PEOPLE DID THEY BUY THE LAND WITH?

I think actually the land had already been bought, and they bought into it. There was six or eight people. Four families, I guess.

WAS IT AN INTENTIONAL COMMUNITY OR WAS IT JUST SHARED LAND?

Just shared land.

IT DIDN'T HAVE A NAME OR ANYTHING?

It did. For a long time it was "Brillig". Then they changed the name at another point. Maybe it was an intentional community.

DID THE FAMILIES SHARE DUTIES, OR SHARE CHILD RAISING, OR SHARE MEALS? OR DID PEOPLE KEEP TO THEIR OWN?

People kept to their own, but they also had to share things as well. We had the waffle breakfast once a week where the parents would all hang out and discuss their beefs with the other people. And the kids would run amok and do kid things. I'm sure there was more to it than that, I just don't remember. I remember them having really long meetings, and hanging off my mom's arm waiting for them to be ready to go.

WHAT DO YOU THINK THE MEETINGS WERE ABOUT?

Well, some of the meetings that I remember were definitely when my parents were deciding to move, when they were deciding to leave the land. About them leaving and the other people moving onto the land. Or them selling out their share.

Meetings about who was planning to log what section of their land, and for what reason. Sharing the roto-tiller, that was always a really big deal, who got the roto-tiller. And animals. Actually, I went back to the land real recently, this last summer. That same land, it's for sale again, my parents' house that my dad built is for sale again, and I went back there for ridiculous reasons and...

YOU WERE GOING TO BUY IT?

No. Uh, I thought about it. But that wasn't the reason, really. I didn't know that it was for sale until I got there. And I found that the land that was at one point a relatively good working community had all these crazy electric fences and barbed wire. It was real weird. And I went to each family one at a time and sort of picked up on the shit about the other family, stuff that I was clueless about when I was younger, but was obviously there. When I went back this last time it was real funny because they were all shit-talking each other, and the people who were still there were just the same as they had been. I mean, they even look-ed the same as when I'd left.

WHAT WERE SOME OF THE PROBLEMS PEOPLE HAD WITH EACH OTHER?

Well, Maureen, the lady who bought the land from my parents, decided she wanted to make an old-age lesbian retreat with her allotted section of land, and she went ahead and logged a huge section of it, and put up a bunch of ramshackle shacks for the old-age lesbians to move into. And I think that definitely disturbed a few of the other folks.

WHY?

Because of lots more people being on the land, and they wanted new road access going through. The division of land, it was shared, but at the same time, each family had their allotted section. So for one person to sort of put their foot in someone else's pie, or whatever you would call it, that's going too far. And, the same thing with water. When people wanted to put a reservoir in one area. One family who had their reservoir here, the ones who are just putting one in fifty feet up, they get all the water. That kind of shit. They didn't have it together, really. I guess they weren't very communicative with each other. You know how a relationship can be weird? You'll never talk to the person you're in a relationship with, you'll go through other people. Maybe it was like that. Even at meetings, when you're supposed to spill your guts, it doesn't really happen because everybody's being real diplomatic.

WHEN YOU WENT BACK TO SEE THEM, THEY REMEMBER-ED YOU AND EVERYTHING?

Oh yeah, it was real funny. I bet they thought I was such a city folk. I'm sure they all were laughing at it, because I was so much different probably than what they would have figured. Because I ran into some of the kids who had also grown up, who were still on that land living with their parents, in their parents' houses. Very socially inept kids, for sure, very awkward to be around.

YOU WEREN'T ABLE TO SHARE YOUR DIFFERENT PERSPECTIVES?

It was too weird for that. It was nice to see them, but one of the kids just wanted to know if I'd brought mushrooms. Had I brought mushrooms from the city? Which is sort of weird. Over and over. Like, "What kind of drugs do you get there?" It was real weird.

NOW YOU WERE LOOKING TO GET LAND YOURSELF NOT SO LONG AGO, RIGHT?

M-hm.

AND WEREN'T YOU LOOKING TO GET A TEEPEE OR A YURT?

Man, you're pushing it. No.

YOU WERE TWENTY MILES OUTSIDE OF TOWN TEEPEE-SITTING WHEN YOU CAME HERE!

No, we yurt-sat. But it was not like that at all. That guy, he coerced us, and we even skipped one weekend. It's true, a yurt is nice, right? But I wouldn't want to live in a yurt. Or a teepee for that matter.

BUT WHEN YOU WERE LOOKING TO GET LAND YOURSELF?

I've had the thought in my mind for quite a while, but last summer is when I tried to pursue it. I went back to British Columbia, because it's where the water is fresh and the land is still for the taking. Still pretty cheap. And I was pretty sure that's what I wanted.

I wasn't looking to go in on land with other people, I was looking to get it myself. I ended up actually going with a few other people and it was really strange because there was a possibility that maybe we would go in on land together if we found just the right piece.

Originally it had been that I was going to get land of my own, and then through a series of letters back and forth with my friends, like me writing and saying, "I'm going to get land. I'm sick of waiting for other people, and I don't think I could cope anyways." And them writing me back, "Yeah, that sounds great! We feel the same way!"

The next thing you know, we were all going back together, and there was the possibility of them getting land with me. It turned out real strange because just going back to the area where I had grown up, and seeing places that I actually did like, and had a feeling for, a passion for, and then having the kids with me who were from other places, and having them discuss their ideas for what they thought would be perfect. I'm sure those things were great, but I just cringed a lot of times. Even though I love those people that I went back with. But some of the ideas were definitely not what I had in mind.

Another thing, I didn't have any close friends living in the area anymore. And I felt maybe in the same situation that my parents were in, where you might have a good communicative relationship with these people, but you're also desperate, right? So you're going to have to make some compromises. Which makes it rea_ weird automatically.

WELL, COMPROMISES CAN BE GOOD. THAT DOESN'T NECESSARILY MAKE IT WEIRD.

I guess. But if you think you have a vision, and somebody else has a vision that is roughly the same but differs in huge ways when it comes down to the nitty gritty, I can just see where it would go wrong if you were to get a piece of land with somebody else. Unless you were all incredibly patient people who were very close. And even then it seems sort of weird.

YOUR BROTHER HAS A LITTLE BIT DIFFERENT VIEW OF GROWING UP ON THE LAND, NO?

Yeah. He's very much bitter about it. He hates the whole thing, his whole childhood. He'd like to think he grew up in a bad, fucked-up way, but in actuality it was one of those, when you talk to kids who've actually had it real bad when growing up, it's one of those things they always think, "Oh, that sounds great!", you know.

My brother's real weird about it.

HE WOULD NEVER BE CAUGHT DEAD GETTING SOME LAND NOW.

No, no. We talked about it, actually. I visited him and he was like, What the fuck? What are you thinking? How could New York not be the place you wanted to spend every minute of the rest of your life in? And I understand it, a little, but not really. We definitely are opposites in a huge way.

I don't know what he thinks. He changed his name, he changed his last name, he doesn't ever talk about his family at all, as far as I know. For whatever reason, I don't know what it is. But he never thinks, at least he doesn't let on that he would ever think of any of that as being a good time. Growing up on a piece of land where you have family and you have a community around. He thinks of it differently. Yeah.

DO YOUR PARENTS LIVE IN VANCOUVER NOW?

No, they're back in Nelson, but only after a huge cycle of events. They've actually ended up back in Nelson twenty-some odd years after they originally moved there.

I'M CURIOUS ABOUT YOUR IDEA OF GETTING LAND COMPARED WITH THEIRS. WHY YOU WOULD WANT TO.

I don't know. I guess the reason why I was thinking of getting land was that I wanted something that would help me get a... something to focus on. Other than that, I thought that maybe the land would be the thing to help me find inspiration. And I don't think that's necessarily what my parents were doing. My main thing when I went back to look for land was that I didn't have any focus on anything except playing in a couple crappy improv bands, and I needed direction of some sort, and I thought maybe that would be it. And also, I like the country. And my parents went to the land because they thought that a simpler life was the way humans needed to live, and they wanted to walk everywhere and be simple folk.

IT'S EASIER TO WALK IN THE CITY.

Yeah, it is. It's true.

BUT I UNDERSTAND WHAT YOU MEAN.

So it's the same thing, but it's also different...

THE LAST CHAPTER OF THIS BOOK IS A CON-
GLOMERATION OF A HALF-DOZEN BOOKS THAT FOR
ONE REASON OR ANOTHER WERE NEVER RELEASED.
"ADD TONER", TOO, COMES FROM ONE OF THOSE ABORTED
PROJECTS, A COLLECTION OF MY XEROX-BASED
ARTWORK WHICH A FINE ARTS PRESS WAS SLATED
TO PUBLISH. THE TITLE DOESN'T ACCURATELY
REFLECT THE CONTENT OF THIS BOOK, SINCE COMETBUS

8 OUT OF 10 DAYS
stories
1993-97

(THESE STORIES ORIGINALLY APPEARED, IN SLIGHTLY
DIFFERENT FORM, IN COMETBUS 35, 37, 38, 41, AND 43)

HAS BEEN PRINTED OFFSET — NOT XEROXED — SINCE
1986, BUT I LIKED THE NAME TOO MUCH TO GIVE IT UP.
AFTER FINDING OUT THE PRESS WAS ONLY GOING TO
PRINT A HANDFUL OF COPIES, TO BE SOLD AT INFLATED
PRICES TO MUSEUMS AND COLLECTORS RATHER THAN
TO REGULAR READERS, I CALLED THE ORIGINAL "ADD
TONER" OFF. WHY HAVE SOMEONE ELSE PUT OUT AN
EXPENSIVE LIMITED EDITION WHEN I COULD MAKE A
CHEAP, MASS-PRODUCED VERSION MYSELF?
   THAT'S ONE OF THE PROBLEMS WITH D.I.Y.: ONCE YOU
FIGURE OUT HOW TO DO THINGS YOURSELF, YOU ASS-
UME OTHER PEOPLE KNOW HOW TO DO THEM, TOO — AND
PROBABLY A LOT BETTER THAN YOU. ESPECIALLY PEOPLE
WITH MORE MONEY, RESOURCES, AND "RESPECTABILITY"
THAN YOU.
   ALAS, IT IS NOT OFTEN THE CASE. THE PEOPLE
WITH MONEY AND RESOURCES TEND TO BE FLAKES.
THEY TREAT PEOPLE AND PROJECTS LIKE TOYS,
QUICKLY GROWING BORED AND CASTING THEM ASIDE.
   AND EVERYONE ELSE? EVERYONE ELSE USES GOOD
INTENTIONS AND LIMITED MEANS AS AN EXCUSE, EITHER
FOR A SHODDY RESULT, A PLAN THAT NEVER COMES TO
FRUITION, OR JUST AN OUTRIGHT RIP-OFF.
   BUT I HAVE WARNED MYSELF TO KEEP THESE
INTRODUCTIONS LIGHT AND BREEZY, AND TO STEER
CLEAR OF BITTERNESS. LIKE OTHER AILMENTS,
BITTERNESS IS INTERESTING ONLY TO ITS BEARER,

AND A BORE TO EVERYONE ELSE, WHICH IS WHY I'VE ALWAYS EDITED OUT THE DARKER, HARSHER SIDE OF MY WORK. AS A RESULT, I'VE KEPT MORE OF MY OWN BOOKS OFF THE SHELF THAN ALL OF THE INCOMPETENT PUBLISHERS COMBINED—A VERITABLE LIBRARY OF GRIPING, SNIPING, RECRIMINATIONS, AND BLAME. FUNNY, THOUGH: I ALWAYS WROTE AND RELEASED MY MOST UPBEAT MATERIAL DURING THE MOST TRYING PERIODS OF MY LIFE. ONLY WHEN THINGS WERE GOING WELL DID I ALLOW MYSELF TO COMPLAIN.

SOMEDAY ALL THAT LEFTOVER NEGATIVITY WILL HAVE TO FIND A RELEASE. BUT WHY START NOW, ON SUCH A SUNNY DAY? THE TRUTH IS, IT'S 4 A.M. IN THE MIDDLE OF A BRUTAL BLIZZARD, AND NO ONE'S SEEN THE SUN IN A WEEK—BUT THAT, TOO, IS BESIDE THE POINT, WHICH IS ALL THE VARIOUS PROJECTS THAT NEVER SAW RELEASE, WHICH NOW PROVIDE THE TITLE OF THIS BOOK AS WELL AS ITS CLOSING CHAPTER.

THE SAGA BEGINS IN 1997, WHEN TWO DIFFERENT MAJOR PUBLISHERS EXPRESSED INTEREST IN MY WORK. I HEADED EAST WITH MY HEAD FULL OF LOFTY DREAMS. GREENHORN THAT I WAS, I WASTED THEIR EXPENSE ACCOUNT DINNERS ON LUKEWARM BORSCHT.

THE NEXT YEAR WAS SPENT WORKING WITH EDITORS FROM THE RIVAL HOUSES. MY PLAN WAS TO PIT THEM AGAINST EACH OTHER, MEANWHILE DANG-LING THE MAJOR PUBLISHER INTEREST IN THE FACE OF A LARGE INDEPENDENT PRESS I PREFERRED, WHO HAD PREVIOUSLY TURNED ME DOWN. HOPEFULLY A LITTLE JEALOUSY WOULD MAKE THEM CHANGE THEIR MIND.

I SHOULD HAVE KNOWN BETTER, HAVING TRIED THE SAME TRICK NUMEROUS TIMES WITH ROMANTIC INTERESTS, ALWAYS WITH DISMAL AND DISASTROUS RESULTS. WITH THE BIG PUBLISHERS, I ENDED UP REJECTING ONE SUITOR ONLY TO GET DUMPED BY THE OTHER, AND IF THE INDEPENDENT I HAD MY EYE ON EVER NOTICED I WAS ALIVE, IT WAS ONLY TO LAUGH AT MY DISGRACE.

I ICED MY BRUISED EGO AND ACCEPTED OFFERS FROM TWO START-UP PRESSES, BOTH FOUNDED BY INDEPENDENT BOOKSTORES I LIKED. ANOTHER TWO YEARS PASSED SPENT WORKING AND WAITING, AND BOTH PROJECTS CAME TO NAUGHT. NEITHER PRESS HAD A SINGLE RELEASE.

MEANWHILE, I HAD BEEN DOWN ON THE LOADING DOCK AT LAST GASP, MAKING A RUCKUS EVERY TIME I DROPPED A NEW ISSUE OFF. LAST GASP HAD REFUSED TO CARRY COMETBUS FOR

YEARS, BUT I WAS PERSISTENT. FINALLY THEY RELENTED AND WERE SOON SELLING THEM BY THE CASELOAD. IT WAS ONLY A MATTER OF TIME BEFORE LAST GASP'S HEAD HONCHO, RON, STUCK HIS HEAD OUT THE WINDOW TO SEE WHAT ALL THE NOISE WAS ABOUT. WHEN HE DID, I YELLED UP, "JUST DROPPING OFF ANOTHER THOUSAND COPIES OF COMETBUS. WHEN ARE YOU GONNA DO MY BOOK?"

AFTER A BIT MORE YELLING BACK AND FORTH, LAST GASP AGREED TO RELEASE "DESPITE EVERY-THING," THE FIRST COMETBUS ANTHOLOGY. I CUT OUT TWO-THIRDS OF THE POSSIBLE MATERIAL, BUT THERE WAS STILL 800 PAGES LEFT—TOO MUCH FOR ONE VOLUME. AND SO, I MADE THREE OTHER PILES. ONE BECAME THE BOOK VERSION OF "DOUBLE DUCE," THE OTHER, "CHICAGO STORIES." THE LAST PILE WAS A SHORT STORY COLLECTION, "8 OUT OF 10 DAYS," FOR WHICH I SET ASIDE SOME OF MY FAVORITE PIECES. IN MAKE-UP IT WAS NOT MUCH DIFFERENT FROM THE MANUSCRIPT I'D ALREADY TRIED TO GET PUB-LISHED TOO MANY TIMES.

"8 OUT OF 10 DAYS" NEVER DID SEE A U.S. RELEASE. IT WAS PUT OUT IN THE U.K., BUT THE ENGLISH PUBLISHER ALTERED THE ARTWORK IN SUCH AN AWFUL WAY THAT I STILL CAN'T BEAR TO LOOK AT THE RESULT. THANKFULLY, THAT EDITION SOON WENT OUT OF PRINT. THE STORIES WERE TRANSLATED INTO FRENCH AND RELEASED UNDER THE NAME "INSTANTANES," AND LATER BY A DIFFERENT PRESS AS "DEVIATIONS." THEY WERE TRANSLATED INTO GERMAN AS WELL, BUT THAT BOOK—LIKE THE CHINESE VERSION OF "DOUBLE DUCE" AND THE SWEDISH VERSION OF SOME EARLIER STORIES—NEVER CAME TO PASS. SO MUCH FOR MY FANTASIES OF ATTAINING A SUCCESSFUL SECOND CAREER OVERSEAS, LIKE THE OBSCURE BAY AREA METAL BANDS I GREW UP WITH.

ONE LAST NOTE: EVEN "LANKY" WASN'T ORIGINALLY INTENDED TO BE AN ISSUE OF COMETBUS. IT WAS SUPPOSED TO APPEAR IN WEEKLY INSTALLMENTS IN A FREE BERKELEY PAPER. WHEN THEY PRINTED THE FIRST SIX CHAPTERS ALL AT ONCE—A MONTH'S WORTH OF WORK—I WAS CRESTFALLEN. THE STEAM I'D BUILT UP WAS COMPLETELY DISPERSED, AND I SHELVED THE WHOLE PROJECT FOR A YEAR BEFORE DECIDING TO FINISH IT AND PUT IT OUT MYSELF.

WHAT IS THE MORAL OF ALL THIS? LUCKILY, THERE IS NONE. SUFFICE TO SAY THAT I'M GRATE-FUL TO LAST GASP FOR BEING THE EXCEPTION TO THE RULE AS FAR AS PUBLISHERS GO, AND FOR GIVING THESE OLD STORIES A SECOND CHANCE.

On the Avenue

SOME DAYS, WHEN I'M FEELING OPTOMISTIC, I SMILE UPON
ALL THE LITTLE SCUMBAGS ON TELEGRAPH. ALL THE GRUMBLY
PUNKS AND SURLY HOODS AND UNFRIENDLY PHONY HIPPIES.
I THINK OF THEM AS PLANTS GROWING OUT OF THE CRACKS IN
THE SIDEWALK. BEGGING FOR WATER, SOAKING UP SUNLIGHT,
LIVING AND DYING RIGHT THERE ON THE STREET. SOME ARE
PERENNIALS, COMING BACK YEAR AFTER YEAR. SOME ARE
UGLY WEEDS THAT WILL NEVER GO AWAY. SOME ARE BEAUT-
IFUL SPRING FLOWERS, IN AN ASSORTMENT OF BRIGHT COLORS,
THAT FILL YOUR HEART WITH DUMB, SIMPLE HOPE. IT
REMINDS ME OF HOW AGING LOCALS USED TO SNEER AT
EACH NEW BATCH OF STREET KIDS, CALLING THEM
"TRANSPLANTS". HOW FITTING.

SOME DAYS, WHEN I'M NOT FEELING SO CHARITABLE, I LOOK
AT THE STREET SCENE FOR WHAT IT REALLY IS: A BUNCH OF
STUPID ASSHOLES WHO WON'T EVEN GIVE ME THE TIME OF
DAY OR THE BENEFIT OF DOUBT. I LOOK AT THE PEOPLE
STANDING RIGHT IN THE MIDDLE OF THE SIDEWALK, BLOCKING
MY WAY, AND I REALIZE THEY AREN'T JUST INNOCENTLY
AND ABSENT-MINDEDLY LOITERING. THEY ARE QUITE PURPOSELY
PULLING A POWER TRIP SO I'LL HAVE TO SAY "EXCUSE ME" OR
WALK AROUND THEM INTO THE STREET. DAYS LIKE THIS I'M
CLOSE TO HAULING OFF AND HITTING SOMEONE. DAYS LIKE
THIS I START YELLING AT PEOPLE WHEN THEY DON'T SAY
HELLO BACK TO ME. IT'S A LITTLE EXTREME BUT THAT SORT
OF THING CAN RUIN YOUR AFTERNOON. WE HAVE A LOT OF DAYS
IN OUR LIFETIME, BUT NOT ENOUGH TO WASTE ON ASSHOLES.

EVERY SPRING BRINGS A NEW BATCH OF THESE SEEDLINGS
TO THE AVENUE TO TRY TO TAKE TO OUR RICH SOIL. A TIME-
HONORED TRADITION, PREDICTABLE AS HICKEYS AND NEW
AWKWARD COUPLES EVERY SUNDAY MORNING AT THE ASHBY
FLEA MARKET. A LITTLE GARDEN OF FRESH SCUMBAGS
EVERY YEAR CROPPING UP THROUGH THE CRACKS, GETTING IN
MY WAY WHILE I TRY TO WALK TO MY P.O. BOX.

WHAT CAN I DO? I GET JADED FROM SEEING NEW PEOPLE
SHOW UP HOPEFUL AND LEAVE JADED. I GET TIRED OF
FINALLY GETTING TO KNOW EACH NEW BATCH OF SCUMBAGS
AND FINDING OUT THEY'RE A LOT NICER AND MORE
INTERESTING THAN THEY APPEARED, ONLY TO HAVE THEM
DISAPPEAR AND BE REPLACED BY A NEW BATCH WHO
LOOK AND ACT JUST AS SNOTTY.

I CAN'T IMAGINE WHAT BERKELEY MUST LOOK LIKE TO
THEM, OR ANYONE COMING HERE FOR THE FIRST TIME.
SOME DAYS I LOOK AROUND AND REALIZE HOW DIFFERENT

IT ACTUALLY LOOKS FROM THE WAY I PICTURE IT IN MY HEAD, MY IDEALIZED VERSION LOOSELY BASED ON A MEMORY FROM TEN OR TWENTY YEARS AGO. I DON'T EVEN SEE ALL THE NEON OR NEW BUILDINGS UNLESS I SQUINT MY EYES. I WONDER HOW IT MUST LOOK TO PEOPLE 25 OR 50 YEARS OLDER, IF THEY STILL SEE GHOSTS OF DAYS MUCH LONGER GONE. I WONDER IF I CAN SEE THE REAL BERKELEY OR IF MY MIND'S EYE IS KEEPING ME FROM SEEING WHAT IT'S REALLY BECOME. I'M JEALOUS OF THOSE WHO COME HERE NOW AND CAN SEE IT FOR THE FIRST TIME, WITH A NEW CHANCE AND A FRESH START. IT'S JUST TOO BAD THAT HALF THE TIME THEY COME HERE BECAUSE THEY DON'T HAVE THE GUTS TO RIOT, OR TO CREATE SOMETHING WORTHWHILE, IN THEIR OWN HOMETOWN.

REALLY, I CAN'T IMAGINE WHAT IT MUST BE LIKE TO COME TO BERKELEY AT ALL. ALL I KNOW IS TRYING TO ESCAPE IT BUT BEING DRAWN BACK EVERY TIME. MY FAMILY AND THE HOUSE WHERE I GREW UP ARE HERE. IT'S MY HOMETOWN. YOU KNOW HOW YOU CAN LAUGH AT AND COMPLAIN ABOUT YOUR FAMILY AND FRIENDS BUT IF ANYONE ELSE DOES YOU WILL LEAP TO THEIR DEFENSE? IT'S THE SAME WAY FOR ME WITH BERKELEY, AND I CONSTANTLY FEEL LIKE I HAVE TO DEFEND IT. PEOPLE MOVE HERE WITH ALL SORTS OF GRANDIOSE GOALS AND THEN, WHEN MIRACLES DON'T HAPPEN, THEY BLAME BERKELEY INSTEAD OF LOOKING AT THEIR OWN SHORTCOMINGS. PEOPLE DO THAT SAME THING WITH PUNK, SO BITTER THAT IT DIDN'T LIVE UP TO THEIR EXPECTATIONS. THEIR EXPECTATIONS. I HATE THAT.

I'D LOVE TO BE ABLE TO JUST COMPLAIN AND TALK SHIT ABOUT BERKELEY. BUT I NEVER GET THE CHANCE BECAUSE SOMEONE IS ALWAYS BEATING ME TO THE PUNCH. I DON'T EVEN CARE IF THEY DON'T LIKE IT HERE, BUT I HATE TO HEAR BERKELEY SO MISUNDERSTOOD. LIKE THIS GIRL I HAD A BIG CRUSH ON ONCE, SHE WAS MY DREAM COME TRUE, EVERYTHING I COULD EVER ASK FOR AND MORE. BUT THEN IN THE MORNING SHE WHISPERED IN MY EAR: "I DON'T LIKE BERKELEY, IT'S SO FAKE".

OKAY, SHE DIDN'T WHISPER IT IN MY EAR. SHE SAID IT OVER BREAKFAST AT THE PATIO OF CAFE DURANT, OVERLOOKING THE AVENUE. MY JAW DROPPED IN SHOCK, AND ALL THE LITTLE BIRDS SEIZED THE OPPORTUNITY TO FLY OVER AND NIBBLE AT MY HOMEFRIES. YOU JUST CAN'T EAT A MEAL ANYWHERE NEAR TELEGRAPH WITHOUT SOMEBODY TRYING TO GET A BITE. IT WAS SAD TO LOSE A GIRL I WAS IN LOVE WITH OVER A CITY I HAVE MIXED FEELINGS ABOUT, BUT WHAT COULD I DO? SHE MIGHT AS WELL HAVE CALLED ME FAKE. I'M A COMPLICATED GUY, WITH CONFLICTING IDEAS AND EMOTIONS AND DESIRES, AND WHAT I THINK I WANT IS NOT ALWAYS WHAT I REALLY WANT. BUT BERKELEY ISN'T FAKE.

a day at the Lake

THIS IS THE PICTURE I PICTURE IN MY MIND WHEN I'M FAR AWAY AND MISSING HOME: THE SIMPLE AND SUNNY DAY OUT STROLLING AROUND LAKE MERRITT WITH EVERY DIFFERENT KIND OF PERSON IN THE WORLD JOINING ME FOR A DAY AT THE LAKE. LIKE THOSE JEHOVAH'S WITNESS PAMPHLETS WHERE THE FAMILY OF MAN IS GATHERED TOGETHER IN HEAVEN FOR A PICNIC, EXCEPT IN MY VERSION WE'RE ALL GATHERED IN OAKLAND AROUND THREE SQUARE MILES OF TOXIC WASTE, AND THERE'S NO PANDAS IN SIGHT.

IT SEEMS TOO COOL TO BE REAL, LIKE AN EQUAL OPPORTUNITY EMPLOYER COMMERCIAL — ALL OF US TOGETHER, INTERACTING SUBTLY WHILE RETAINING OUR INDIVIDUAL CULTURE AND GLORY. BUT IT IS REAL, AND IN IT'S FUNKY OAKLAND WAY, IT IS BEAUTIFUL. OTHER PLACES HAVE THEIR SPECIAL QUALITIES BUT NOWHERE I'VE FOUND HAS THE DIVERSITY AND THE PARTICULAR SPIRIT OF THE BAY AREA, AND NOWHERE IS IT SO LOUD AND IN BLOOM AS A SUMMER DAY AT THE LAKE.

THERE'S MUSIC AND MOVEMENT EVERYWHERE, LIKE SOME BIG, WILD, CHOREOGRAPHED DANCE. WINOS SIT ON THE BENCHES WITH LITTLE RASPY RADIOS PLAYING KFRC WHILE JOGGERS LOOP AROUND THE PATHS PANTING IN RHYTHM. A BIG GUY SITS IN THE SHADE OF A TREE PLAYING CONGAS ALONG WITH A BOOMBOX BLASTING OPERA MUSIC. NEARBY, AGING HIPPIES DO THEIR CREEPY TAI-CHI AND VIETNAMESE YOUNGSTERS PLAY SOMETHING LIKE VOLLEYBALL, USING FEET INSTEAD OF HANDS AND JUMPING IMPOSSIBLY HIGH. PEOPLE STRUT AND PROMENADE TO AN IMAGINARY BEAT AND WALK BY SINGING SONGS ACCOMPANIED BY AN IMAGINARY BAND. SOME JUST CARRY ON A HEATED ARGUMENT WITH AN IMAGINARY FRIEND.

CHILDREN PLAY IN FAIRYLAND, AN ACID CASUALTY'S VISION OF A CHILDHOOD NIGHTMARE. THE TYKES HAPPILY CRAWL THROUGH TUNNELS FILLED ANKLE DEEP WITH PISS AND PUKE FROM OLDER REVELERS OF THE NIGHT BEFORE. AFTER ALL, THIS IS OAKLAND, NOT DISNEYLAND. GEESE AT THE DUCKPOND CHASE DOWN BIRDFEEDERS AND DEMAND THEIR FOOD UP FRONT, IN ONE LUMP SUM. OCCASIONALLY, A HUGE GRUMPY STORK COMES AND SITS DOWN ON THE BENCHES WITH THE LITTLE GRUMPY OLD WOMEN AND THEY EYE EACH OTHER WITH STUDIED INDIFFERENCE. FAMILIES STAND AND STARE INTO THE RARE BIRD CAGE WHERE THE ONLY BIRDS LEFT ARE A FEW STRAY PIGEONS. I EXPLAIN THAT THESE ARE VERY SPECIAL PIGEONS, GATHERED FROM ALL CORNERS OF THE WORLD. THE ADULTS NOD KNOWINGLY AND TURN TO EXPLAIN THIS TO

THE CHILDREN WHO LOOK AT ME AND SHAKE THEIR HEADS.

THE OLD LAKE MERRITT BANDSHELL, WHERE OAKLAND PUNK LEGENDS KWIKWAY AND THE SPEED QUEENS ONCE PLAYED, IS NOW ROPED OFF — CLOSED FOR SEISMIC RETROFITTING, PERHAPS PERMANENTLY. BUT NEARBY, IN THE OPEN FIELD, AN OLD TIME ORCHESTRA IS PLAYING. THE MUSICIANS AND THEIR CROWD ARE ALL OVER SIXTY AND WITHERING AWAY IN THE UNUSUALLY BLAZING HEAT. I SIT AT A DISTANCE WATCHING THE GUY PLAY THE HUGE KETTLE DRUMS, FEELING IT IN MY GUT EACH TIME THEY THUNDER OUT THEIR OMINOUS, YET REASSURING, SOUND OF DOOM. WATCHING THE OLD COUPLES AND THE WAY THEY LOOK AT EACH OTHER AND DANCE TOGETHER; THINKING HOW THERE IS NOTHING SWEETER IN THE WHOLE WORLD, AND THINKING ABOUT MY GIRL.

THE BAND GETS TUCKERED OUT FROM PLAYING IN THE HEAT AND DECIDES TO TAKE A LITTLE BREAK, JOINING THEIR FAMILY AND FRIENDS SPRAWLED OUT IN THE SHADE. I READ MY BOOK WHILE HALF-LISTENING TO THE BANDLEADER ENTERTAIN THE CROWD: OLD PEOPLE JOKES AND LITTLE STORIES OF GROWING UP IN OAKLAND MANY YEARS AGO ON HIS DAD'S FARM. THE WAY YOU COULD TELL HOW HOT IT WAS BY LOOKING OUT THE WINDOW AT THE CHICKENS. ON A DAY LIKE THIS, HE SAYS, THEY WOULD GO OUT AND HOSE DOWN THE CHICKENS.

THE CROWD SIGHS, WANTING TO BE HOSED DOWN THEMSELVES. NOT ME, THOUGH. I'M HAPPY TO STAY HIGH AND DRY. I DON'T EVEN WANT TO COME CLOSE TO THE WATER TODAY FOR FEAR IT MIGHT JUMP ME AND PULL ME IN, AS IT DID TWO WEEKS AGO WHEN ME, JED, AND LITTLE SUICIDE RENTED A CANOE. WE HAD TO BE RESCUED BY A LIFEGUARD IN A SPEEDBOAT AND PICKED OUT FROM AMONG THE DEAD BODIES, BROKEN BOTTLES, AND DIRTY NEEDLES. NOW I KNOW: THE LAKE RESEMBLES OUR HOUSE. THAT'S WHY I'M CAREFUL TO KEEP A SAFE DISTANCE FROM BOTH.

she

SHE KISSES WITH HER MOUTH OPEN. SHE DOESN'T WEAR UNDERWEAR. ON YOUR FIRST DATE TOGETHER YOU BOTH GET SCARS. ON YOUR SECOND DATE, YOU MAKE OUT AT THE LAKE. ON YOUR THIRD DATE WHEN SHE SAYS IT'S NOT NORMALLY LIKE THIS, IT'S A COMPLIMENT. BUT THINGS ARE AWKWARD AFTER THAT, SO YOU GIVE HER A CHANCE TO DUMP YOU NICELY. YOU ASK IF SHE WANTS YOU TO STOP CHASING HER. TO YOUR SURPRISE, SHE SAYS NO. YOU PICK ORANGES TO

GIVE HER ON THE FOURTH DATE BUT THEY TURN GREEN WAITING FOR HER TO CALL.

SHE IS THE BEST THING THAT'S HAPPENED ALL YEAR. SHE GETS YOU DRUNK IN HER BED AND YOU ARE IN HEAVEN. WHEN YOU'VE GOT YOUR HEADS PRESSED TOGETHER, SHE DOESN'T LOOK LIKE A BLURRY ONE-EYED MONSTER LIKE EVERYONE ELSE DOES THAT CLOSE. YOU BLINK AND SHE DOESN'T SUDDENLY APPEAR TO BE YOUR TENTH GRADE ENGLISH TEACHER OR YOUR SISTER OR YOUR WORST NIGHTMARE, LIKE EVERYONE ELSE. YOU BLINK AND SHE LOOKS LIKE A MOVIE STAR. YOU BLINK AND SHE LOOKS LIKE YOUR SECRET CRUSH. YOU BLINK AND SHE LOOKS LIKE AN OLD FRIEND, THEN LIKE A RAD GIRL YOU SAW ONLY ONCE YEARS BEFORE. SHE LOOKS LIKE EVERYONE YOU'VE EVER WANTED TO BE IN BED WITH, AND IT'S GETTING WEIRD, AND YOU CAN'T EXPLAIN WHY YOU KEEP BLINKING AND STARING AT HER. SHE FALLS ASLEEP BEFORE YOU AND SHE IS SO FUCKING BEAUTIFUL SLEEPING, SHE IS RADIANT. SHE IS DIFFERENT IN THE MORNING, THOUGH. SHE HAS CHANGED HER MIND AND YOU HAVE TO FIND ANOTHER PLACE TO STAY. YOU HAVE FAILED HER TEST. SHE ADDS INSULT TO INJURY BY TRYING TO SET YOU UP WITH HER FRIEND. SHE MAKES PLANS TO SEE YOU THE NIGHT BEFORE YOU LEAVE ON A LONG TRIP. SHE DOESN'T SHOW UP AND DOESN'T CALL. YOU REMEMBER WHEN SHE SAID SHE WAS FROM HELL AND WOULD RUIN YOUR LIFE, AND YOU'D THOUGHT IT WAS A JOKE.

SHE CAPTURES YOUR ATTENTION AND THEN YOUR IMAGINATION AND THEN YOUR HEART. SHE TELLS YOU ABOUT LIVING IN THE BUS STATION WHEN SHE WAS FOURTEEN. SHE TELLS YOU ABOUT DOING SO MANY DIFFERENT THINGS IN SO MANY DIFFERENT PLACES THAT SHE'S EITHER 40 YEARS OLD OR ONE HELL OF A LIAR. SHE IS ONLY 23. SHE LIVES IN A CLOSET. DOWN ON THE WATERFRONT, SHE TEACHES YOU HOW TO USE OIL PAINTS, THE DARK COLORS FIRST. SHE DIGS THE VEGETABLES OUT OF THE DUMPSTER AND TOSSES THEM OVER THE FENCE TO YOU. SHE FINDS CLOTHES BUT THEY'RE TOO NEW AND UNCOMFORTABLE, SO YOU BOTH PUT THEM ON AND GO DRAGGING EACH OTHER AROUND TOWN, THROWING EACH OTHER IN PUDDLES, WRESTLING EACH OTHER IN THE DIRT; THEN THE CLOTHES ARE FIVE SIZES BIGGER AND WORN IN JUST RIGHT. SHE STARTS HANGING OUT WITH YOUR WORST ENEMY, BUT SAYS IT'S NOT LIKE THAT. THREE DAYS LATER IT IS, AND SHE SAYS IT'S YOUR FAULT. SHE LEAVES ON AN AIRPLANE WITH YOUR WORST ENEMY. IT WOULD BE NICE TO BE HOME WITH BOTH OF THEM OUT OF YOUR WAY, BUT YOU'RE ALSO LEAVING THAT DAY, FIVE HOURS LATER, ON AN AIRPLANE HEADING THE SAME DIRECTION. ON THE AIRPLANE RADIO, HER SONG COMES ON.

SHE IS THE LAST GIRL IN THE WORLD YOU SHOULD EVER

FALL IN LOVE WITH, BUT IT'S TOO LATE. SHE TELLS YOU SHE LOVES YOU, THEN IN THE MORNING SAYS SHE WAS ON DRUGS AND DIDN'T MEAN IT. SHE TAKES THE PRESENTS YOU GIVE HER AND GIVES THEM TO OTHER GIRLS WHO SHE SAYS LIKE YOU MORE. SHE TAKES THE LIST OF YOUR WORST FEARS AND USES IT AS A CHECKLIST, MAKING THEM HAPPEN ONE BY ONE. YOU LOSE, AND THEN YOU LOSE HER TOO, AND LOSING HER FEELS LIKE HAVING EVERY GIRL IN THE WORLD AND THEN LOSING THEM ALL. SHE BRINGS YOU TO LIFE AND THEN BRINGS YOU TO DEATH. SHE SAYS THAT AS LONG AS YOU LOVE HER AND SHE LOVES YOU, ALL THE SHIT THAT'S HAPPENED DOESN'T REALLY MATTER. UNFORTUNATELY, IT DOES MATTER TO YOU.

eyes

MAYBE IT'S JUST COINCIDENCE THAT HE REMINDS ME OF HER. THE WAY HE SWAYS BACK AND FORTH DRUNK, EYES CLOSED AND ROLLING BACK IN HIS HEAD, ALMOST FALLING OVER, QUIVERING WITH EMOTION. THE WAY HIS WHOLE BODY LEANS INTO HIS MOUTH, PUSHING ALL OF ITS WEIGHT AND FORCE INTO HIS LIPS. WE'RE MAKING MUSIC TOGETHER, SCREAMING AND BANGING AWAY FURIOUSLY. IT'S SOMETHING COMPLETELY DIFFERENT THAN WITH HER BUT THERE'S THOSE SAME FEELINGS OF ANGER AND HOPE, PASSION AND FRUSTRATION. WITH HIM I PLAY DRUMS WHILE HE SINGS AND PLAYS GUITAR. WITH HER IT'S MORE COMPLICATED. WE TAKE TURNS PLAYING DIFFERENT ROLES.

SHE LOOKS AT ME, WONDERING WHY I LOOK SO HAPPY. LIKE THERE MUST BE A SECRET REASON, OR LIKE I'M STUPID TO BE SO HAPPY AND NOT REALIZE SHE ISN'T. SHE LOOKS AT ME LIKE IT WILL NEVER WORK OUT BETWEEN US, OR LIKE WE WILL ALWAYS BE TOGETHER. I CAN'T TELL. I LOOK INTO HER EYES FOR AN ANSWER BUT JUST SEE MORE QUESTIONS.

ALL I SEE IS THAT NO MATTER HOW MUCH WE STARE INTO EACH OTHERS EYES, NO MATTER HOW CLOSE WE PULL OURSELVES, NO MATTER HOW MUCH TIME WE SPEND TOGETHER, WE WILL NEVER REALLY KNOW EACH OTHER. WHEN I LOOK IN HER EYES I CAN FEEL SOME OF THE THINGS SHE HAS SEEN, SOME OF THE PLACES SHE HAS BEEN. BUT I CAN NEVER REALLY SEE OR UNDERSTAND THEM. THAT'S WHY I'M HAPPY, BECAUSE SHE WILL ALWAYS BE A MYSTERY TO ME.

SHE CLOSES HER EYES. I CLOSE MY EYES AND CAN FEEL HER LOOKING AT ME. SHE THINKS I AM OBSESSED WITH

HER EYES, ALWAYS STARING AT THEM, BUT REALLY I'M LOOKING RIGHT THROUGH THEM INTO SOMETHING ELSE. I DON'T EVEN KNOW WHAT COLOR THEY ARE. IT'S THE SAME WITH HIM BECAUSE HIS EYES ARE ALWAYS CLOSED. HE GETS THE NOTES ALL WRONG AND KNOCKS OVER MY BEER. THE WAY SHE LOOKS AT ME LIKE SHE DOESN'T KNOW ME, THE WAY HE KEEPS HIS EYES CLOSED LIKE I'M NOT EVEN THERE. YET WE PLAY SO TIGHT TOGETHER, NEVER MISSING A BEAT.

me and my stubborn Pride

SHE SAYS SHE HAD A DREAM ABOUT ME LAST NIGHT. SHE WAS TALKING TO ME, TELLING ME HOW HANDSOME SHE THINKS I AM, AND OTHER MUSHY STUFF. WHEN SHE WOKE UP SHE WAS IN BED NEXT TO SOMEONE. AT FIRST SHE WAS HAPPY BECAUSE SHE THOUGHT IT WAS A GIRL. THEN SHE REALIZED IT WAS HER BOYFRIEND.

SHE CALLS ME IN THE LATE AFTERNOON AND WAKES ME UP TO GO OUT DRINKING. I BRING HER TO THE LUSH GREEN HIDDEN VALLEY, THE BEST DRINKING SPOT EVER. IT WAS THE SECRET SPOT I HAD FOUND AND WAS SAVING FOR THE PERFECT PERSON AND THE PERFECT TIME. IT WAS SUCH A PERFECT PLACE THAT IT MADE ME TERRIBLY SAD, BECAUSE I KNEW THAT THE PERFECT PERSON AND TIME WOULD PROBABLY NEVER COME. THEN SHE SHOWED UP.

I AM SO HAPPY TO HAVE SOMEONE TO BRING TO THE PERFECT SPOTS AND TO SMASH BOTTLES WITH AND TO HIDE WITH IN A STINKY DUMPSTER WHEN PEOPLE START YELLING AT US FOR SMASHING BOTTLES. WE SNEAK THROUGH THE GRAVEYARD AND UNDER FENCES AND ONTO A ROOFTOP WHERE YOU CAN SEE ALL THE LIGHTS GOING ON AND OFF IN THE DOWNTOWN WINDOWS AS THE NIGHT JANITORS DO THEIR WORK. WE SNEAK INTO AN OFFICE BUILDING AND UP TO THE ELEVENTH FLOOR EXECUTIVE MEETING ROOM WHICH IS A GREAT PLACE TO VIEW THE CITY, ALSO A GREAT PLACE TO WRESTLE AND ROLL AROUND. WE ARE SNEAKY AND I AM HAPPY.

I AM FALLING FOR HER IN A BIG WAY. MEANWHILE, SHE GOES OFF TO L.A. FOR THE WEEKEND TO DO HEROIN. I HATE IT WHEN THAT HAPPENS. I'M LEFT TO THINK ABOUT HER AND CREATE SILLY FANTASIES. SHE'S GONE LONG ENOUGH FOR US TO HAVE A WONDERFUL COURTSHIP, A TORRID ROMANCE, AND A SAD, SWEET

BREAK-UP, ALL IN MY MIND. MY FANTASIES GET SO LOFTY THAT I BECOME TERRIBLY DEPRESSED KNOWING THAT THEY'LL NEVER HAPPEN. SHE RETURNS AND FINDS ME MISERABLE, AND HAS NO IDEA WHY. I TRY TO EXPLAIN BUT OF COURSE IT DOESN'T MAKE ANY SENSE. FINALLY I GIVE UP EXPLAINING AND SETTLE FOR JUST MAKING HER AS CONFUSED AS I AM. I TELL HER I'M IN LOVE WITH HER BOYFRIEND.

SHE TELLS ME ABOUT HER WEEKEND AND THE DRINKING AND FIGHTING AND TRAVELING AND PILLS AND SCARS. SOON ALL HER SCARS WILL CONNECT AND SHE WILL BE ONE BIG SCAR. ONE BIG SCAR, WALKING WITH ME, TRADING OFF GIVING EACH OTHER PIGGYBACK RIDES. I MAKE THE MISTAKE OF LOOKING OUT MY WINDOW AND SEEING HER WALK IN MY GATE AND UP THE STEPS. AFTER THAT I CAN'T LOOK OUT THE WINDOW WITHOUT HOPING TO SEE HER WALKING THROUGH THE GATE AGAIN. WHEN SHE DOES SHOW BACK UP, THE STRAY CAT WALKS OUT THE DOOR AND NEVER RETURNS. IT'S A GOOD TRADE-OFF BECAUSE THE CAT WAS ANNOYING AS HELL AND ALWAYS TOOK A SHIT IN THE KITCHEN RIGHT WHEN YOU SAT DOWN TO EAT.

WE MEET IN THE PARK OR AT THE CHURCH OR IN THE BAR. I HAVE TO DRAG HER OUT OF THE BAR OFTEN TO GO DRINK AT REAL DRINKING SPOTS. ONE NIGHT RIDING DOUBLE ON THE WAY TO THE TRACKS, WE GET CAUGHT IN THE MIDDLE OF A HUGE RAINSTORM. WE SIT SOAKING WET AT THE TRAIN TRACKS, TRYING TO KEEP WARM WHILE SINGING OUR THEME SONGS. SHE ASKS ME A SCARY QUESTION AND I SING MY THEME SONG, "YOU DON'T HAVE TO LIE BUT YOU DON'T HAVE TO TELL THE WHOLE TRUTH." SHE SINGS HER THEME SONG, "I NEED ANOTHER BEER." THEN WE BOTH SING ONE OF OUR FAVORITES, "HALF-ASSED IS AS CLOSE AS WE COME TO DOING ANYTHING IN THIS LIFE." WE DON'T HAVE VERSES YET OR EVEN TUNES, BUT STILL YOU CAN TELL THAT THOSE ARE OUR ANTHEMS.

I DREAM ABOUT HER A LOT: FINDING HER JACKET IN AN ALLEY; HANGING OUT WITH HER IN OTHER CITIES; COLLECTING NEAT THINGS TO PUT IN A BOOK TO GIVE TO HER. ONE NIGHT I DREAM ABOUT HAVING A DATE WITH HER WHERE SHE DRAGS ME TO THE WORST PLACE IN THE ENTIRE WORLD, BUT SOMEHOW WITH HER THERE IT'S NOT SO BAD. THE NEXT NIGHT THE DREAM COMES TRUE, AND SHE DRAGS ME TO THE WORST PLACE IN THE ENTIRE WORLD. SHE SAYS THAT WITH HER ON MY ARM WE CAN GO TO HELL AND IT WILL BE OKAY. SHE IS RIGHT. AFTER STOPPING BY HELL, WE WALK DOWN THE ALLEY ARM IN ARM. WE GO TO HER FAVORITE ROOF SPOT, BUT ON THE WAY BACK DOWN THE FIRE ESCAPE, SOMEONE YELLS, "WHO THE FUCK IS ON THE ROOF?", CHARGES OUT THE FIRE ESCAPE DOOR, AND IS ABOUT

TO HIT US WITH A METAL PIPE. THEN HE REALIZES
THAT HE KNOWS HER, SO HE INVITES US IN. SHE
WHISPERS TO ME THAT HE KNOWS HER BECAUSE SHE
OWES HIM TWO HUNDRED DOLLARS. HE IS VERY PLEAS-
ANT AND DOESN'T MENTION THE MONEY, BUT STILL
WE ESCAPE AT THE FIRST CHANCE WE GET.

I FIND MYSELF ALL OUT OF FOOD STAMPS AND
ALMOST OUT OF FOOD. I SPEND THE LAST OF MY
CHANGE ON A STICK OF BUTTER FROM THE CORNER
STORE, BUT EVERYTHING I COOK WITH IT TASTES
WRONG, ALL SICKLY SWEET AND SOAPY. I AM SO
BUMMED: THE "NEW" BUTTER I'VE BOUGHT IS ANCIENT
AND ROTTING. SHE BRINGS OVER FRESH MILK AND
MARGARINE AND SAVES THE DAY. I COMPLAIN
ABOUT EVERYTHING WHILE COOKING BREAKFAST.
I'M IN A LOUSY MOOD, AND SHE WANTS TO WALK
AROUND WITH ME ANYWAY. WE WALK AROUND,
THEN SHE BUYS ME BEER AND BEATS ME AT POOL.
I'M NOT IN A LOUSY MOOD ANYMORE.

I ALWAYS FELT SO GODDAMN PROUD WHEN I WAS
WITH HER, SO I STARTED CALLING HER MY PRIDE.
MY PRIDE NEEDS A BEER. MY PRIDE IS WOUNDED.
MY PRIDE IS WITH HER BOYFRIEND. SWALLOW
MY PRIDE. ME AND MY PRIDE ALWAYS HAD A GREAT
TIME HANGING OUT. BUT SHE NEVER STAYED LONG
ENOUGH. I MISSED HER. I EVEN SENT HER SAPPY
POSTCARDS FROM FIVE BLOCKS AWAY. I WAS LOSING
MY PRIDE. SHE SAID SHE WOULD REALLY MISS ME
WHEN I LEFT.

SO I LEFT.

the Sweating Contest

ONE VAN, TWO BANDS, AND WE WERE ROLLING ALONG JUST
FINE UNTIL THE THIRD FLAT TIRE IN ONE NIGHT, WITH NO
MORE SPARES. MAYBE I DIDN'T KNOW THEM WELL ENOUGH YET
TO LAUGH OUT LOUD AT SUCH A STRESSFUL TIME, BUT IT WAS
HARD NOT TO. THE GRAFFITI STILL LOOKED FRESH FROM WHEN
ME AND ANGIE HAD BROKEN DOWN AT THAT EXACT SAME SPOT
JUST THREE MONTHS PREVIOUS: MILE MARKER 124, MONTANA.

3:00 IN THE MORNING AND EVERYONE WAS PREPARING TO
CATCH SOME SLEEP IN THE VAN, STALLING FOR TIME UNTIL
THE AUTO SHOPS OPENED. I SUGGESTED WALKING TO MILES
CITY INSTEAD, SEVENTEEN MILES AWAY, TO GET SOME COFFEE.
TO MY SURPRISE, TWO OF MY VANMATES TOOK ME UP ON THE
OFFER. IT WAS SO NICE TO BE OUT WALKING UNDER THE BIG

WIDE OPEN NIGHT INSTEAD OF JUST DRIVING THROUGH IT.
WHAT A PERFECT WAY TO START A TOUR.

THE SHOWS WERE ALWAYS A CHALLENGE AND NOT ALWAYS
FUN. I BARELY KNEW THE SONGS. I ONLY HAD ONE
REHEARSAL TO LEARN THEM, THEN A SHOW EVERY NIGHT
AFTER THAT. FOR ME, THE BEST PART OF THE TOUR WAS
JUST GETTING TO KNOW THE BOYS IN BOTH BANDS. CONCEN-
TRATING ON THE PEOPLE I WAS WITH FOR A CHANGE,
INSTEAD OF THE PLACES WE WENT. TALKING UNTIL DAWN
EVERY NIGHT, PLAYING RUMMY 500 IN A HUNDRED DIFFERENT
DINERS AND IN THE BACK OF THE VAN WITH THE DISCO
LIGHTS ON, CARDS SLIDING EVERYWHERE. DANCING, DRINKING,
PUSHING OUR LIMITS THROUGH A PARADE OF LOUSY SHOWS
AND SILLY PARTIES.

IT WAS GOOD JUST TO BE AROUND BOYS AGAIN AFTER BEING
THE ONLY BOY IN ALL-GIRL HOUSES. NOT THAT IT MATTERS
MUCH, BUT IT DOES IN LITTLE WAYS. MAYBE IT WAS BECAUSE
WE WERE BOYS THAT A COMPETITION SEEMED LIKE THE
NATURAL, AND FUN, WAY TO BOND. I DON'T KNOW. I HAD MY
OWN REASONS FOR SUGGESTING THE IDEA; IF A SHOW WAS
GOING TO BE AWKWARD FOR ME, I FIGURED IT MIGHT AS WELL
BE AWKWARD FOR EVERYBODY.

IT STARTED WHEN I CHALLENGED THE DRUMMER OF THE
OTHER BAND TO A SWEATING CONTEST. WE CONSULTED
WEATHER MAPS AND OUR TOUR SCHEDULE AND DECIDED ON
BILOXI AS THE HOTTEST SPOT FOR THE SHOWDOWN. THEN
I ENCOURAGED THE REST OF THE BANDMEMBERS TO
CHOOSE THEIR OWN CONTESTS, THREATENING THAT I WOULD
CHOOSE THE CHALLENGE IF THEY FAILED TO. EVERYONE
LIKED THE IDEA, BUT AS THE DAYS ROLLED BY AND THE VAN
ROLLED FURTHER SOUTH, ONLY THE BASSISTS ANSWERED THE
CALL. IT WAS SORT OF A GROSS IDEA, BUT AT LEAST IT WAS
THEIR OWN. SOMETHING ABOUT TAKING FIFTEEN EPHEDRINE
EACH BEFORE PLAYING AND THEN COMPARING BODY PARTS.

I HAD SOME LONG NIGHTS IN THE VAN THINKING OF
DIFFERENT POSSIBILITIES FOR MISERABLE, HUMILIATING,
AND UNHEALTHY CONTESTS. I SETTLED ON TWO IDEAS THAT
WEREN'T EXACTLY CONTESTS, BUT WERE CERTAINLY ALL
THOSE OTHER THINGS.

THE SINGER/GUITARIST OF EACH BAND WAS TO BE BLIND-
FOLDED, AND THEIR FEET TIED. BOTH RHYTHM GUITARISTS
WOULD BE TIED, TOO. TIED TO EACH OTHER, FOR THE
DURATION OF BOTH SETS.

HA HA HA. THIS WAS GOING TO SUCK.

WHEN WE PULLED INTO BILOXI IT WAS ONE HUNDRED
DEGREES IN THE SHADE AND PERHAPS ONE HUNDRED AND
TWENTY DEGREES IN THE TRAILER WHERE THE BANDS

WERE GOING TO PLAY. THE AIR IN THE TRAILER WAS STEAMING AND STALE, BUT THE PROMOTER SAID ALL DOORS AND WINDOWS HAD TO REMAIN SHUT OR THE NEIGHBORS WOULD COMPLAIN.

I STOOD WITH THE OTHER DRUMMER, DRINKING AS MUCH WATER AS WE COULD STOMACH. THEN, STRIPPED DOWN TO OUR UNDERWEAR, WE WEIGHED IN.

MY BAND WAS SET TO PLAY FIRST. THE SMALL CROWD PACKED IN, AS EXCITED AND CONFUSED AS WE WERE. NEVER HAD THEY SEEN A SHOW LIKE THIS. THE SINGER WAS BUMPING INTO THINGS, SINGING AT EVERYTHING BUT THE MICROPHONE, ALMOST FALLING OVER. THE BASSIST WAS BUG-EYED, PACING AROUND LIKE HE WAS INSANE. THE RHYTHM GUITARIST HAD SOMEONE TIED TO HIS BACK. THE DRUMMER, YOURS TRULY, WAS WEARING THERMALS, A SWEATER, A WINTER COAT, AND TWO HATS.

WITH ALL THE DISTRACTIONS, THE CROWD PROBABLY DIDN'T EVEN NOTICE THAT WE SOUNDED LIKE HELL. WHOEVER THINKS THAT PEOPLE COME TO SHOWS TO LISTEN TO THE BANDS IS KIDDING THEMSELVES ANYWAY. PEOPLE COME TO SHOWS TO SEE THAT THEY AREN'T THE ONLY FREAK IN THE WORLD, TO SEE OTHER PEOPLE EVEN MORE OUT OF PLACE THAN THEY FEEL. FOR ONCE I FELT LIKE I WAS PROVIDING A REAL SHOW, EVEN PROVIDING A SERVICE.

I WAS SEEING SPOTS, BLACKING OUT. I WAS DRENCHED IN SWEAT AND SO WAS A FIVE FOOT RADIUS AROUND ME EVEN BEFORE I BROUGHT OUT MY SECRET WEAPON: A FULL POT OF HOT COFFEE.

THERE WAS NO AIR AT ALL LEFT IN THE TRAILER WHEN THE NEXT BAND BEGAN. THE DRUMMER WAS WEARING THERMALS PLUS A PLASTIC JOGGING SUIT. HE SHOWED NO SIGN OF DISCOMFORT, BEING MORE ACCUSTOMED TO EXTREME TEMPERATURES THAN I WAS. HE HAD WARNED ME OF THAT, SAYING HE WORE THE SAME PLASTIC JOGGING SUIT THROUGH FREEZING MIDWEST WINTERS AND BLAZING SUMMERS. THIS WAS GOING TO BE A CLOSE CONTEST.

I WAS OUTSIDE SPRAWLED ON THE GRASS TRYING TO CATCH MY BREATH WHEN SUDDENLY THE TRAILER DOOR BURST OPEN AND THREE PEOPLE RAN OUT. THEY WERE CARRYING THE LIMP BODY OF SLIM, THE RHYTHM GUITARIST OF THE SECOND BAND. HE WAS OUT COLD, MAYBE NOT EVEN BREATHING.

IT TURNED OUT THAT SLIM HAD PASSED OUT STANDING UP, TIED BACK TO BACK WITH RICHARD, THE GUITARIST OF MY BAND. RICHARD DIDN'T NOTICE, AND HE CONTINUED JUMPING UP AND DOWN, KNOCKING MORE WIND OUT OF SLIM. THE SINGER DIDN'T NOTICE EITHER, BECAUSE HE WAS BLINDFOLDED. THE BASSIST AND DRUMMER WERE TOO PREOCCUPIED WITH

THEIR OWN PREDICAMENTS TO SEE WHAT WAS GOING ON.
SOMEONE IN THE CROWD FINALLY POINTED IT OUT IN
BETWEEN SONGS.

EVERYONE RAN AROUND TOSSING WATER IN SLIM'S FACE,
TRYING TO CHECK HIS PULSE, GETTING READY TO GIVE HIM
MOUTH TO MOUTH. WE WERE ABOUT TO DRIVE SLIM TO THE
EMERGENCY ROOM WHEN HE OPENED HIS EYES AND SAW
THE CROWD GATHERED AROUND HIM. POOR GUY, HE JUST
WANTED TO BE LEFT ALONE. HE WAS GOING TO BE ALRIGHT.

I FELT TERRIBLE ABOUT THE CONTEST, THE WHOLE
STUPID RECKLESS IDEA THAT HAD ALMOST ENDED IN
THE HOSPITAL. BUT SLIM TOOK IT IN GOOD HUMOUR, ONCE
HE HAD GOTTEN HIS BREATH BACK. THERE WAS NO DENYING
HE WAS THE WINNER. THEIR DRUMMER ALSO WON HANDS
DOWN, LOSING SIX POUNDS COMPARED TO MY FOUR. OUR ONLY
WINNER WAS THE INCREDIBLE SHRINKING BASSIST, AND
THAT WASN'T MUCH.

WE WERE ALL COMPLETELY EXHAUSTED. WHAT A MESS.
WE WENT SWIMMING, BOTH BANDS IN A LITTLE PLASTIC
POOL, AND THEN SNUCK OUT TO THE CASINOS. IT WAS THE
FIRST TOUR I'D EVER BEEN ON WHERE I LIKED EVERYONE
EVEN MORE AT THE END.

Hot Cars

I NEEDED A LITTLE SPACE, SO I PACKED UP
AND MOVED AWAY. KISSED ANGIE GOODBYE. IT WILL
BE NICE MISSING EACH OTHER, I SAID.

LIFE IN THE NEW TOWN WAS JUST WHAT I
NEEDED. QUIET, CONTEMPLATIVE SOLITUDE. IT LASTED
A WHOLE WEEK BEFORE ANGIE SHOWED UP AND
FOUND ME.

JESUS CHRIST, GIRL, I SAID. I MEAN, I MISSED
YOU TOO. I LOVE YOU. I'M SO GLAD YOU CAME.

WHAT ELSE COULD I SAY TO SOMEONE WHO'D
JUST SPENT THREE DAYS CAMPING OUT IN BUSHES,
COVERING THE TOWN IN CHALK MESSAGES, SEARCHING
FOR ME? DRIVEN FIFTEEN HOURS, ACROSS STATE
LINES. IN A STOLEN CAR.

YOU REALLY SHOULDN'T HAVE, I SAID. I MEAN,
STOLEN A CAR.

SHE BEAMED. GUILTY AND PROUD.

ANGIE WAS JUST VISITING, THAT'S WHAT SHE
SAID. VISITING FOR A FEW DAYS. A VISITOR. HARMLESS.
BUT EVERY DAY, THERE WAS SOME REASON TO STAY.
AT FIRST IT WAS BECAUSE WE ALWAYS WOKE UP
TOO LATE. SHE COULDN'T DRIVE AT NIGHT. MORE
CHANCES OF GETTING PULLED OVER. STOLEN CAR,
CROSSING STATE LINES, A FELONY. KISSING FROM

OPPOSITE SIDES OF THE GLASS IN A VISITING ROOM.
CAN'T HAVE THAT.

THEN ONE NIGHT WE WERE IN THE LIBRARY AND
A VOICE BOOMED OVER THE INTERCOM: "ATTENTION,
LIBRARY PATRONS. AN IMPORTANT ANNOUNCEMENT.
IT'S SNOWING OUTSIDE."

SNOW? IN SEPTEMBER? WELL, WE TUMBLED
OUTSIDE, TRIPPING OVER EACH OTHER, ROLLING AND
RUNNING AROUND GETTING IN SNOWBALL FIGHTS WITH
INNOCENT PASSERBY. GOOD TIMES. COLD HANDS,
WARM MOUTHS, WINTER ROMANCE. THEN WE WENT
TO THE CAR AND FOUND THAT THE LOCKS WERE
ICED OVER AND FROZEN SHUT.

NO PROBLEM, I SAID. I'LL JUST REACH MY ARM
IN LIKE THIS, HOLD THE COAT HANGER LIKE THIS.
VOILA! THE WINDOW SHATTERED.

OH, MAN. A HOT CAR WITH FROZEN LOCKS AND
A BROKEN WINDOW FOR THE SNOW TO BLOW IN,
PARKED JUST DOWN THE BLOCK FROM MY HOUSE.
GETTING RISKIER WITH EACH PASSING DAY, ESPECIALLY
WITH MY NEIGHBORS WATCHING. TWO FREAKS OUT IN
THE SNOW HOLDING COAT HANGERS AND SMASHING
CAR WINDOWS, LAUGHING. LOOKS SUSPICIOUS. AND
NOW, ON TOP OF EVERYTHING, WE HAD TO BUY
CHAINS FOR THE TIRES.

WE FELT SO GUILTY. GUILTY BECAUSE ANGIE
HAD HOTWIRED A STRANGER'S CAR, DESTROYED IT,
AND KEPT IT FOR TWO WEEKS INSTEAD OF TWO DAYS
LIKE SHE'D PLANNED. BUT MOSTLY GUILTY FOR
HAVING THE TIME OF OUR LIVES.

Midnight Movies

THIS IS THE ONLY TOWN I'VE EVER LIVED IN THAT HAS MIDNIGHT
MOVIES SEVEN NIGHTS A WEEK, AND I'M PRETTY HAPPY ABOUT
THAT. I'M PRETTY HAPPY ABOUT A LOT OF THINGS, MOSTLY
INCONSEQUENTIAL LITTLE THINGS, BUT THEY ADD UP. THE ONLY
THING I COULD ASK FOR, BESIDES A RICEMAKER, WOULD BE
ALL-NIGHT MOVIES. AT LEAST THIS TOWN HAS LOTS OF ALL-
NIGHT COFFEE, AND THAT I COULDN'T GET IN THE LAST TOWN
OR THE TOWN BEFORE THAT. THOSE WERE NICE PLACES TOO,
IT'S JUST THAT I LIKE TO DRINK COFFEE LATE AT NIGHT.

THE ALL-NIGHT MOVIE THING, THOUGH, I'VE NEVER BEEN ABLE
TO UNDERSTAND. THERE'S ALL THOSE SONGS AND STORIES THAT
TALK ABOUT BEING DOWN AND OUT AND GOING TO THE ALL-
NIGHT MOVIES TO SLEEP OR JUST STAY WARM. YET I'VE
NEVER BEEN ABLE TO FIND ALL-NIGHT MOVIES IN ANY CITY,
NOT EVEN NEW YORK, AND IT WASN'T FOR LACK OF TRYING.
I'VE BEEN DOWN AND OUT AND NEEDING SLEEP OR WARMTH

IN MORE CITIES THAN I CAN REMEMBER, AND ALL-NIGHT MOVIES NEVER MAGICALLY APPEAR. MAYBE IT USED TO BE DIFFERENT OR MY IDEA OF ALL-NIGHT IS DIFFERENT. MAYBE THEY MEAN PORNO MOVIES. I'M TOO SHY FOR THAT.

I'VE BEEN GOING TO THE MIDNIGHT MOVIES AND I HAVE YET TO SEE A BAD ONE. IN FACT, I'VE ONLY SEEN A COUPLE BAD MOVIES IN MY LIFE. I'M NOT VERY PICKY WHEN IT COMES TO MOVIES, LIKE I AM WITH EVERYTHING ELSE. EVEN STUPID MOVIES ALWAYS REMIND ME OF SOMETHING EXCITING, OR I CAN LOOK AT THE CAMERA ANGLES, OR I CAN THINK ABOUT WHAT IT LOOKS LIKE UP IN THE PROJECTIONIST BOOTH. MY LIFELONG FANTASY OF WHAT IT'S LIKE UP IN A PROJECTIONIST BOOTH IS STILL ONE FANTASY UNTARNISHED AFTER EXPERIENCING THE REAL THING. MY FREIND SEAN USED TO WORK AS A PROJECTIONIST, AND I WOULD GO UP THERE AND HANG OUT WITH HIM, AND IT WAS ABOUT THE COOLEST PLACE IN THE WORLD. HE EVEN SET UP TWO LITTLE DESKS SO WE COULD WORK ON OUR ZINES WHILE THE FILMS RAN. HE TAUGHT ME A LITTLE ABOUT HOW TO THREAD THE FILM AND FOCUS AND DIM THE LIGHTS AND STICK YOUR HEAD OUT THE PROJECTIONIST WINDOW TO MAKE SURE THE VOLUME WAS RIGHT. HE DECIDED TO GIVE ME THE FINAL CRASH COURSE ONE NIGHT. "PUT ON BATMAN 2", HE SAID, "IT STARTS IN FIVE MINUTES". I SCREAMED "NOOOOOOO" AS SEAN ESCAPED OUT THE DOOR AND RAN THROUGH THE ENDLESS LABRYNTH OF PASSAGEWAYS. HE DISAPPEARED INTO THE MYSTERIOUS DEPTHS OF THE THEATRE WITH HIS LOUD LAUGH ECHOING. SOMEHOW I GOT BATMAN 2 UP AND RUNNING AND IN FOCUS, BUT HOW I DID IT I'LL NEVER KNOW.

LATELY, INSTEAD OF THINKING ABOUT ALL OF THE THINGS I'VE DONE THAT I WISH I'D DONE DIFFERENTLY, OR ALL THE THINGS I NEVER DID, I'VE BEEN THINKING ABOUT ALL OF THE THINGS I'D DO AGAIN THE EXACT SAME WAY. SOME OF THEM I'D REALLY LOVE TO DO AGAIN. I COULD SPEND A YEAR OR TWO HAPPILY RELIVING SOME DAYS OF MY LIFE THE EXACT SAME WAY. IT'S NOT THAT I REALLY WANT TO, BUT THINKING ABOUT IT HAS MADE ME REALIZE I'VE DONE BETTER THAN I THOUGHT. EVEN THE DAYS I'VE BEEN HAVING LATELY, I WOULD DO AGAIN GLADLY. SIMPLE DAYS BUT WITH LITTLE SUPRISES AND LONG WALKS AND GOOD LUCK. FOR INSTANCE, I FOUND A HUGE BLOCK OF CHOCOLATE IN THE DUMPSTER, AND EVERY TIME I GO TO THE DONUT SHOP WITH MY GIRL AND ORDER ONE DONUT, THEY SNEAK IN A SECOND ONE FOR US. THIS IS NOT THE BIGGEST DEAL IN THE WORLD, BUT PRETTY NICE CUZ WE'RE BOTH BROKE. THE MIDNIGHT MOVIES ARE OUR ONE BIG EXTRAVAGANCE. WE ARE PRETTY LUCKY

BECAUSE THIS IS AN EASY TOWN TO BE BROKE IN. ONE LOCAL PUNK CLUB SOMETIMES HAS SHOWS THAT COST ONE PACK OF RAMEN TO GET IN AND ANOTHER SOMETIMES HAS SHOWS THAT COST SOME DUCT TAPE OR ONE SHARPEE TO GET IN. SERIOUSLY, IT IS ALMOST TOO GOOD TO BE TRUE, BUT IT IS TRUE.

I Blame You

THE MORE I THINK ABOUT IT, THE MORE IT MAKES ME MAD. HOW YOU CAME TO OUR HOUSES WHEN YOU NEEDED A PLACE TO CRASH, SOMEONE TO TALK TO, SOME EXCITEMENT, SOME SYMPATHY. YOU SUCKED UP OUR WORLD, ALL THE LATENIGHT PLANS AND ANGRY BANDS AND OUR FAMILY THAT WAS MORE OF A FAMILY THAN YOU'D EVER HAD. BUT WHEN IT CAME TIME FOR YOU TO MAKE YOUR OWN MOVE INTO THE WORLD YOU GOT A LITTLE SINGLE ROOM WITH YOUR GIRL AND STARTED ACTING LIKE MOM AND DAD. YOU CUT US OUT AND LEFT US IN THE COLD. WHO DO I BLAME WHEN I COME BACK TO MY TOWN AND THERE'S NOT AN OPEN DOOR TO BE FOUND, NOT EVEN A FUCKING FLOOR? I BLAME YOU.

WHEN I THINK OF THE CHANCES WE TOOK, THE LENGTHS WE WENT TO CREATE SOMETHING MEANINGFUL, SOMETHING WE COULD TRULY CALL OUR OWN. MAYBE IT DIDN'T ADD UP TO MUCH MORE THAN A COUPLE DINGY CLUBS, A FEW FUCKED UP HOUSES, SOME IDEAS AND SILLY SLOGANS ABOUT HOW TO LIVE. BUT WE TOOK ALL THE INSPIRATION AND ENERGY WE GOT FROM THE WORLD AND THREW IT RIGHT BACK TWICE AS HARD. YOU CAME INTO IT ALL WIDE-EYED AND SO HUNGRY, AND WE KEPT ON DISHING IT OUT. BUT YOU ATE AND ATE UNTIL YOU'D HAD YOUR FILL AND NEVER EVEN CONSIDERED TURNING AROUND AND GIVING ANYTHING BACK. YOU WATCHED US GET TIRED AND INSTEAD OF PICKING UP THE BALL, YOU JUST LET IT FADE AWAY, SO HAPPY AND CONTENT THAT YOU COULD TELL THE NEXT WAVE YOU'D BEEN THERE "BACK IN THE DAY". YOU DIDN'T HAVE THE GUTS OR EVEN THE DECENCY TO KICK OUR ASS BY DOING SOMETHING WAY BIGGER, WAY WILDER WHICH WOULD MAKE WHAT WE DID LOOK TAME. YOU COULDN'T EVEN MUSTER UP ONE GREAT BAND. SHIT, YOU STOPPED DANCING EVEN BEFORE MOST OF US DID. WHO DO I BLAME WHEN SHOWS JUST AREN'T MUCH FUN ANYMORE? I BLAME YOU.

YOU HAD YOUR FUN BUT NOW IT'S THE REAL WORLD, NOT LIKE OUR WORLD WHICH I GUESS WAS SOMETHING ENTIRELY DIFFERENT. FUNNY HOW WHEN YOU'RE DEPRESSED

OR HAVING TROUBLE WITH YOUR GIRL YOU COME BACK TO OUR WORLD, WHERE EVERYTHING DOESN'T HAVE TO BE TAKEN SO SERIOUSLY. WHERE YOU CAN GET TRASHED AND SO CAN OUR HOUSES. BUT CAN'T YOU SEE, THIS IS OUR ONLY WORLD AND WE'RE STUCK IN IT—A CHOICE WE MADE OR A CHOICE MADE FOR US LONG AGO. WE CAN'T JUST COME AND GO AS WE PLEASE, AND SOMETIMES, BELIEVE ME, WE WISH WE COULD. OUR DOOR IS ALWAYS OPEN AND YOUR DOOR IS ALWAYS LOCKED. WHO DO I BLAME WHEN EVICTION COMES AND THERE'S NOWHERE LEFT TO GO? WHEN NOTHING SEEMS LIKE MUCH FUN AND WHAT WE HAVE IS ONLY A SHADOW OF OUR FORMER GLORY? WHEN EVERYTHING IS FALLING APART AND THERE'S LESS OPTIONS AND LESS PEOPLE TO COUNT ON THAN THERE USED TO BE? I BLAME YOU, THEN I BLAME EVERYONE ELSE WHO CAME BEFORE OR AFTER YOU, AND THEN AFTER A WHILE THERE'S NO ONE LEFT AND I HAVE TO BLAME MYSELF, AND I'M TIRED OF BLAMING MYSELF.

Dylan + Falena

DYLAN WORKED AS A SECURITY GUARD DOWNTOWN, JUST ANOTHER DEAD END JOB. SO DID FALENA BUT THEY DIDN'T KNOW EACH OTHER YET. THEN ONE FINE DAY DYLAN HAD TO EVACUATE THE BUILDING. FALENA HAD TO RUN UP AND DOWN THE STAIRS LOOKING FOR EXPLOSIVES. SOMEONE HAD CALLED IN A BOMB THREAT. THE BUILDING DIDN'T BLOW UP AFTER ALL, BUT OUT ON THE STREET IN ALL THE PANIC THEY MET, AND FELL IN LOVE.

IMAGINE MY SURPRISE WHEN I GOT A LETTER IN THE MAIL FROM MY LONG LOST FRIEND. GOOD NEWS, HE WASN'T IN JAIL, JUST BAD AT KEEPING IN TOUCH. THE WEDDING WAS SET FOR JULY SO I HOPPED ON AN AIRPLANE AND ME AND ANGIE TOOK THE FERRY TO THE ISLAND WHERE THE WEDDING WAS GOING TO BE.

AT THE FERRY TERMINAL WE FOUND DAVE AND ANNA. WE WERE ALL DRESSED IN THE VERY BEST (MOSTLY BORROWED) SUITS, LOOKING MORE LIKE MAFIOSO THAN DISTINGUISHED GUESTS. ONCE WE GOT TO THE BEACH WE FOUND THAT IT WAS A CASUAL AFFAIR AND WE WERE ACTUALLY OVERDRESSED, THOUGH I KNOW THAT'S HARD TO BELIEVE.

OUT ON THE BEACH IN THE RAIN IT WAS A BEAUTIFUL DAY AND THE WEIRDEST MIX OF PEOPLE I'D EVER SEEN GATHERED TOGETHER UNDER THE CANOPY. IT WAS A SMALL

INTIMATE CEREMONY. DYLAN STAMMERED. FALENA BLUSHED. THE JUSTICE OF THE PEACE WAS LATE. I INSTRUCTED THEM TO FEED EACH OTHER CAKE BUT INSTEAD FALENA'S LITTLE SISTER GRABBED SOME AND CHASED AFTER ME TRYING TO THROW IT IN MY FACE. A REAL DEMON CHILD, MOST LIKELY POSSESSED, BUT VERY SWEET NONETHELESS.

THEY KISSED AND EVERYONE TOOK PHOTOS AND PROCEEDED TO GET DRUNK. WE ALL HUGGED AND WISHED EACH OTHER THE BEST OF LUCK. THE BRIDE'S DAD HAD A STASH OF CHEAP BEER IN HIS TRUNK. THE PUNCH MUST HAVE HAD SOMETHING IN IT TOO, FOR EVERYONE STARTED TO MAKE AISLE EYES AT EACH OTHER. ME AND ANGIE WANDERED OFF TOGETHER. A LOCAL DOG ADOPTED US. WE DECIDED TO TAKE HIM FOR A WALK BUT IT TURNED INTO A LONG MUDDY CHASE ALONG THE WATERFRONT.

WHEN WE RETURNED, THE PARTY WAS FINISHING. IT WAS A REAL D.I.Y. WEDDING. DYLAN AND FALENA WERE CARRYING LEFTOVER FOOD THROUGH THE RAIN WITH THE REST OF US, LOADING IT ALL INTO THE BACK OF A PICKUP TRUCK. IT WAS MONUMENTAL, A WONDERFUL LITTLE DAY IN OUR LIVES WHICH ARE GOING BETTER THAN EXPECTED, THANKS TO THE DEAD-END JOB AND THE MYSTERY CALLER, THE WOULD-BE BOMBER WHO HAD BROUGHT DYLAN AND FALENA TOGETHER AND ALL OF US TOGETHER AGAIN.

the Unheard Music

THERE ARE WORSE TRAGEDIES THAN DEATH, ALTHOUGH THERE WAS PLENTY OF THAT GOING AROUND TOO. LYON GOT BEATEN TO DEATH BY REDNECKS. NICK OVERDOSED IN A GREYHOUND STATION BATHROOM. JAKE BURNED DOWN WITH HIS HOUSE. BROUGHT DOWN IN THE PRIME, AND TIME, OF THEIR LIVES. THE MEMORY OF THEM AND THE MUSIC THEY MADE WOULD NEVER BE FORGOTTEN, AND IN THAT MEMORY WAS A DIFFERENT KIND OF TRAGEDY: THE TRAGEDY OF WASTED TALENT, FAILURE, AND REGRET. NOT OF THOSE DEPARTED BUT AMONG THE LIVING. GETTING OLDER AND BITTER AS THEIR DREAMS WENT ONE WAY AND THEIR LIVES WENT THE OTHER.

ALL OF THE BANDS FROM ALL OF THE SHITTY SMALL TOWNS AROUND. EACH ONE A STORY, EACH ONE A STR- UGGLE TO BOND TOGETHER AND OVERCOME THEIR ISOLATION. EACH ONE SOUNDING THE SAME AS THE LAST, SCREAMING ABOUT HOW ANGRY THEY WERE BECAUSE THERE WAS NO FUTURE, REALLY JUST TERR- IFIED BECAUSE THEY KNEW THAT THERE WAS. EVERY ONE A FAILURE, NEVER CHANGING THE WORLD OR

MAKING THE KINDS OF REAL CHANGES IN THEIR LIVES THAT THEY DEMANDED IN THEIR SONGS. ALL THE PROMISE AND HOPE, ALL THE FIERY PASSION, AND SOMEHOW IT DIDN'T ADD UP TO ANYTHING AT ALL.

TEN YEARS LATER AND YOU WONDER IF IT EVER REALLY HAPPENED. HARDLY A TRACE CAN BE FOUND ASIDE FROM YELLOWING FLIERS WITH A THOUSAND FORGOTTEN BAND NAMES. SOMEWHERE OUT THERE ARE THE FORGOTTEN PEOPLE BEHIND THOSE BAND NAMES, AN ARMY OF FORMERLY WILD YOUTH, NOT TO MENTION YOUTH CRISIS, YOUTH AUTHORITY, AND YOUTH YOUTH YOUTH. "KIDS OF THE 80'S" NOW ADULTS OF THE 90'S STUCK WITH THE SAME OLD BORING STORIES AND UGLY TATTOOS.

I WOULD HAVE FORGOTTEN THEM TOO, EXCEPT THAT MUSIC HAS A WAY OF HOLDING ON TO MEMORIES, AND I STILL HAVE THEIR MUSIC: A BIG BOXFUL OF DEMOS, REHEARSAL TAPES, AND CASSETTE COPIES OF RECORDS THAT WERE SUPPOSED TO COME OUT BUT OF COURSE NEVER DID. SHORT BURSTS OF HOPE AND RAGE, OVER BEFORE THE BOMB HAD A CHANCE TO DROP. SONGS SO MUCH PART OF THAT TIME, AND YET TIMELESS THE WAY MUSIC CAN BE, NEVER GETTING OLD THE WAY THAT PEOPLE DO.

THE WEIRD THING ABOUT MEMORIES IS THAT THEY AREN'T REALLY THE PAST, BECAUSE YOU EXPERIENCE THEM IN THE PRESENT, JUST AS REAL AS ANYTHING ELSE. FOR ME, IT'S THE SAME WITH THE OLD MUSIC, BUT TRYING TO EXPLAIN IT IS LIKE TRYING TO EXPLAIN A MEMORY: ALWAYS OUT OF CONTEXT, ALWAYS MIS-UNDERSTOOD. TO ANYONE ELSE, IT JUST SOUNDS LIKE THE PAST. BETTER TO KEEP IT TO YOURSELF.

ALL THE PEOPLE WHO LIVED TOO FAST, BURNED OUT TOO FAST, MADE IMPORTANT DECISIONS TOO FAST. ALL BECAUSE THEY WERE TERRIFIED WHAT THE FUTURE WOULD BRING. THAT SENSE OF URGENCY PRODUCED SOME GREAT MUSIC BUT DESTROYED SOME GREAT PEOPLE. THE FUTURE NEVER HAD A PLACE FOR THEM, AND STILL DOESN'T. ALL THE UNHEARD MUSIC. FOR-GOTTEN BANDS SCREAMING TO BE HEARD, BEGGING TO BE REMEMBERED.

8 out of 10 days

I'VE BEEN HERE LONG ENOUGH NOW TO START TO FEEL AT HOME. I HAVE MY REGULAR HIDEOUTS AND HANGOUTS. CLERKS KNOW MY NAME AND ORDER, WAITRESSES FLIRT WITH ME, AND ONE PLACE EVEN LETS ME RUN A TAB. NONE OF THAT STUFF EVER HAPPENED TO ME BACK IN MY HOMETOWN, WHERE I HADN'T BEEN ALIVE LONG ENOUGH TO ACHIEVE "REGULAR" STATUS. HERE, EVEN THE CRANKY OLD REGULARS IN THE DONUT SHOP TALK TO ME AND TREAT ME LIKE

A LOCAL. THEY TALK TO ME ABOUT LOVE, OR THE WEATHER, OR REIN-CARNATION. THEY SAY, IF I HAD ANOTHER CHANCE, IT WOULD BE TOTALLY DIFFERENT. DO YOU KNOW HOW? I'D DO IT EXACTLY THE SAME WAY, THAT'S HOW. EXCEPT NEXT TIME I'D GET A DOG. A COLLIE. I'D BE A TEAMSTER. I WOULD BE SEVEN FEET TALL, SO I COULD PLAY A MEAN GAME OF BASKETBALL.

THE OLD GUYS TALK CYNICALLY, TOO, BUT THEY LAUGH IN A WAY THAT BELIES THEIR GRUMPY ACT. I ADMIRE THEM. THEY'RE SO SHARP AND QUICK. NOT JUST SHARP IN STYLE, BUT SHARP IN THEIR MINDS AND QUICK WITH THEIR WIT. I'M ALSO SHARP AND QUICK, BUT IN ALL THE WRONG WAYS. I WALK SO QUICKLY AND QUIETLY THAT PEOPLE ALWAYS TURN AROUND IN SHOCK, THINKING I'M SNEAKING UP ON THEM. I'M QUICK TO THINK UP A MILLION THINGS TO SAY AND DO, BUT NOT SHARP ENOUGH TO FIGURE OUT THE RIGHT ONE AT THE RIGHT TIME. I'M SHARP LIKE KNIVES AND NERVE ENDINGS ARE SHARP. INSANELY HIGH-STRUNG, HYPER-TENSE, BUT AT THE SAME TIME NOT EXACTLY STRESSED OUT. MAYBE I SHOULD DRINK LESS COFFEE. IT'S HARD TO EXPLAIN.

I REMEMBER THIS ONE OLD CLASH INTERVIEW WHERE THEY GET ASKED, SIMPLY, "ARE YOU WORRIED?" JOE SAYS "YEAH", AND MICK SAYS "WE'RE DESPONDENT, UH, 8 OUT OF 10 DAYS. PRINT THAT". I THINK ABOUT THAT CUZ IT'S THE SAME FOR ME

I FOUND A NEW PLACE TO LIVE, AT LEAST. IT'S A SECOND-FLOOR WAREHOUSE ON THE OTHER SIDE OF THE FREEWAY, A GOOD HALF MILE FROM MY LAST MISTAKE. WE CALL THIS ONE "THE ARK," FOR OBVIOUS REASONS. TWO COUCHES, TWO DRUMSETS, TWO BATHTUBS, TWO STEREOS, TWO CATS, AND TWO DOORS. ONE FRONT DOOR AND ONE BACK DOOR, NONE IN BETWEEN. JUST ONE BIG ROOM WITH NO DOORS OR WALLS OR EVEN CURTAINS TO SEPERATE THE KITCHEN, BATHROOM, REHEARSAL SPACE, AND SLEEPING QUARTERS. THERE'S NO WINDOWS EITHER, JUST EMPTY HOLES THE WIND BLOWS THROUGH WHERE GLASS USED TO BE. IT'S ACTUALLY KIND OF A SHITHOLE, BUT I LIKE IT. I TELL MYSELF THE PLACE IS FUNNY AND COLD AND LOUD AND CRAZY LIKE LIFE ITSELF, AND ONLY SOME OF THE TIME DOES THAT SEEM LIKE A BAD REASON TO LIVE SOMEWHERE.

I DON'T MISS MUCH ABOUT MY OLD PAD. I DON'T MISS THE VICIOUS DOGS AND THEIR LIKE-MINDED OWNERS. I DON'T MISS THE CHURCH BELLS AND THE SOUNDS OF MY NEIGHBORS KILLING EACH OTHER. BUT I DO SORT OF MISS WARMTH, PRIVACY, AND MY OLD ROOMMATE JACK. WE GAVE UP THE APARTMENT WHEN HE FINALLY SAVED UP ENOUGH TO BUY A TRAILER. NOW JACK AND HIS GIRL ARE TRAVELING AROUND THE COUNTRY, WORKING ODD JOBS AND SENDING

ME POSTCARDS FROM DIFFERENT TRAILER PARKS THEY STAY IN ALONG THE WAY. MY NEW ROOMMATE IS BRADLEY, A KINDHEARTED LOUDMOUTH WHO DRINKS TOO MUCH AND LIKES TO SING ALONG WITH SINATRA'S "IN THE WEE SMALL HOURS".

LATELY THERE'S BEEN A LOT OF WET CEMENT AROUND TOWN. WHAT COULD BE BETTER? PUTTING YOUR NAME DOWN IN A NICE STRETCH OF WET CEMENT CAN REALLY BRIGHTEN EVEN THE LOUSIEST OF DAYS AND FINISH OFF THE LONGEST OF NIGHTS. I USED TO ALWAYS WALK AROUND TRYING TO FIGURE OUT THE PERFECT WORDS AND PHRASES TO IMMORTALIZE FOREVER WHEN I NEXT FOUND WET CEMENT. I GAVE UP ON THAT, THOUGH. NOW I JUST WRITE MY NAME, AND MAYBE ANGIE'S TOO, DEPENDING ON WHETHER OR NOT WE'RE TOGETHER THAT WEEK.

ONE NIGHT I FOUND THESE ANCIENT HIDDEN ARMY BUNKERS, BUILT FOR THE CIVIL WAR AND NEVER USED SINCE. THERE WAS GRAFFITI CARVED INTO ONE CRUMBLY WALL DATING BACK A HUNDRED YEARS. "GAP AUG 1951", "BALES AUG 1917", "TIM 68", "TEX KID APRIL 1942", AND HUNDREDS MORE. "VINCE+SHERYL 1915" AND OTHER FADED HEARTS WITH PLUS SIGNS OF COUPLES LONG SINCE DEAD. MAYBE THEY GOT MARRIED AND THEIR GRANDCHILDREN ARE AROUND NOW, OR MAYBE THEY WERE ONLY A COUPLE FOR ONE NIGHT OUT AT THE HIDDEN ARMY BUNKERS. EITHER WAY, THEIR GRAFFITI LASTED LONGER THAN THEY DID.

USING ROCKS, I CARVED "COMETBUS 1995" IN BOLD LETTERS RIGHT NEXT TO "JM MARCH 13, 1924 – FOOLS WITH MONKEY FACES PUT THEIR NAMES IN PUBLIC PLACES". I LOOKED AT IT PROUDLY FOR A WHILE, THEN REALIZED SOMETHING WAS MISSING. IN ANOTHER SEVENTY YEARS PEOPLE WOULD KNOW EVEN LESS ABOUT ME THAN I KNEW ABOUT JM. I WANTED TO GIVE THEM SOMETHING TO BE CURIOUS ABOUT. I SETTLED ON ADDING "SWAMP PUNKS" UNDERNEATH THE "COMETBUS 1995". THERE WAS JUST ONE PROBLEM. MY NAME WAS NOW THREE TIMES AS BIG AS ANY OF THE OTHERS, AND I FELT LIKE A JERK. OOPS. SORRY TEX, JM, BALES, AND VINCE PLUS SHERYL.

THIS WEEK I AM EXTRA TENSE BECAUSE THIS IS RUSH WEEK FOR ALL THE LOCAL FRATS AND SORORITIES. BUT SINCE I GREW UP IN A COLLEGE TOWN, I AM ALSO PREPARED. I CARRY A GOOD ROCK IN MY POCKET AND WAIT FOR THE FRAT BOYS TO THROW EGGS OR SPRAY WATER AT ME SO I CAN SMASH OUT THEIR CAR WINDOW. NOT NECESSARILY A GOOD IDEA, BUT IT DOES SOUND LIKE FUN. I'VE BEEN THINKING ABOUT IT A LOT, PLANNING ESCAPE ROUTES AND STUFF. I'M DISSAPOINTED CUZ IT HASN'T HAPPENED YET. I EVEN

WROTE "FUCK YOU, HICK" ON MY ROCK, BUT FOR NOW IT'S JUST WEARING A HOLE IN MY POCKET.

I GUESS I HAVE BEEN SORT OF OBSESSIVE LATELY, ABOUT SMASHING HICKS' WINDOWS AND WALKING EVERYWHERE AND TRYING TO DO EVERY SINGLE THING AT ONCE. IT'S NOT THAT OLD OBSESSION WITH DEATH, I'M PRETTY MUCH OVER THAT — THE THING WHEN YOU WANT TO DO SEE TOUCH BE KISS EXPERIENCE EVERY SINGLE THING, PLACE, AND PERSON BECAUSE IT MAY BE YOUR LAST CHANCE BEFORE YOU OR THEY ARE GONE. NOW IT'S MORE A FAITH IN THE FUTURE AND WORKING TOWARDS IT, BUT THAT FEELING IS SO STRONG IT BORDERS ON OBSESSION.

THERE'S JUST SO MUCH IMPORTANT STUFF TO DO. EVERY DAY I RUN LIKE AN IDIOT BACK AND FORTH ACROSS TOWN TRYING TO DO ALL THE USEFUL THINGS ON MY LIST, CROSSING THEM OFF ONE AT A TIME. I WAKE UP LATE, AND EVERYWHERE I AM, I'M ALREADY LATE TO GET TO THE NEXT PLACE. THERE'S NEVER ENOUGH TIME, AND THE ONLY WAY TO SOLVE THAT PROBLEM IS TO MOVE FASTER.

BY THE TIME I GET BACK TO THE ARK IT'S 1:00 OR 2:00 IN THE MORNING AND I'M A TOTAL EXHAUSTED MESS, SORE AND COMPLAINING AND NEEDING A BEER. BUT THEN I LAUGH AT MYSELF, THE WAY THE OLD MEN LAUGH AT THEMSELVES COMPLAINING. I SOUND LIKE A TYPICAL WAGE SLAVE AFTER A HARD DAY'S WORK, AND I DON'T EVEN HAVE A JOB. I LOVE LIFE SO MUCH IT'S KILLING ME. DUH.

BRADLEY WORKS SWINGSHIFT AS A FRY COOK, THEN COMES HOME LATE AT NIGHT WHEN I'M FINALLY DONE MAKING NEW LISTS AND WALKING THE STREETS LOOKING FOR WET CEMENT AND PONDERING THE CITY AND MY FUTURE. BRADLEY COMES HOME AND WE SHOOT THE SHIT AND PLAY DRUMS AND COOK BREAKFAST AND FINISH OFF THE BEER, AND IT'S SO LATE I MAYBE HAVE TO SKIP SLEEP AND GET COFFEE AND START SCRATCHING OFF THE NEW LIST.

LAST NIGHT WHEN I WENT OUT TO GET A BOTTLE, THERE WAS NO ONE IN THE SUPERMARKET. I WHISTLED FOR THE CLERKS IN THE BACK TO COME OUT AND RING ME UP, BUT NO ONE DID. I GOT IMPATIENT WAITING AND OPENED THE BOTTLE, SNEAKING A FEW GULPS. STILL, NO ONE CAME. AFTER A WHILE I WAS SITTING AT THE CHECKOUT COUNTER ENJOYING MY 40 AND READING A COPY OF THE NATIONAL ENQUIRER. THEN I FINISHED THE RAG, PUT THE EMPTY BOTTLE BACK ON THE SHELF, AND WENT OUT TO WALK THE STREETS. IT'S HARD FOR ME TO RELAX, BUT THIS WAS VERY RELAXING.

I STAYED UP ALL NIGHT AGAIN, BUT TODAY SOMETHING DIFFERENT HAPPENED ON MY WAY BETWEEN COFFEE AND THE POST OFFICE. I LOOKED UP AND NOTICED THOUSANDS AND THOUSANDS OF BIRDS FLYING TOGETHER OVER DOWNTOWN, FLYING IN CRAZY BEAUTIFUL FORMATIONS LIKE I'VE NEVER SEEN BEFORE. A MASSIVE SWARM CROSSING ACROSS THE SKY, GATHERING TO HEAD SOUTH FOR THE WINTER. PEOPLE DOWNTOWN STOPPED THEIR RUSHING AROUND AND STARED UP AT THE SKY IN AWE. ME AND DIANNE ALMOST LITERALLY BUMPED INTO EACH OTHER, BOTH ABSORBED IN STARING UP AT THE BIRDS.

I HADN'T SEEN DIANNE IN WHAT SEEMED LIKE A LONG TIME. SHE SAID SHE'D BEEN OUT ON THE WATERFRONT GETTING HER HEAD STRAIGHT. SHE JUST SAT AT THE SAME SPOT FOR THREE DAYS, NOT EATING ANYTHING BUT A BAG OF COOKIES, NOT GOING ANY- WHERE EXCEPT OCCASIONALLY INTO THE BUSHES TO PISS OR SLEEP. SHE SAT THERE AND THOUGHT THINGS OUT AND CLEARED ALL THE POISON AND BULLSHIT OUT OF HER HEAD. NOW SHE WAS DONE WITH THE SELF-PITY AND HALF-TRYING AND WAS READY TO TAKE ON THE WORLD. SHE TOLD ME HER NEW PLANS WHILE WE WATCHED THE SWARM OF BIRDS AS THEY BROKE APART THEN REFORMED, TURNED DIRECTION SO THAT THEY DISAPPEARED FROM OUR SIGHT, THEN TURNED AGAIN AND BLOCKED OUT WHOLE PARTS OF THE SKY. I THOUGHT ABOUT HOW SO MANY OF US ARE ON THE VERGE OF SOMETHING GREAT BUT ALSO ON THE VERGE OF NERVOUS BREAKDOWN. I THOUGHT, WHICH WILL COME FIRST?

safety pins

ANOTHER GOOD THING ABOUT SAFETY PINS IS THAT WHEN THEY BOOK YOU AND TAKE AWAY ALL YOUR POSSESS- IONS AND THROW YOU INTO A LITTLE CELL, YOU CAN USE SAFETY PINS TO SCRATCH NOTES INTO THE LINING OF YOUR JACKET. THEY TOOK AWAY ALL MY PENS AND PAPER AND CIGARETTES. THEY EVEN TOOK MY SHOELACES SO I COULDN'T HANG MYSELF. AT LEAST THAT WOULD BE SOMETHING TO DO. THEY TOOK ALL THE SAFETY PINS THEY COULD SEE ON ME, LEAVING MY CLOTHES BARELY HANGING OFF MY BODY. HOWEVER, THEY DID NOT KNOW THAT MY UNDERWEAR IS ALSO HELD TOGETHER WITH SAFETY PINS. BOY, I REALLY GOT ONE OVER ON THEM THIS TIME.

"WHAT'S SO FUNNY, AARON?" ASKS THE HUGE BEARDED

JAILER. I DON'T LIKE THE WAY HE KEEPS SAYING MY NAME. HE'S BROUGHT ME OUT OF MY CELL NOT TO RELEASE ME, BUT TO FINGERPRINT ME ONE MORE TIME. THIS IS THE SIXTH TIME. THE FIRST THREE TIMES I TRIED TO GIVE BAD PRINTS, MOVING OR PRESSING DOWN HARD TO SMUDGE OR SMEAR THE INK. THAT WORKED, BUT THEY KEPT DOING IT OVER UNTIL THEY GOT IT RIGHT. THE LAST TWO TIMES I TRIED TO GIVE THE BEST PRINTS I COULD, BUT HEADQUARTERS SAID THEY WEREN'T GOOD ENOUGH, AND THE JAILER CAME AND GOT ME OUT OF MY CELL AND TRIED AGAIN. I DON'T KNOW WHAT IS WRONG WITH MY HANDS, BUT I HOPE HEADQUARTERS IS SATISFIED THIS TIME. THE JAILER SAYS IT'S BECAUSE I HAVE "WORKINGMAN'S HANDS."

I CAN HEAR OTHER PEOPLE SCREAMING, BUT THE ONLY PEOPLE I'VE SEEN IN THE LAST FEW HOURS ARE THE JAILER AND THE GUARD AT THE DESK. THE GUARD SAYS, "ONE WOMAN SAID SHE HAD NO ILLNESSES AND NOW SHE KEEPS CALLING FOR A GUARD, SAYING SHE'S SICK AND NEEDS ALL KINDS OF MEDICATION. WHAT'S WRONG WITH THESE PEOPLE? THEY'RE ALWAYS DEMANDING EVERYTHING. WHY CAN'T THEY BE REASONABLE?" HER JOB IS TO DEMAND INFORMATION FROM PEOPLE, ORDER THEM AROUND, INSULT AND LAUGH AT THEM, AND THEN LOCK THEM IN A CAGE. SHE WONDERS WHY THEY'RE UNREASONABLE. THE PHONE RINGS AND SHE PICKS IT UP, ANSWERING WITH JUST ONE WORD: "JAIL."

FUNNY, ISN'T IT? ALL THE THINGS I HAVE DONE WORTH GOING TO JAIL FOR, AND NOW I AM IN JAIL FOR WHAT? A BROKEN BIKE LIGHT. AN ASSHOLE COP WHO DECIDED TO TEACH ME A LESSON WHEN I WOULDN'T LET HIM SEARCH MY BAG. WHAT A DRAG. IN A WAY, THOUGH, IT'S SORT OF A RELIEF. JAIL IS NOT AS BAD AS I THOUGHT IT WOULD BE. I WOULDN'T SAY I'M LUCKY, BUT I KNOW IT COULD'VE EASILY BEEN A LOT WORSE. INSTEAD OF TRANSFERRING ME TO PRISON, THEY'VE DECIDED TO CITE ME OUT IN THE MORNING AND GIVE ME A COURT DATE. SO, FOR NOW, IT'S JUST A MATTER OF WAITING.

WAITING WAITING WAITING, LOSING TRACK OF TIME. SLEEPING A LITTLE, DRUMMING ON THE TABLE, SCRATCHING THE WALLS, LOOKING OUT THE WINDOW. WAITING FOR THE JAILER TO COME LET ME OUT. THE WORST SOUND IN THE WORLD IS THE ECHO OF HIS KEYS RATTLING IN THE HALLWAY EVERY FIFTEEN MINUTES. EACH TIME YOU WONDER IF THIS IS THE TIME HE'S COMING TO UNLOCK YOUR DOOR AND SET YOU FREE. BUT EVERY TIME IT'S JUST SOMEONE NEW GETTING THROWN IN THE HOLE.

said + Done

I WAS TIRED OF THE SMALLTALK. INSTEAD OF BRINGING
US CLOSER TOGETHER IT JUST MADE US FEEL MORE ALONE.
CONVERSATIONS STARTED TO SEEM MORE LIKE SPORTS AND
SOUND MORE LIKE ARGUMENTS. I CRAVED A SILENT
TOGETHERNESS, TIME TO THINK. A SENSE OF PRIVACY
WITHOUT BEING ALONE. BASICALLY, I WANTED TO GO
INTO THE KITCHEN TO MAKE TOAST WITHOUT ANYONE
TRYING TO TELL ME THEIR LIFE STORY. SO I MADE A NEW
HOUSE RULE: NO TALKING ABOUT WHAT YOU DID THAT DAY.
IF POSSIBLE, NO TALKING ABOUT WHAT YOU DID THAT YEAR.

THAT CUT OUT HALF THE IDLE CHATTER, AND EVERYONE
WAS HAPPIER. ONE PROBLEM THOUGH, AND THAT WAS BRAD.
THE DETAILS OF BRAD'S DAILY LIFE HAD ALWAYS BEEN A
CLOSELY GUARDED, AND MUCH-SPECULATED, SECRET. THE NEW
RULE DIDN'T AFFECT HIM. HE CONTINUED TALKING TWENTY
HOURS A DAY, ONE LONG STREAM OF JUMBLED IDEAS AND
EMOTIONS IN THE FORM OF RHETORICAL QUESTIONS.

I POSTED A NEW RULE. QUESTIONS ONLY ALLOWED EVERY
HALF HOUR. THAT PUT A SERIOUS DENT IN BRAD'S MONOLOGUES,
AND ALSO HELPED TO CUT DOWN ON THE GENERAL WISHY
WASHY QUALITY OF OUR LIVES.

WE SAT AROUND TALKING ABOUT NEW PERSPECTIVES,
INSIGHTS, AND IDEAS, BUT NOT THE EVENTS THAT BROUGHT
THEM ON. TALKING ABOUT QUALITIES IN PEOPLE WE LOVED
OR DISLIKED, WITHOUT MENTIONING NAMES. ANOTHER RULE.

BRAD SAT NEARBY FURIOUSLY SCRIBBLING OUT PAGES OF
NOTES, WAITING FOR THE CLOCK TO HIT SIX OR TWELVE.
OCCASIONALLY HIS EXCITEMENT COULD NOT BE CONTAINED
AND HE BLURTED OUT A LONG LINE OF QUESTIONS. ON
THESE OCCASIONS I CHARGED HIM A NICKEL PER QUESTION
AND PUT THE MONEY TOWARDS OUR HOUSE FUND.

SOMETIMES I WOKE UP TO FIND LUMBERJACKS IN THE
LIVING ROOM, EATING PANCAKES. SOMETIMES ITALIAN
CHEFS BENT OVER A BIG VAT OF SAUCE. SOMETIMES
HOUSEWIVES WEARING LIPSTICK, ROBES, AND TOWELS
AROUND THEIR HEAD. IT WAS TRICKY BUSINESS BECAUSE
EACH OF US HAD ONLY ONE SET OF CLOTHES, AND FAKE
MOUSTACHES COULD ONLY GO SO FAR. BUT IT WAS A HOUSE
RULE: WHATEVER WAS ON THE STOVE, EVERYONE MUST
DRESS ACCORDINGLY.

WE BEGAN PLAYING CARDS TWICE A WEEK, MOSTLY SPADES,
A GOOD GAME WITH LOTS OF RULES. THE KIND OF SUBTLE,

SILENT BONDING BETWEEN PARTNERS THAT IS IMPORTANT NOT ONLY IN CARDS BUT ALSO IN FRIENDSHIP AND ROMANCE. STILL, THERE WAS SOMETHING MAKING IT HARD TO CONCENTRATE. TOO MANY WORDS BEING HASTILY THROWN AROUND THE TABLE. I FELT THEY SHOULD BE CHOSEN WITH MORE CARE. HENCEFORTH, A NEW RULE: EACH PERSON ALLOWED ONLY TWENTY WORDS WHILE PLAYING CARDS.

AMOS CAME OVER TO TEACH US HOW TO PLAY PINOCHLE. HE WAS ALLOWED TO TOSS AROUND WORDS LIKE WISHES, BUT THE REST OF US HAD OUR SEPARATE LISTS, CAREFULLY SELECTED. "IS THAT YOU?", I ASKED. "COFFEE THIS I AM PINTO" SAID ANGIE. "FUCK YOU I WIN" SAID COURTNEY, WHO WAS ACTUALLY LOSING, BUT HADN'T PICKED THAT WORD. WE ALL UNDERSTOOD PERFECTLY, EXCEPT FOR AMOS. POOR GUY, HE WAS A LITTLE SHORT-TEMPERED AND IMPATIENT. WE NEVER DID LEARN HOW TO PLAY PINOCHLE, BUT WE DID GET A TASTE OF WHAT IT'S LIKE TO ASK DIRECTIONS IN A FOREIGN COUNTRY.

SINCE QUESTIONS WERE ONLY ALLOWED EVERY HALF HOUR, THERE WAS PLENTY OF TIME TO THINK OF THE RIGHT ONES. HOW HAVE EACH OF YOUR FRIENDS INFLUENCED YOU? WHAT DO YOU LIKE BUT PRETEND TO HATE? WHAT WAS THE BEST MOMENT OF YOUR WHOLE GODDAMN LIFE? WHO DO YOU SECRETLY PLAN ON GETTING BACK TOGETHER WITH, FOR RICHER OR FOR POORER, IN SICKNESS AND IN HEALTH? WHAT WOULD YOUR NAME BE IF YOU JOINED THE RAMONES? WHAT HAVEN'T YOU DONE? THAT ONE WAS MY FAVORITE.

EVERYONE WAS SURPRISED TO FIND OUT ALL THE SIMPLE THINGS THAT THEIR FRIENDS HAD NEVER DONE. FOR INSTANCE, I HAD NEVER PUKED OFF ALCOHOL, WORN DEODERANT, RODE A ROLLERCOASTER, DROVE A CAR, PLAYED SPIN THE BOTTLE, OR MADE OUT IN A MOVIE THEATRE. ONLY ONE OR TWO OF US HAD EVER DRESSED IN DRAG, HAD SEX AT OUR HIGH SCHOOL, GOTTEN DUMB TATTOOS WE REGRETTED, LEARNED A SECOND LANGUAGE FLUENTLY, OR BROKE THE WINDOW OF A COP CAR. I WAS AMAZED THAT BRAD AND MATTHEW HAD MISSED OUT ON SIMPLE PLEASURES LIKE SKINNYDIPPING AND STAGEDIVING, WHILE THEY WERE AMAZED THAT NEITHER PEDRO OR I HAD EVER HAD A MOHAWK.

PEDRO CHECKED IN AT ONE OF THOSE HUMAN LAB RAT PLACES WHERE THEY LOCK YOU UP AND PAY YOU LOTS OF MONEY TO DO DRUGS. TWICE A WEEK HE HAD ONE HOUR FOR VISITORS. HE WAS ANXIOUS TO TALK AFTER BEING ALONE ALL WEEK IN THE LITTLE PADDED CELL. WHEN I WALKED INTO THE VISITING ROOM AND SAW HIM SITTING THERE IN THE HOSPITAL GOWN, I WAS SO PROUD. PEDRO HAD GIVEN HIMSELF A MOHAWK.

RECENTLY I SAW PEDRO AGAIN. HE PRESSED HIS HAND IN MINE AND THANKED ME. COMING TO VISIT HIM IN THE LOCKDOWN WAS ONE OF THE NICEST THINGS ANYONE HAD EVER DONE, HE SAID. THERE HE WAS, IN THE HARDEST TIME OF HIS LIFE, SO BROKE AND HUNGRY AND DESPERATE THAT HE HAD TO RESORT TO BECOMING A HUMAN LAB RAT, AND IT MEANT SO MUCH JUST TO SEE A FAMILIAR FACE.

I FELT TERRIBLE. I HAD NO IDEA HE WAS GOING INSANE BACK THEN. I DIDN'T EVEN KNOW HE WAS BROKE. PEDRO HADN'T MENTIONED IT AND I HAD NEVER THOUGHT TO ASK.

Born to drive

WE FELT LIKE LEMMINGS. TWO LEMMINGS ON OUR WAY TO THE COAST, JUST TRYING TO FULFILL OUR DESTINY: GET TO THE OCEAN, JUMP OFF A CLIFF, AND DIE. WE WERE GONNA CHEAT, THOUGH, AND GET THERE FAST. CRUISE DOWN THE HIGHWAYS AND BYWAYS WITH THE WIND IN OUR HAIR WHILE ALL THE OTHER LEMMINGS WALKED. HUH. EXCEPT, WE KEPT GETTING LOST.

TWO LEMMINGS IN A CHEVY VOLARE, STOPPING EVERYONE ON EVERY CORNER IN EVERY SMALL TOWN IN AMERICA TO ASK, "WHICH WAY TO THE MOTHER-FUCKING COAST?" TWO LEMMINGS AND A DOG. A GOOD SOMBER, THOUGHTFUL, UNTALKATIVE DOG. IT JUST STARED STOICALLY OUT THE WINDOW AS ANGIE DROVE AND I HELD THE MAP UPSIDE DOWN.

ANGIE DICTATED NOTES FOR HER NOVEL. "SEVENTEEN," SHE SAID. "IGLOOS, STIR-FRY, FIVE-YEAR PLAN, TRADING CARDS. COMMUNITY OUTREACH, STEP-DAD, WALMART, DEAD FRIENDS." WRITING IN THE DARK ON THE BACK OF MY HANDS, SOMETIMES ALL THE WAY UP TO MY ELBOW, THE NOTES ENDED UP EVEN MORE CRYPTIC BY THE TIME I RECOPIED THEM BY DAYLIGHT. I WORKED ON TURNING THEM INTO SONGS SO WE COULD BETTER REMEMBER THEM.

"THE ROAD TRIPS AND PIÑATAS AND FIVE-YEAR PLANS," WE CROONED TOGETHER WHILE I DRUMMED ON THE DASH. "IGLOOS FUCKED UP, SOMETHING'S WROOOONG, SOMETHING'S WROOOONG." ON THE LONG NOTES THE DOG WOULD STICK ITS SNOUT IN MY MOUTH.

ECCH, LEMMINGS ON A SUICIDE MISSION, BORN TO DIE, AND YET, WE WEREN'T GETTING ANYWHERE. WE KEPT HAVING TO STOP, AND EVERY STOP LED TO UN-FORESEEN COMPLICATIONS. WE WENT TO A DINER JUST TO GRAB A QUICK CUP OF COFFEE, AND ENDED UP IN A CONTEST TO SEE HOW MANY WORDS YOU COULD FIND IN "MERRY CHRISTMAS" IN TEN MINUTES.

WITH SEVENTY-THREE WORDS, ANGIE AND I WERE
THE WINNERS. NOT ONLY DID WE GET TWO FREE
MEALS ON THE HOUSE, WE ALSO GOT A WHOLE APPLE
PIE FOR FINDING THE SECRET BONUS WORD. FILTHY
ANIMALS WITH A DEATHWISH, AND THERE WE WERE,
APPLAUDED BY A DINER FULL OF CHRISTIANS FOR
BEING THE ONLY ONES SICK ENOUGH TO FIND "MASTER".

WYOMING, LIKE NO OTHER PLACE ON EARTH. IOWA,
YOU MAKE ME SMILE. UTAH, STILL THE RIGHT PLACE.
WE WERE GOING IN CIRCLES, WIRED OUT OF OUR
MINDS, DRIVING ALL DAY, AND THEN DRUNK OUT OF
OUR GOURDS AT REST STOPS EVERY NIGHT. FALL
LEAVES STARTED TO FALL, AND THE SNOW CAME AND
LAID A BLANKET ON THE GOOD EARTH. CURSES. WE
HAD MISSED OUR CUE.

WE WERE BEARS, TWO BEARS AND A DOG, IN A
CHEVY VOLARE. FOLLOWING OUR NATURAL INSTINCTS
TO DRINK BEER AND SLEEP IN THE BACK OF THE CAR
ALL WINTER. BIRDS, GATHERING STUFF FOR OUR
NEST. PARKING TICKETS, CIGARETTE BUTTS, COUNTRY
MUSIC TAPES. WE WERE BIRDS, TWO BIRDS, HEAD-
ING EAST FOR THE WINTER. NO, THAT WASN'T RIGHT.
TWO STARS. TWO TWINKLING LITTLE STARS IN THE
AMERICAN NIGHT, GOING AROUND AND AROUND
THE EARTH, SHINING BRIGHT. PERHAPS DESTINED
TO DIE, PERHAPS JUST BEING BORN. PERHAPS
ALREADY DEAD, BUT NO ONE WOULD KNOW FOR
SURE FOR TEN THOUSAND YEARS.

just keep driving

WE WAITED WAITED WAITED FOR A YEAR, THROUGH ALL
KINDS OF HELL, FOR THE DAY WE WOULD FINALLY GET TO
GO EAST. GET A QUIET LITTLE ROOM TOGETHER AND CATCH
UP ON ALL THE READING AND WRITING WE HAD MISSED
WHILE RUNNING AROUND LIKE IDIOTS WORRYING ABOUT
EVERYONE ELSE'S PROBLEMS. GO TO THE 24-HOUR LIBRARY
AND ALL THE FREE MOVIES AND LECTURES. IMMERSE
OURSELVES IN QUIET STABILITY AND ACADEMIA.

I DIDN'T WANT TO TRAVEL. I JUST WANTED TO GET TO
BOSTON AS SOON AS POSSIBLE. LARAMIE LOOKED SO GOOD AT
NIGHT THAT WE THOUGHT ABOUT JUST MOVING THERE.
THERE WAS A SUBLET OPEN IN LINCOLN. AH, ST. LOUIS.
THERE WERE BASEMENTS IN INDIANA AND MINNEAPOLIS
THAT WEREN'T BAD. BUT WE SAID NO. JUST KEEP DRIVING.
WE HAVE TO GET TO BOSTON.

WE SLEPT MOSTLY AT REST AREAS, THE THREE OF US IN

THE BACK OF THE TRUCK. ME, ANGIE, AND ANGIE'S DOG.
IT WAS LATE OCTOBER AND SNOWING. THE DOG TOOK UP
HALF THE FUCKING BED. I ALWAYS WOKE UP COLD AND
SORE. ANGIE AND THE DOG WOULD BOTH GROWL AT ME
WHEN I TRIED TO STEAL THE BLANKETS.

BY THE TIME WE GOT TO BOSTON WE WERE DEHYDRATED,
EXHAUSTED, DERANGED, CONFUSED, SUICIDAL, AND A LITTLE
WORRIED. I HAD TOLD ANGIE NOT TO WORRY; IT WOULDN'T
BE THAT HARD TO FIND A PLACE TO LIVE WHICH WOULD
ALLOW DOGS. I, THE GUY WITH A GOLDFISH AND NOWHERE
TO LIVE, HAD BECOME AN EXPERT ON DOGS AND REAL
ESTATE. I HAD A LIST OF TEN DIFFERENT PEOPLE WHO
HAD OFFERED US A COUCH WHILE WE LOOKED FOR A STEADY
PLACE TO RENT. I CALLED ALL TEN AND THEY ALL SAID THE
SAME THING: NO DOGS.

WE WENT TO A SHOW AND ASKED EVERY STRANGER IN THE
AUDIENCE IF THEY KNEW OF A PLACE FOR RENT. A GIRL
OFFERED TO TAKE ME HOME. I ACCEPTED, BUT SAID IT
MIGHT GET CROWDED IN BED WITH ANGIE AND THE DOG.
A GUY SAID I COULD MOVE INTO HIS BEDROOM IN THE
SUBURBS. HE AND I COULD SHARE THE ROOM AND DRINK
BEER AND TALK ALL NIGHT AND LOOK AT HIS COMIC BOOKS.
THEY DIDN'T UNDERSTAND. I DIDN'T WANT TO TALK TO,
OR EVEN FUCK, ANYONE. NOT EVEN ANGIE. I WANTED A
PLACE WHERE WE COULD BE STUDIOUS AND PRODUCTIVE
AND IGNORE EACH OTHER, RIGHT IN THE HEART OF A
THRIVING CITY.

THE NEXT MORNING I WOKE UP AND WAS IN A MEAN MOOD.
I FELT HUNG OVER, BUT IT WASN'T FROM THE ONE BEER.
IT WAS FROM BOSTON, FROM OUR STUPID PLAN AND ALL OUR
HOPES. IT WASN'T GOING TO WORK.

I BOUGHT A COPY OF THE BOSTON GLOBE AND HEADED TO A
DINER TO READ THE ELECTION RESULTS. CITIZEN FISH WERE
THERE. I SAT DOWN AT THE NEXT TABLE, FACING THE OTHER
DIRECTION. NO POINT DISCUSSING PRESIDENTIAL ELECTIONS
WITH A BUNCH OF ANARCHIST FOREIGNERS.

THEY WERE HAVING BREAKFAST BEFORE HEADING ON TO
NEW YORK. I WISHED I WAS ON TOUR AGAIN AND COULD
GET IN THE VAN AND SAY, "JUST KEEP DRIVING. FUCK THAT
TOWN." I WISHED IT WAS THAT EASY. THAT'S WHAT I HAD
DONE EVERY OTHER TIME IN EVERY OTHER TOWN, AND NOW
WAS IT CATCHING UP TO ME. GNAWING ON SOME RUSTY EGGS,
I RETRACED THE PAST TWO YEARS. SPENDING THE FIRST YEAR
TRYING TO GET TO A NEW CITY, EVEN JOINING A BAND SO
I COULD DO A CROSS-COUNTRY TOUR AND GET DROPPED OFF
THERE. FINALLY ARRIVING AND HAVING IT ALL FALL APART,
THEN SPENDING THE NEXT YEAR TRYING TO GET TO BOSTON.
HELLA DUMB.

MY MOOD WENT FROM BAD TO WORSE. FRUSTRATION TO ALL-OUT STABBING SPREE. AFTER AN HOUR AND A HALF, I HAD ONLY GOTTEN ONE REFILL. ONE REFILL. I LEFT AND WENT TO A DINER DOWN THE STREET WHERE I SAT FOR AN HOUR AND GOT NO REFILL. I WAITED ON THE CORNER TO MEET ANGIE. ANGIE NEVER SHOWED UP.

BY THE TIME I FOUND HER JUST WAKING UP BACK AT THE TRUCK, I WAS SO ANGRY I COULD BARELY SPEAK. STILL, WHEN A PEN-PAL OF MINE APPROACHED US, I MANAGED TO SCREAM AT HIM TO GET FAR, FAR AWAY. ME AND ANGIE JUMPED IN THE TRUCK. I WAS FOAMING AT THE MOUTH. I DIDN'T KNOW EXACTLY WHY, BUT THERE WERE PLENTY OF REASONS TO BE ANGRY, HOPELESS, AND INSANE.

WE DROVE TOWARD A RECORD STORE, "BELOW ZERO", TO DROP OFF MAGAZINES. WE WENT SOUTH ON 93 LOOKING FOR THE TREMONT STREET EXIT. WE KEPT DRIVING SOUTH. AS THE CITY DISAPPEARED BEHIND US, MY BAD MOOD WORE OFF. THERE WAS NO TREMONT STREET EXIT.

"JUST KEEP DRIVING", I SAID.

"FUCK BOSTON", ANGIE SAID, AND WE DROVE ON TOWARD CAPE COD.

End of the Road.

IT WAS EARLY MORNING AND I WAS WALKING OUT ALONG THE ROCK PATH AT LAND'S END. OCEAN ON BOTH SIDES, WAVES CRASHING BY MY FEET, WATCHING ANGIE AND THE DOG UP AHEAD IN THE DISTANCE, AND I GOT STUPID WARM ALL OVER JUST THINKING ABOUT HOW THE TIME RIGHT NOW IS ONE OF THE GREAT TIMES IN OUR LIVES. ONE OF THOSE TIMES LIKE AN ISLAND IN YOUR MEMORY THAT YOU LOOK BACK ON WITH WONDER, CRAVING THE SIMPLICITY AND INNOCENCE.

IT DOESN'T MAKE SENSE BECAUSE WE SPEND ALMOST ALL OUR TIME HERE WORRYING, FREEZING, COMPLAINING, AND BEING CONFUSED. IT'S NOT THE PICTURE-POSTCARD SCENERY THAT FOOLS ME. THAT ONLY MAKES IT FUNNIER, BECAUSE OUR REAL LIVES ARE SO OUT OF PLACE IN THE PICTURE. IT DOESN'T MAKE SENSE THAT WE'RE HERE AT ALL. THAT'S THE BEST PART, AND WHY I KNOW I'LL MISS THIS LATER.

IT'S NO SECRET: LIFE DOESN'T GET ANY EASIER EVEN IF YOU DO GET MORE USED TO IT. IT IS ALWAYS MAKING FUN OF YOU KILLING OFF PEOPLE THAT YOU LOVE, FORCING YOU TO MAKE DECISIONS YOU DON'T WANT TO MAKE. SO WE BOTH HAD A HARD YEAR, THAT'S ALL. NOT AS HARD AS OTHERS, BUT THER

IS SORT OF A CUMULATIVE EFFECT WHEN THE YEARS COME ONE AFTER THE OTHER.

SO IT'S NICE TO RUN THROUGH THE FOREST WITH THE DOG, TO RIDE MY BIKE OUT ALONG THE OLD HIGHWAY WITH ALL THE BOARDED UP SUMMER COTTAGES. IT CLEARS OUT MY BRAIN. NOT HAVING TO TALK TO OR DEAL WITH ANYONE ELSE, NOT HAVING TO TRY TO EXPLAIN OURSELVES. IT'S SHOCKING HOW DIFFERENT DOING EXACTLY WHAT I WANT TO DO IS FROM THE WAY I USUALLY LIVE.

WE WERE WALKING ALONG THE BEACH, BY THE LIGHTHOUSES AT THE VERY END OF THE CAPE, AND I SAID, WOULDN'T IT BE NICE TO HAVE A BOAT. WE LOOKED OUT OF THE CORNER OF OUR EYES AND, YES, THERE WAS A LITTLE BOAT WASHED UP RIGHT THERE ON THE BEACH—'THE JOLLY ROGER' BATTERED AND FILLED WITH BROKEN GLASS, BUT STILL SEAWORTHY. WE CROWDED IN AND SET SAIL ACROSS THE LITTLE CURL OF THE CAPE. HEADED TO PROVINCETOWN, JUST LIKE THE PILGRIMS FOUR HUNDRED AND FIFTY YEARS AGO.

ANGIE AND I HAVE BOTH STAYED IN PLENTY OF SQUATS, BUT NEVER HAD ONE OF OUR OWN. WE'RE SO FUCKING PROUD. A THREE-STORY HOUSE, NOT TRASHED AT ALL BUT OBVIOUSLY VACANT FOR AT LEAST A YEAR. DESKS AND CHAIRS, BEDS AND CLEAN BLANKETS, EVEN ELECTRICITY. BETTER THAN A HOTEL. BETTER THAN THE PLACE WITH BRADLEY THAT I'D BEEN PAYING RENT ON.

WE HIDE IN THE TOP ROOM, WARMING OURSELVES OVER A BROKEN TOASTER, KEEPING THE LIGHT FROM BEING SEEN OUTSIDE WITH FOUR LAYERS OF BLACK FABRIC OVER THE WINDOWS. WE WORRY ABOUT THE OWNER OF THE HOUSE, THE NEIGHBORS, THE HUNTERS IN THE FOREST, THE COPS, AND THE DOG WHEN IT FREAKS OUT AND ALMOST TIPS OVER THE BOAT. BUT AT LEAST WE DON'T HAVE TO WORRY ABOUT FINDING A PLACE WHERE A DOG CAN STAY. HERE, SHE HAS HER OWN BED.

I'M SURE THE COMING YEARS WILL BE A LANDSLIDE OF SHIT. OH, GOOD THINGS WILL COME TOO, BUT, OPTIMIST THAT I AM, I'M ALREADY EXPECTING THE GOOD THINGS ANYWAY. IN THE MEANTIME IT'S NICE TO TAKE TIME IN BETWEEN THE LAST SET OF CATASTROPHE, ROMANCE, MURDER, BETRAYAL, AND TEARFUL REUNIONS, AND THE NEXT.

TIME TO RUN BAREFOOT ON THE BEACH LIKE IDIOTS, TO SIT AT THE LIBRARY READING FRISCO NOVELS OR AT THE DINER WITH THE WHOLE PLACE TO OURSELVES. EVERYONE ELSE LEFT TOWN FOR THE WINTER. WALKING BACK THROUGH THE GRAVEYARD TO SPEND ANOTHER NIGHT AT HOME, SITTING AT OUR DESKS, MAKING CORNBREAD AND COOKIES AND BAKED POTATOES. SOME SQUATTERS WE ARE. WE EVEN HAVE AN ESPRESSO MAKER.

credits:

TITLE PAGE ART BY FLY, CB44 COVER BY
PHIL LOLLAR. CB46 COVER AND ALL ART-
WORK BY NATE POWELL, "AT WORK ON
LANKY" PHOTOS BY KATIE GLICKSBERG.
"COMETBUS COPIES" PIC BY IDON, BRUCE
ANDERSON INTERVIEW BY LAWRENCE
LIVERMORE AND MICHAEL SILVERBERG.
ALL OTHER WRITING, INTERVIEWS, LAYOUT,
AND ART (BESIDES FOUND PHOTOS) BY AARON.
HEAPS OF THANKS FOR ALL THE HELP
FROM THOSE WHO'VE PROVIDED SUPPORT!

After seeing anti-war protesters Thursday like Aaron Cometbus, foreground,
children Hannah Collins, 10, and Kayla Boren, 10, talked their mothers, Darla
Collins and Lisa Boren, into showing support for President Bush.